Sick Heroes

Louis Léopold Boilly, French, 1761–1845, *Moving Day at the Port of Wheat*, Paris (Les Déménagements sur le Port au blé), oil on canvas, 1822, 73 x 92cm, Harold Stuart Fund, 1982. 494. Photograph © 1996, The Art Institute of Chicago. All Rights Reserved.

Sick Heroes

French Society and Literature in the Romantic Age, 1750–1850

Allan H. Pasco

UNIVERSITY
of
EXETER
PRESS

First published in 1997 by
University of Exeter Press
Reed Hall, Streatham Drive
Exeter, Devon EX4 4QR
UK

British Library Cataloguing in Publication Data
A catalogue record of this book is available
from the British Library

Hardback ISBN 0 85989 549 1
Paperback ISBN 0 85989 550 5

Typeset in 10 on 12½pt Plantin Light
by Greenshires Icon, Exeter

Printed and bound in Great Britain
by Short Run Press Ltd, Exeter

S. D. G.

Dallas

Contents

Illustrations   viii

Acknowledgments   ix

Conventions   xi

Introduction   xii

1 Moving   1

2 The Unrocked Cradle   31

3 Doddering Paternities   54

4 The Unheroic Mode   84

5 Incest in the Mirror   109

6 Death Wish   134

7 An Ending: Julien among the Cannibals   157

Notes   179

Bibliography of Primary Sources   217

Bibliography of Secondary Sources   225

Index   243

Illustrations

Frontispiece:
Louis Léopold Boilly, *Les Déménagements sur le Port au blé*
(*Moving Day at the Port of Wheat*), 1822, Chicago Institute of Art

1   Louis Léopold Boilly, *Les Conscrits de 1807 défilant*
devant la Porte de Saint-Denis (*Draftees of 1807 Filing Before*
the Saint-Denis Gate), 1808, Carnavalet   20

2   Jean-Baptiste Greuze, *Les Sevreuses* (*The Nursemaids*),
1765, Nelson-Atkins Museum   30

3   Edgar Degas, *Portrait de famille* also called *La Famille Bellelli*
(*Family Portrait* also called *The Bellelli Family*), 1860–67,
Orsay   53

4   Anne Louis Girodet-Trioson, *Scène de déluge*
(*Scene from a Flood*), 1806, Louvre   78

5   Hubert Robert, *Vue imaginaire de la grande galerie du*
Louvre en ruine (*An Imaginary View of the Louvre's Great*
Gallery in Ruins), 1796, Louvre   83

6   Jean-Baptiste Greuze, *La Cruche cassée (The Broken Pot)*,
1771, Louvre   108

7   Henry Wallis, *The Death of Chatterton*, 1856, Tate Gallery,   133
London

Acknowledgments

Although the original understanding of the Romantic hero as an "unrocked" creature of his time came in the quiet of my study, the working out of that idea was not a solitary enterprise. As I followed the scintillating but languorous waltz of these eighteenth- and nineteenth-century creations, I was joined by numerous superb studies of literature and society. The fact that I have referred to many in the following pages is insufficient indication of my debt and very real gratitude to them.

I have several reasons to be grateful to the Hall Family Foundation, first of all for the endowment that gave me time to pursue this project and, secondly, for the Hall Center fellowship granted by the Joyce & Elizabeth Hall Center for the Humanities that released me for a semester from teaching and administrative responsibilities.

I also want to thank various journals and presses that have allowed me to use material that they originally published. Much abbreviated, early versions of chapters two, five, and six appeared, respectively, in the *Journal of European Studies* 21 (1991): 95–110, the *Cincinnati Romance Review* 14 (1995): 58–72, and *The French Novel from Lafayette to Desvignes: Collected Essays to Mark the 60th Birthday of Patrick Brady*, edited by Sharon Diane Nell, Bernadette C. Lintz, and George Poe (Knoxville: New Paradigm Press, 1995) 77–87. Portions of chapters four and six came out originally in the *Philological Quarterly* 70 (1991): 361–78, and in *L'Esprit Créateur* 35.4 (1995): 28–37, respectively. And, finally, early work on the failing epic was published in the volume *Epic and Epoch*, edited by Steven Oberhelman, Van Kelly, and Richard J. Golsan (Lubbock: Texas Tech University Press, 1994) 233–47.

In addition, lively audiences at the University of Kansas, Kansas State University, Whitman College, the University of Texas, Texas A & M University, the University of Tennessee, the University of Connecticut,

ACKNOWLEDGEMENTS

Randolph-Macon College, the University of Virginia, and the 1994 Taft Lecture of the University of Cincinnati Conference on Romance Languages occasionally made me change direction significantly and regularly provided new insights. More specifically, I would like to thank Mary Donaldson-Evans and Sara Melzer, who made a number of useful suggestions on reading an early version of the "Cradle" chapter, Van Kelly who has provided me with a broader perspective in countless conversations, and Mary Cordaro, Richard Burton and Barbara Cooper who read and significantly improved the entire manuscript. James Smith Allen, Robert Anderson, Max Aprile, Reed Benhamou, James A. Brundage, Rae Beth Gordon, Richard Grant, Lois Cassandra Hamrick, Al Hamscher, Claude Pichois, and Laurence M. Porter, put me onto a number of very helpful texts. David Dinneen and Stephen Kellogg helped me with a particularly muddy etymology. But most of all, I want to thank my wife and partner Dallas C. Pasco. Not only did she welcome all those Romantic heroes and heroines into our private and social life, she read and reread the parts and parcels of my own account as they came out of my computer. To her I dedicate this book.

Conventions

Unless otherwise indicated, all references to poems, plays, novels, and autobiographies are indicated parenthetically and briefly in the text. Complete bibliographical references for the editions I used are found in the "Bibliography of Primary Sources" at the conclusion of the volume. Where it seemed to me that a writer cited in the text was particularly obscure, I add a brief, biographical footnote. With very few exceptions that are clearly labelled, all translations are my own.

Introduction

How did French people live a hundred and fifty or two hundred years ago? What were they like? What were their states of mind, their conscious and unconscious assumptions, attitudes, prejudices, and emotions? Historians have long been able to tell us about important events of the period between 1750 and 1850, and writings about the French Revolution would fill a substantial library. Add to this the biographies of important people, studies of philosophical movements, histories of wars, in addition to considerations of political forces loosed in France during the Industrial Revolution, and we might be said to know quite a lot about the country and its citizens. Recent historians have gone further, and begun to give us snapshots of the people themselves: the things that filled their homes, how often they moved, the diseases that afflicted them, the number of times they attended religious functions, how many of the youth were drafted, what books attracted them and how they were distributed, even the recipes urban bakers used. From this we can construct a partial portrait of the typical French person. Still, the picture remains out of focus.

Were these people much like us? Did they have similar worries? Or did the times they lived through isolate them from future generations? Did the urban riots make them fearful? How were they affected by numerous public executions? Were personal lives upended by the stupefying disruptions that took place in the governments and men that ruled them? How did young soldiers feel about the draft? What were the effects of moving from country to city? Was loneliness a problem? What happened when people got sick? What were their pleasures and escapes? Was crime related to alcohol and drug addiction? How did changes in work and the opportunities to amass wealth affect particular men and women? Such curiosity arouses frustration today, since the archives of the period bear at best tangentially on such matters. We have occasional letters and diaries, the odd bundle of police reports, scattered attempts by such writers as Restif, Mercier, Jouy* to describe the life of the times, but if we wish to become truly acquainted in any detail with these people and with what the French call their *mentalités*, we remain overall unsatisfied.

The importance of the printed word has not had as much attention as it should, despite excellent work by Robert Darnton and others. Decade by decade there was a steady increase in the numbers of novels, poems, plays, and essays that found their way into print. Roughly twice as many novels appeared in the 1790s as in the 1750s, for example. In the following pages, I will turn to these novels as an important lens that brings the individual reality of the period into focus. Although as the bibliographies at the end of this volume will show, I have taken advantage of the marvelous work done by historians over the last half-century, I have concentrated on the period's novels, many of which no longer have enthusiasts, some of which are masterpieces. I have been drawn to the way these literary works bring people from the mid-eighteenth to the mid-nineteenth century into view. For the purposes of this study, the aesthetic value of the work matters little—Mme Cottin's† sentimental drivel has as much diagnostic value as Balzac's masterpieces. Poems, plays, essays, but particularly novels are my archive. The picture they capture is illuminating.

Art exposes a society's conscious and unconscious reality in all its glory and shame. Recent historians like Eugen Weber have demonstrated that literature constitutes a body of cultural materials that often appears historically trustworthy. Granted, the creations are presented as fiction or, at best, romanticized autobiographies, and one must read between the lines, interpreting in accordance with facts that come to us from other sources. The story may not be true in detail, but the background most frequently seems to be. When using creations as a means of insight into

---

* Nicolas Restif de La Bretonne (1734–1806) was an incredibly prolific writer of quasi-autobiographical works that are extremely useful for their penetrating observations of the life and social conditions of French people at the end of the eighteenth century. Although Louis Sébastien Mercier (1740–1814) was an active dramatist and critic, today only his long *Tableau de Paris*, composed of numerous vignettes describing life in late eighteenth-century Paris, is appreciated. Joseph-Etienne Jouy (1764–1846), who often wrote under the name of Monsieur de Jouy, authored vaudevilles, comic operas, a tragedy, and several novels, but he is best known for his satirical sketches of Paris and the provinces during the Empire and Restoration.

† Sophie Cottin (1770–1807) was widowed young, then moved to the region of Paris, where she wrote five novels in a sentimental, moralizing vein. She is thought to have committed suicide.

the people who wrote and read them, someone who wishes to bring the mind–set of the day into focus looks especially for the repetitions, for salient elements, indeed for the obsessive features, those qualities and images that recur in the works of numerous artists. Such factors must be perceived in the light of other things we know about the period. There is surprising consistency in these repeated elements, because they are connected to the public's dreams, fears, compulsions, customs, and manners. Julie's problems with her father in *La Nouvelle Héloïse* are doubtless imaginary, but the attitudes that he and she reveal towards each other are historically typical and accurate. We know so because they recur in many other novels. Similarly, Sir Ralph's and Indiana's pact to commit suicide together is fictive, but their obsession with death was a common reality. Although of a particular kind, the literary information that deals with attitudes, fears, manners is generally accurate and provides helpful insight into the period of its publication.

I have selected over two hundred literary works published between 1750 and 1850 that serve as my "archive" and a means of conceptualizing the period. A surprisingly consistent portrait of the people's collective mentality arises from these works. It is only reasonable to conclude that it tells us something about the people that used their money to purchase contemporary novels, poems, and plays. While it may be an exaggeration to suggest that the novels portray with precision and in detail the people who walked the streets, bought groceries, established homes, and struggled to survive, the fact that such people read these literary creations indicates that they found something appealing in them. I have found that the Romantic hero is recognizable in virtually every one, and I have come to believe it was because people of the day identified with the character. Writers and readers found themselves reflected in these strange, alienated, and depressed characters that distill the dominant traits of the reading public and increasingly of the public at large. It offers a convincing explanation for the plethora of Romantic heroes that populated over one hundred years of French literature.

What follows is thus history of a sort; one might call it psychological history or perhaps sociological, anthropological, or even environmental history. Because of the subject matter, however, it views the period from limited perspectives. Very little will be said about Marie Antoinette or, even less, about Louis XV or XVI. I am interested not in them either personally or as rulers, but rather in whether people felt insecure as their leaders and government appeared increasingly untrustworthy, ineffective, and ephemeral. Although as a background reality I am throughout conscious of the various wars as of the revolutions of 1789, 1830, and

1848, and while I would not join Richard Cobb and suggest that the Revolution of 1789 is a "magnificent irrelevance," very little will be explicitly said about either notable events or notable people, not only because so much has been written about them, but especially because they are only a few of the numerous crises that raised uncertainty and fear in the populace. It is the effect of the many changes that were occurring in French society, of the revolutions, the riots, and the many wars that concerns me here. How was the way French men, women, and children lived affected? From the point of view that governs the following pages, migration, street violence, and the appalling conditions of the major cities were as important as the more grandiose subjects that traditionally fill our history books. As Toqueville and many others have pointed out, across these often startling events there was a continuity from the monarchy through the Revolution and on into the modern age. I am convinced that as the middle class took over, as the Industrial Revolution took hold, as France moved towards capitalism a radically different kind of person was being created. This new personage is characterized by the Romantic hero.

This study consequently looks at Romanticism in an unusual way, and the result is surprising; it might even be called *anti-Romantic*, since I have been forced to redefine Romanticism as a social phenomenon extending from before the Revolution to well into the nineteenth century. Under the general rubric of the Romantic hero, I have chosen six topics that seem to me particularly useful in gaining insight into the psychological reality of French people between 1750 and 1850. In the first chapter I consider migration. While France had for centuries been "sedentary," as Jacques Dupâquier puts it, largely because of the Industrial Revolution people were leaving home by the mid-eighteenth century in search of better conditions and a better future. The particular practices of child care, where most French infants were sent away from home for between two to four years, makes it legitimate to talk of maternal deprivation for much of the French populace. To missing mothers was joined a kind of paternal deprivation, since fathers were also drawn out of the home to support their families. More significant is the fact that the whole paternal system had come into question, and the authority of fathers, priests, and the king had been radically weakened. The Revolution of 1789, and the other revolutions that followed, resulted from this crisis of authority that I call "Doddering Paternities." Migration and parental deprivation represent causes, important causes that modern psychology helps explain when they are viewed in relation to the defining traits of the incredibly popular Romantic hero.

With the fourth topic, the innovative and adventuresome if not confusing structures that increasingly appear in literature, I want to turn to effects. As society seemed more and more unstable, with the disruption of families, the disintegration of the monarchy, and the weakening of the church, so people felt adrift, and writers reflect the instability in their works by searching for new orders, new organizations. I doubt that they hoped, like artists after the First World War, to bring salvation to humankind, or even that they were conscious of what impelled them. Given the confusion reigning in society together with the new structures in literature, it seems possible that the latter is an effect of the first.

Separating causes from effects is impossible, however. Especially in a society where the seeds of instability and fear have been sown, ideas are as infectious as the typhoid, syphilis, cholera, tuberculosis that afflicted the population. In chapter five I point as an example to incest. We know that it has long-lived effects on victims and that it tends to run in families. Consequently, the social and psychological factors that create incest also tend to reproduce the psychological traits that encourage incest, as well as the same factors that began and continue the chain. Severe depression is common among abusers, as it is among the victims. Furthermore, victims tend to become abusers. Likewise, in chapter six, it is well known that suicides taint the surrounding friends and families, sometimes for generations, producing the depression and helplessness that encouraged the original suicide. Well-documented suicide "showers" that are the undoubted result of such influence mark suicide as a cause as well as, or rather than, an effect. To what degree did incest and suicide, or for that matter education, books, illness, and persistent malnourishment, cause the Romantic hero? Should one rather see such problems as the results of the practices initiated by depressed, chronically ill, lonely, and alienated people? In 1832, Alphonse Karr* suggested that "novels create behavior" (*Sous les tilleuls*, 236). Is literature a cause or a reflection? Surely it is both, and while the concepts of causation and result can be useful when distinguished from each other, in a tumultuous world such as that found at the end of the eighteenth and beginning of the nineteenth centuries, cause and effect feed upon each other.

Looking at society from the footnotes, if not the underside, through its art rather than in the eyes of its official historians gives one a different view. I have then been led to redefine Romanticism with less emphasis on

---

* Alphonse Karr (1808–90) wrote several Romantic novels filled with frenzied love and vengeance, but he was also a journalist, a dramatist, and an accomplished satirist. Today he is remembered, if at all, for the books reflecting his horticultural interests.

the traits that are normally cited than on the feelings of helplessness and insecurity that cause them. Because my work has given me a new perspective, in the last chapter I have turned again to Stendhal's *Le Rouge et le noir*, one of the period's unquestioned masterworks, one that has long elicited scholarly attention and legions of commentaries. I use what I have learned both to understand how the novel reflects its period and how the topics treated in preceding chapters cast new light on the work itself. I hope that the various perspectives opened by this study will add both plausible insights and conclusions and a new dimension to the full-length portait of Romanticism and the Romantics that is coming into focus.

CHAPTER 1

Moving

If Romanticism began after the Revolution with the birth of the new century, as Pierre Moreau believes,[1] it grew out of the terrible deceptions that greeted aristocrats as they returned legally and illegally to France. Committed to the monarchy, they had spent years in poverty far from the pleasures of home, dreaming of victoriously regaining their rightful place in government and society. For most, of course, that was not to be, and on coming back to the motherland, they found they had wasted their youth in futile dreams of what was irrevocably past. Some family estates were lost, and neither Napoleon nor the increasingly powerful middle class were particularly interested in reversing the Revolutionary confiscations. The returning nobles had no profession, no position, no connections, and they must have greeted with disillusion the thought that the sacrifices of their long absence had been not only in vain but for a chimera. Most of them were, as Sainte-Beuve put it, "despoiled and proscribed" (*Volupté* [1834] 1.95). Chateaubriand admirably represents the lamentable situation of the *émigrés* when he returned to Paris in 1800, although he eventually gained considerable importance through the brilliance of his numerous, influential publications. No one could question the salience of his writings. The famous portrait by Girodet of Chateaubriand standing on a prominence above ruins and greenery, with wind-swept hair and a Napoleonesque hand tucked in his waistcoat, is the very image of a Romantic hero and has come to symbolize Romanticism. Certainly, for the avid youth of the 1820s, Chateaubriand's deliciously autobiographical *René* (1802) became the movement's proto-text.

Further reflection on the personages of the period turns one also to Mme de Staël as a quintessential Romantic. She likewise was exiled, much traveled, and had enormous influence in her day. Gérard did her equally impressive, though less famous, portrait. It shows her seated near Mount Vesuvius, high above the bay of Naples on the rubble of antiquity, and

1

surrounded by adoring gazes. While her hair is quite restrained if compared to Girodet's representation of Chateaubriand, the volcano and the wind-blown scarf wrapped around her neck serve equally well to portray subjection to the violent movements of nature. There is little doubt that Staël's essay, *De l'Allemagne* (1808–10), was important for bringing German Romanticism to France. Her novels *Delphine* (1802) and *Corinne ou l'Italie* (1807) offer vivid examples of full-blown Romantic heroines, and the widely publicized events of her life—especially the long and troubled love affair with Benjamin Constant—not only blurred the line between reality and fiction but make her seem an excellent image of Romanticism itself. Other names come readily to mind as typical representatives of the Romantic period, though none more than Chateaubriand and Staël, and even they merely approximate what we know of this extraordinarily tumul-tuous era in France.[2] While Romanticism has generally been considered a literary movement, I suggest that it was rather a larger, cultural reality given birth by widespread social factors and sustained by a mass market. Imaginary creations, however, offer in the period's predominant literary type a remarkably suitable characterization of the age, and I would suggest that the best representation of Romanticism occurs in the characters that acted out their pathetic fates in hundreds and hundreds of poems, plays and novels, not merely subsequent to the Revolution but well before.[3]

The character was eventually known as the Romantic hero—or heroine (his spiritual sister was exempted from few of his virtues and flaws). Toward the mid-1700s, these remarkably troubled, often offensive, though strangely appealing personages appeared in European literature. Contrary to any reasonable expectation, since the characters are neither examples of normalcy nor unreservedly attractive, they began to multiply, swarming throughout literary and other art forms. For something like one hundred years variations on the type dominated in literature. For this reason, I have come to see that Romantic heroes' personality traits and more material features like appearance and wealth are a key to major social movements spanning the last two centuries in the Western World. I focus on France where the dominance of such characters was longer and more intense than elsewhere. I turn to psychologists for insight into individuals. And because "Every period mentally constructs its own universe," as Lucien Febvre said,[4] I turn to sociologists for ways of relating those individuals to society. By paying close attention to the imaginative creations of the Romantic world and to the relationships of cause and effect, it may also be possible to understand somewhat better both this period and how literature is related to people's lives. The Romantic hero distills a multitude of life experiences and expectations.

Studying what was happening in the individuals who lived from the 1750s through the 1850s presents difficulties because of the paucity and unreliability of information remaining to us. Even where some attempt had been made to keep registers, changing regulations, invasions, and civil insurrections played havoc with the records. Statistics on death, for example, were only compiled after 1825, those on migration have so many variables that we are left with little more than guesswork. As a means of exposing the fantasies, beliefs, fears, and loves, and illuminating what facts historians can provide us, the following study turns to novels, plays, and poems of the period, many of which include extensive social commentary. As the considerations of Lucien Febvre, Robert Mandrou, indeed the entire Annales school, and others have shown, literature is particularly important for broadening our understanding of other periods,[5] and it is no longer possible to deny that creative works form an important, well-integrated part of that web of a period's economic and social structures and mentalities that mold individuals into a society. No document, whether aesthetic, cultural, or more purely historical, can be interpreted outside its social context. Ideas do not exist in a vacuum. While all texts coming to us from the past must be read with considerable care in the light of their function, acceptable considerations of the past may not be limited to the historical accounts of kings and queens, the chronicles of wars and crusades, or the statistics of infant mortality and coal production.

Philippe Van Tieghem suggests that the enormous success of Rouseau's *La Nouvelle Héloïse* (1761) grows from its recognition of the public's aspirations. Rousseau did not invent these desires and needs, Van Tieghem is careful to point out, but rather the novel elucidates and justifies them to readers (*Romantisme*, 7–8). I wish to go further: *La Nouvelle Héloïse* and other such works were not only important in their revelations to the men and women of their day; when read carefully, they also provide us with means of understanding these people of long ago. The novel genre was a particularly popular form designed for a mass audience and written for the general public. Because of the length of novels and the temptation they offer authors to expand on their insights and ideas, long fictions are more useful as investigative tools than the other genres, but other forms of art join as well to make literature and the arts wonderfully fertile sources for accurately understanding the mind-set and cultural reality of the Romantic period. They frequently include long, detailed descriptions and commentaries. Although the imaginative creations of Romanticism must be tested against contemporary documents, studies, and the subsequent work of historians, the insights of "fiction" into attitudes, customs, and the details of everyday life are often not just verisimilar but true. As Georges May argued in his *Le Dilemme du roman*, novels of the seventeenth and eighteenth centuries make it clear that the public had less and less patience with the improbable.[6] Unlike Hayden White who insists that history is a story that reveals the story-teller, I want to suggest that stories frequently reveal history, especially in its motivations and cultural reality. In addition, while the arts are always to some degree a result of the forces at play in society, occasionally they also influence society, perhaps even cause certain actions, patterns of behavior, fashions, and optics of viewing and understanding.

Freud argued that the creative works, or fantasies, of a writer provide a reliable indication of what goes on in the most private, most personal, most real levels of his or her psyche, what the psychoanalyst called "the deepest stratum of impulses in the mind of the creative poet."[7] At first he felt this was only true of less expert writers, those who lacked the aesthetic control to create great masterpieces. Subsequently, however, he expanded his argument to the work of all artists.[8] For later psychological critics, when a writer reveals the same "psychic structure" repeatedly in his works, the reader-analyst is considered to be on firm ground to assume the discovery of something important about the artist's subconscious.[9] Mauron suggests the need for constant, indeed incessant comparison of an author's creations in order to discover "the unconsciously obsessive, thus structural, traits" (Mauron, 31). He carefully considers the aesthetic works' characters, the feelings that animate them, and the words and actions that they manifest, as well as the system of relationships making up the whole and which moves toward the conclusion (32). It is rather like taking a number of photographic negatives, stacking them one on the other, and holding the pile up to the light. One assumes that the clearly configured images that are apparent are those with particular importance. Although it is true that the individual works thus lose the individual traits that often give them aesthetic value, there is no reason why readers may not return to the specific texts by once again isolating each of the "negatives" for a more appropriately aesthetic reading. Sometimes the images, relationships, or patterns revealed through the comparison or general view permit a far more valid understanding of an isolated work.

While I am well aware of the dangers of psychoanalytic over-generalization, of reducing works to fuzzy outlines where real distinctions become difficult, I am unwilling to follow Goldmann and conclude that such a psychological approach is more "rash" than a similar method consecrated to sociology.[10] What I hope to accomplish nonetheless resembles the psychological analysis suggested by Freud and Mauron. It differs in that I hope to examine and reveal (possibly even "psychoanalyze") not a writer but a period and to suggest the causes for the some of the more important characteristics of the Romantic age. Perhaps particularly in the Romantic period, when reading was an increasingly important part of the social fabric,[11] literature provides an invaluable tool for plumbing the anxieties, the dreams, the realities of a people. Not only is there some chance that the writers had actually experienced the dreads and hopes, held the views, dreamed the dreams, perceived the realities that they describe, but there is also the fact that some publisher or producer thought that the particular novel, poem, play would appeal to many others who would pay for the privilege of reading or watching it. Republication is even more significant, since it proves the work previously succeeded in establishing resonance with a public. When the same images, descriptions, or fantasies reappear in numerous works by different authors, we may reasonably conclude that it was important to French people of the time.[12]

In preceding periods, authors could get by if they could satisfy a wealthy patron or a small group of like-minded people, but it was no longer enough for a scribbler to find a Maecenas who would pay for publication, with a little extra for the author's living expenses. Publishing had changed. Now successful writers depended on mass markets of people who would purchase or rent their published wares. Novelists and playwrights in particular were required to attract readers and spectators or, to be more precise, they had to write works that would appeal to others, many others, and bring an audience with money in hand. As Balzac put it in his preface to an early version of *Les Employés* (1838): "The destiny of French literature is today fatally linked to the bookstore and the newspaper" (7.892).[13] It is subjected to "the capricious laws of taste and the preferences of merchants" (7.890). Authors who could not seduce the rather large and rapidly growing general public were not welcomed by publishers, since paper and presses were expensive. Bankruptcy awaited those who could not successfully predict reading tastes and, so to speak, take the public pulse.

Despite the new importance given to the imagination and to sentiment, one of the topics that most interested this public was its own culture. From Restif and Mercier at the end of the eighteenth century to Jouy and the extraordinarily popular realistic sketches called *physiologies* of the early nineteenth century, a substantial sub-genre described the surrounding world.[14] Realism was a well-prepared outgrowth of Romanticism. People looked to novels to teach them about their society, to reveal it as it truly was, to explain things so that readers would be more able to cope with the turmoil they saw and sensed around them.[15] Fantasy did exist, and the tremendously successful translations of E. T. A. Hoffmann's tales leave no doubt of its attraction, but stories of the super-natural were most often set solidly in reality. Shepherds and shepherdesses loving in bucolic if pasteurized Arcadia were no longer acceptable. Even during the Restoration's neo-classical revival, unques-tionably including the painter David's Greek and Roman heroes, the subject matter was directly tied to the political and social life of the period. Jonathan P. Ribner has, for example, shown conclusively how the paintings decorating the suite of rooms where the Bourbon Council of State met "were as inescapably tied to France's heritage of revolutionary violence as the regime for which they were painted."[16] Most often, if writers were to situate their adventures in the past, it was to be an European or, better, a French history, and it must deal with problems of current interest. Increasingly, however, literature treated the events of the present. Manuals of literary history talk of "local color," or the little details that give the flavor of a period or a place, but immersion in the actual works of pre-Romantic and Romantic literature makes it clear that writers were struggling to portray the reality that surrounded them, the *hic et nunc* (May, 49). The plot might be more or less invented, and it became more simplified (May, 62), but, increasingly across the eighteenth century, the characters were realistic and the backdrop was a verisimilar reflection of the customs, events, and décor of the contem-porary world (May, 163). There were exceptions, but the nominally creative works of this hundred years portray a surprisingly consistent picture of a turbulent, unsettled society with weak foundations, great anxiety, and only tatters of joy. In short, the literary Romantic hero fleshes out what history tells us about French life in the late eighteenth and early nineteenth centuries.

Excessive individualism, acute self-consciousness, and neurotic intro-spection make Romantic heroes moody, unstable, and passive, capable of little but momentary paroxysms of desire or revolt. When they do act, they habitually set themselves up for failure and for victimization. Bernard Stamply in Sandeau's* *Mademoiselle de La Seiglière* (1848) is only an apparent exception in that he actively pursued glory by following the emperor. After almost dying in a Russian prison camp, he makes his way home, where he curses himself for having abandoned his now dead

---

* Jules Sandeau (1811–83) had a reasonably good reputation as a novelist and dramatist, but he is best known as for his collaboraton with George Sand and Emile Augier.

father to seek glory in the emperor's train (163). Then he falls in love with an aristocrat who is already committed to another man from her own class and, in despair, kills himself. Some scholars conclude simply that Romantic heroes are ill. Stendhal wrote, however, that they suffer "from no other sickness than that sort of discontented, judgmental sadness that characterizes the young people of [the impotent Octave de Malivert's] day and circle" (*Armance* [1827] 31). Though defeated, rejected, and impotent, literary Romantic heroes are usually portrayed as above the common herd, either because of their great intelligence, acute sensitivity, or heightened powers of insight or wisdom, and they are not at all adverse to being set off as an astonishing if not admirable spectacle. Almost always physically attractive, they come from the aristocracy or the upper reaches of the middle class.[17] Despite the fact that they are often orphans and virtually without exception in their late teens or twenties, seldom do they have to work for a living. Nor, indeed, do they wish to find a useful occupation. They see themselves as misunderstood outsiders, fated to be imprisoned within their situation, and are unequivocally impressed with their own singularity (despite their remarkable resemblance to each other). In words that could have been addressed to hundreds of others, Lamartine's Jocelyn (1836) feels he hears the morning star tell him, "Your life is a desert, your heart is an abyss" (*Jocelyn*, 174). Enmeshed in a society with values and attitudes they cannot accept—and given that their misanthropy is universal, they have no friends with whom they may share their own—most passively accept what life dishes up for them as they float forlornly along their way. In an amusing parody of John 17.14–16, Chateaubriand says that "they remained in the world without giving themselves to the world."[18] Although they would love to belong somewhere, to someone, to something, they would never accept membership in what is available. The father, mother, family is too base, the neighbors too vile, the surrounding reality too dull. Romantic heroes live "like someone set apart, isolated from other men" (*Armance*, 1.36). As their most notable trait, one would point to pride—excessive, over-weaning, self-centered pride.

Hungry for new experience, they view the future with skepticism if not despair (historians talk of *Weltschmerz* and, Rose's term, *Ichschmerz* or ego suffering). When they fail to establish a comforting religious faith, they concoct vague ideals and eventually decide to settle for the love of a woman (or man) who for one reason or another is inappropriate and unavailable. It is even useful to note with Lilian Furst that as Romantic heroes arrogate to themselves "the role of divinity, God is removed from the universe" (48). When reality fails to measure up to their hopes, they

7

fall prey to melancholy. When reason betrays them, they turn to imagination and dreams. Frequently they come to yearn for death. Their sensibilities are easily offended, and their solitude has the advantage of
marking their difference from the common run of human beings.
Constant's description of Adolphe serves for legions of these heroes: "I
wanted to paint in Adolphe one of the principal, moral illnesses of our
century: this fatigue, this incertitude, this absence of force, this perpetual
analysis that puts an after-thought beside every sentiment and that consequently corrupts each one from birth. Adolphe is . . . incapable of consistency, of sustained devotion, of calm generosity; only his vanity is
permanent" (*Adolphe*, 304). Frederick Garber's shrewd insight that the
self-absorbed Romantic heroes typically have difficulty distinguishing
themselves from the "other"—and are regularly brought up short when
others resist being absorbed—gives an accurate indication of their
general, emotional immaturity.[19]

Of course, while the above description of the Romantic hero characterizes the literary type that with few variations appears in hundreds of
contemporary works, the flaws in these selfish, vain heroes did not await
the insightful explications of modern critics. Contemporary writers were
perfectly competent to analyze their own creations, and did. In *Suzanne*
(1840), for example, the novelist Ourliac* points explicitly to Lareynie's
cowardice, laziness, and base, parasitic nature (177–79, 194, 200).
Edouard Alletz's† *Maladies du siècle* (1835) terms Madame de
Villecourt's complaints about her husband a "sickness . . . I mean the
sufferings of a captive imagination, the uneasiness of a disappointed
sensibility, the vague irritation of a soul tormented by the wounds that she
gave herself" (81–82). Fromentin's Dominique (1863) discovers himself
in preceding Romantic books, but "[t]heir example taught me nothing;
their conclusions, when they concluded, did not correct me either. The
harm [*mal*] was done, if you can call harm the cruel gift of looking at
one's life as though it were a show put on by someone else, and I entered
into life without hating it, though it had made me suffer a great deal, with
an inseparable, very intimate, and positively mortal enemy that was
myself" (80). Balzac's irony is patent when he discusses feckless poets
like Lucien in *Splendeurs et misères des courtisanes* (1838–47): "These

---

* Edouard Ourliac (1813–48) had some success as a novelist, and, for a time, his stories
were frequently anthologized. He was known for his ironic wit, his sincerity, and his fine
observations of contemporary life.

† Alletz (1798–1850), a diplomat and man of letters, was known for his essays attempting to
find a ground for the conciliation of philosophy and religion, though he also wrote fiction
and some poetry.

handsome geniuses are so rarely understood that they spend themselves in false hope; they are consumed in a quest for their ideal mistresses; they almost always die like beautiful insects marvelously adorned for love festivals by the most poetic of natures, and who are crushed while still virgins beneath the foot of a passer-by" (6.475). Still, it remained for Flaubert to paint with devastating clarity the essence of Romantic delusions in *Madame Bovary* (1857).

Though hundreds of tireless pens recorded these strange heroes' plaints of lassitude and ill-defined ambitions, the testimonies would have only passing interest except for the fact that they long continued to attract readers and because writers were not alone in their obsessions. A whole society supported the literary creations featuring Romantic heroes by purchasing or renting in numerous reading rooms the novels and newspapers where their demoralizing adventures were performed. Octave de Malivert's mother expresses the fears of right-thinking people before this flood of print when she wails: "God only knows the repercussions of all your reading" (Stendhal, *Armance* 34). Indeed, flesh-and-blood readers and spectators assured long life for the fictional species when they bought legions of artistic representations and paid hard-earned money to watch them act out their lives on stage. Why were so many people willing to pay to witness these litanies of self-centered despair? Most likely it is because the Romantic hero incarnated and played out deep-seated needs, concerns, and dreams of the men and women of the day.

The special cast of mind we have come to think of as Romanticism has numerous distinctive features. Seldom has such an encompassing world view swept a significant portion of the globe in so short a time and with such widespread and notable impact. Doubtless what we might call "romantic" exists in every epoch and in every mind, but there was something special about the movement that began in the middle of the eighteenth century and peaked a hundred years or so later, though with occasionally long-lived progeny. To a degree, Romanticism can be understood as an opposition to Classicism—the claims of the imagination, the individual, and emotion in confrontation with reason, universals, and discipline.

The particular spirit of the eighteenth and nineteenth centuries had something that set it apart, however. People increasingly held a quasi-religious belief in individual human beings as the be-all and end-all, in Man as the captain and benefactor of his own vessel. The nineteenth century believed that man was capable of bringing his ship to harbor, and, when he did, that he deserved the rewards. The exigencies of the community were subordinated to the rights of the individual. Not surprisingly, Romantics had a difficult time empathizing with the problems of others. Perhaps as a consequence, conditions for working people, the impoverished, the desperately ill were generally inhuman. If God was not dead, the grasping apostles of the new creed were determined to act as though He were. Increasing numbers of ego-centric people were aggressively looking out for "Number One." The Revolution of 1789 was thus the symptom of a disturbing conflagration: that burgeoning collectivity of egos we have come to know as the middle class was taking over. The "proletarian" revolution was short-lived indeed. Monarchies around Europe were determined to stamp out the fire. They ganged up on France in the attempt, and while the French as a nation were eventually brought to heel, the bourgeoisie merely solidified its position. Although various individuals sported the trappings of power within the country, the middle class was in fact king.

A new religion had been adopted by the Western World. While its temple was France, its impact was by no means limited to that country or, indeed, to the Old World. Today we have a hard time remembering the degree to which the new paradigm was revolutionary. The ruling parties of Europe had no misconceptions. It was a time of rebels and zealots. In passing but nonetheless destructive outbursts, individuals were willing to trample tradition, absolutes, institutions, civilization itself in order to make their own heaven and indulge themselves in it. Bonaparte effectively epitomized the bourgeoisie when he crowned himself, disdaining the whole religious superstructure that sanctioned some political appointments, happy to make his own traditions.

Distance in time and space gives a certain objectivity which allows us to see that the Industrial Revolution, as Albert Joseph George argued, and the rise of the middle class go far in explaining much that characterizes Romanticism. The social cataclysm was accompanied by a vague religiosity that informed (if not inspired) a great deal of the activity. The old God had been well defined. People knew what He stood for, and they wanted no more of it. They sealed the decision to be done with divine right by spilling the monarch's blood, and then, for good measure, by helping themselves to the church's lands (somewhere between 6 and 10 percent of France). The new god had yet to be characterized. The deism of the eighteenth century was turned into a vague humanitarianism. The vagueness of a relative truth which felt good was much more palatable than the old beliefs. When Auguste Comte tried to become more systematic by inventing philosophical dogma, canonizing great men as saints, and installing Man as god incarnate, the new church was revealed in all its doddering ridiculousness.

For all the philosophical and social influences on Romanticism, it was nonetheless to a large degree a literary phenomenon. Authors often described their characters in terms of other literature. Maxime du Camp's Jean-Marc, for example, is described in *Mémoires d'un suicidé* (1853) as the "illegitimate son of René, raised by Antony and Chatterton!" (18). He envies René because the latter has true misfortune causing his unhappiness (114), whereas he has only his own imagination. Even literary characters explicitly read, reread, and imitated each other. As Chateaubriand put it in the *Génie du christianisme*, "[T]he multitude of books that treat man and his feelings make people skillful without experience. They are disabused without having enjoyed; they remain with desires, and they have no more illusions. Imagination is rich, abundant and marvelous, while existence is poor, dry and disillusioned. You live with a full heart in an empty world, and without having worn anything out, you are disabused of everything" (2.218). And as literary heroes imitated, so the public. Literature unquestionably influenced the suicidal, for example, through the power of art to encourage self-destruction. Termed the "Werther effect," it has been exaggerated. Perhaps more important than literature as a cause, the long-lived literary emphasis on suicide reflected a societal obsession that was discussed repeatedly and at length. In some instances, literature's reflection of reality was more subtle. There is no question, for example, that the widespread portrayal of sickness reflects the reality of burgeoning French cities in the horrendous sanitary conditions of pre-Pasteurian society, but in novels it normally appears as the guarantee that the character's emotions are sincere. The intensity of the passion often results in the woman's collapse, whether the outcome is happy or not.

The most commonly cited explanation for the Romantic hero comes from Musset, who in his *Confessions d'un enfant du siècle* (1836) ascribed such characters to the frustration of the generation raised under Napoleon, who were encouraged to dream of glory but then had no opportunities when they reached maturity. Still, there are other explanations having to do with widespread social unrest, the breakdown of families, and the weakening of religion.[20] It seems impossible to deny such explanations, at least as contributing factors, though the thought comes immediately to mind that no one cause can by any means be considered discrete and that the causes previously suggested are simply not sufficient to explain the Romantic hero. Social, political, and religious insecurity have occurred with some frequency in the Western World without producing a Romantic hero. And while there has only been one Napoleon, many others have like him promised glory and produced chaos. Society's fickleness despite the most certain assurances is neither new nor even unusual. Many young people in many periods have been encouraged to believe in a rich future, only to learn that the dazzling image leading them down their path was a mirage. Only in the period from 1750 to 1850, however, have such influences resulted in legions of Romantic heroes in literature.

What makes the Romantic period different is the particular concatenation and combination of pressures that were at play. Although many periods have something resembling factors like the Industrial Revolution, extreme political instability, social unrest, migration, weakened religious and ethical foundations, changing aesthetic canons, endemic illness growing from poor sanitation and malnutrition, wide spread methods of child care that exacerbated psychological problems, and rapid dissemination of information and commentary, only the Romantic period has them all. Significantly better communication, which came from much improved printing presses, cheap paper, and the rapid expansion in number and size of newspapers, was also particularly important. Because of increasingly inexpensive and available means of publication, people rapidly learned of the problems confronting society and had plenty of opportunity to fear the consequences.

Most historical, sociological, and literary studies leave the causes aside and have been content merely to describe the Romantic movement and its various manifestations. Such practice produces a shallow conception of the literature, the society, and the period, whereas focusing on changing social realities like the treatment of infants, education, and suicide offers a more adequate understanding of the causes of Romanticism and the Romantic hero. Emile Durkheim's classic sociological text, *Le Suicide, étude de sociologie* (1898), describes moreover the egoistic and anomic types that we can recognize in the heroes of Romantic fiction and theater. While Durkheim's theory was based on questionable statistics, such recent sociologists as Whitney Pope claim the theory has been substantiated by later studies, and it consequently serves as an excellent means of setting off recent historical research and my own study of literary texts. I use the resultant triadic vision of literature, history, and social sciences to consider the causes, the aesthetic reflections, and the creation of a society. By looking at certain events, problems, and themes, in some cases for the first time, or, in others, from a different angle, I believe that it is possible to draw important conclusions about major forces set in motion by pre-Romantics and Romantics. It also permits a more adequate definition of the movement: *Romanticism is a sense of insecurity, both widespread and profound, that grows from a tumultuous personal, public, and natural world, marked by acute awareness of reality, extreme self-consciousness, and a desire to escape.* In that it affected the whole of society, this mind-set was new to Europe, and to France, in the late eighteenth and nineteenth centuries.

Just as Romanticism is the predominate way of looking at the world, so depression is the predominate trait of Romantics. Many scholars have mentioned the prevalence of melancholy in the art of the day, but I want to go further and suggest that the depressive feelings described and represented at such length and with such frequency, and categorized under the rubric of "melancholy," are the motive cause of Romanticism and the reason Romanticism differs from both classicism and baroque. Neither depression nor melancholy was unique to Romantics, but at no other time in the known history of the Western World has such a large proportion of the population suffered so severely. It is not far wrong to say that society was depressed. I suspect that the endemic depression derived primarily from childhood neglect, in particular from the absence of parents in the lives of children. Resulting feelings of insecurity were exacerbated by the turmoil of this turn-of-the-century world. In the attempt to find a way of organizing the constant agitation and change, artists indulged in radical experimentation of art forms and attempted to develop new modes of expression. With, moreover, the evisceration of the patriarchy, the individual was deified, giving rise to an ethos of self-indulgence and to the cultivation of self-destruction.

The Romantic hero gives a pulse to what history tells us about the society. As the Industrial Revolution spread and capitalism slowly moved to the fore, the agricultural economy of France was disrupted. Cities were not prepared for mass migration from the countryside. The new urban populace was undernourished, overworked, and unresistant to the epidemics of typhus, cholera, syphilis, and tuberculosis. Many lived in incredible squalor. As ecclesiastical, aristocratic, and paternal authority weakened, French people were left with little spiritual and physical support and diminished ethical standards.[21] People moving away to the city cut themselves loose from the familiar network of family, friends, priest, and local aristocrats that had provided a certain amount of stability in agricultural communities. It would be wrong to suggest that the feudal and seigneurial culture of the countryside was heavenly or even trouble-free; it was merely reasonably stable in comparison with the incredible turmoil of the aborning society of the Industrial Revolution. Although urban immigrants rapidly made new contacts, as Thomas Brennan and others have argued, the supportive ties of such new and shifting groups were shallow and weak. On the public scene, revolutionary governments executed the aristocrats who had once provided governmental stability; they also attacked the institutional church that had offered the cement for social authority and standards by which acceptable life and government were possible. Olwen H. Hufton describes in dire detail the catastrophic results for those who were destitute—whether deranged, abandoned, or merely incapacitated through sickness, age, or injury—when the social services were disrupted.[22] Novels like Picard's* *Le Gil Blas de la Révolution* (1824) and Ourliac's *Suzanne* (1840) bring palpitating life to poverty and madness.

This period from the mid-eighteenth to the mid-nineteenth century goes under many labels. Depending on one's orientation, it may be termed pre-Romantic and Romantic, or the early Industrial Revolution, or the Enlightenment and the Revolution, or simply the transition period from Early Modern to Modern Europe. The label does not matter all that much, though each of these terms brings attention to an important facet of the day. I want to suggest that under all of these rubrics, there was a set of motive factors that caused the distinctiveness of this epoch. Romantic heroes represented in literature are particularly important to understanding what was going on in France itself. Blown by the winds of every passing doctrine, these verbose, feckless interlocutors of their age, constantly seeking apparently lonely but violent and exotic scenes where they could be at center stage, gave imaginative shape to the hopes and fears of real people who struggled in the midst of revolutionary changes. The character of modern France, in a large degree even of the Western World, and many of the attitudes that we readily recognize as our own became realities at the turn of the eighteenth and nineteenth centuries. We are familiar with all too many of the terrors. Our own affection for these most unlovable of heroes may come from the anguish generated in our own society as we move from the Industrial Age that the Romantic hero observed to the equally tumultuous "Information Age," or however we ultimately designate this new complex society that currently seems to be rising around us.

Life in nineteenth-century France was riddled with anguish. The Revolution and especially the Terror gave people in all classes reason to fear for their lives, though a less apparent but no less real apprehension of the future was perhaps responsible for the most pervasive and long-lived dread. Paintings of shipwreck, floods, catastrophes flooded the market, and are one indication of the distress.[23] The aborning Industrial Revolution brought turmoil to the whole of society; significant portions

---

* Now forgotten, Louis-Benoît Picard (1769–1828) had considerable success in the early nineteenth century with his vaudevilles and comedies. As can be seen in the novel mentioned here, he was particularly adept at portraying everyday life.

of the population moved from the countryside to the city in search of a better life; and major political and economic changes shifted civilization's power base. What had been an agrarian, land-based society turned capitalistic as money became a commodity. While the terms "political and economic changes," "power base," "land-based society,"[24] "capitalistic" are abstractions, each marks very basic changes for real people. Men, especially, but increasingly women and children as well, poured into cities poorly prepared to receive them. With the urban influx of population came loneliness, squalor, and disease, since the rudimentary sanitation systems, social agencies, and available housing were incapable of taking care of the increased demands. Especially after the revolutionary government disenfranchised the church, which had previously looked after many of the sick, old, and hungry, conditions rapidly worsened. It took little intelligence to see that the old ways were dying and that new and unpredictable forces were making the future problematic.

As wars were won and lost, rulers peacefully or violently enthroned and deposed, new power structures elbowed their way into place. Unpredictability and seemingly universal capriciousness left many men and women traumatized by unbearable anxieties. Fear was engendered by the weakening structures of traditional religion and by the growth of strange supernatural beliefs, by the unknown, by poverty, by a loss of identity, in short, by change that produced conditions differing significantly from the comfortable, well-known, and understood realities of the past. It was bad enough that the familiar was changing, but the fear that the unfamiliar might hide malignity was worse. For every awful reality there were dozens of prospective dangers. Many Frenchmen found no deliverance. Timorous and alarmed, they had little choice but to suffer in a shifting, even convulsive and destructive world. Some subsided into despair and found escape through alcohol, drugs, or suicide. Others proclaimed new hope through various social movements, through equality of the sexes, through democracy, through the invention of new truths.

Whatever the period from 1750 to 1850 is called, it was a time of incredible change: change in religion, government, education, transportation, and economic system. Virtually every phase of life was radically affected by the violent agitation and disruptions that characterize these years and raised an anxious sense of accumulating change in individuals. Like Balzac's Lucien de Rubempré, people were "dizzy from the rapidity of the Parisian whirl" (*Illusions perdues*, 5.264). A number of issues were particularly important and obvious in France. Moreover, historians' considerable, often admirable work to bolster our understanding with facts drawn from French civil and ecclesiastical records is frequently persuasive. Still, historians do not have certain knowledge about a great deal of this reality, because statistics are rare and unreliable. Indeed, in many instances my own and others' views are reasonable hypotheses drawn from miscellaneous documents that have survived in part and seemingly by accident from the past. The existence, depth, and pervasiveness of change, however, is not in doubt.

Perhaps most obviously, the migration of people exemplified this change. Individuals left their places of birth and moved, usually to a nearby city, then again to another urban area, frequently to Paris. Until fairly recently, as Michael W. Flinn has pointed out, "there was a tendency to assume that the population of early modern Europe remained relatively static." We are now aware, however that "in some areas there was an astonishingly lively movement of population."[25] It is true that in regions of France where the population was tied to the land—one thinks for example of eighteenth-century Normandy—seventy-five percent of the small landholders born in a typical parish were still there at the time of their marriage (Flinn, 67). Moreover, seventy percent of the males died in the parish of their birth (ibid.). To some degree, the surprisingly large twenty-five percent to thirty percent balance who disappeared from the parish registers is to be explained by the fact that younger sons and daughters were often forced to leave to find employment, but this migration also included predictable kinds of displacement, like a woman moving to join her new husband, a young person going elsewhere to take up an apprenticeship, or an elderly person seeking long-term medical help. One quarter of a province's population is not, however, a negligible figure, and, in fact, the agricultural regions of Flanders, Normandy, Dauphiné, and the Massif Central regularly produced significant numbers of people that moved towards Lyons, Rouen, Nantes, Bordeaux, and Paris in search of a livelihood, most often to labor in domestic service and the textile industry or as apprentices (Flinn, 67–68).

Military service was also important, for France was frequently at war in the seventeenth, eighteenth, and nineteenth centuries. Corvisier estimates that over sixty percent of those who enlisted never returned home.[26] In Zola's novel *La Terre* (1889), the character Jean Macquart, who found himself in a area far from home and stayed (4.273–74), was typical. If one of the wars left an area devastated, the people brought in to repopulate and to seal the victor's rights of ownership were generally from rural areas, thus moving the new inhabitants from one rural region to another. Most migration was nonetheless from the country to cities or urban areas, a migration that accelerated after epidemics of cholera or typhoid created vacancies in the labor force that needed to be filled.

16

Particularly after the Saint Bartholomew's night massacres in 1572, significant numbers of Protestants left France and abandoned positions in the trades and professions for others to fill, which of course encouraged further urban immigration. As Flinn concludes, however, rural overpopulation and the threat of consequent poverty was the primary source of most of this movement, whether the migratory streams resulted directly from religious persecution, war, the quest for profit, or, simply, the need for a job (72). Daniel Roche emphasizes the importance of the fascination exerted by the city, the desire for anonymity and freedom that urban areas made possible, the hope of permanent rather than temporary employment, and the dream of rising in society.[27] Like Ourliac's fictional but typical Lareynie, immigrants came from across France "to make [their] fortune in Paris."[28]

Much of the migration was temporary.[29] Far-ranging peddlers persisted in their search for customers; craftsmen looked for opportunities; agricultural workers followed the harvest. Restif's quasi-autobiographical *Monsieur Nicolas* (1790–97) describes young artisans who enjoyed the excitement of travel and who moved from job to job before finally settling down in one city or another. Most migrants were between the ages of 15 and 29 (Flinn, 68). It is also notable that much of this migration occurred in stages: people who eventually ended up in Paris usually stopped for a year or more at several intermediary places. To some degree the ebb and flow of migration reflects the fact that the early stages of the Industrial Revolution took place primarily in small cities and certain rural areas,[30] but it also reflects a fear of the unknown—at least for the first displacement. People did not want to get too far from family and friends, from the places and customs in which they were reared. The novelist Picard pointed to an important aspect of migratory reality when in 1824 he wrote, "Poor people never move far."[31] A job within a comfortable day's travel from home was much to be preferred to something farther afield, though subsequent moves surely reflect the continuing attraction of the metropolis as people dreamed of the prosperity that seemed possible there. This widespread and continuing displacement affected many aspects of daily life. It doubtless accelerated the weakening of the church, since relatives and neighbors had less influence on the attendance of young people at mass and the practice of the faith. Restif illustrates in *Monsieur Nicolas* how increasingly transient lives surely had much to do with the illegitimate birthrate almost doubling (from 2.9 per one hundred live births prior to 1750 to 4.7 per hundred in the 1780–1820 period—Flinn, 118). The significance of the migration is highlighted on realizing that 60 to 78 percent of the inhabitants of typical quarters of Paris and its suburbs were born in the provinces.[32]

Louis Henry estimates that from 1740 to 1792 when the population of Paris was between 500,000 and 600,000, something like 7000 people moved to Paris every year ("Volume," 1084). Some left, of course, but many stayed. It is startling to realize that with 7000 new inhabitants per year (much less the 14,000 of some estimates) the population of Paris should have increased to 1,300,000 by the 1790s. In fact, it did not come anywhere near that figure. Though Paris, Lyons, Nancy, Nantes, Toulon, and Versailles had doubled in size from 1600 to 1750 (de Vries, 140), from the mid-eighteenth century to 1789 the population of Paris only increased by 100,000 to an estimated total of 620,000 people (Roche, 7; Dupâquier, 2.94). Figures for Parisian live births and deaths leave no doubt that the city would have lost population in substantial numbers without the constant influx of people. Clearly, cities had grown beyond their capabilities, and, for natural and unnatural reasons, urban life was now mortally dangerous. It also seems that during the five revolutionary years, France itself which began the Revolution with something like 28.5 million inhabitants, lost half a million people by 1795 (Dupâquier, 2.65).

The figures given here are only estimates. Although attempts to divine population early and late in eighteenth-century Paris vary by as much as 400,000 people,[33] they nonetheless give a sense of how important migration was during the early years of the Industrial Revolution. Most of these immigrants came from the lower, working classes, but individuals from educated, professional, and aristocratic families were far from unrepresented.[34] Multitudes of fictional characters—like Marivaux's Marianne in *La Vie de Marianne* (1731), Restif's Edmond in *Le Paysan et la paysanne pervertis* (1787), and Balzac's Rastignac in *Le Père Goriot* (1834–35)—follow their flesh and blood counterparts by immigrating to Paris.

What the figures do not give us is a sense of the living reality of these people moving into major cities like Paris. For that we turn to the arts. Louis Léopold Boilly's canvas, *Les Déménagements* (*Moving House*), reproduced as the frontispiece of this book, vividly configures the aspirations that impelled moving, the hardship involved in the displacement, and the desperate realities that all too often awaited the migrants when they finally settled down. Some years after completing and exhibiting the painting in the official Salon exposition of 1822, Boilly wrote or perhaps only authorized the following explanation: "[I]t was just a slice of Paris life: A wagon (loaded with furniture), hand-carts, stretchers, porters, cross a public place and go to the new residences of the tenants; here is another exact picture of Paris, when the rent terms expire."[35] The description comes from the catalogue for the sale that Boilly organized in 1829, and it has been taken pretty much at face value. Because it was written some seven years after the painting was finished, however, one might not wish to grant the catalogue entry absolute credence. Boilly's written emphasis on realism may have had less to do with accurately conveying his thoughts when he was in the throes of creation than with a sale-oriented desire to exploit the subsequent popularity of *physiologies* and their pseudo-scientific studies of people in various trades, professions, and locales. Whatever the case, there is no doubt that the painting's depiction admirably represents migration. While the artist says he was portraying those moving from one place to another within the city and its environs as their leases ended, it is also possible that it includes representatives of those new arrivals coming from without, all with the hope of something better in Paris. The glowing faces of several people portrayed, which markedly differ from more serious expressions in an earlier sketch,[36] give some indication of the dreams that stimulated this displacement.

The activity portrayed in Boilly's painting was not unusual in the streets of the early nineteenth century. When Clara, the title character of Auguste Ricard's* novel *La Grisette* (1827) is abandoned by her lover Oscar, she decides to change her residence to another part of Paris. Ricard's description of his character moving from one apartment to another leaves no doubt that Boilly's painting represents a common occurrence: "Do you see that little two wheeled cart, drawn by a skinny old nag loaded with a bed, a chest of drawers, chairs, a pair of tongs, bellows, water pots, etc., etc., which is slowly going down Saint-Jacques Street, crossing the bridges, and about to be lost in the mass of cabriolets, carriages, carts, hackney cabs, drays that create unending congestion at the entrance of Saint-Denis and Saint Martin Streets. . . . Behind the cart comes Clara, walking with a pensive, melancholy air, and carrying her money, jewelry, and the last letter from Oscar in her purse" (*Grisette*, 2.172–73). Does the large, two wheeled cart in Boilly's painting depict a young mother and a cartman, or should the fact that the latter appears much younger than in the earlier sketch (Siegfried, 136, fig. 8), thus about the age of the woman, imply that a young family is moving from the country in search of a better life?

As Carol Eliel has shown, the long-proclaimed realism of Boilly's genre paintings of scenes from Parisian life needs to be nuanced. We must "read" the paintings. They are by no means a simple slice of life. As an example, Eliel points to another of Boilly's paintings, *Les Conscrits de 1807*

---

* Ricard (1799–1841) was a prolific novelist in the popular vein. His novels are usually set in the lower middle or working classes.

1. Louis Léopold Boilly. *Les Conscrits de 1807 défilant devant la Porte de Saint-Denis* (*1807 Draftees Filing Before the Saint-Denis Gate*), 1808, Carnavalet. © Photothèque des musées de la ville de Paris/cliché . . . by SPADEM.

défilant devant la Porte de Saint-Denis (*Draftees of 1807 Filing Before the Saint-Denis Gate*, 1808—plate 1). The work's composition cuts off the arch's entablature, which seems strange until we remember that the friezes and sculpture that were lopped off honored the Emperor Napoleon. By thus effacing the arch's surmounting art work, which celebrated the Empire's military glory, and consequently by eliding the most grandiose elements one would expect to see in this particular location, the painting uses a kind of minus device to emphasize a group of young draftees being led off by a soldier whose exaggerated enthusiasm draws attention to the paucity of excitement behind. The huge piers of the Saint Denis arch dwarf the conscripts just as they must have felt overwhelmed by the forces leading Napoleon to continue his wars and the very unpopular conscription. Some of these young men will surely die in the battles of Eylau or Friedland.[37] The anecdotal understanding encouraged by the scenes from family life, that John Stephen Hallam calls Boilly's first manner,[38] continues into the second that concentrates on genre paintings, though the subject matter changes. From domestic tableaux designed to produce moral lessons, the painter shifted to panoramas that elicit social commentary. "Readings" of Boilly's paintings after 1800 that neglect the social and cultural realities of the contemporary scene are much impoverished if not completely misconstrued.

Joseph Ballio used contemporary drawings to identify the site of Boilly's *Les Déménagements*. It is now indisputable that the square encumbered by carts, wheel-barrows, and people and the buildings in the background right were in the Port-au-Blé, a Parisian working-class area not far from the Pont Notre-Dame.[39] The accuracy of the depiction renders the hazy but nonetheless easily recognizable church in the left middle ground all the more startling, for it is Santa Maria del Popolo, and it belongs not in Paris but in Rome.[40] The painter blurred the sharp lines and dampened the clear colors used for the other buildings, making the Roman church seem dreamlike, a distinct contrast from the realism of the rest of the painting. I would suggest that the anomalous church symbolizes the Holy City and thus implies the aspirations, the hopes, the dreams of the thousands upon thousands of people in this period who continued to move in the attempt to situate themselves for the new world that they watched being born around them. Most of them would be disappointed, since Paris could be and often was a harsh and bitter experience. The resulting hard reality conflicting with their dreams was perhaps symbolized by the black hearse in the right middle ground that seems to be moving toward the "church of the people."

Until the radical restructuring of Paris in the second half of the nineteenth century, conditions for immigrants were at best frightening, at worst devastating. When one was not wealthy enough to purchase protection from the harsher realities, life in Paris was appalling. Louis Sébastien Mercier, the peripatetic witness of late eighteenth-century life in Paris, called it very simply "the filthiest city in the world"; Pierre Chauvet, despite the restraint imposed by his scientific pretensions, calls it "the center of stench."[41] In places, he adds, the fetidity made flowers wilt (38n1). The city streets served as the receptacle for the waste of industrialization. Domestic brooms pushed household garbage into the thoroughfares, though at Balzac's Vauquer boarding house an abundance of water was used to flush the garbage under the gate and out into Neuve-Sainte-Geneviève Street (*Père Goriot*, 3.52). Dishwater, which particularly exercised Parent-Duchâtelet* in 1824 (1.219–20), was simply tossed out of convenient windows and doors. The offal of businesses like butcher shops assailed passers-by with the odors of blood and putrescence and left the shoes of the unwary red. It was not just that refuse littered the paving stones; it was that these streets were in fact open sewers. Although an ordinance against emptying chamberpots out of windows was passed in 1780, latrines continued to feed into gutters which occasionally burst allowing the contents to run down walls, and in one way or another end in the streets. Passers-by were often drenched with the miry liquid descending from dark corners of neighboring buildings. Sudden, particularly plentiful downpours were known to collapse umbrellas and cause thunderous reverberations in passing carriages. If one were near public facilities that held a particularly high density of people and lacked cesspools, like the Ecole Militaire, the Hôtel des Invalides, or the hospital of la Salpêtrière, the gutters and streets were unspeakable (Parent-Duchâtelet, 1.215). Nor was the dung from horses and other animals a negligible item (Ronesse, 7). Paris had over 20,000 horses alone. Unpaved streets were disgusting cesspools that on bad days came up to the knees of those who could not avoid them; paved streets were dangerously slippery when it rained. The wheels of carts and carriages constantly stirred the stew.

Theoretically the garbage was collected, while the effluent moved regularly into sewers (described at length by Parent-Duchâtelet) and then into the Seine. Reality, however, was another matter entirely: "This

---

* Alexandre-J.-B. Parent-Duchâtelet (1790–1836) was a well regarded physician who devoted himself to public health. He was particularly admired for his studies of the Parisian sewer system and of prostitution.

appalling residue makes its way slowly along the streets toward the Seine River. . . . where water porters fill their buckets in the mornings with water that the insensitive Parisians are obliged to drink," as Mercier recounted (*Tableau*, 1.117). The "black streams of *boue*" (*Père Goriot*, 3.50) might be along the edges of the street or down the middle, wherever the lowest path happened to be. If the street was poorly engineered, the foul, black water might not flow at all and formed instead stagnant pools that could cover the entire block (Ronesse, 74–75). In narrow, crooked, dark streets, high buildings prevented the sun from ever reaching the muck, which in some cases like the Rue aux Fèves where Sue's Fleur-de-Marie lived in *Les Mystères de Paris* (1842–43), never dried out.[42] It did not help that Paris was built on low, swampy ground. Some buildings had cesspools, but even when such receptacles did not filter into neighboring basements or wells, cleaning them was a hazardous, messy endeavor that left spilled residue throughout the city as carts carried the effluent away. Overflowing cemeteries likewise had to be cleaned up, especially when the common graves became so full that the weight broke down the sides and spilled corpses into adjoining basements. Rectifying the situation required carting the bodies through the streets before being dumped in old quarries like that at Denfert-Rochereau. Mercier wondered how anyone could live in this "filthy den of vice and ills . . . in the middle of air poisoned by the putrid odors of butcher shops, cemeteries, hospitals, sewers, streams of urine, piles of excrement, chemists, metalworking shops..." the list continues *ad nauseam*, and he marveled at what Parisians could get used to (*Tableau*, 1.122).

In the eighteenth century before the authorities encouraged more extensive use of sewers, and thereby turned the Seine into an indescribable cesspool for half a century, the city employed *boueurs* (mudders) whose task it was to remove the accumulations from the streets. Whilst the dried sewage was sold for fertilizer, the efforts of the *boueurs* were by no means effective, their carts frequently slopping over and providing another hazard for pedestrians. Mercier said with resignation, "It does you no good to walk on tiptoe. Being watchful and quick doesn't keep you from getting splattered" (*Tableau*, 1.1255). In the streets, where Baudelaire saw "old tramps" and "consumptive negresses" "trudging through the *boue*" (*Fleurs du mal*, 83, 123), the filth provided a means of income for some homeless people. Armed with planks that could be lowered for a contribution, beggars helped wealthier citizens cross the streams of sewage. Another painting by Boilly called *L'Averse ou Passez-Payez* [*The Shower or Pass-and-Pay*], dating from around 1805, portrays the common occurrence. Other beggars armed with brushes served as dedungers [*décrotteurs*], though those pedestrians who followed Mercier's advice and wore only black could dispense with the service (*Tableau,* 1.200–01).

The result of all this was *boue*. The dictionary says the word means "mud" or "sludge," but in Paris of the pre-Romantic and Romantic periods it was, as Mercier put it, "a really special *boue*" (*Nouveau Paris,* 1.xx). It was a fetid, black, sticky substance that would occasionally eat through clothing. Although many of the sources for the above description of Parisian streets come from the late eighteenth century, conditions did not change until after the middle of the next century. As Eugène Sue testifies in 1842, the black sewage water continued to splash up and thus color the houses in dark, vile avenues (*Mystères,* 1.2). Whether or not Lutèce, the name of the primitive village on the site of Paris, meant "city of mud," as Mercier and others have believed,[43] Paris was unquestionably a city of *boue*. Balzac calls it a quagmire or *bourbier* (*Père Goriot,* 3.89— the word's relationship with *boue* is obvious). While it is true that most European cities had serious difficulties with sewage and sanitation, the *boue de Paris* was particularly vile. F. Chon, on attempting to find words to depict the indescribable filth of one of the worst streets in Lille, was reduced to comparing it to the Parisian Rue Mouffetard.[44] Paris was, so to speak, the standard, and it is virtually inconceivable that a Parisian would have been as offended as a certain Grugnet of Libourne when Bernard Thomas dumped a bucket full of dirty water in the gutter upstream from his residence. Grugnet blackened Thomas's eye, knocked him down, and thus covered him "with muck and mire from head to feet."[45] "Parisian streets are generally disagreeable," Mercier said with wonderful understatement, "but in certain [rainy] months they are ghastly" (*Nouveau Paris,* 5.40).

If there had been any precipitation at all, there was simply no avoiding *boue*. When children played in the streets, they would be covered with it (Ricard, *Grisette,* 1.xxii–xxiii). Pedestrians were inevitably going to be splashed. Occasionally, the victim kept his or her good humor. Restif tells about the time when, all dressed up and walking gaily to see his mistress, a coachman purposefully sent four of his horses' large hooves through the muck, showering the narrator "with thick water as black as ink. Good-by beautiful white stockings! good-by beautiful luster suit! Everything was dirtied, even my beautiful, embroidered cuffs" (*Nuits,* 11.2519). He wipes his face and makes things worse. At first he is furious, but he decides that the splashing was a good corrective for his pride. Now, humbled, he and his mistress have a good laugh. The experience teaches him to wear stockings dyed black and to avoid wearing his best clothes in the streets. Not everyone took it so well. In Lesuire's* *L'Aventurier français* (1782) Rolfe laughs uproariously when her bumbling suitor's foot slips on the paving stones as he bows "energetically" to her. It takes no imagination to know that with "his nose in the *boue*" (1.94) he has trouble seeing the humor. Sensible people simply did not choose to walk in these streets. That Stendhal's Henry Brulard does so in the early 1820s merely marks his naïveté, which is emphasized when he then makes the mistake of stopping off afterwards to visit Mme Cambon. Stendhal did not need to describe either the young man's odor or the state of his clothing. He merely tells us that Henry came "on foot in the *boue*" (*Brulard* 357), and readers of the day knew why Mme Cambon would make him understand his "foolishness" (ibid.).

Symbols often begin rather prosaically as common, everyday things that take on meaning because of their qualities, use, or context. One of the marvels of Baudelaire's poetry comes from his ability to sense the way the objects of our world affect us, to recognize the poetry of everyday things, whether cracked bells or orange skins discarded on the street. When he proclaims to Paris, "You gave me your *boue*, and of it I made gold," or, elsewhere, "I kneaded your *boue*, and of it I made gold,"[46] he takes an everyday reality to play on the *nigredo* or blackness that was the initial state of chaos and dissolution from which the alchemists hoped to bring *aurum philosophicum*. Romantic writers did not wait for Baudelaire to exploit the larger implications of *boue*, however. When Baculard d'Arnaud's† cowardly Mylord Thaley agrees to a counterfeit marriage in order to get the virtuous Fanni into his bed and then abandons her, her father James writes to the scoundrel, "You have dishonored my old age. You have covered a man, an entire family with the *boue* of infamy" (*Fanni* [1764] 47–48). Similarly, when the life of Boulay-Paty's‡ title character begins to fall apart, and he fears he will sink to crawling in the *boue*, he clings to the remnants of his Catholic faith (*Elie Mariaker* [1834] lxxxii). In the same period, Balzac referred to the low-class bars as a "band of *boue*" around the city. He is of course thinking of their location in the surrounding, unpaved, poorer areas, but he wants it understood in a moral sense, as well: it is a "belt of the most

---

* Robert-Martin Lesuire (1737–1815) was a prolific author of essays, poetry, and, especially, popular novels marked by numerous peripeteia.
† François-Thomas-Marie de Baculard d'Arnaud (1718–1805) wrote very moralistic, sentimental novels and plays. Specialists of popular theatre mention his melodrama *Le Comte de Comminges* (1764) as a particularly horrifying example.
‡ In his day, Evariste Boulay-Paty (1804–64) was a reasonably well-known poet, though little of his verse would attract a modern reader.

shameless of Venuses" where working people lose their week's wages ("Fille aux yeux d'or" [1834–35] 4.1041). One of Sue's characters wants to prevent the memory of her brother from being dragged through the *boue* (*Mystères*, 3.101), and Sue's narrator terms the prisoners of Saint-Lazare "gangrenous hearts" and "loathsome *boue*" (ibid., 2.251–52).

Ricard provides a more subtle example that serves as a means of foreshadowing: M. de Saint-Germain sent his carriage away, since he thought Clara would invite him to stay the night. When she did not, the count, "obliged to return home on foot, felt the rain stream over his clothing. His fancy slippers [and] the openwork of his stockings left his feet and legs exposed to the abuse of the *boues de Paris*. Soaked to the skin, squelching through the gutters that had turned into torrents, he felt a glacial chill slip into his veins" (Ricard, *Grisette*, 4.59). A rapidly traveling carriage "covered him with a flood of water and *boue*. Soaked, covered with manure, frozen," the amorous count needs help undressing when he finally arrives home (ibid., 4.60). While Clara's resistance doubtless made her seem more desirable to the count, readers would have understood the adumbrative function of the foul drenching. The love affair that M. de Saint-Germain is so excited about will not prosper. Rather, it draws him into an inappropriate marriage with a low-born grisette, Clara. As a new countess she will find herself at loose ends in the foreign world of aristocratic wealth (4.35) and, tragically, will not just betray her husband but will do so with an unworthy lover. Later Barbey d'Aurevilly's Duchess de Sierra-Leone explains how she is getting revenge on her husband: "I swore that I would soak his name in the most vile of *boues*, that I would turn it into shame itself, into filth, into excrement! To do that, I became what I am: a common whore" ("Vengeance" [1874] 2.253). *Boue* stands as much for the vile, for shame, for failure as it does for sludge. When Count Norbert takes Julien Sorel riding, the latter "thought he rode superbly. But coming back from the Bois de Boulogne, right in the middle of Bac Street, he fell . . . covering himself with *boue*" (*Le Rouge et le noir* [1831] 2.36). The story comes out, and excites the hilarity of Mathilde de La Mole. Though Julien carries it off with aplomb, no one could mistake his mortification. Lucien Leuwen does less well when *boue* is thrown in his face. He is "covered with *boue*" (1.805). *Boue* symbolized poverty, disgrace, moral degradation, failure in all its forms. Musset's narrator returns to the city and seems to hear, " 'Debase yourself, debase yourself! and you will no longer suffer!' That's what . . . is written on walls with soot, on streets with *boue*" (*Confession*, 62).

I have gone on at some length about this one aspect of eighteenth-and nineteenth-century Paris because I want to insist on the indescribably horrible reality that confronted, and unquestionably affected, immigrants. Perhaps the most vivid descriptions of what it was like to arrive a stranger in Paris come from the pens of the quintessential outsiders, Stendhal and Balzac. The latter, who considers the experience repeatedly, thinks the most discouraging sight is the population itself. Visibly unhealthy, you can read the danger of death in their contorted, cadaverous faces. Seeing such people and perceiving clearly both their exhaustion and greed, newcomers "initially experience a movement of disgust for this capital city, a vast workshop of sensual pleasures, where they themselves will soon be caught and willingly deformed" ("Fille aux yeux d'or," 5.1039). "[I]t is not just a joke to call Paris a hell" (ibid.). Those who come to the city will certainly be marked by the experience. They may like Paul de Manerville and Victurnien d'Esgrignon be bankrupted, or like Lucien de Rubempré end up a pathetic, jailhouse suicide, or like Rastignac or Bianchon they may gain fortune and fame. Of course, for Rastignac, it was at the price of total corruption.

Illusions perdues (1837–43) tells the story of a handsome young poet, Lucien de Rubempré, who is carried off to Paris by the provincial beauty, Mme de Bargeton. Lucien's arrival in Paris is prepared at length and in detail. Though something of a 'swell' back home in the provinces and able to engage in an affair with the socially prominent Mme Bargeton, he lacks the funds to keep up appearances in the capital city. Indeed, the trip itself takes most of what he planned to live on for his first year there (5.256). Things cost more away from home and a good deal more in such a tumultuous city as Paris during the age of Romanticism and the Industrial Revolution. Indeed, "Paris is not beautiful for the little things to which people of limited means are condemned" (5.257). Those who had a certain importance in the provinces cannot avoid being impressed as they look around them, on the one hand, by the incredible luxury and affluence and, on the other, by the extreme poverty. It affects one's view of oneself. In Paris, Lucien is a nobody; poorly dressed, miserably lodged, he "experiences an immense, personal diminishment" (5.264). He spends his limited funds on new clothing, but with no understanding of fashion, he chooses unwisely and wastes his money. To keep himself from being splattered, he takes cabs. Without connections, except for his provincial mistress who quickly realizes that she has made a mistake, he commits one faux pas after another. On becoming discouraged he comforts himself with a decent meal, only to realize that the cost is exorbitant and that such indulgences only accelerate his impoverishment.

The moment finally comes when Mme de Bargeton snubs him, and he rages in the letter he sends: "After the beautiful dreams you pointed to . . . I see the reality of poverty in the *boue de Paris*. While you, brilliant and adored, move across the heights of this society, I am shivering on its threshold in a miserable garret where you threw me away" (5.291). Lacking the persistence and drive to turn his apparently real talent into work of artistic genius, he compromises by turning to journalism and, eventually, to prostituting himself.

Rastignac has several advantages. He initially makes the acquaintance of Paris as a student, where it is unnecessary to spend considerable sums to move in style. Even when "[t]he demon of luxury bit him at the core, the fever of gain caught him, the thirst for gold dried his throat" (*Père Goriot*, 3.107), he has family connections that are willing to guide him into the society where he may make essential contacts. He already knows that if you wear finery in the streets, you will inevitably get manure (*se crotter*) on your stockings and ruin your shoes (3.76), and on his way to visit Mme de Restaud he "takes great precautions to avoid getting dirty [*se crotter*]" (3.94). It is all for nothing, though, and he tries to brush the muck off before arriving. "If I were rich," he says to himself. "I would have come in a carriage" (ibid.). Balzac insists on the street filth, on Rastignac's lack of fortune, and on his ignorance. The engaging young man needs to get the manure of the provinces off, *se décrotter*. His soiled boots and pants are simply the prefiguration of what is to come. Because he lacks knowledge, he offends the Restauds, and when he later decides to spare his clothing by hiring a carriage, he picks a rental coach that still carries the decorations from a lower-class bridal party. He sees his mistake only on hearing the laughter of the valets as he steps to the ground and compares his conveyance with the elegant coupé waiting in Mme de Beauséant's courtyard. Rastignac, however, is determined not "to remain in the *boue*" (3.120). He extorts money from his family by threatening suicide (ibid.). Then he uses his mistress mercilessly, and he allows himself to be used in a swindle that leaves him very wealthy. Of course, in the process, he becomes what Bixiou calls "a profoundly depraved gentleman" (6.337). At the end of *Le Père Goriot*, he not only knows but he accepts that society is like "an ocean of *boue* in which a man plunges up to his neck if he so much as dips his foot in it" (3. 262). He is precisely the kind of person that Gobseck describes: "So as to avoid being splattered with manure by going on foot, the great lord or the one who apes him takes a thorough bath in the *boue!*" (2.974).

When Stendhal's Henry Brulard comes to Paris sometime in the first quarter of the nineteenth century, he is depressed by the absence of mountains and by "[t]he *boue de Paris*" (*Brulard*, 332–33). An entry in Stendhal's diary for 10 September 1811 is more anguished: "We should yell at the inhabitants of Paris . . . 'You are savages, your streets give off a loathsome stench. A person can't take a single step in them without being covered with black *boue*. . . . That comes from your absurd idea of turning your streets into a public sewer'" (10 sep. 1811, *Journal*, 1.1088). Not only were the streets disgusting, they must have been terrifying, for they dramatically illustrated the price of failure. No one coming to the city from the provinces can have failed to feel the fear and anguish of any newcomer, but there was something particularly terrible about the bustling city of Paris. Success could mean great wealth; failure often meant death. And people were formed to a considerable extent by the society, by the physical surroundings, the everyday reality, and the customary practices of mothers, fathers, tradespeople, police, in short, of the bustling populace as almost everything changed in the creation of a new world. In this mass of scurrying creatures, there were many Romantic heroes. Certainly, readers recognized themselves in the literary type. Many were depressed and lonely if not sick. Many had significant doubts about their ability to succeed. Indeed, many would fail. Their success and their failure, I suggest, was a function of their society.

2. Jean-Baptiste Greuze. *Les Sevreuses* (*The Nursemaids*), 1765, The Nelson-Atkins Museum of Art, Kansas City, Missouri (Purchase: Nelson Trust).

CHAPTER 2

The Unrocked Cradle

Ducray-Duminil's* novel, *Lolotte et Fanfan* (1788), tells that when Charlotte Blett-Winzel (Lolotte) and her brother the Chevalier Roselle d'Oresty (Fanfan) were unceremoniously abandoned with the dying Derly on a small island in the West Indies, they were virtually without resources. They were only three years old, and their protector died almost immediately of the wounds he received in their defense. Nonetheless, they live, the novel maintains, and show remarkable resourcefulness. Very early on, for example, they begin cutting a mark on a big tree each and every day to mark the passage of time (1.57). Consequently, they are able to ascertain that it is four years, two months, and eight days later when Milord Welly is shipwrecked on their island. He finds the children, whom he takes under his wing for an energetically English upbringing. The task is daunting, since despite their gentle characters Lolotte and Fanfan are unquestionably savages, but Welly accepts the responsibility. He tells them, "[I]f I must finish my days on this island. . . . my sweetest occupation will be to raise you and form your hearts to embrace virtue" (1.14). They respond by bringing Welly "tortoise eggs, birds' eggs, jujubes, dates, yams, and some liqueur in a shell that tastes like something from palm trees" (ibid.). Despite his weakness from the stress of shipwreck, strength returns "after having eaten a little of these simple, frugal dishes" (ibid.). Welly does not doubt that the Supreme Being has sent him to the island to bring the children up properly (1.18), and he soon goes off with Lolotte and Fanfan to explore this "new Eden" (1.21).

The miraculous fact that the children are still alive is explained at length. Shortly after making land, a remarkably benign, undomesticated nanny

---

* François-Guillaume Ducray-Duminil (1761–1819) was the author of a number of very popular novels that were laden with sudden changes of fortune and other melodramatic elements and were frequently adapted for the stage.

goat came by with her kid, and the children drank their fill. Subsequently, they lived in a cave, and they ate fallen fruit and birds' and tortoise eggs. Only later, when they were bigger, were they able to throw rocks and kill birds, which they ate on the spot (1.22, 50–61). From a partially legible letter found on Derly's mummified body, Welly learns that the children come from Piccadilly, a rich section of London inhabited by nobles, where he is well acquainted. Suddenly, he and the children are forced to interrupt their conversation, for a whale arrives with Welly's boat on its back, and Welly is able to extract an abundance of materials to facilitate life on the island. From observing the hardship of living like miniature Robinson Crusoes, the reader is invited to see the development of a new Swiss Family Robinson. Welly even moves them out of the cave into a proper hut. As Providence would have it, he manages to rescue a number of books from the boat: Shakespeare, Addison, Richardson, Pope, Young, Milton, Voltaire, J.-J. Rousseau, Prévost, Le Sage, and others. It will consequently be possible to give the children a suitable education (1.71). Life becomes especially good four years later when Welly's servant Jerwik arrives, having escaped from the devil-worshipping Indians that had found and enslaved him.

The adventures of the little family are far from over. We learn the terrible story of Milord Welly and hear of evil stepmothers, adulterous passions, a vile son lusting after his own sister, stolen inheritances, false accusations, abduction, attempted murder, poison, evil suborners, suicide, pirates, slaves, rejected children, virtuous women, and righteous men (the list could easily be extended), as Welly, Jerwik, and the children escape from the island, and with many adventures make their way back to England where all is eventually resolved. Lolotte marries Welly's son; Fanfan takes as his bride the daughter of the minister who has been signally helpful in saving Welly's offspring. The British monarch then sends the lot of them back with 200 settlers to found a new colony on their island, now renamed the "Island of the Twins"—"in memory of abandonment of the two children and of Heaven's visible protection in withdrawing them from this deserted place" (2.185). Naturally, "All our heroes finally met happiness and peace there in this country setting" (ibid.).

To dismiss Ducray-Duminil's fiction as an unrealistic descendant of the Gothic novel would be a mistake, for it offers insight into the psychological life of the period's readers. From early in the eighteenth century, the new field of anthropology was raising interest in human beings and how they differed from animals. The so-called "natural man" that had not been infected by civilization was particularly fascinating to readers. Both scholars and ordinary people joined Rousseau in wondering what made human beings human, how they differed from animals, whether there was such a thing as natural morality, and whether it could be found and studied. By mid-century, Defoe's *Robinson Crusoe* (1719) had been translated into French several times, and then reprinted in dozens of editions. As the nineteenth century approached, new adaptations and translations appeared and republication continued at an energetic pace that showed no signs of abating in the 1800s. As Roger Shattuck put it, "The Romantics loved Defoe's book."[1]

Robinson's story is closely related to the tales of Lolotte and Fanfan and to the "enfants sauvages" abandoned in the woods. They too were miraculously kept alive by wolves or other animals that were willing to nurse them. Europe as a whole, and France in particular, had long been extremely interested in wild or "wolf" children, supposedly nourished by animals, and capable of sustaining themselves from their youngest years. In 1766 Linaeous cited nine cases of such children, and in 1775 Rousseau's *Discours sur l'origine et les fondements de l'inégalité parmi les hommes* mentioned five.[2] Many of the travel memoirs published in the eighteenth century told stories of children that had been raised by animals (Shattuck, 195). The documentation was very scanty, but the fascination was real. Ducray-Dumisnil was merely exploiting a topic of great interest, and it is not surprising that his *Lolotte et Fanfan* was reprinted in at least ten different editions, with numerous other apparently unauthorized reprintings between 1788 and 1812.

Why was there such interest in *enfants sauvages*, in wild or merely abandoned children? The attraction was so widespread and so strong that anthropological interests do not in themselves seem a sufficient explanation. One may wonder whether the very subject of being lost or abandoned might have touched some particular emotional chord in the people of the day. Abandonment is, of course, a basic fear of all human beings. It is, for example, an essential element of the Oedipal archetype, since the myth suggests that when Oedipus was left to die in the hills around Corinth, it caused a deep-seated sense of loss that could only be satisfied by a renewed intimacy with his mother. It is a curious fact that the people of the late eighteenth and early nineteenth centuries were obsessed with abandonment, motherlessness, orphans, and, as will be pointed out in a later chapter, with incest.

Modern psychology leaves no doubt that abandoning a child can cause a lifelong sense that something desperately irreparable has happened. Children who have lost a parent through death commonly feel that they have been abandoned and, however irrational it may be, are often angry with the parent that died. The knowledge that the death was unintentional does not change the very real sense of deprivation and need. The orphan

33

feels abandoned, left behind, even rejected, and the resulting anger and resentment can have a significant impact on the personality and behavior of the individual involved. For my purposes, this theme of abandonment may provide insight into the strange and seemingly inexplicable popularity of *Lolotte et Fanfan*. It is almost certainly related to the legions of motherless children and orphans that populate the period's literature.

The impact of Jean-Jacques Rousseau's incredibly popular autobiography might be cited to explain the fact that mothers dying in childbirth became a commonplace in later literature. Early in the *Confessions* of 1782, and early as well in the formation of the Romantic hero, Rousseau wrote: "I was born feeble and sick. I cost my mother her life, and my birth was the first of my misfortunes" (1.7). Rousseau was not the first to turn an orphan into a hero. Marivaux's Marianne (1731–42), for example, lost both of her parents in a highway robbery while she was still a baby, and the title of Crébillon *fils*'s* four volume (but still uncompleted) *Les Heureux Orphelins* (1754) merely makes the theme obvious. Though Rousseau does not have the virtue of precedence in the death of his auto biographical character's mother, his phrase resonated in the hearts and minds of readers and recurs with little change in numerous later novels and plays. Parental loss continues throughout the literature of the next century and a half. Brouard-Arends even views Diderot's *La Religieuse* (1760/1796) as "the novel of the absence of maternal love."[3]

Maternal death in childbirth recurs with such frequency in subsequent literature that, without taking anything from Rousseau's undoubted influence, one should suspect that it might also have much to do with some emotional factor. Certainly, such events were commonplaces in popular novels. Milord Welly tells in the already cited *Lolotte et Fanfan* of 1788 that his mother "lost her life in giving it to [him]" (1.183), and he is not alone. Mme de Senneterre's birth, as well, "cost my mother's life" on the first page of Fiévée's† *La Dot de Suzette* (1798). The title character of Madame Cottin's frequently reprinted *Claire d'Albe* (1798) also lost her mother while still in the cradle. One is hardly surprised to hear Chateaubriand's René say several years later in 1802, "I cost my mother her life on coming into the world" (185). And, as a means of indicating

---

* Claude-Prosper Jolyot de Crébillon (1707–77), known as Crébillon *fils*, wrote dialogues, tales, and novels, one of which was considered lewd and led to his imprisonment. His masterwork, *Les Egarements du coeur et de l'esprit* (1736), continues to be admired.

† Joseph Fiévée (1767–1839) wrote several popular novels, which have now fallen into oblivion. Primarily a newspaperman, he became editor of several major papers, and he was one of Napoleon's special counsellors, responsible for keeping the emperor abreast of public opinion.

the theme's resiliency, just as in 1827 Ricard's banker, M. Dupont, tells his daughter, Claire, "My wife died in giving you life" (*Le Portier*, 2.129), so in 1836 Laurence's "young mother died in giving him [we later learn the character is really female] birth" (Lamartine, *Jocelyn*, 60). Laurence returns to the terrible event and its results:

> My mother, who died in giving me birth,
> Withdrew from me too soon the shade of her love... (ibid. 228)

After Rousseau, the mother's death while giving birth to the child was used often as a formative event in the psychological make-up of a character. It is of course only one variation of parental death, and it was not alone. The title character of Ducray-Duminil's *Victor ou l'enfant de la forêt* (1797) was abandoned as an infant, and he was long left with nothing but monthly subsidies to indicate that someone, somewhere remembered him. In a later novel, Joseph Fiévée's Frédéric (1799) eventually uncovers his parents. The topos is even more noticeable in Balzac's *La Comédie humaine*. From the beginning in 1829 to the end in 1847, there is an epidemic of real and functional orphans. Dumas *père*'s Antony (1831) was also bereft of parents and, moreover, ignorant of their identities. He has various reactions to what was clearly meant to come across as a life-long sense of loss. At one point, he is ready to ask any woman he crosses, "Could you be my mother?" (Act 2, Scene 5, p. 163). I have let this catalogue go on at some length, since I want to give a sense of the enormous quantity of examples that exist.[4]

Even when heroes of the period have a mother, they commonly feel deprived, for she is often absolutely unmaternal, ignorant of and perhaps uninterested in a role as nurturer. Esmeralda's mother in Victor Hugo's *Notre-Dame de Paris* (1831) is insane. In Balzac's "La Fille aux yeux d'or" (1834–35), Henri de Marsay's natural mother unceremoniously washes her hands of the child; Paquita's mother sells her daughter into slavery and, finally, death. Victor, the illegitimate hero of *L'Enfant du carnaval* (1796), was left at the wet nurse's for six years. Other fictional mothers, like Balzac's duchesse de Cadignan of 1840, develop postiche maternity only after all other means of self-expression have been foreclosed. Typically, the main characters of late eighteenth- and nineteenth-century French fiction are separated at a young age from their mothers. They are frequently orphans. And the refrain of motherlessness continues in so many imitators that it should be recognized as a nineteenth-century topos, a commonplace among the devices, information, and attitudes that were the conventional stock-in-trade for writers of the period.

The "monster mother" theme continued to be developed later in the century. Des Esseintes, for example, whose "mother, a long, silent, white woman, died of exhaustion. . . . had kept only a fearful memory of his parents, without gratitude, without affection. His father, who ordinarily lived in Paris, he hardly knew; his mother, he remembered motionless and bedridden in a dark room of the château de Lourps" (*A rebours*, 28). Maupassant's women include several who give birth to monstrously deformed children. One could mention "La Mère aux monstres" (1883), "Un Fils" (1882), and "Le Champ d'oliviers" (1890). For Maupassant the best mother seems to be the one who, as in "Aux champs" (1882), gives away her child so that he may then succeed in society. Even when the main characters of Romantic novels have parents, as Glyn Holmes has pointed out, they most often suffer from a poor relationship and a lack of understanding.[5]

The anguish of the protagonist at the beginning of Proust's *A la recherche du temps perdu* (1913) when he is separated from his mother marks a reaction to this long-lived literary phenomenon. Against the backdrop of the Romantic hero (it should be remembered that the protagonist's grandmother presents the boy with a selection of George Sand's novels), the episode of the nightly kiss turns into burlesque, and the grandiose posturing of the main characters of countless works is revealed in all its childishness. Proust's little boy disobeys, lies, and cries. To the child's misfortune, he succeeds in breaking the established rules and is allowed to spend the night with his mother. Of course, the episode has other functions within the novel, but it serves as a convenient summation for the kind of personage that interests me here. By Proust's day, motherless heroes and unnatural mothers had for some time been less common in literature, as were the petulant, self-centered complaints of the Romantic hero. The phenomenon of the maternally-deprived literary character became noticeable in the late eighteenth-century, rose in frequency, reaching a high point in the 1820s, 30s, and 40s, before declining and virtually ending by the 1880s and 90s.

There are a number of explanations that could be advanced to explain the motherless children and orphans so prevalent in French literature of the late eighteenth and early nineteenth centuries. Almost certainly, they are a reflection of several converging social forces. Because of the Industrial Revolution and the change from an agrarian to a capitalistic economy, populations massed in the cities. Disease was rampant, malnutrition the norm, and mortality at every age and in every class was high.[6] Giving birth was so dangerous that many women died in the process, leaving children without mothers.[7] As any woman knew, to love a man

36

was to run a very real risk of death. The historian Michelet encapsulated the feeling when he wrote, "Love is the *brother of death*" ("L'amour est le *frère de la mort*"—*L'Amour*, 119). Clearly, the homophonous coupling of *l'amour /la mort* (love and death) was more than a pun. In short, realism is one possible explanation for the presence of orphans in the poems, plays, and novels of the day. Still, it does not suffice: although giving birth was so dangerous that many women died in the process, leaving children without mothers, the undoubted results of the dangers of childbirth are far less significant than Romantic representations would indicate. About one in a hundred births resulted in the death of the mother.[8] However distressing this figure may be, and in comparison with today's figures it is indeed appalling, it is a striking fact that eighteenth- and nineteenth-century mothers died no more frequently during childbirth than they had for hundreds of years. Why then does Romantic literature make us think the rate was far higher?

Of course, writing about orphans provides authors with certain advantages. The orphaned characters are unencumbered by family. They are then free to make their own way and establish their own standards of behavior. Should the heroes also be ignorant of their past, they provide authors with numerous opportunities for subsequent intrigue and surprising changes of circumstance. Such possibilities were soon exhausted, however, and occur less frequently after the turn of the century. Rousseau's example may be important. He did not allow his autobiographical character to dream about a possibly magnificent heritage. He insisted rather, as did most other authors, on feelings of loss and a sense of foreshadowing misfortune. Another possibility seems worth considering. Could it be that the multitudinous, fictional children without mothers mirror not so much real orphans, which had occurred at a relatively constant rate for hundreds of years, but rather reflect more recent, widespread feelings of parental rejection and loss? Fictional orphans would then be less a reflection of a physical than of a psychological reality. They join with other literary and social currents to form a pattern of considerable significance. Stories of orphans were so widespread and marked in so many literary works that it seems only reasonable to assume it appealed to a deep sentiment in the people who purchased the works. Perhaps the possibly temporary willingness to share the orphan's fate imaginatively indicates that people felt orphaned. Did these authors and readers feel rejected, lost, abandoned? Was there something going on in this society that would produce such widespread, apparently unmotivated malaise?

The frequency and long life of the literary Romantic hero is very difficult to explain. Especially in his aggressively voluble pessimism, he seemingly has little to do with the most frequently cited causes for Romanticism: the rise of the middle class, the Industrial Revolution, capitalism, and the major social movements of this society. In general he was portrayed as an aristocrat. One can perhaps see in the various authors' personal lives of the period why Byron invented Childe Harold, Chateaubriand René, Goethe Werther, for the world had changed and there was no longer an assured place for the likes of them. Chateaubriand, for example, sees the fact that he had scarcely left his mother's womb when he was shipped off to a wet nurse as a prefiguration of the exile of poverty and emotional distress which were to characterize much of his life. At one point, convinced that the aristocracy's last hour had struck, he contemplated suicide. Although he had a manuscript of genius when he returned to France, he had no real assurance of position or success. He felt both rejected and displaced. And there were hundreds of equally alienated young nobles. Some who had emigrated to support their king came home to find their wealth confiscated; all found their future subject to a society controlled by the middle class. As Lloyd Bishop points out in his reappraisal of *The Romantic Hero and His Heirs in French Literature*, "René's malady . . . is that not only of a unique individual but of a social class: the aristocracy rendered obsolete and useless by the Revolution."[9] It is indeed difficult to understand why the displaced Chateaubriand's characters, Chactas, Atala, and René, were not painted in even darker colors. Such aristocrats could see that events had made them obsolete.

While one can sympathize with the feelings of despair in aristocratic writers, one cannot help but marvel that, especially after 1820, *René* became a key text for a whole generation of young people and that a rather large public of middle-class readers was willing to read and share his and other similar sufferings at second remove. Certainly, René was a peculiar creation, and when viewed dispassionately, rather disagreeable; hardly the sort of character one would expect to elicit widespread reader sympathy or, as indeed was the case, identification. Like others of his breed, his obsessive focus on his own needs and emotions would in the real world make him insufferable. Frequently depressed, the typical Romantic hero swings from dreams of power and glory to passive complaints that he is not appreciated as he should be. Moody, unstable, and capricious, he generally drifts with the current, though he is capable of unpredictable, violent activity on behalf of an impossible dream. Convinced that he is so superior that society should place him by acclamation in a position of power and authority, he so disdains his peers that he is certain—correctly—that they will not do so. The resulting

Weltschmerz, a combination of egregious egotism and fatalism, leaves him incapable of desiring anything sufficiently to move him to effective action. He is an outcast, a pariah. Too young to have experienced his society, much less the world, he has judged it and found it wanting. He masks his self-doubt with arrogance, and, most importantly, his conviction that society will not have him becomes self-fulfilling prophesy. He sets himself up for failure. Taciturn only whilst among his fellows, when he manages to surround himself with a solitary wilderness blanketed by rain and clouds, he is recorded by a faithful scribe as he relentlessly whines of his lassitude, vague idealism and ambitions, uncertainty, languor, and melancholia. Of course, the wilderness is where he should be. The combination of megalomania, paranoia, and depressive passivity would have made him a trying companion. Even the saintly Father Souël found René's presence burdensome. For all this, the wonder is not that writers created so many offspring of Rousseau in the *Confessions*, of René, of Werther, of Manfred, the wonder is that so many people were willing to read the resulting litanies of self-centered despair.

There were hundreds of variations on the model. Joseph Fiévée's Edouard de Rulsberg of 1803 emphasizes Germany and the undoubted importance of German Romanticism. Edouard has traveled relentlessly "in the hope of dissipating his melancholy which was all the more painful as it was unmotivated. Born in the midst of abundance, he had not yet desired anything passionately. Nonetheless, his mind was ardent and his heart capable of a great love. The arts had seduced him for a time; the sciences had occupied him in turn without being able to fix his vague imaginings. If fortune had treated him well, nature had been no less favorable. Rulsberg had an advantageous stature, and his face could have served as a model to paint the sublime calmness of sorrow. It was impossible to see him without feeling an indefinable interest. One hoped that he would have the happiness that his virtues merited, but in considering him with attention, you could not avoid the presentment that he was destined to be unhappy" ("Jalousie," 1.1–2). Other heroes might be marked by other characteristics—an aristocratic lineage, for example, personal beauty, or great wealth—but all share the defining traits of solitary natures and melancholy with the unmistakably delicious perfume of coming disaster.

Enumerating the Romantic hero's qualities makes it especially difficult to explain his long, literary life. He was usually a noble, while the reading public was for the most part middle class. Why were low-born readers so avid to spend their money and read of aristocratic anguish? Why were members of a class whose potential was virtually unlimited so willing to wallow in the pitiful cries of a highborn depressive? After all, the middle class now filled the positions and owned the land which had once belonged to the aristocracy. The existence of Romantic heroes—or heroines—and their complaints across hundreds of best-selling books to a middle-class audience proves that something about these characters spoke to certain needs in the rapidly enlarging reading public. One would like to know what those needs were. Musset blamed the generation's bleak outlook on young people's disappointed dreams of glory when Napoleon was finally defeated and died (or was murdered, as has been suggested). Musset's is an enticing explanation, until one recalls that the Romantic hero began appearing well before Napoleon and the turn of the century, though the period of intense popularity did not come until the early 1820s. Rousseau's *Confessions* (1782, 1789) and the French translation of *The Sorrows of Young Werther* (1776) provided important stimuli. Etienne Delécluze* testifies that the "moral malady" associated with the Romantic hero was fashionable late in the eighteenth century. It encouraged a number of suicides.[10] Further consideration of the Romantic hero's qualities may suggest another explanation for the appeal to such a wide reading audience. With the exception of his extraordinary intelligence, the Romantic hero resembles someone suffering from maternal deprivation.

To lose one's mother while very young or, worse, to go without the specific, focused attention and love of someone in the early years of one's life has terrible consequences. Babies who are not handled, cuddled, played with become apathetic. The lack of parental attention is, moreover, considered one of the most important factors in faulty psychological development, as the directors of infant wards, nurseries, and orphanages are now well aware. Children's emotional reactions, their attitudes toward themselves, their relationships with others, their development, and even their physical health can be severely damaged by a lack of care and affection. The nurturing, care provider need not be a mother, need not even be a parent. Anyone will do, as long as the person offering the love and nurture remains consistent in their presence and in their love. Often infants deprived of such care waste away and die. As M. A. Ribble showed in classic studies, the children of indifferent or antagonistic mothers are similarly affected.[11]

Despite the availability of adequate food, neglected children become tense, negative, restless, and withdrawn within a few weeks of birth. Many

---

* Etienne-Jean Delécluze (1781–1863), a minor painter and one-time pupil of David, became a well-known art critic and intellectual. His *Souvenirs* provide a valuable witness of the Restoration.

even refuse to nurse, and develop such symptoms as muscular rigidity, shallow breathing and constipation. Most are apathetic and depressive, with little interest in food or other stimuli. The biggest dangers are to children under six months of age. As H. Bakwin pointed out, when neglected these infants are generally listless, emaciated, febrile, pale, relatively immobile, unresponsive to communications like a smile or a coo, and with obviously unhappy appearances.[12] Subsequent studies made it clear that neglectful homes can be as dangerous as institutions. Furthermore, in a publication by the World Health Organization, Mary D. Ainsworth found that the effects of little or no parental care and love occur not just in institutionalized children or the offspring of bad parents, but even in those infants who suffer through a series of separations from the mother figure.[13] Other studies leave no doubt that those children who live may have serious psychological problems. These effects are not universal, since the susceptibility of children to the stress of deprivation varies considerably, yet many are seriously and permanently maimed. Adults who have lived through inadequate physical, social, emotional, or intellectual nurturing as infants tend, like Romantic heroes, to be restless, pathologically inattentive, anxious, depressed, irritable, withdrawn yet avid for attention. They have difficulty concentrating, on the one hand, and establishing relationships with people, on the other. These early experiences are crucial, since it is now clear that they permanently mark the individual; neglected children, for example, suffer from life-long feelings of rejection.[14]

Unlike England and Germany, where by 1800 high-born mothers had by and large moved from wet-nursing and, when possible, were nursing their own babies,[15] France of the late eighteenth and nineteenth centuries became increasingly committed to hired nurses and thus institutionalized a society-wide phenomenon of unbonded children. Because of the wet-nursing practices of France from the mid-eighteenth through much of the nineteenth centuries, they are a promising field for investigation. They provide a plausible explanation of why the Romantic hero was especially multitudinous, long-lived, and welcome in the literature of France. Not only are the qualities of someone who has suffered from such deprivation similar to those of the typical Romantic hero, there was a very close chronological relationship as well. From the 1760s though the 1850s most French children were wet-nursed, though by the 1840s the practice of wet-nursing had begun to wane. Upper-class women were either nursing their own babies or insisting that the nurse live beneath the parental roof.[16] By 1870, a Parisian obstetrician can say, "Comfortable families put their children with a nurse only if it is physically impossible to do otherwise."[17]

Reform in other classes did not take hold until 1874, when the Roussel Law required medical surveillance and the registration of nurslings, and the 1890s Pasteurian revolution leading to sterilized feeding methods.

For almost a hundred years the majority of French infants were put into situations which, in the light of modern psychology, seem destined to create a nation of unbonded children. Current clinical thought would give reason for believing that the treatment of French children in the period from Rousseau to Flaubert would have resulted in serious, psychological problems that appear remarkably similar to the identifying traits of the Romantic hero. Those children who were in many cases deprived of the focused love of a nurturing adult, and who survived, became either authors that created a plethora of Romantic heroes in literature or members of a receptive public that avidly purchased the newspapers and books featuring them. When we look at the plight of mothers, nurses, children, and of the adult lives that resulted, as well as the reflections in literature, it seems possible that we have been taken to the cradle of the French Romantic hero, one of the most important, and puzzling, literary phenomena of the nineteenth century, and to a set of phenomena that remarkably resemble the well-documented effects of maternal deprivation.

From antiquity, wet-nursing was a part of the class structure.[18] It was attractive for a number of reasons. Nursing and the attendant care were very time consuming, physically demanding, and disruptive of normal relationships—people believed, for example, that sexual intercourse spoiled the milk and impeded the flow. Such beliefs are occasionally revealed in literature. The hero of Pigault-Lebrun's* *L'Enfant du carnaval* (1796) explains: "[L]egally married women . . . who become legal mothers never fail to send their children to the wet nurse, if they have any care for their bust and any indulgence for their lovers" (27).[19] Previously, only the wealthy could afford to "spare the mother's health" by hiring wet nurses, and, of course, wet nurses were enlisted from the impoverished classes. For the wealthiest of the high-born, as had been common in aristocratic homes from antiquity, the nurse lived in the family's home or, like the nurse of Madame de Souza's† Eugène de Rothelin ([1808] 244), nearby in the neighborhood, thus under supervision (which may account for the rarity of characters resembling the Romantic hero in the writings

---

* Pigault-Lebrun was the pseudonym of Charles-Antoine-Guillaume Pigault de l'Epinoy (1753–1835). His mildly libidinous novels and comedies were very popular.

† Madame de Souza was the pen name of Adélaïde Filleul, marquise de Souza-Botelho (1761–1836). After her first husband was guillotined, she supported herself by writing sentimental romances that are usually set in the aristocratic society of pre-Revolutionary days.

of those earlier aristocrats who became creative writers). Periodically, wet-nursing was criticized, but the practice was common among the well-to-do from at least the time of Rome. We know that starting in the thirteenth century, the children of French royalty were entrusted to closely supervised wet nurses (outside of France, the practice was more varied; the Hapsburg empress, Maria Theresa, for example, nursed her many children). So, through the eighteenth and nineteenth centuries wet-nursing became more common in French society, particularly in the middle class where it seems to have been to some degree caused by a desire to keep up with Lady Jones, to some degree for the sake of convenience. In Restif's *Ingénue Saxancour* of 1789, for example, Moresquin sends his new daughter to a wet nurse, so that he may prostitute his wife, the title character (124, 130). Balzac claimed that the typical middle-class family left their children with the wet nurse until they could be packed off to school ("Fille aux yeux d'or," 5.1046). The poorer *petite bourgeoise* and working classes needed wet nurses because families could not live without the incomes of both husband and wife.

There were other things which made nurses desirable. Nancy Senior argues that medical opinion undermined the confidence of young mothers in their ability to nurse a child. When, moreover, mothers persisted in their desire to nurture their own babies, they were expected to wait several says before beginning, which made success problematic.[20] The high rate of infant mortality was perhaps even more important. Philippe Ariès suggests, in his authoritative study of childhood under the monarchy, that children were so fragile that people put little value on them until they had lived long enough to prove viability. Though there were exceptions in individual cases, the vast majority of parents apparently felt that it was foolish to invest oneself in a creature that might well, and often did, die. Not until children could take a place with adults did they really join the family. In the meantime, they were frequently neglected, abandoned, or put out with the wet nurse. Only after what Ariès calls "the discovery of childhood" that began to take place in the Romantic period does this attitude start to change.[21]

France of the late eighteenth and nineteenth centuries extended wet-nursing with decreasing supervision and increasing personal and social damage. From a relatively small, aristocratic class (that produced few authors) it spread through most of French society. Almost everyone was affected—both writers and readers. Sussman quotes a 1780 statement by Jean-Charles-Pierre LeNoir, lieutenant-general of the Parisian police: Of the 20,000 to 21,000 children born in Paris each year, "[o]ne thirtieth at most sucks the mother's milk, an equal number is nursed in the mothers' and fathers' homes. Two or three thousand, belonging to the class of the well-to-do citizens, are dispersed around the suburbs and environs with wet nurses. . . . But the least wealthy and consequently the most numerous class was necessarily forced to take wet nurses at more considerable distances and in some ways at random."[22] Using these figures, we can then say that in 1780 between 19,400 and 20,000 Parisian children were put with a wet nurse; about 19,000 were sent out of the parental home; from 2,000 to 3,000 of these were nursed in the Parisian region; and over 16,000 were sent far enough away so that any supervision was difficult or non-existent.[23] That was only for one year. In parts of Lyon seventy-five percent of newborns were sent to the country for commercial nursing. In Marseilles fifty percent (Fildes, 229).

Because of the enormous, widespread need for wet nurses, they were in short supply. As birth rates increased conditions worsened. Although Galliano estimates that the late eighteenth-century death rate of infants in their first year of life was only 17.7 percent, his study was conducted in an area that was close to Paris where one would expect more supervision than further afield.[24] Sussman establishes "three different levels of infant mortality for children born in the cities of late eighteenth-century France. The lowest, perhaps 180 to 200 per 1,000 (or a little higher), was the normal for a baby nursed by its mother, a pattern that was rare in the largest cities. In the middle, perhaps 250 to 400 per 1,000, was the infant mortality of babies placed at birth with rural wet nurses. The highest level of infant mortality, perhaps 650 to 900 per 1,000, prevailed among newborns abandoned at the foundling hospitals."[25] Jacques Houdaille hazards that fifty percent of all eighteenth-century rural children died before the age of ten.[26] Many of these children would have come from the cities for nursing. Consequently, the rates for the whole of France were probably about the same. Half the children died.

For the nineteenth century, Sussman's tables listing the placements of Parisian wet-nursing bureaus are an indication of the entire society. They show mortality rates of around twenty-five percent for 1789–92. By 1815 and from then until the early 1870s infant death rates were regularly above thirty percent, some years well above (*Selling,* 116–17). Emile Duché estimates that from 1839 to 1859 twenty-nine percent of all French babies died before their first birthday.[27] Jacques Donzelot says simply, "[T]he death rate of children entrusted to nurses was huge: around two-thirds for nurses living at a distance and one-fourth for those nearby."[28] As in the preceding century, approximately half of all children died before the age of ten, and the mortality rate rose steadily until the 1860s. Faÿ-Sallois cites Monot and Brochard, who in 1866 and 1867 state that in some areas the infant mortality rates exceeded seventy percent (73–76). Other studies leave no doubt that though the percentage of children wet-nursed declined through the nineteenth century, the actual numbers of nurslings and the mortality rates did not. By 1869, there were 54,937 births in Paris (which had been somewhat enlarged geographically). Mothers in the middle and upper classes were increasingly breast-feeding their own babies, and the commercially nursed had decreased to forty-one percent, that is, 22,529 children, of whom fifty-two percent died (Sussman, *Selling*, 111–12).

The variation in these figures indicates how difficult it is to know precisely what was going on. Their similarly high numbers makes it possible, however, to estimate conservatively that approximately two thirds of all infants born from the late eighteenth century through the mid-nineteenth century were wet-nursed and that of these at least one-third died. If the nurse did as was expected, and weaned her own child as soon as she took on another's, death was the common result for the prematurely weaned infant.[29] As the practice of commercial nursing spread downward through society, it became increasingly difficult to find suitable wet nurses in the neighborhood, and more and more infants were sent to the countryside far from their families. In some cases, the deaths resulted from fraud or neglect: the wet nurses had taken too many nurslings, gave preference to their own children, stopped lactating, or were themselves too busy, ignorant, or careless to provide minimal care. Using cow's or goat's milk for artificial nursing was disastrous, given the lack of sanitation, as was entrusting more than one child to the same nurse (the practice in the hospices with abandoned children where up to ninety percent died[30]), since sickness was then spread by the nurse. The conclusion is inescapable: the rising infant mortality rate during the eighteenth and nineteenth centuries was directly tied to the increasing practice of wet-nursing.

Rousseau's *Emile* (1762) praised the practice of mothers' keeping, nursing, and caring for their children and was doubtless responsible for a short-term reversion to maternal breast-feeding in the upper classes, but by 1783, according to Louis-Sebastian Mercier, the fashion of familial infant care among Parisian women had passed.[31] In general, unless the nurse's milk supply ceased—and if she was honest or responsible enough to inform the family—the child stayed with her until death or weaning, usually at around two years of age. Athénaïs Mialaret (1828–99), who became the wife of the French historian Michelet, was not, she says, "remembered" and reunited with her family until she was four years old.[32] Chateaubriand was left until he was three.

Today the horrors of such practices seem evident. There was the likelihood of sickness, either due to infection or negligence, which could lead to death. Sanford Kanter claims, "The Franco-Prussian War reduced infant mortality in France during the war from 33 percent to 17 percent because . . . actual or feared disruption . . . caused bourgeois mothers to suckle their own children."[33] In respect to psychological damage, we do not know how harmful it may be for a child to be given up at two or three days or at a week, though studies indicate that infants are astonishingly perceptive, thus susceptible to the harm inflicted through maternal rejection and loss. Sir Ralph, the morose hero of George Sand's *Indiana*, says, for example, "Scarcely was I born when I was repulsed by the heart I needed the most. My mother sent me away from her with disgust" (321). If taking a baby from its mother within the first few weeks of birth is not a problem, others remain. Careless or neglectful nurses are the most obvious, but a loving nurse might cause even more serious scars, for at two to four years of age the weaned child was usually separated from the nurturing figure, often with little ceremony or preparation. Such children might suffer doubly for mothers twice lost. In Sophie Gay's* *La Comtesse d'Egmont* (1836), which examines rejection from a number of different angles, Séverin illustrates the point. He tells about being taken away from his nurse: "When I woke up . . . I tearfully called for my nurse. Alas! this excellent woman, the first affection, the first regret of my life, the person who replaced my mother... I was not to see her any more!" (173).[34]

As appalling as the infant mortality rates were, it is perhaps worse to consider those children who lived. To put the figures given before in a somewhat different way: out of every ten infants, 6.6 were sent to the wet nurse. Only 3.3 lived. Of the 3.4 children that were maternally nursed, approximately twenty percent or 0.66 children died, leaving 2.7 living children. As a result, of the original ten children, something like 5.9 were still living at the end of the first year. More than half of these living enfants had survived wet-nursing. In short, slightly more than fifty-five (55.9) percent of the population of late eighteenth- and early nineteenth-century France lived through commercial nursing, where, as the deaths indicate, a standard of neglect prevailed. Many of these children were emotionally maimed, physically neglected or abused and, as adults, would undoubtedly have borne the psychological scars of the treatment they received. Rachel G. Fuchs' statistics indicate that the damage done to

---

* Sophie Gay (1776–1852) wrote more than twenty works, including novels, stories, and plays, of no particular note. She was more important as the hostess of an influential Romantic salon.

nineteenth-century children who received minimal care and attention was indeed as serious then as it is today. Looking at the prison population, she takes the number of criminals relative to the population as a whole and compares that to the incarcerated "enfants assistés" (welfare children) relative to all such wards of the state. The comparison is instructive. In 1860, one abandoned child out 350 had become a condemned criminal, while for the rest of the population the figures were only one in seven hundred. A further breakdown for such wards in 1849 is even worse. "[T]here were 130 'vicious' or bad youths out of 9,000 or one in sixty-eight."[35] Institutionalized infants made do with whatever the state or church could provide with wet-nurse wages that were often far from competitive. Those infants who lived until they got a nurse were usually sent where the conditions (and viability) were the least favorable, that is, far from Paris with little or no supervision. In short, the children whose maternal deprivation is best documented produced significantly higher levels of social misfits or criminals. Two writers whose psychological aberrations are extraordinarily well documented in their own writings may serve as examples. Restif de la Bretonne was wet-nursed for a short time (see n19). Given the date of his birth and his class, the Marquis de Sade almost certainly was as well. As Jean-Jacques Pauvert observes, "While we do not know enough to judge Sade's feelings about his mother, it is difficult not to notice how many mothers are mistreated in the course of his oeuvre."[36]

Wet-nursing is by no means absent from literature, but the idyllic visions of the earlier Dumas and Sand give way to a far less pleasant portrayal. In a now famous passage of *Madame Bovary* (1857), Flaubert's narrator follows Emma when, on a whim, she goes off to the wet nurse's squalid house to see her child.[37] "At the sound of the gate, the wet nurse appeared, holding a nursing child in her arm. With her other hand, she pulled along a sickly looking brat, whose face was covered with scrofula and who had been left in the country by his parents, Rouen hosiers, too busy with their business."[38] When Emma's baby, the third child in the nurse's care, vomits on her mother's collar, Emma unceremoniously flees, the wet nurse trailing behind to beg for soap, coffee, and brandy. The child, Berthe, is pictured here and there across the rest of the novel, wan and silent, eventually employed in a cotton mill. Pigault-Lebrun's previously mentioned *L'Enfant du carnaval* describes at length the way a wet nurse takes—in addition to her wages—all the money, food, wine, clothing meant for the child's care, to lavish on her own family. The nursling was left with only one set of clothing in case there was a family visit and, otherwise, went naked (30–37).

Writers apparently suspected that there might be a connection between antisocial behavior and wet-nursing practices, since they not infrequently link the two. Balzac, for example, tells in 1840 that the "dreadful" Rogron brother and sister who as adults abused Pierrette, were as infants "put with a low-cost wet nurse in the country. These unfortunate children returned with a horrible village education, having long and often cried for the breast of their nurse who had gone off to the fields and who, meanwhile, locked them in one of these dark, humid and low-lying rooms where French peasants live" (*Pierrette*, 4.40–41). The belief in the formative influence of wet nurses gave rise to occasional humor: Alexandre Dumas *père*, suggests, for example, that Eugène Sue "was nursed by a goat and long retained the brusque and jumpy ways of his nurse."[39] It is of course true that people had long believed infants ingested characteristics of the nurse. Consequently, using animals was traditionally frowned on. Fildes quotes a fourteenth-century Tuscan moralist, who warns that a child "nourished on animal milk . . . always looks stupid and vacant and not right in the head" (46; see also Fildes, 73). Some diseases, like syphilis, were unquestionably spread through nursing (Fildes, 72). Although direct links between negative personality traits and wet-nursing are difficult to find, there is an abundance of texts toward mid-century where such characteristics are found with maternal deprivation. Théophile Gautier's Paul d'Aspremont, for example, who realizes that "[h]e was a monster," since he is afflicted with the evil eye, "remembers his mother who died in giving him birth" ("Jettatura," 204–5).

Perhaps no one created quite so many Romantic heroes as Balzac. Certainly there is no one who seems so clearly aware of the personal and social problems of wet-nursing. In *Le Lys dans la vallée* (1836), for example, Félix de Vandenesse says,

> What poet will tell us about the pain of a child whose lips suck a bitter breast and whose smiles are repressed by the devouring fire of a harsh eye? . . . What vanity could I, a newborn, have wounded? What physical or moral flaw earned my mother's coldness? . . . Sent to a nurse in the country, forgotten by my family for three years, when I returned to my father's house, I counted for so little that people felt sorry for me. . . . Disinherited of all affection, I could not love anything, and nature had made me loving. . . . Although neglected by my mother . . . she occasionally talked of my education and expressed the desire to attend to it herself; I shook with horrible shivers on thinking of the agony that daily contact with her would cause me. I blessed my abandonment. (9.970–71)

But then Balzac knew from personal experience the scars his own infancy left. Late in his life, on January 2, 1846, he wrote Mme Hanska: "I never had a mother; today, the *enemy* declared herself. I never revealed this wound to you; it was too horrible, and you have to see it to believe it. As soon as I came into the world, I was sent off to a wet nurse . . . and I stayed there until I was four."[40] His torment, and that of his period, is revealed most clearly in the Romantic heroes populating the books and stories he and others like him created for the delectation of readers, whether serialized in newspapers or published between hard covers.

The Romantic author Chateaubriand was ambivalent about what he considered René's progeny:

> An episode from the *Génie du Christianisme*, which at the time aroused less fuss than *Atala*, determined one of the characteristics of modern literature; still, if *René* did not exist, I would no longer write it; if it were possible for me to destroy it, I would destroy it. . . . A family of René-poets and René-prosewriters pullulated: people heard nothing but disconnected and lamentable phrases. . . . There was not an aspiring writer leaving school who did not dream of being the unhappiest of men, not a child who at sixteen had not exhausted life, who did not believe himself tormented by his genius, who, in the abyss of his thoughts, did not give himself over to the *indefiniteness of his passions* [*vague de ses passions*], who did not strike his pale and disheveled forehead and stupefy men with an unhappiness whose name he did not know, no more than they.[41]

While there is no doubt that *René* had considerable influence, especially after 1820, there is likewise little doubt that this society would have produced something similar whether or not Chateaubriand had written this particular work. Plenty of other authors had been maternally deprived and were then ready, if not driven, to give written form to their terrible malaise, thus responding to the apparently unconscious cravings of a large and growing reading public. Society required a Romantic hero.

Given the intimate relationship of artistic creations to the world in which they appear, it seems logical to look for pervasive conditions or movements which encouraged authors to continue multiplying the Romantic hero in their writings and, perhaps even more surprisingly, find readers wanting to read about him. Given both the Romantic hero and the equally numerous instances of motherless children in French Romantic fiction, poetry, and drama, it is plausible to seek at least a partial explanation in a social phenomenon which had profound physical and psychological impact on the people in late eighteenth- and early nineteenth-century France: the infants routinely taken from their homes as newborns, left with a wet nurse, recovered and removed from that environment two to four years later, and reintroduced into the now strange parental home made maternal deprivation and deep-seated feelings of personal rejection a systematic fact of French life and provided a stimulus for that tormented literary creature, the Romantic hero. When Marivaux's "poor orphan" (*Marianne*, 35) cried out in 1731: "I have no one on earth who knows me; I am neither the daughter nor the relative of anyone at all! From whom will I ask for help? Who is obliged to give it? What will I do when I leave here? My money won't last long, someone could take what I have" (25), her words clearly foreshadowed the agony that would rise in the hearts of many if not most French people.

The realities I have discussed are particularly important when considered together. As wet-nursing, frequently attended by maternal deprivation and the resultant unbonded children, moved down from the aristocracy through the middle to the lower classes, it first affected the upper segment of the middle classes, the part of society from which the bulk of the writers was drawn. The merchant and professional classes, which had long produced most of the writers, were turning increasingly in the late 1700s to hired nurses. For the first time, in short, it was common for those who would be the authors of poems, novels, and plays to be given to wet nurses, and these infants would come of age from the late 1790s through the early years of the nineteenth century. As already mentioned, because of Rousseau's *Emile*, there was a brief respite in the 1770s; otherwise, the use of wet nurses continued in the comfortable levels of French society until the mid-1800s. With the establishment of universal education and the advent of modern journalism, the numbers of writers and also readers increased considerably in the early nineteenth century. This is the period during which the Romantic hero and heroine appear increasingly in literary works, though their popularity and extra-ordinary multiplication did not occur until the 1820s. The period from 1820 to mid-century corresponds to the maturation of a vastly enlarged reading public, peopled by members of the rapidly expanding middle class who had been affected by rising levels of literacy resulting from Napoleon's institution of universal education and psychologically impaired if not maimed by practices of infant care.

As authors created legions of works that displayed the creatures we term Romantic heroes and heroines, it is particularly significant to note that the public supported the Saint-Preux, Delphines, Corinnes, Renés, Obermanns, Adolphes, Joseph Délormes, Julien Sorels, Antonys, Louis Lamberts, Chattertons, and so on, by purchasing the newspapers and volumes featuring them, by frequenting the reading rooms that made them available, and by attending the plays that gave them voice. Serialized novels were a major factor in the success or failure of newspapers. By the 1840s the upper middle class and aristocrats were having serious doubts about the benefits of hired nurses. When wet-nursing declined among aristocratic and upper middle-class families, so too the frequency of the Romantic hero in literature declined fifteen to twenty years later. A charted curve of the literary phenomenon, though with a delay of a decade and a half, follows and closely resembles the curve representing the spread and diminution of wet-nursing. The concordance of these social factors is persuasive. In addition, present psychological knowledge points to strong social pressures as influence on the birth and popularity of the Romantic hero in literature.

There is then good reason to suggest that France's institutionalized maternal deprivation of the late eighteenth and early nineteenth centuries was a significant impetus for both the Romantic hero and for its appeal to a French reading public that was eager to share its anguish. Because one can correlate certain traits of this character type with that of authors (increasingly from classes where wet nurses were used) and readers, there seems little doubt that French Romanticism's astonishing success as a movement is due in part to the fact that it spoke to the deep, psychological wounds suffered by the burgeoning middle class. Author and audience shared certain psychological traits and needs because of this widespread social phenomenon; indeed, the survivors seem to have been traumatized by the neglect that killed from a third to half of their generation. Different parenting practices would have reduced the psychological need for this literary mode, in both its expression and reception. When aristocrats began to take better care of their children, thus curbing the tendency towards neglect in the upper middle classes as well, they began the lingering death of the Romantic hero. It seems equally possible that had they done so a century earlier, that strange and unpleasant literary creature might have miscarried.

Literature reflects the society that gives it birth. As Elme Caro put it in 1869, "[T]rue poets are . . . the interpreters of the universal soul, in both its inspiration and suffering, at a given moment in history. They are great only to the degree that they are able to translate the general emotions. They experience the influence of their period's or their country's ideas and sentiments, and it is because they discovered how to make the human heart talk, which before them had neither words nor voice, that humanity consecrates them as the aristocrats of poetry."[42] The public, moreover, supports such work in the marketplace. A novel which is completely out of line with prevalent thought will not sell, and society prevails in a belated way. In like manner, plays are performed to empty auditoriums when their themes are ahead or behind their time. There are exceptions, of course, but as a general rule, there is no doubt about the symbiotic relationship between literature and society. While writers probably echo their world more commonly than they create new sounds, as Trotsky realized in *Literature and Revolution*, writers can and sometimes do help form a people (one remembers the classic example of *Uncle Tom's Cabin* and its limited but nonetheless influencial role in bringing about the American Civil War). More often, of course, as Lucien Goldmann argued in *Pour une sociologie du roman*, artists are merely sensitive to social impulsions and somehow crystallize them in their art, thus encouraging the age to move in a particular direction. Readers are not always conscious of the commitments they express when they buy books and newspapers, patronize reading rooms, or go to the theater. Nonetheless, their beliefs, penchants, perversions, and glories often seem clear if not obvious to subsequent generations. The Marxist György Lukács, for example, perceptively studied nascent capitalism in the work of such novelists as Balzac. Nineteenth-century readers would doubtless have been astonished and perplexed by what modern students view as their manifest economic views. The arts provide a means of diagnosis. No other tool serves this function as reliably or as clearly. The artistic works of an age reveal the secret reality of a people, show what they are, whether or not they themselves recognize its truth. Literature likewise provides a plausible key to understanding that bizarre creation that dominates Romantic poems, novels, and plays. Rarely in the entire course of Western literature does one find such unpleasant heroes. Never does one find such a plethora as in late eighteenth- and nineteenth-century France. But then there have seldom been so many people who could readily sympathize with the disagreeable, petulant, and self-centered Romantic hero. William Ross Wallace once asserted, "The hand that rocks the cradle is the hand that rules the world." Here we have a contrary case. For almost a century the cradle was unrocked, and for almost a century, not the mother, but the unbonded child reigned.

3. Edgar Degas. *Portrait de famille* also called *La Famille Bellelli* (*Family Portrait* also called *The Bellelli Family*), 1860–67, Orsay. © Photo RMW—Jean Schormans.

CHAPTER 3

Doddering Paternities

Sophie Gay's novel, *La Comtesse d'Egmont* (1836) tells of two bad fathers. The first, M. de Richelieu, forces his daughter Septimanie into a loveless match with the Count d'Egmont and thus obliges her to reject Louis de Gisors, the love of her young life. Although already a duke and a marshal, the dissolute father expects to use his daughter's marriage to further his still unsatisfied, selfish, and exaggerated ambition. Septimanie de Richelieu is so distraught that she considers suicide, until a forceful priest turns her away from the idea. But Louis is not to be dissuaded: he seeks and finds death as a soldier in battle. M. de Richelieu illustrates a dichotomy between the moral and the legal standards of the day. By law, he is perfectly within in his rights to choose Septimanie's mate. Ethically, however, he is in the wrong because of his dishonorable motives. As the Chevalier de Jaucourt wrote in the *Encyclopédie*, "It is shameful [for a father] to sacrifice children to his ambition."[1] Richelieu's self-serving is repugnant, but it is doubly unacceptable in that it strikes against true love. The novel punishes him terribly. First of all, his military genius is unappreciated and repeatedly frustrated in the dissolute court of the ineffective Louis XV. Eventually Richelieu is forced to abandon the career for which he sacrificed his daughter. In addition, Septimanie's marriage of convenience with Egmont sets in motion a chain of tragedies that bring death to Louis de Gisors and to Septimanie herself. As the book ends we are given a glimpse of Richelieu's despair: "[I]n the funereal, candlelight of the mortuary chapel, they saw. . . . a despairing father near his dead daughter... VANITY weeping over its victim" (307).

Sentimental love was the source of conflict in numerous Romantic novels and plays. Fathers seldom imitate M. d'Etanges in *La Nouvelle Héloïse* [1761] and beat their daughters into submission (though M. de Méran follows this pattern in Pigault-Lebrun's *Adélaïde de Méran* [1815]

54

19.153–54), but the heads of families commonly impose their will, either under threat of disinheritance, as in Bernadin de Saint-Pierre's *Paul et Virginie* [1787], or by one form of persuasion or another, as in Sandeau's *Mademoiselle de La Seiglière* (1848). Fathers are occasionally shown to be too weak and in the wrong when they permit their children to marry against their better judgment, as when the title character of Sophie Gay's *Léonie de Montbreuse* (1813) is allowed to marry a scoundrel. But for the most part novels leave no doubt that true love has more importance than the family's previous commitment, fortune, or social conventions. Fathers who oppose it are usually revealed as villains. The new importance given to sentimental love, which took nothing but individual feelings into consideration, represented a significant change for the Romantic period.[2] It raises not just love but the individual above family and even above the church. In Du Camp's* *Mémoires d'un suicidé* (1853), Suzanne even tells Jean-Marc that if she dies during his absence, "I give my soul to you, and not to God, since you created me, and it is by you alone that I have lived" (144). Romantic love was more important than religious strictures against incest, as in Etienne Jouy's *Cécile, ou les passions* (1827), more important than vows to the Virgin, as in Camille Bodin's† *Etrennes morales* (1840), more important than commitment to a religious order, as in Balzac's "La Duchesse de Langeais" (1834), more important than class, as in Mme de Duras's‡ *Edouard* (1825), more important, in general, than anything. It was individualistic, and it regularly occurred not in accordance with but in opposition to society and social considerations, as in *Adolphe* (1816), and to fathers, as in *Eugénie Grandet* (1833). Consequently, "true love" is but one of the indications that the Romantics had embraced individualism as an absolute value.

In *La Comtesse d'Egmont*, after Septimanie has come to terms with her loveless marriage and her life as a beautiful but rather withdrawn woman of the court, an old family friend puts her in touch with a young man named Séverin de Guys. It turns out that both Séverin, an illegitimate child, and Septimanie's now dead lover, Louis de Gisors, were sired by M. de Belle-Isle. Séverin, who yearns especially to know his father,

---

* Maxime Du Camp (1822–94) was a journalist and the author of a few novels, some memoirs, and books of travel, history, and art criticism.

† Camille Bodin was the nom de plume used most often by Jenny Bastide (1792–1854), a minor novelist whose novels for young women had some following.

‡ An important literary salon gathered in the home of Madame Claire de Duras (1778–1828) during the Restoration. She also wrote three novellas of love made impossible (in two cases, because of differences of race and class—with additional hints of affinitative incest making the loves doubly impossible—and, in one, which has only recently been published, because of impotence).

suspects that the imposing man he remembers making occasional visits in his childhood must have been his sire, and nothing but the chance to uncover his roots will do. Like Telemachus, whose story had previously nourished his imagination (194), he sets out to find his father. As he explains to Septimanie,

> You have to have lived in ignorance of who you are, of who you might be, to understand how much trouble the vaguest conjecture can bring to the soul of a poor orphan. Being subjected to the will of a barbarous father, deploring the loss of an adored father are doubtless two great misfortunes, but to be yourself abandoned and left to seek the father who denies you . . . , to dream of him occasionally as though he were the way a son would like him to be, to believe you have surprised him in a sympathetic look, to recognize his voice in a tone of pity, to feel yourself . . . sympathetically attracted [to] an unknown person, then to see the smile of disdain or irony respond to your exaltation... you have seen land, then, but you find yourself in the middle of the ocean of society in a lonely bark. That is the torment no courage can confront, that is the desert where there is no consolation. (171–72)

Although Séverin is correct to believe he has found his father in the Marshal de Belle-Isle, by law fathers need not recognize their illegitimate offspring.[3] To avoid any unpleasant confrontation, M. de Belle-Isle arranges a *lettre de cachet* and has Séverin imprisoned, perhaps killed since he is never heard from again. To add to the complications, Septimanie falls in love with Séverin, as she did with his half-brother. Unfortunately, because her husband remains alive, she is still not free to do anything but die of grief, which she does with considerable elegance.

The text never makes it completely clear why M. de Belle-Isle refuses to recognize Séverin, though it makes no difference. He need not justify himself. Before the law, as Mulliez explains, an illegitimate child "has no father: the only father is the [legal] father of a family, at once engendering source, teacher and vector of both patrimony and name" (281). M. de Belle-Isle then feels no need to continue supporting the fruit of his adultery when he no longer loves Séverin's mother. Of course, the ethical situation is quite different. The novel leaves no ambiguity about that. Like Richelieu, though in a different way, Belle-Isle is a bad father, and even Louis, the latter's legitimate son, is repelled when he hears Séverin's story. He says to himself, "[T]o abandon him like that!. . . to deny his child. . . to give him over to utter destitution. . . I would never have thought him capable of such a thing" (215). And Septimanie terms Belle-Isle "a despicable man who flouts his most sacred duty [of fatherhood]" (258). Belle-Isle nonetheless has all the power that *ancien régime* fathers had by law: "The father ruled his wife, children, and servants like a domestic monarch, and the divinely ordained monarch ruled his subjects like a royal father. Disobedience and impropriety in the household were regarded as public offenses because families provided the model for the hierarchical relations of subordination and authority that ordered French society."[4] Already in 1731, when the Abbé Prévost's Des Grieux responds to his angry father by calling him "barbarous and unnatural" (*Manon Lescault*, 172), the pattern for the next century was established. Exceptionally rigorous, often harsh and unjust fathers were an unattractive commonplace in literature. When literary characters mention fathers in the Romantic period, the fathers are in general egregiously egotistical, with rights but without responsibilities.

Though both Richelieu and Belle-Isle are within their legal rights, they are equally reprehensible on ethical grounds, since they use paternity to gratify their own selfish desires. They thus illustrate one form of Romantic hypertrophy of the self: fatherhood subjected to self-interest. Patriarchs no longer enjoyed good press. Belle-Isle joins multitudes of unworthy fathers in the period's literature. Mme de Tencin's★ *Mémoires du comte de Comminge* (1735) tells of brothers who destroy their respective children by refusing them permission to marry one another. Ducray-Duminil provides a number of other examples: because Elina's father opposed her marriage, he is "barbarous" (*Lolotte et Fanfan* [1788] 1.154), whilst Victor's father, Roger, is a notorious bandit who murders his own wife (*Victor* [1797]). And Fiévée's M. de Miralbe shuts his daughter Adèle up in a convent so he may have free use of her inheritance (*Frédéric* [1799]). Internal justification and common literary practice validated the decision of Fiévée's Adèle and Frédéric to choose other families and thus to deny the importance of paternity. Bonnet believes, in addition, that the common use of pseudonyms in both literature and reality, and the Convention's decree of 1793, which allowed people the freedom to change names as they wished, indicate the continuing dissolution of families.[5]

Posterity has not had a high regard for *La Comtesse d'Egmont*, but it was republished at least four times in the nineteenth century and was, then, reasonably successful. For the present purposes, it provides a good

---

★ Mme Claudine-Alexandrine Guérin de Tencin (1682–1749) hosted a salon and occasionally wrote a novel, the best known of which is mentioned here. In 1764, Baculard d'Arnaud turned her Mémoires du comte de Comminge into a horrifying melodrama that people found very satisfying.

example of the period's perceptions of fathers and kings, and it sets the stage for a consideration of paternity and the family across the eighteenth and nineteenth centuries. Prior to the mid-eighteenth century, an individual was situated in a reasonably well-defined place, as a member of a nuclear family under a father, in a parish under a priest, in a community under a lord, as well as, under the authority of an aristocratic and ecclesiastical hierarchy. While I do not wish to paint too bucolic a picture of this feudal, seigneurial, patriarchal world, since there was an abundance of dissatisfaction, exceptions, and, as the mid-eighteenth century approached, widespread controversy and trouble. It was only comparatively stable. In contrast with the new, urban, industrial society, however, it seems very peaceful indeed. Virtually all the fiscal, social, and spiritual aspects of his or her life were established and defined by the traditional dependencies of this web of authority (Mandrou, *Introduction,* 77–138). The three pillars of what had been a paternalistic society were closely connected, each affecting the other, and all—father, church, and king[6]— were being undermined and brought into disrespect. In Romantic novels and in life, bad and absent fathers joined an ineffective church and an enfeebled, dissolute, vacillating royalty. The patriarchy was dying, with such significant effects as the widespread revolutionary activity and the Revolution of 1789. From the crisis of authority that I have dubbed "doddering paternities" profound changes racked society. Written in the mid-1830s, when Romanticism was in full bloom, *La Comtesse d'Egmont* deals with the earlier period of Louis XV's reign (especially the last half of the 1750s) and thus, from setting to composition, spans much of the period when both monarchy and patriarchy were falling into disrepute. Unfortunately, there was nothing to replace the patriarchial system of authority that had for many centuries governed the French. The traditional form of power, canonized in the Civil Code, remained through the various governments that succeeded one another. Lacking respect and credence, however, the form lacked strength, and the people regularly took to the streets. With some frequency, governments fell.

One might validly emphasize the revolutionary activity, given the revolutions of 1789, 1830, and 1848, and more needs to be said about the frequent disturbances, riots and, especially, the wars. From 1792, when France declared war on Austria, for the next twenty-two years and, indeed, for much of the nineteenth century, France was at war with one or more European powers. But whether the focus remains on one form of violence or another, it is important to recognize that as paternity weakened both in reputation and in strength, violence exploded.

58

Perhaps most important of the paternities was the case of the family father, since it serves as the dominant model for the whole of Romantic society. As Cabantous puts it, "The profound economic, social, political, cultural modifications that were transforming French society between 1750 and 1920 affected the father by diversifying his function and his image. From then on, at the side of the *pater familias* dominating his household, emerged little by little the migrant father, the divorced father, the absent father."[7] The traditional model for the patriarch had been one of self-sacrifice. The Bible instructed husbands, for example, to "love your wives, even as Christ also loved the church, and gave himself for it" (Ephesians 5:25). The decline and passing of the patriarchal model is indicated by the literary parade of ignoble if not maleficent father figures. Saint-Albin's early (1758) cry, "[Fathers] gave us life only so we would be at their disposal. . . . Fathers! Fathers! There are none... there are only tyrants" (Diderot, *Père de famille*, 233), results from a momentary misunderstanding, but it signals the dominant attitude of the future. It was far from uncommon for characters to curse their fathers. Jean-Marc, for example, smashes a bust of his long dead father and screams, "May you who engendered me be damned, damned!" (du Camp, *Mémoires*, 38). Most of literature's "bad" or "unnatural" fathers are represented as bad primarily because they oppose their children's wishes. Romantic novels no longer describe fathers as invested with a position and powers instituted by God and under the self-sacrificing father's control. In 1803, for example, Botte is unable to convince the Marquis d'Arancey that a father's task is not self-satisfaction but to make his child happy (Pigault-Lebrun, *Monsieur Botte*, 3.143). During the period starting in the mid-eighteenth century, individualism with all its rights to the pursuit of happiness joined sentimental love as a societal goal. Fatherly love and self-sacrifice became lost in the shuffle.

Even when Nicolas Restif's grandfather Pierre tricked his son Edmond into returning home by telling him that he was sick (which in fact was clearly true, since he died shortly thereafter), and then forced Edmond to forsake his heart's choice for his father's, the text makes Pierre's perhaps ill-conceived, paternal love clear. Pierre does not select his child's mate on the basis of his own ambition, as did Septimanie's father. Restif de La Bretonne's fathers exemplify the patriarchal model. Edmond says, for example, "I obeyed, my God! I obeyed you in your noble reflection, in my father" (*Vie de mon père* [1778] 73). "Edmond's father [Pierre] was for him a visible God" (ibid., 78–79). The major difference between Pierre Restif and Belle-Isle lies in the latter's lack of a father's love, while there is no doubt of the paternal love motivating Restif's fathers. Belle-Isle's treatment of Séverin is in another category altogether. Although Louis feels there may be some justification for his father's discarding Séverin, the abandonment and subsequent repression qualify him abundantly as an inadequate father. By opposition, he highlights what a father should be.

Traditionally, fathers had a number of roles. They were leaders, charged with the family's direction and also its material and spiritual well-being. They were to provide and protect, and they were to teach. Private, home-based instruction had been a major feature of education since the Renaissance; one thinks of Montaigne's and Pascal's private tutorials, not to mention those of Rousseau's Emile. In addition, boys were normally taught the father's skills, trade, or profession at the patriarch's knee, and girls learned both from fathers and mothers, as they shared the mother's responsibilities. Diderot's M. d'Orbesson, for example, is proud of his paternal behavior: "I did not abandon you to the care of mercenaries," he tells his son. "I taught you myself to speak, to think, to feel" (*Père de famille*, 228). Paternal teaching was, however, brought into question when after four years of debate, and over the objections of such major figures as Talleyrand and Condorcet, obligatory public education was instituted by the Revolutionary government in 1796. As Danton put it in a widely cited statement: "Children belong to the Republic before they belong to their parents" (Mulliez, 291).

The changes in no way benefited young women. In aristocratic France, upper-class girls had been educated in convent schools and by mothers and tutors at home. Standards were long set by the outstanding convent school at Saint-Cyr, founded in 1686 by the pietistic Madame de Maintenon for the indigent but proud daughters of the nobility. It had been advantageous to educate the aristocracy's daughters, since the business of nobles frequently required the attentions of both spouses. The increasingly powerful middle class was, however, convinced that girls needed very little in the way of academic training. After the revolution, under the prevailing influence of Rousseau, who touched on raising Sophie in book five of *Emile* (1762), pre-Romantic and Romantic young women were educated more and more at home with emphasis on sewing, cooking, housekeeping, and music. The intellectual content of their training seems, moreover, to have diminished and the standards degraded. Indeed, Restif de La Bretonne felt in 1777 that women of the merchant classes might be taught to read and write in a rudimentary way to conduct business, but upper-class women should under no circumstances be taught to write.[8]

Michelet avowed that the Revolution dismantled the construct of *ancien régime* paternity.[9] Lynn Hunt goes on to argue that around 1750 the "bad" father was replaced by a "weak," but "good" father who had lost his authority. For Hunt impotent fathers augur the end of fatherhood, which will be replaced by revolutionary fraternity.[10] My own research, however, would suggest that no such chronology leading from loveless, tyrannical paternity, to feckless fatherhood, to brotherhood can be sustained. As a reading of Marcel David's consideration of post-Revolution fraternity indicates, neither the word nor the concept of brotherhood had much significance beyond the rhetorical realm of the workers' movements. "Fraternity faded away during the Consulate and Empire," David summarized in his earlier study of Revolutionary fraternity, "until you would have been justified in believing that it had had its day."[11] Furthermore, legions of weak, selfish, and cruel fathers continue to occur regularly and in no discernible order in novels throughout the eighteenth and nineteenth centuries. They appear well beyond the Revolution, and they make way not for fraternity as Hunt believes but for extreme forms of individualism. Along with many other examples, some of which I have already mentioned, Benjamin Constant's sister Louise d'Estournelles creates M. de Laval who opposes the love match between his son and Eugénie in *Pascaline* (1821), Stendhal's hated father figures in the 1820s and 30s are too vivid to need highlighting, and in Flaubert's novel published in 1857, Charles Bovary's appalling behavior as a father comes readily to mind.

In addition to numerous bad fathers, there is a particularly telling and growing disappearance of fathers from Romantic literature. Not only do fathers vanish from material written for children, either because they are said to be too busy with various affairs to take a significant part in the central adventure of the fiction or because they are off on a trip, they also constitute a remarkable absence from the majority of novels as well.[12] The paternal departure marks what was happening in reality as seasonal migration, numerous wars, and business removed fathers of all classes increasingly from the home. As pointed out in chapter two, there was moreover the problem of wet nurses, which took children from their mothers and thus deprived many infants of both parents. Even after children returned home the father was commonly unavailable.[13] I also suggested that the numbers of orphans in Romantic literature may indicate widespread feelings of abandonment. Certainly, as Kathryn Norberg summarizes, "Before our eyes, patriarchal authority dwindles until it almost disappears."[14] Whereas just a hundred years before, no one would have thought to deny that the family was a formalizing, foundational institution for society itself, since rule of law and theology insisted on its importance, literature represents that by the 1750s the previously stable family was precariously perched on a crumbling cliff. As porches, rooms, and pillars of the societal house slid into the turbulent sea of Romantic change, traditional values came into question as well.

As fathers disappeared from literature, so they also disappeared from families, not usually as it is in our own age because of divorce, but rather because the new industrial society drew fathers away from the home. Until the mid-eighteenth century, fathers were indisputably care-givers, protectors, and educators, in addition to being the heads of the family and the breadwinners. With the turmoil of a changing economy, however, fathers often had to leave home and family for months at a time either for work or, for one of the seemingly endless wars; or, at the very least, in order to work a twelve-hour day at the factory, shop, or office. In the past, members of the extended family could and did take over in the case of absence or emergencies. As emigration to the urban areas left families without the familiar, local web of relationships, and fathers were unable to carry on their traditional responsibilities, especially in regard to the children's care and education, such obligations increasingly fell entirely to mothers or employees.

Recent studies leave little doubt of the father's crucial role in the education of children. They have enormous importance in forming in the child a firm sense of their own identity, a commitment to ethical standards of behavior, and general competence in constructing a viable social role.[15] While the studies that give rise to these conclusions are recent and based on our own society where single-parent homes are fast becoming the norm, the results would lead us to expect that with an increasing number of fatherless homes there would also be an increase as the children came of age of predatory and casual sex, violence, child and domestic abuse, and emotional problems. Although I have not been able to find credible evidence of an increase in domestic violence or rape, the existence, in 1832, of an estimated 30,000 prostitutes in Paris with a population of approximately 800,000 people does indicate a certain amount of sexual license.[16] As for violence, it seems safe to say that pre-Romantic and Romantic France was one of the most violent of societies. The shocking bloodletting of the Terror in 1793 is but one example. Although Napoleon managed to control the people's propensity for sanguinary revolts, his constant wars eventually brought his downfall, and both revolts, revolutions, and wars regularly mark the century. I will look into the question of child abuse in chapter five. Suffice it to say for the moment that it seems to have increased significantly, just as the entire body of Romantic literature testifies to significant amounts of depression and other forms of emotional disturbances.

As Blankenhorn summarizes, the result of fatherlessness is "narcissism: a me-first egotism that is hostile not only to any societal goal or larger moral purpose but also to any save the most puerile understanding of personal happiness. In social terms, the primary results of decultured paternity are a decline in children's well-being and a rise in male violence, especially against women. In a larger sense, the most signif- icant result is . . . society's steady fragmentation into atomized individuals, isolated from one another and estranged from the aspira- tions and realities of common membership in a family, a community, a nation, bound by mutual commitment and shared memory" (*Fatherless*, 4). Blankenhorn is discussing, of course, the late 1980s and 90s in the United States, but his description is appropriate for the French Romantics as well. At best, as depicted in Edgar Degas's portrait of *La Famille Bellelli* (1860–67) (plate 3), separation was occurring between fathers and their families. In addition, as pointed out in the preceding chapter, the Romantics lacked more than a father. In the formative, early years of their existence, many also lacked a devoted nurturing care-giver: they lacked a mother. Although the absence of fathers may not be so immediately damaging as motherlessness, there can be no doubt that the combination had enormous impact on the psychological health of industrializing France.

The patriarchy did not die overnight. Ghosts of fathers-past continued to have rhetorical and legal reality. Michelle Perrot argues that "the newest political idea of the [post-revolutionary] day probably was that the family was the basic cell of society. Domesticity had a fundamental regulatory function: it played the role of the hidden god."[17] The family unquestionably provided the vehicle for the rise of the middle class in the eighteenth and nineteenth centuries, and Napoleon's Civil Code attempted to replicate the patriarchal patterns of authority within the family unit. I nonetheless argue that the family was merely a holdover from the past, important only because it served as a transition to the centrality of the individual. Balzac's M. de Chaulieu shows considerable insight: "In cutting off Louis XVI's head, the Revolution cut off the heads of all fathers. Families no longer exist today; there are only individuals. In wanting to become a nation, the French renounced being an empire. In proclaiming equality of rights to the paternal estate, they have killed the spirit of family!" ([1842] 1.242). Family honor, which had once been of enormous importance to members of the specific families, decreased in value. Individuals considered it important to the degree that it facilitated or impeded the acquisition of personal wealth, whether through business or a suitable marriage. The most salient events of the late eighteenth and nineteenth centuries can be seen as a series of attempts to take authority away from the church, from the king, from fathers, then from the family proper. As Hunt believes, the abuse of *lettres de cachet* intertwined royal and familial power, and in denouncing them Mirabeau and others were in effect attacking paternal power and privileges (*Family*, 20). The major battles of the century—in regard to primogeniture and the rights of younger sons and daughters to inherit property, separation of wealth to protect wives from profligate husbands, women's suffrage, divorce, marital separation, family councils (*tribuneaux de famille*) that took power away from fathers—inevitably weaken the rights of the family in favor of the individual. Balzac's *Le Père Goriot* (1834–35) suggests a series of substitute fathers: the arch-criminal Vautrin wants to own a few hundred slaves, so as to indulge his "taste for a patriarchal life" (3.141), and Rastignac is delighted to find a tailor "who had understood the paternity of his trade."[18]

Attacks on fatherhood continued while attacks on the other two institutions of patriarchy, the church and royalty, increased. One of the more obvious alterations, as the power of the church and belief in God weakened, occurred in the view people had of marriage. It was no longer considered a sacrament. Mulliez points out that "everything is new from the point when marriage changes its nature and stops being an indissoluble family pact, to become a contract resting on love that lasts only as long as that love."[19] The revolutionary government legalized divorce for the first time in 1792, and such novels as Louvet de Couvay's *Emilie de Varmont* (1791) extolled it as "necessary." The guarantor of the family unit was no longer a higher authority in the person of either God or society or, even, the relatives involved, but rather individual love—and such love, as Denby's *Sentimental Narrative and the Social Order* makes patently clear, constitutes a very unstable pillar for society.

Jeffrey W. Merrick's splendid book *The Desacralization of the French Monarchy in the Eighteenth Century* chronicles the long process of self-centered and self-destructive political maneuvering that fatally weakened the Gallican church, the second pillar of the French patriarchy. As he demonstrates, the bishops worked in conjunction with legislators in the various national parliaments to attack the doctrine of *Unigenitus*. It was not that they wanted to have the doctrine of salvation by works revoked, and thus institute the Jansenistic doctrines of uniquely efficacious predestination and divine Grace. The controversy was simply to enhance their own corporate power by making the king accountable to the parliament. "The bishops consecrated the king, and the judges burned books that impugned his sacred character. Both acknowledged in principle that he was answerable only to God but disowned this axiom of absolutism in practice by exploiting it to justify their resistance to the crown."[20] After 1750, when the conflict became particularly strident, although direct attacks on Louis XV and royal abuses were generally avoided, the king's fiscal and ecclesiastical policies were constantly highlighted as magistrates, legislators, and clergy attacked his ministers.[21] The primary result of the continuing controversy, which descended too often to the level of undignified bickering, was to undermine the doctrines of divine ordination and divine right of kings in favor of national sovereignty. Merrick claims that by the time of the ascension of Louis XVI in 1774, the concept of divine right was politically dysfunctional (*Desacralization*, 132). The rhetorical posturing of the king as the nation's father was continued by both the king and the parliamentarians, but the rhetoric had less and less substance. The stage was set for the Revolution to remove the king and turn the priesthood into a cadre of governmental functionaries.

Olwen Hufton, while arguing that between 1796 and 1801 the laity made the restoration of the church a political necessity, recognizes that the church would never again have the power it enjoyed during the *ancien régime*: "The revolutionary decade [1789–1801] emphatically severs a world of almost unquestioned obeisance to Catholic teaching from one in which significant sectors of the populace slipped away into indifference."[22] When church and king lost their power, there really was nothing to serve as a rallying point, no effective vehicle for collective ideals. As Merrick points out, Catholicism had effectively served to preserve social order. As it weakened, so too did the standards taught by the church. When the National Assembly confiscated the church's property in 1789 and then in the following year passed the "Civil Constitution for the Clergy," which reorganized the Gallican church, severed direct ties with the Vatican, and forced priests to swear allegiance to the state, the legislators proclaimed publicly that the Catholic faith had lost power over the French but there were also many other indications. Merrick provides a list of symptoms of the profound change:

> More delayed baptisms, indifference concerning burial, omissions of religious invocations and intercessory clauses from wills, bequests to subsidize charity for the living rather than masses for the dead. More novels, newspapers, historical and scientific works, and unorthodox books, but fewer theological titles in print. More Sabbath-breaking, blasphemy, suicide, premarital sex, illegitimate births, abandoned children, contraception, adultery, prostitution. Less regularity in attendance at Sunday mass and fulfillment of paschal obligations,

fewer confraternities and ordinations, more friction between clergy and laity over tithes, ecclesiastical fees, parish expenditures, administration of the sacraments, observance of holy days, and standards of moral conduct.[23]

The long-held belief that all kings ruled by divine right was not enough to prevent Louis XVI's execution and, consequently, is an important sign that the old religion had lost much of its sway. Attacked economically through property confiscation, its authority over the aristocracy vitiated, its independence from the French government nullified, and with an increasingly indifferent flock, the formerly mighty church triumphant became debilitated and indigent. Balzac describes her in *Jésus-Christ en Flandre* (1830–31) as a fleshless old crone.[24] Increasingly, the faithful among the Romantics were like Boulay-Paty's title character Elie Mariaker (1834) "hanging on with all their strength to the ruins of Catholicism" (lxxxii), but without real conviction.

The third patriarchal institution, the aristocracy, fared no better, in fact, even worse. Grumbling against the rulers of society has unquestionably continued from the early days of civilization, though the higher ranking members were usually preserved from public caricature and vilification by the power of their position. Molière and others demonstrated that it was acceptable to satirize the "little counts" who lacked importance, but not until the late eighteenth century would it become commonplace to dare broaden the comedy to include dukes and duchesses, princes and kings and, indeed, to take aim at the entire ruling classes of church and state. True, for the four or five year period of the Fronde, as the agitation and insurrection during the minority of Louis XIV was called, the regent Anne of Austria and her advisor Mazarin were subjected to a heavy barrage of vile satire. Attacks on Mazarin were so incredibly vicious that a term, Mazarinade, was coined to describe them. Nonetheless, the political satires of the later period starting in the early 1770s and continuing through the 1790s (though with decreasing volume after the Terror in 1793) were particularly startling, since they call the very principle of absolute power into question. The negative commentary continues over many years, and it vilipended not just individuals, quite a number of whom are clearly named or graphically portrayed, but it expressed profound skepticism and disdain toward the governing hierarchy of aristocrats and clergy. In the early 1790s, the National Assembly itself was portrayed as a brothel where unrestrained libidinousness reigned. Pornography enjoyed enormous success because of increased literacy and because the economics of printing brought notable growth in the publishing business,[25] but also because censorship and royal propaganda were ineffective and unable to counter the widespread opposition to absolutism (Merrick, *Desacralization*, 21–22). Perhaps most important, as one bookseller explained, authorities were frustrated in their attempts to control the dissemination of pornographic materials, "because people are set on obtaining them at any price. And who? The very people who, given their birth, their status in society, their faith, their learning, and their zeal for religion, ought to be the first to condemn them."[26] Reasons for the changing perceptions and attitudes have been touched on above in the discussion of the weakening church. In addition, the regency of Philippe d'Orléans and the reign of Louis XV the "Well-Beloved" were notably dissolute and bear no small part of the responsibility in discrediting the monarchy. Louis XV's profligate philandering was well publicized, and the fact that his mistresses Mme de Pompadour and Mme du Barry were believed to have considerable influence increased the scandal and the outrage, further weakening royal authority.

A swelling body of political invective in the form of pamphlets, cartoons, and engravings thus joined genuine scandals. Scurrilous pamphlets attacking the aristocracy, the clergy, the members of parlement increased steadily in number from the early 1770s until the Revolution took to the streets and effectively wrested power from the aristocracy. Some of the worst of these were directed at the crown. After 1789 porno-graphic attacks on the king and queen turned from a steady flow into a flood. While it is no doubt true as Hunt has suggested that Marie-Antoinette "was the emblem (and sacrificial victim) for the feared disin-tegration of gender boundaries that accompanied the Revolution" (*Family Romance*, 114), such scatological material served to attack and undermine the monarchy and also, the institutions—church, academies, salons, aristocracy, parliaments—that supported the individual rulers. Even in the case of pornography with no observable political intent, like Andréa de Nerciat's* *Félicia, ou mes fredaines* (1775) or Restif's *Anti-Justine* (1798), lubricious clergymen were depicted as significant partici-pants. Peter Wagner maintains that the anticlerical satire, much of which was salacious, "contributed decisively to the abolishment of religious orders in France in 1790" ("Anticatholic Erotica," 180). Marie-Antoinette was said to be both sexually voracious and indiscriminate. Even after Louis XVI's impotence was taken care of by a minor operation to repair his phimosis and some explicit instruction, he was held up for ridicule both as a cuckold and as the pathetic tool of aggressive women.

---

* André-Robert Andréa de Nerciat (1739–1800) wrote primarily licentious, and some unequivocally obscene, novels that had considerable success.

While Louis XV's turpitude was eminently deserving of such treatment, Louis XVI "tried to make his own family a model of domestic felicity and devoted himself to the happiness of his subjects" (Merrick, "Sexual," 81). Neither he nor Marie-Antoinette were without flaws—far from it—but neither deserved the treatment they received in these publications that took slander to new depths. As Antoine de Baecque explains, the myth was that the "'Ancien Régime' was defeated because of debauchery, its downfall hastened because of sex" ("Livres remplis," 147); the reality was that the scurrilous publications with no apparent concern for truth, which Robert Darnton calls Grub Street, constitute a significant factor in the discreditation of royalty (Merrick, *Desacralization*, 21–22).

The king and queen were not alone in being pilloried by the pamphleteers. A panoply of diseased and degenerate nobles, magistrates, and clergy illustrated the virulent drawings, poems, songs, and squibs, which increasingly signaled that the entire system was under attack. No one should dispute Darnton's contention that such obscene lampoons of highly placed people constituted a far more dangerous attack than the more intellectually acceptable writings of the philosophes, though it is equally certain that the political, philosophic, and pornographic writings that poured from the underground press were but three manifestations of the same impulse. The ruling class was portrayed as utterly ineffective and dissolute, the males impotent or effeminate, the over-sexed females desperately turning to masturbation, virile working men, members of their own family, and other women.[27] As Baecque says, the underlying assumption was that debauchery "goes hand in hand with moral turpitude and political duplicity" ("Pamphlets," 170). It became increasingly difficult, indeed impossible, to maintain and protect the trust and reverence that had allowed the monarchy to rule. For all Napoleon's later efforts and the solemn pomp of the subsequent Restoration, whether newly turned or polished with age, France's nobility would in the future remain bereft of its resplendent aura and authority.

The mere quantity of cartoons, songs, poems, pamphlets in this flood of what Mercier termed "repugnant" pornography in his *Le Nouveau Paris* of 1798 (3.178–79) differentiates it from preceding periods. Pornography has always existed, though it blossomed with the invention of the printing press. Politically motivated and oriented pornography multiplies only in times of social turmoil. Still, it was just one of a number of unquestionably important factors in the midst of a turbulent social context particular to the late eighteenth century. Merrick insists, "The protracted disputes involving the monarchy, the parlements, and the clergy, not the debauchery of the Parc aux cerfs [where Louis XV and his friends disported themselves], undermined the juridical principles of kingship 'by the grace of God'" (ibid., 22). If not a direct cause of the Revolution, however, no knowledgeable person would dispute Hunt's claim that the proliferation of pornography in the 1780s was "the harbinger of a broader social crisis" ("Pornography," 301–7). It is also undoubtedly true that it "contributed . . . to the destruction of the feeling of deference and decorum which the Parisian citizen felt for his leaders" (Baecque, "Livres remplis," 129). Pigault-Lebrun's M. Botte tells M. d'Arancey, "Dazzled by passing glamour, you thought yourself well above [my son]; despoiled of your entourage and appreciated for your true worth, today you find him well above you" (*Monsieur Botte*, 3.142).

Despite the apparent tameness of Figaro's celebrated monologue, we can recognize the wisdom of Louis XVI's decision to prevent Beaumarchais from performing *Le Mariage de Figaro* (1784). Figaro is not merely holding a foppish, minor noble up for laughter, he has the entire aristocratic class in view: "No, Sir Count, you will not have [my Suzanne] . . . you will not have her . . . Just because you are a great Lord, you think you are a great genius! . . . nobility, fortune, rank, position, all that makes a person so proud! . . . What did you do for so many good things? You took the trouble to be born, nothing more" (5.3). Without question, Figaro's words heralded the coming Revolution and marked the diminished authority of the patriarchy. Romantics were increasingly free from the domination of fathers, church, and nobles. In 1793, under the initials of N.-E.R.**D.*-L*-B.*** the easily discernible Restif de La Bretonne started publishing part three of the forty-two volume work, *Les Contemporaines*. Some of the volumes showed a significant change in subtitle. Part I had been titled, *Les Contemporaines ou avantures des plus jolies femmes de l'âge présent* [Female Contemporaries or the Adventures of the Prettiest Women of Our Day]; part II announced the adventures of *belles marchandes, ouvrières* [beautiful women merchants, workers]; part III, on the other hand, promises stories of *jolies femmes de la noblesse, de la robe, de la médecine et du théâtre* [pretty women from the nobility, magistracy, medicine and theatre].[28] The collection's narrator assures us that the frequently licentious stories give reliable information about a broad range of French society.

In and for itself, the title of one of the "adventures," "La Duchesse," does not startle; one would merely assume that the well-known author has broadened his compass somewhat. But the story immediately begins to criticize the aristocratic title itself. The narrator finds the very word "duchess" ridiculous, since a duke should be the captain of an army, and his wife could in no way share his military responsibilities.[29] While he

69

explains that "two or three" duchesses distinguished themselves by their virtue, others indulged themselves. As an example, he tells of Duchess Maclovie-Louise-Caroline-Céleste M****, who encouraged the debauchery of her ladies-in-waiting, while she herself corrupted her male servants. Like others of her quality, "she seemed to resemble Divinity" (3.9), but "[s]he is truly the Queen of Animality" (ibid.). After the Revolution, legions of Romantic authors wrote lengthily and emphatically that nobles of any rank were no better than the rest of us,[30] although just a generation before such a statement in a signed work would have been altogether too dangerous for any sensible writer. Perhaps not countesses, but duchesses and queens were so powerful that writers who did not wish to fall victim to a *lettre de cachet* and, like Beaumarchais, spend time in prison knew that aristocrats might as well be divine.

Restif was, of course, not alone. Floating, so to speak, on top of the tide of anonymous political satire, were a considerable number of increasingly explicit and negative observations in Romantic books and plays where the identities of authors, directors, and printers could be easily established. Moreover, the ridicule continued. In Dumas's *Le Collier de la reine* (1849–50), for example, readers are treated to an amusing little domestic drama which, with different characters, would earlier have provided meat for writers of fabliaux or farces. It deals with Louis and Marie-Antoinette, the King and Queen of France. The King, concerned about his wife's night-time excursions, has her loyal servant replaced at the entry to her apartments with a soldier. "I will not open," the soldier responds to the whispered demands for entrance. The Queen begs, "But, my friend, don't you know that Laurent normally opens for us?" The soldier is unimpressed: "To hell with Laurent! I have my orders" (1.134–35). The comedy continues as the Queen stands outside her own door in the middle of a cold night, trying unsuccessfully to bribe the mutton-headed guard, unable to convince him to open since the King himself has organized the scene. The Queen is forced to spend the night in one of her profligate brother's hideaways.

Few Romantic novels lack examples of what today would be called anti-heroes. Stendhal's main characters are regularly unhorsed and allowed to fall into the splattering *boue* of the streets. On remembering what *boue* meant with respect to the overflowing sewers of French cities, we move away from farcical pratfalls to the vulgarity of the *fabliaux*. Balzac has an impoverished descendent of the Valois living in a brothel in *La Vieille Fille* (1837). M. Jules penetrates his wife's *cabinet* in Balzac's "Ferragus" (1834), from where she had previously come like an angelic visitation. The most intimate secrets of her artifice are revealed, and she is destroyed by the realization that the purity of ideal love is no longer possible. Indeed, as I shall suggest in the next chapter, all heroes became problematic.

Balzac's perception of this debasement shows uncommon perspicacity. He maintained that "[a]n aristocracy is in a way the thought of a society" (5.925). What he meant was that they represented the ideals of the country, but I suggest that his words were more accurate than his intended meaning. In fact, as Romantic literature denied ideal traits to aristocrats, to the church, and to fathers, and suggested that all three institutions of the patriarchy were degraded, there seems to be a significant decline in belief in the ideal, indeed in any ideal. It becomes easy to revolt against the empty forms of the patriarchy. To imply that aristocrats and churchmen might be bestial marks a radical change from the grumbling of the preceding half-century. For Balzac the most elevated aristocrats, whether ecclesiastical or otherwise, should be above ordinary laws and dispensed from ordinary obligations. They should cultivate their minds and spirits. Of course, with rare exceptions, they do not correspond to the ideal. Likewise, in the parallel institution of the church, Balzac regularly created unbelieving priests. The abbé de Maronais, for example, was a "true priest, one of those ecclesiastics made to be a cardinal in France or a Borgia beneath a tiara" ("La Fille aux yeux d'or" [1834–35] 5.1055). Father de Maronais was "vicious but political, unbelieving but learned, perfidious but likable, apparently weak but as vigorous mentally as he was physically," and he successfully raised Henri de Marsay to believe "in neither men nor women, in neither God nor the devil" (5.1056–57). As the novelist wrote some years later when rehearsing the failures of the aristocracy, "[E]verything should raise a person's soul who, from youth, possesses such privileges; everything should impress him with great respect for himself, the least consequence of which is a spiritual nobility in harmony with the nobility of his title" (5.927). Balzac thought that the aristocracy should be distant from the rest of the nation, since this materially consecrates "the moral distances which should separate them" (5.926). Of course, he was well aware that the aristocracy had failed. He repeatedly pointed out that French nobles were petty, stubborn, undisciplined, self-centered, united only in their desire to prevent the talented and capable from entering their class. More greedy than bourgeois parvenus, they sold the lands on which their power was based to play the stock market. In effect, they peddled their birthright and condemned themselves to futility. Fiévée's M. de Montluc analyzes the situation:

> [I] think it is too bad that there is nothing above wealth. . . . Look at the Romans. When the patricians were above their fellow citizens, daring members of the lower classes only struggled to be admitted among then. [Later, w]hen the patriarchy was debased, ambition

could only be satisfied by subjugating Rome, and Rome was subjugated. . . . [A]s patricians saw their rights restrained, they looked for compensation in wealth and in the brilliance that it procures. The same reduction of power among nobles in France has brought a similar love of riches." (*Frédéric*, 3.56–57)

Besides, he explains a few pages previously, "There is no longer any such thing as nobility in France. . . . Since it can be bought, it is beneath money. . . . The prince sells privileges, and their multiplicity removes the glory from them" (ibid., 3.53–54). Balzac summarizes the accusations and condemnations of the previous several generations: "[W]hatever form the *Government* takes, as soon as the patricians do not fulfill the requirements of complete superiority, they lose their force, and the people soon overthrow them" (ibid.).

The Marquis de Sade poses as a philosopher when he ties the death of the king to the death of God. "Let us believe," he intones, "that a people wise enough and brave enough to take an impudent monarch from the summit of grandeur to the foot of the scaffold, a people that in these last few years has been able to overcome so many prejudices and do away with so many ridiculous constraints will be sufficiently wise and brave to finish the affair and, for the republic's well-being, immolate a mere ghost after having beheaded a real king" (3.485–86). By "ghost," of course, he means God. The results of these real and asserted deaths were many and profound, in both the nineteenth and twentieth centuries.

Many people, like Fiévée's Mme de Sponasi, "made a religion of not believing in God. That may seem extraordinary to you," says the narrator, "but it is a fashion that passes from the boudoir to the salon, from the salon to the anteroom, and from the anteroom to all the classes of society" (*Frédéric*, 1.101). Interestingly enough, most literary commentaries of the day were concerned not because of potential blasphemy, but rather because they feared the impact of such atheism on the people. Mercier worried at some length in 1798: "The hotchpotch of the doctrines of Rousseau, Voltaire, Helvétius, Boulanger, Diderot had formed a sort of dough. . . . that ordinary minds were unable to digest and that became harmful for them. Old, fundamental truths [were] ridiculed, [and] people denied them, abandoned them. They did more: a mob of scatterbrains went beyond the great minds and substituted the system of atheism and license for the philosophical ideas. This 'philosophism' owed its origins to poorly read books that were poorly understood. . . . Ignorance engenders barbarity, but half-knowledge does even worse. It causes a crowd of errors to circulate through all the veins of the political body. In the name of humanity, it does all sorts of harm to humanity" (*Nouveau Paris*, 2.121–22).

Some basic assumptions within a society are so diffused, so taken for granted that the people making up the society never even think to formulate them, probably because the paradigms of principles and values on which they build their lives are so pervasive as to be invisible. These may include "assumptions . . . about the nature of reality, about the organization of experience, about the function of language and its capacity to express reality, about the operations of society and the kinds and strengths of the pressures it exerts."[31] When we read the works of a former age, we need to identify what thoughts, influences, inclinations constitute undeclared givens. We need to focus on what is most often only implicitly present. Only then can we make out the basic, unstated, perhaps unperceived impulsions of the artist. Without such insight, we are likely to misread the work. There are many examples. I think for instance of Boccaccio's tale of Gualtieri and Griselda, long misunderstood by a public unacquainted with the book of Job and thus unable to perceive the *Decameron*'s allusion,[32] or, for a different kind of example, of the belief that the child of the husband will bear the traits of the woman's first lover in Emile Zola's *Thérèse Raquin* (1867). When Thérèse discovers she is pregnant, she is terrified that her child will resemble Camille, the husband she and Laurent murdered: "The thought of having Laurent's child seemed monstrous to her. . . . She was vaguely afraid of giving birth to a drowned person. It seemed to her that she felt the cold of a disintegrated and limp corpse in her entrails" (117). The pregnancy is but one more exacerbating factor in the progressing insanity that will eventually drive the main characters to suicide. Today, the "scientific fact" behind this passage seems ludicrous and might recall that Zola failed his baccalaureate examination, though it was in fact an accepted theory among Zola's contemporaries. Even someone as learned (and still highly regarded) as Michelet once wrote, "Widows frequently give children who resemble the first husbands to their second."[33] Believing that such a concept results from the writer's stupidity or lack of education brings one sort of misconception. More dangerous, I think, is the possibility that these or other erroneous beliefs will become important in and for themselves, and thus govern our appreciation of the work. *Thérèse Raquin* is not absurd just because it incorporates what we now hold to be an absurd idea. To the contrary, as Michel Claverie said, it is "Zola's first masterpiece."[34] Future scholars who consider our own age will have similar problems. They are going to have to be conscious of the extreme forms of individualism rampant in Western society (one might think of the egotistically titled, popular magazine *Self*). Surely we are all affected, however little time we spend analyzing it.

As has been recently pointed out, Romantic literature frequently secularized divine images and thus manifested the emptying of traditional religious symbolism. Angels continue to appear in stories and poems, for example, but they have lost much of their spiritual content. They have been naturalized. Women might be ethereal, but they are human, and when the word angel appears, it is seldom more than an epithet meaning kind, or charitable, or beautiful.[35] Among the many images of Moses, the Ten Commandments were usually replaced by the Rights of Man, or, in one stunning medallion that shows how the world has been upended, Napoleon hands tablets containing the Napoleonic Code to a kneeling Moses.[36] Despite the aggressiveness of such images, deep down, people feared they had sown the seeds of their own destruction. As Balzac put it, "In all creations, the head has its indicated place. If by chance a nation drops its head to its feet, it will sooner or later notice that it has committed suicide" (5.926).

The people had lost their ideals. As Romanticism opposed universals, so it emasculated the patriarchy and favored individual experience and values. As family, church, aristocracy were undermined, so too the vehicles for transcendent values. The *ancien régime* had maintained that God had set up the patriarchy and that within the overriding structure of the institution he guaranteed both the permanence and the justice of the three patriarchal pillars. Every institution must have a superior power that serves as authority and guarantor. The great banking families of the fifteenth and sixteenth centuries were able to move money around the Western World because the family name of Melser or Fugger guaranteed the transaction. Although monarchies later managed to subdue these mercantile families, they were still forced to rely on families like the Rothschilds, who had maintained their independence by remaining transnational and, thus, above individual governments. Every institution must have a guarantor. For the *ancien régime* the individual was regulated primarily as a member of a family. Families were governed and protected by the oldest, most powerful male and by rule of church and state. The monarchical system was anointed by the church, which was in turn considered to be guaranteed by God Himself. The hierarchy was maintained only as long as the superior forces were able to protect subordinate authority and, thus, maintain trust. The monarchy could not continue when it was without a higher order, whether Rome, Avignon, or heaven, for there was no one and nothing to guarantee the king's acceptable performance. In China, Japan, Rome, and Egypt emperors and pharaohs were able to serve as their own guarantors by insisting on their divinity. In Europe the ploy was unsuccessful, probably because none were able to retain power long enough to gain sufficient confidence to continue despite passing problems. Within the French hierarchy of the late eighteenth and nineteenth centuries, when trust failed, either because of prolonged or unsuccessful warfare, unacceptable regulation or taxation, famine, or simple loss of respect, the subordinate authorities retired to wait, to watch, and with remarkable frequency to revolt. Other aspects of society rapidly reflected the inoperative institutions: royalty was inattentive if not inept, priests failed to perform as expected, people withdrew, and money went into hiding. Nothing remained to prevent the Revolution.

In the pre-Romantic and Romantic period, as fathers, church, and the aristocracy were undermined, the entire, monolithic hierarchy was called into question. The philosophes had long been hinting that there might not be a God, that at best there was a distant Supreme Being or something called Providence. Henri Peyre is nonetheless correct to claim that the loss of religious faith was not sufficient cause for the *mal de siècle*.[37] It was only one element in the midst of an entire society embroiled in tumultuous transition. Some clergy were in hiding; many had fled the country; some were willing to swear allegiance to the nation and thus become state employees. The Catholic church itself had been despoiled and disenfranchized. The institution of monarchy had been taken apart, and the king executed. Aristocrats either tried to keep a low profile, or they emigrated, or they joined with the regicides and tried to gain power and wealth through politics, none of which brought them glory. In fact some middle-class fathers seemingly held them in such contempt that they would not allow their daughters to marry them. Claude Tillier's* *Mon oncle Benjamin* (1843), for example, tells that M. Minxit brought about his daughter's death when he refused her permission to marry an aristocrat. "My daughter is dead," he says, "because I did not love her enough. I acted toward her like an execrable egotist. She loved a noble, and I didn't want her to marry him, because I detested nobles" (264).

The Revolutionary government promised a new society, but the frequent changes of leadership, the inconsistent often capricious laws passed by the National Assembly, and the abuse of the power to mint money brought the new system into bankruptcy and disarray. In essence,

---

* Claude Tillier (1801–44) was a provincial journalist who turned his pen frequently to controversial subjects and to novels where irony plays a key role. Today he is remembered only for this work, which affectionately mocks life in the provinces.

everything regularly and repeatedly came to a standstill. The people had no bread, and they rioted. Inflation devalued revolutionary money daily, and people engaged in wild spending, gambling, and frenetic parties before their assignats became absolutely worthless. The middle class went into the mode of protecting capital, hiding their funds in flowerbeds, quietly disdaining the bloodthirsty brutes who had taken power and terrified everyone. When Napoleon came on the scene, promising peace and stability, he attempted to highlight his function as a reliable guarantor by taking the crown in his own hands and crowning himself. Unfortunately, there was nothing above him, nothing that guaranteed either his effectiveness or his permanence. He was not pharaoh, and not surprisingly, he was only one of a long string of more or less rapidly changing rulers. In every case throughout this century of revolutions, when rulers were proven untrustworthy, they fell. People were no longer governed by a triadic world view of God/man/beast. Since they had done away with God, they were left with nothing but the two lower orders. More important, without the sustaining institutions, there were no vehicles for collective ideals, no standard bearers for normative behavior. That this created a significant, long-lived problem may be indicated by one of Maurice Barrès's young "heroes" late in the nineteenth century: while listening to the future assassin Racadot rant against injustice, he muses, "There is truth in what he says; we need to find a new basis for ethics."[38]

Unfortunately for France, ideals are neither self-generating nor self-sustaining. They only exist within the framework of institutions, and without higher authorities to act as guarantors, institutions, beliefs, standards, and ideals have a very short life. Michelet, who understood the importance of this vacuum, wanted to replace God with the new mystical entity of Nation (Dunn, *Deaths*, 51–52), but there was nothing to make Romantics believe in the reality, much less the long life of Nation. And governments continued to fall. What was one to believe in? The Revolution proclaimed "Liberty, Equality, Fraternity." Then the blood-letting began, proving that people in the grips of fear were neither free, nor equal, nor brotherly. As Edgar Quinet* explained, "[A]s long as Louis XVI lived, factions were united in their hatred for him; they were brought together if only to fear and accuse him. After he died, those same parties no longer agreed on anything; among them was not a moment of truce; all that was left was for them to destroy one another."[39] In short, as long

---

* Quinet (1803–75) was a historian primarily interested in the philosophy of history. Among his many historical, philosophical, and religious writings, there were several prose epics.

as the old, God-ordained king and monarchy lived, there was a guarantor that unified the nation. When he died there was nothing.

Musset notes the dearth of possibilities: "Everything that was is no longer; everything that will be is not yet," and he compares the Romantic to "a man whose house was falling apart. He tore it down to build another. Rubble covers his field, and he waits for new stones to build a new edifice. Just when he is ready to shape the stones . . . someone comes to tell him that they are out of rock" (*Confession,* 20). Should one elevate love as a value? Musset's *La Confession d'un enfant du siècle* (1836) turns on Octave's refusal to accept what his friends believe: that love is fleeting. Nonetheless, when Brigitte commits herself totally to him, when Constant's Elénore commits herself irrevocably to Adolphe (1816), when Ourliac's Suzanne commits herself completely to Lareynie (1840), in fact, when hundreds of Romantic characters commit themselves to their lovers, love dies. Marriage? In a country that had legalized divorce, it was manifestly difficult to take wedding vows as seriously as does the monk in Ducray-Duminil's *Cœlina* ([1799] 6.234–35).

Friendship? Octave saw one of his "most intimate friends. . . . caressing my mistress" (*Confession,* 24–25). Alletz's Préval seduces the wife of a friend ("L'Isolement" [1835]). And when Alphonse Karr's Edward steals Magdeleine from his friend Stephen and marries her, Stephen then exacts revenge by killing Edward in a duel before seducing his widow (*Sous les tilleuls* [1832]). So it went with other Romantic ideals. Happiness was subject to too many variables and seldom continued beyond the closing pages of the chapter. Glory lasted no longer, whether it came from politics, the military, or the arts.[40]

Lamartine, Michelet, Hugo, and legions of social thinkers formulated a new humanitarian ideal (Dunn, *Deaths*), but it never took root.[41] As Camus pointed out repeatedly in, for example, *L'Homme révolté* and *La Chute,* our humanitarian ideology seems to justify murder and all too often leads to tyranny. Besides, as Sartre long proclaimed, nothing proves that human beings are worth sacrificing for. Individuals might be good or bad, but the generalizations of "humanity" or "brotherhood" were not real. Collectives were only as good as the benefit they produced. As Madelyn Gutwirth demonstrates, people were adrift, at sea. The feeling of helplessness, of engulfment, of being overwhelmed fills the art of the day. One of the most popular artistic subjects was the biblical flood, but there were also numerous representations of wild tempests, shipwrecks, capsizing boats, the flotsam of a vessel's wreckage, pathetic survivors, the dead and dying (e.g., plate 4). It was not so much *Oedipus Rex* that drew this public (though as I shall mention in chapter five it had an important

4. Anne Louis Girodet-Trioson. *Scène de déluge (Scene from a Flood)*, 1806, Louvre. ©
Photo RMN–R.G. Ojeda.

following), but *Oedipus at Colonus*, where they could focus on the helpless
despair of the blind patricide, Oedipus, and his frail guide, Antigone.[42] To
some degree, such subjects merely indicate the value of sentiment. It may
even be, as Peter Brooks has suggested, that they demonstrate that
sentiment has replaced religious morality and philosophical ethics.[43] If we
can weep over the lot of another, perhaps we are not absolutely selfish,
perhaps we really do have values. More than anything else, however, these
pathetic subjects represent people without stability in a world of turmoil.

And that, of course, is precisely what we find at the core of Romantic heroes in all their manifestations.

When people have gone adrift, when their institutions no longer sustain them, when they are baffled and lost, they then become very self-protective. Whatever freedom they have is committed to their personal well-being. Benjamin Constant equated liberty and individualism: "[B]y liberty," he said, "I mean the triumph of individualism, as much over authority that would like to govern through despotism as over the masses that demand the right to subject the minority to the majority."[44] And Mercier explains the meaning of liberty: "What is a people suddenly freed from the political and religious yoke? It is no longer a people, it is rather an unrestrained populace, dancing in front of the sanctuary, screaming the words to the carmagnole, dancing so wildly (I'm not exaggerating) that they almost lose their pants, collars undone, chests exposed, stockings around their ankles, turning so rapidly that they look like whirlwinds, precursors of tempests that bring devastation and terror" (*Nouveau Paris*, 4.140). Individualism reigns. In a passage that shows his recollection of Exodus 3:14 where "God said unto Moses, 'I AM THAT I AM,'" Samuel Taylor Coleridge explains, "We begin with the I KNOW MYSELF, in order to end with the absolute I AM."[45] The *moi* is no longer detestable.

The heroes of novels and plays of the period believe themselves justified in seeking their own happiness, in pursuing their personal benefit. In *Berthe et Louise* (1843), for example, Camille Bodin recounts that Berthe feels no guilt for abandoning her mother (32), and Fernand seems oblivious to the fact that he might dishonor his father (45–46). Though the narrator makes it very clear that such decisions will degrade the characters, myriads of Romantic heroes are demonstrably not prevented from the continual impulsion to gratify or fulfill themselves in successions of Romantic plays and novels. Although the commitments of Berthe and Fernand are perhaps more obvious than those of many Romantic characters, they differ little in primary allegiance to number one. As Lilian R. Furst pointed out, "It is no coincidence that so many works of this period bear as their title simply the name of the main character. . . . He holds the centre of works whose primary purpose is the presentation of his character."[46]

Louis Reybaud★ presented a typical image of the age with *Jérôme Paturot à la recherche d'une position sociale* (1842). As the comic Paturot shifts with the wind of every passing doctrine, joining every ephemeral

---

★ Reybaud (1799–1879) was a many faceted man of letters who is most remembered for his novels that satirize contemporary France and the aborning middle-class society.

movement, only in the end to settle down and become a successful shopkeeper, we have the essence of the nineteenth century. Elsewhere, Louis-Benoît Picard describes Laurent Giffard in *Le Gil Blas de la Révolution* (1824). Poor Giffard both emigrates, thus proclaiming his loyalty to the monarchy, and collects the credentials of an ardent revolutionary, as he struggles to make ends meet by embracing every movement from 1789 through the Restoration. The difficult feat leaves him both impoverished and exhausted. Clearly he has no real commitment to anyone or anything but himself and whatever temporary advantage presents itself. Still, I do not want to suggest that people of the period had no aspirations or personal ideals, for that was not the case. They had individual feelings, hopes, and dreams. They were often individually faithful to their families, to their country, to their church. But they did not have collective ideals to provide the architecture of societal support. Like us, they suspected scandals of plagiarism or perversion behind public figures, and without the threat of star chambers, gulags, and death squads even the illusion of true heroism remained impossible. Weakening the authority of aristocracy and aristocrats, church, and clergy might be compared to what would happen if dictionaries no longer functioned as standards of word forms and meanings. The language would not disappear; it would simply change more chaotically and rapidly. Likewise, ideals did not disappear with the devitalization of the nobility. Nor did the Christian faith dissolve with the weakening of the church. Beliefs merely fragmented and mutated with increasing rapidity. As Giffard explains, "The fact is that during the day I changed my opinion three or four times, and when evening came I had none at all" (Picard, 5.44).

Balzac's Raphaël de Valentin is typical. He dreams of surmounting great obstacles and accomplishing great things: "I will wrestle with yellow, blue, green fever, with armies, with scaffolds" (10.203). Despite his poverty, he is such a devoted son that for years he sacrifices pleasures to help his father, and he eventually sells his small inheritance to pay the family debt. He retains nothing but the small island where his mother's tomb is located, thus highlighting his filial virtues and commitment to traditional values. Convinced that he is destined for great things (10.128), that he can cover himself with glory (10.132), he prepares to "scramble to heaven without a ladder" (10.133) by means of his philosophical treatise, *Théorie de la Volonté (Theory of Will Power)*. Determined to live a life of significant service to humanity, he plans to lay out "a new path for human science" (10.138). Still, all these good intentions were before he was given the *peau de chagrin*, the ass's skin which gave him the power to have his wishes fulfilled. Then, rather than solve enduring problems of hunger or sickness, rather than making a significant mark on the world, he chooses self-gratification. His "first desire is vulgar" (10.88). He settles for luxury, a life of egotistic pleasure, selfishness that is emphasized both by the sale of the island where his mother's tomb is located (10.201) and by the duel in which he kills a young man. Balzac says of his class as a whole, "An aristocracy held in low regard is like a lazy king, a husband in skirts; it is void before becoming nothing" (5.927).

A literature filled with the self-seeking "heroes" would have little to admire, and indeed the literary portrait of the Romantics is discouraging. While one would have trouble believing that corruption has not always existed, for example, it is seldom as unremarkably and unimaginably banal as in Lamothe-Langon's* cynical *Monsieur le Préfet* (1824). The results of the changes in contemporary society were many and frequently remarked by the writers. In *Le Curé de village* Balzac, for instance, notes that a "proletariat no longer accustomed to sentiment, with no other God than Envy, with no other fanaticism than the despair of hunger, with neither faith nor belief, [is a proletariat that] will come forward and place its foot on the country's heart" (9.820). Pierre Saint-Amand, moreover, would have us believe that the Marquis de Sade does not represent an anomaly. "All he did, as a good reader and anthropologist of his century, was to expand on the terror of relations. . . . In retrospect, Sade can be seen to represent a logical outcome—but of a process already corrupt. All that was necessary was to rip off the veil, to reveal the formulae concealed beneath the layers of makeup."[47]

The social reformers did not hesitate to point to society's many problems, but they held out a new hope. If the world left much to be desired, surely things would improve. With individual good will and man's superior intelligence dedicated to science, there would be progress toward a better future. The doctrine of progress enjoyed considerable currency until about the time of the disastrous Franco-Prussian War, when people began to look around and catalogue the continuing abuses. Fin-de-siècle neo-Romantic and naturalistic writers and the general public recognized that the much hoped for new world had not arrived. Progress had not brought a new heaven on earth.

Prior to the Revolution man might have his feet in the *boue*, but it was at least possible for him to raise his head to the clouds. Unfortunately, when the heroes of 1793 began closing the churches, seizing the church's

---

* Etienne-Léon de Lamothe-Langon (1786–1864), while writing a few Romantic novels, served as a subprefect in several places under the Empire. He was dismissed early in the Restoration, after which he wrote false memoirs and novels that catered to public taste.

lands, and perhaps most significant, when Napoleon crowned himself, the mythology governing men's lives lost an important element that was belatedly announced by Nietzsche: God was dead, and heaven had, so to speak, come down to earth. Since it clearly did not exist here, people were asked to believe in progress that would, in some distant future, manifest an earthly paradise for humanity. Their inability to continue such faith was incarnated in tepid epics that I shall discuss in the next chapter, as well as in riots and widespread pessimism. The hierarchical relationship of God/man/beast that had defined men became bipolar: man/animal. If there were no gods then the concept of godlike was meaningless. Human beings in their pathetic weakness had no place to rise, no higher realm, and Romantic heroes were left yearning for a vague ideal, destined for disappointment. Sadly, however, they could nonetheless fall to the maudlin, the laughable, or the bestial. Melodrama, comedy, and the novel then became the defining art forms, the lens through which humankind saw and understood themselves. Neither the patriarchy nor the noble genres were credible.

5. Hubert Robert. *Vue imaginaire de la grande galerie du Louvre en ruines* (*An Imaginary View of the Louvre's Great Gallery in Ruins*), 1796, Louvre. © Photo RMN.

CHAPTER 4

The Unheroic Mode

Hugo's *Hernani* (1830) gives an important example of how crumbling institutions during the Romantic era were reflected in a literature that was holding noble genres up for mockery. In the first scene, Hugo treated the public to a womanizing king, so besotted that he would sneak into a young woman's home uninvited and unwanted, so undignified that he would forget his station and hide in a broom closet, even after he has recognized that it served to store the most common implements. "Would this be the stable where by chance you put/Your broomstick" (1.1), he asks the girl's governess before squeezing into it. Respect for royalty was for all intents and purposes dead. Not surprisingly, only a few months after the first performance of *Hernani*, many in Hugo's audience would man the barricades and chase a king from his throne. It was by no means an accident that the comic, theatrical incarnation of King Don Carlos soon to be Charles V, emperor of the Holy Roman Empire, was Hugo's most important tool for humbling the canons of classical theatre. In the midst of twelve syllable alexandrines that would make one expect a classical tragedy, the king asks prosaically, "Quelle heure est-il? [What time is it]" (2.1), and he is answered even more unimaginatively, "Minuit bientôt [Soon midnight]" (ibid.). Hugo proudly points to the line in "Réponse à un acte d'accusation" (1854): "They heard a king say, 'What time is it?'" (v. 92), but the real crisis came when Hernani was so crude as to confront Don Ruy Gomez and yell, "Stupid old man!" (3.7). The absolutely unacceptable prosaicness of the inelegant cry brought the audience to their feet in a riot. Today it is hard for us to grasp the impact of such seemingly banal verses, but in 1830 both the audience and the wider public understood that Hugo was purposefully debasing the classics, the standards against which everything had been judged. Hugo and his many friends who had come to cheer on the desecration were proclaiming the

84

new Romantic aesthetic. Théophile Gautier's leonine mane and bright green doublet were a further offense to the conservatively dressed *amateurs* of classical theater. As Hugo later explains, he is not only a simple spectator of previous revolutionary acts against literature— "Drinker of the blood of phrases, I clapped my hands" ("Réponse," v. 134)—he himself carries the revolution to poetry: "I blew a revolutionary wind./I put a red [revolutionary] hat on the old dictionary" (ibid., vv. 65–66). "In the chaos of this century which wrings your heart,/I trampled good taste and the ancient French verse,/beneath my feet..." (ibid., vv. 1–3). As Jean Viennet, a contemporary witness, put it in 1830, "Racine and Voltaire are held up for ridicule" (*Journal*, 96).

During the course of the eighteenth century the traditional genres had a steadily diminishing ability to speak to people. Artists demanded more freedom, devising new rules for old, established genres and introducing new art forms. What was called "drama" arose, according to Michel Lioure, in opposition to the traditional forms of dramatic art.[1] Writers were looking for something else, something different. It was no longer sufficient to amaze audiences with the stately beauty of one's verses. Spectators and readers demanded to be touched or, at least, to be educated about the fearsome society growing up around them. In the face of tradition, lachrymose comedies, bourgeois dramas, philosophical novels, and memoirs by unimportant witnesses of banal events sold well. Novelty was a virtue. Especially as the nineteenth century opened and blossomed, literature was graced with new verse forms and unusual topics, while melodramas and novels became the genres of preference. Napoleon encouraged the great genres consecrated by the classics, but he was only partially successful and that only for a while. Mme de Staël served as a clarion to announce that "[i]n France, our greatest tragedies no longer interest people" (*De l'Allemagne*, 189). She explained the failure of tragedy by its inability to touch people, but it was more than that. Fundamentally, tragedy and epic failed because Romantics no longer believed in heroes and the heroic. Although epic poetry continued to wheeze along for almost a century with decreasing credibility, it was in fact moribund and, like tragedy, destined for the dust heap of libraries— or for burlesque.

The tragic loves of antiquity are replaced in Paul de Kock's comic novels by the amours of a buffoon like Raymond. All the great themes are degraded. There is, for example, the narrator of Paul de Kock's "La Voiture du farinier" ('The Flour-merchant's Cart,' 1844), who, "does not have a taste for solitude" (*Tyler*, 151). He sets off with his mistress in search of adventure. "We were finally in the season where you desire ardently to leave the big city, to go afar, far from the world" (150). Repelled by the thought of noisy, crowded, public conveyances, and lacking "golden carriages [and] magnificent horses" (159), the hero and his beloved are forced by financial considerations to settle for the cart of the flour-merchant returning home to Ermenonville after selling his goods. The down-to-earth hero takes care of the preparations by buying a nice *pâté*... after all, you have to "think about something solid" (159). Unfortunately, when he and his "little friend" confront danger, he realizes that he has forgotten the essential: "I don't have any [weapons]... nothing, not even a cane" (210). It is hard to be a hero in the everyday life of the nineteenth century.

Other writers use the grand works of the past to highlight an opposition. Zola's *La Curée* (1872), for example, uses a magnificent performance of *Phèdre* to set off Renée's sordid affair with her step-son Maxime. "How petty and shameful was her drama beside the ancient epic!" she thinks (1.509). *Nana* (1881) raises the curtain on Venus cavorting in theatrical floodlights with Mars, and where antiquity's Aphrodite was only mocked by the gathering gods and goddesses, Zola's Venus is exposed to the ridicule of mere men, since she was caught in an all too human act. The comic *in flagrante delicto* descends a notch, and the goddess in rut appears not merely human but bestial. Writers seem to have heard Sade's cry: "[N]o more gods, Frenchmen, no more gods" (*Philosophie,* 3.491).

Daniel Madelénat summarizes the common understanding of "epic": "The definitions usually include two 'semes': narrativity (long), exceptional action and themes (heroic and wondrous), like that of the Academy: 'A grand composition in verse, where the poet tells of some heroic action that he embellishes with episodes, fictions, and wondrous events.'"[2] Not everyone would agree. Madelénat cites Zumthor and Etiemble who would downplay one or the other of these traits, but examples of the epic in nineteenth-century France could be called on to suggest that when the epic (1) loses its elevated style, (2) breaks up into short narrations, (3) fails to find heroic or exceptional events to recount, and (4) cannot construct personages that are convincingly heroic, it has reached an impasse.

Although the nineteenth-century desire to resuscitate the epic resulted in a surfeit of wan counterfeits, the authors occasionally discuss the genre's problems. Edgar Quinet, for example, wonders in his "Préface" to *Merlin,* "Why would the French, who created vast inventions in the middle ages, no longer be capable of doing as much? Why should they resign themselves to producing nothing but fragments? . . . . The public, they say, is too weak, too corrupt, too worn out; it can no longer either support or understand grand compositions" (1.ix–x). His narrator begins with: "And I also am looking for a man, a hero. . . . All that I ask is that he be very real, not even a strong penchant for materiality would be super-fluous, so much are the men of our day annoyed with ideal creatures" (1.1). Sadly, Quinet's Merlin makes a wooden hero, and though the author avoids fragmentation, his "vast invention" is written in prose, rather than the traditional verse, and never succeeds in lifting the reader's imagination beyond the earthly to the rarefied heights of the ideal. The hero's crown should belong to the reader who manages to get through the turgid composition.

As I have noted, the epic was not the only noble genre to become problematic in definition and occurrence as the Revolution approached. The decline in tragedy also paralleled the attacks on the aristocracy and the divine. Because God and king, on the one hand, alexandrine and *bienséances* (roughly translatable as decorum), on the other, had been the guarantors and the vehicles of collective ideals, the standard bearers of everything noble and heroic, when they were debased in comedy and pornography they lost their effectiveness. The newspapers of the Romantic period indicate conclusively that the nineteenth century believed in progress, at least for a while, but authors were unable to incarnate progress heroically. Neither *Merlin* nor most other such works were meant to be burlesques. In *Jocelyn* (1836), Lamartine portrays a prophet of the people, an evangelist of a new religion that envisaged humanity moving toward a future of brotherly reconciliation. Though it had some success, it resembles an epic less than a long idyll and is today virtually unreadable. The poem's recent editor, Jean des Cognets, maliciously comments, "In composing *Jocelyn* [Lamartine] was delighted to discover that it is only a short distance from prose to verse" (xv). Prosaism is, as Madelénat points out, an important feature of the passing epic.

If *Jocelyn* were not enough to prove that it is difficult to deify man, Quinet's grandiose, syncretistic compositions use prose to invent a new garden of Eden where Adam appears with a pantheon of gods. The inferior quality of the artistry might be blamed for the aesthetic failure of Lamartine's *Jocelyn*, Quinet's *Ahasvérus ou le Juif errant* (1833), the *Génie des religions* (1842), and *Merlin* (1860), but another explanation must be found for Hugo's *La Légende des siècles* (1859–83). Gide's famous quip when asked to name France's greatest poet, "Victor Hugo... Alas!" rings not over Hugo the poet (despite the work's significant fragmentation), but over Hugo the pontificating philosopher/preacher. While Hugo's poetry saved *La Légende des siècles*, Zola's messianic *Les Trois Villes*

(1894–97) and, worse, *Les Quatre Evangiles* (1899–1903) have few if any redeeming features. Zola's previously admirable workmanship no longer produces major poetic movements, the characters and actions seem but pale exemplars of the author's messages, and the result appears, in short, regrettably formulaic and pedestrian.

Eugène Sue had great popular success with novels that deified the worker and mankind in general. His readers' interest grew, however, not from Sue's pompous pronouncements about Humanity's laborers, but rather from the sympathy that Fleur-de-Marie and other pathetic characters elicited in unending volumes of melodramatic novels. Unlike Lamartine's *La Chute d'un ange* (1838), which failed to please, his earlier *Jocelyn* succeeded like Sue's novels by playing on the heart strings of its enchanted public. While these decadent epics cannot stir a people to heroism, and indeed I am not at all sure that was their purpose, their Romantic sentimentalism very successfully touched readers and elicited very satisfying tears.

Where eighteenth- and nineteenth-century writers who were skeptical about both the aristocracy and the divine replaced heroes with more down-to-earth individuals, thus rendering literary heroes less convincingly admirable, previous classical literature rigorously separated the higher realms of power, thought, and poetry from comedy and the realities of bodily functions. "There are no lavatories in tragic palaces, but from its very dawn, comedy has had use for chamber pots," says George Steiner.[3] Aristotle had no difficulty keeping the elevated where it was supposed to be, that is, away from the debased: "[C]omedy represents the worse types of men; worse . . . in the sense that the ridiculous is a species of ugliness or badness. . . . Epic poetry agrees with tragedy to the extent that it is a representation, in dignified verse, of serious actions" (ch. 5). Rabelais, after all, whose interest in fundamental matters is well known, was well aware that you could not have heroes or gods going to the toilet, and, as undergraduates have long noticed, the utopian Abbey de Thélème lacks the necessary.

Gods knew it as well. Aphrodite understood that her reputation would never recover from her being exposed with Ares. No wonder she pursued Phaedra's offspring for generations. Where human beings had occasionally been able to compare themselves with the gods, as the Romantic era unfolded they could only envision themselves with animals, or as Gide had Pasiphaë complain on considering the Minotaur, "It is rather vexing (and it wasn't easy!), I was hoping that a god was hidden in it.—If Zeus had been involved, I would have given birth to a Dioscuri; thanks to that animal I only put a calf into the world" (*Prométhée*, 341).

This was the problem of the Romantics. Gods were revealed in their bestiality, heroes no longer had godlike models, and when Romantic heroes tried to pose statuesquely on the slopes of Mount Olympus they tumbled face down, nose in the comic. It is not necessary to repeat the litany of Romantic failures. Seldom do these pathetic heroes even die in noble causes. Death by suicide, death by wasting away, death by despair. While they often sounded admirable when enumerating their goals, on looking closely we cannot fail to note that these characters would be happy in bed with someone else's spouse or with sufficient funds to live a life of relative ease. Gilbert Durand has concluded that this was a period when "[a]ll heroes are from another epoch, from the species of demi-gods, from an ancient race."[4] But it was worse than that. Aristocrats demanded to be reinstated to all their former wealth and privileges, apparently satisfied to neglect the essential values of courage, talent, intelligence, and spiritual nobility for the form. Indeed, the nineteenth century lost faith in the very possibility of heroes and heroism. Consequently, neither they nor we have effective epics or tragedies.

The changes taking place in the epic are marked in Marmontel's* essay on the epic genre late in the eighteenth century. For him, the epic "is the imitation, as a tale, of an interesting and memorable action,"[5] terms considerably more humble than words like "greatness and importance" that one would expect and that only appear later as phantoms of former glory (13.353, 354). This is not the only evidence of Marmontel's compromise of the traditional conception of the epic with literary reality. He goes on to say that "it is not necessary for characters to be noble, provided that the action is itself elevated" (13.356) and that "[n]othing is more useful . . . than the mixture of supernatural beings with men" (13.368). There seems to me no question that nineteenth-century experiments with the epic form indicate conclusively that Marmontel was wrong in believing epics were possible without gods and exceptional men. Still, the thought of a new definition that would be more suitable for the nineteenth century has certain attractions. If the epic could be understood, not as a lengthy "representation, in dignified verse, of serious actions," with Aristotle, but rather as what Lukács called "the epic of a world that has been abandoned by God"[6] or, perhaps, what I would term

---

* Jean-François Marmontel (1723–99) was a major writer in last half of the eighteenth century, known across Europe less for his tragedies than for his philosophical novels and "moral" tales. The articles he wrote for the Encyclopédie made up the Eléments de littérature which includes the essay I refer to here.

a "lengthy, serious portrayal of humanity's degradation," then Balzac and Zola become the century's greatest epic writers.

Madelénat suggests that the epic moved into its twilight because the most objective of genres could not sustain Romantic subjectivity. I would go further and propose that Romantic individualism, like private sentiment and the rage for unbridled liberty of action and expression, could brook no competition. Romantics were driven to pull down the old gods, and, as the aristocracy was humbled, as God and gods were denied and ridiculed, as noble poetic forms and rhythms were mocked, all standards were called into question. Without the noble vehicles that had served to bear the ideal, the epic as previously understood had effectively become impossible.

Allegory fared no better than the epic and tragedy. Edwin Honig has argued that "the Romantic esthetic broke off the chain relating man to other creatures and to the inanimate world. It jettisoned not only the traditional symbolism of Christian analogy but also the cosmology of the natural sciences along with its humanitarian ideals and its belief in the possibility of controlling nature unaided by providence. In losing its objective character, the symbol became a simulacrum, a disembodied form in which ideas or feelings were arbitrarily substituted for real events, persons, and things. The symbolism of the French symbolists became another version of the reality-drained personification allegory of the Middle Ages."[7] For authors faced with forms and genres that were no longer capable of touching and moving their audiences, there were other options. They could either find new forms, like verse with an uneven number of syllables, or they could rethink the existing genres and, in effect, reinvent them to render their art more effective and depict the social upheaval of the Romantic period.

From our perspective at the end of the twentieth century, the early eighteen hundreds look very exciting. Revolutions had upended societal structures in France and the United States; Europe was shifting from an agricultural to an urban, capitalistic society; enormous numbers of people were migrating to the cities to provide labor for the rapidly expanding industrial revolution; population was exploding; lands were being conquered and colonies established; networks of canals and railroads were being built; science was perfecting its methods of research, and its discoveries were changing the face of the world, while promising more radical improvements in the human condition for the future. Though such changes do indeed encourage excitement, they also cause keenly felt uncertainty and fear, even anguish. Certainly, the terrible plight of the lower classes, literally plagued with disease, poorly nourished and overcrowded, made the results of failure in this society evident. These things history can tell us is in all too vivid detail.

It is less easy for historians to tell us how people experienced these changes. For that we must turn to the arts, for it is literature, painting, sculpture, architecture, music that crystallize the feelings, yearnings, and fears. Given the apparent excitement about progress, which we can see in the newspapers and essays of the day, it is perhaps surprising to find so little reflection in literature.[8] Many poets turned away from a disagreeable present to sing of ancient days and ways; others, like Baudelaire and Nerval, openly disdained middle-class success; but many provide glimpses of the monstrous terrors prowling in the secret thoughts of men and women. Vigny captures the nightmare in "La Maison du Berger," giving form to the invisible forces responsible for the vertiginous changes:

> On the iron bull that smokes, blows and bellows,
> Man climbed too soon. No one yet knows
> What storms this coarse, blind thing bears within itself,
> And the gay traveler gives it his treasure;
> His old father and his sons, he throws them as hostages
> In the burning belly of the Carthaginian bull,
> Which casts them up as ashes at the feet of the Golden God.
>
> vv. 78–84

Aberrations similar to those of this poem may be revealed by what we can see in the incapacities and failures of so many Romantic characters. It may well be that for most of these people who yearned for a stable, ordered life, the most terrifying things were the changes and convulsions themselves. However that may be, even before trains and other machines came to represent the obsessive reality of death,[9] novelists managed no less vividly to render palpable their readers' most hidden fears. The plight of the masses of urban poor was indeed so appalling that failure to succeed was unthinkable for the middle and upper classes. To sink to that level was to lose one's humanity. As I shall discuss in chapter six, for many, suicide was preferable. Raymond Giraud puts it nicely: "We are again reminded that there is an economic floor below which the Stendhalian hero is extremely reluctant to descend. He is a bourgeois, as Stendhal was. To be unduly concerned with money is in poor taste; to seek one's happiness in it is unheroic. But heroism is not worth the price of poverty."[10] Fear of being subordinate, dependent, poor, spattered with *boue* can provide a powerful stimulus, but it can also paralyze. When Balzac's previously mentioned Lucien Chardon arrived in Paris, he was particularly struck by the extremes of ostentatious luxury and wretched poverty, and he "was left feeling diminished" (5.264). Wherever they looked, young people saw the maw of poverty gaping at their feet, waiting for them to stumble.

Perhaps because Stendhal's Fabrice stumbles so often, an examination of *La Chartreuse de Parme* (1839) may provide insight into the particularly unheroic heroes that abound in Romantic novels. Readers have been surprisingly uncertain of *La Chartreuse*'s true subject. In 1840, Balzac wrote that Stendhal erred in not ending the work with Fabrice's rehabilitation, which indicates that the two novelists differed markedly in their opinions of what the novel is about. For Balzac, it was a study of a particular segment of society, and, as he put it, "Despite the title, the work is over when Count and Countess Mosca return to Parma, and Fabrice is archbishop. The important comedy of the court is finished."[11] If the novel does not stop there, and it does not, Balzac is either wrong or important structural flaws exist. Zola expanded on the master's strictures: "There is no need to prove the lack of logical composition in Stendhal's novels; this lack of composition is obvious, especially in *La Chartreuse*. Balzac, so enthusiastic, felt very clearly that the novel had no center; the subject shifts according to the episodes, and the book which began with an interminable introduction, ends suddenly at the moment when the author has started a new story."[12] Or, as the critic Elme Marie Caro put it in 1855, "I wonder where the interest is in the *Chartreuse*. It is an accumulation of disorganized scenes without a hint of unity."[13] Readers have therefore found it difficult to ascertain what *La Chartreuse de Parme* is about. While it is not necessary to reread William Empson's *Seven Types of Ambiguity* or to review the more recent comments on the polyvalent in order to realize that ambiguity can allow particularly interesting aesthetic effects, it is also true that some shifts of focus are distracting, even destructive. Because the apparently faulty construction of Stendhal's novel continues to bedevil critics, there is reason to suspect an instance of confusion within the work itself rather than aesthetically successful ambiguity. Most recent readers would nonetheless agree that the novel is a masterpiece.[14] They apparently discern some underlying armature or logic that makes sense of the work.

Stendhal's response to such reservations as those just cited was unequivocal, even though it was not written for public consumption. In a now published but then discarded draft of his bread-and-butter letter to thank Balzac for the latter's review-essay, he asked, "Haven't I written Fabrice's life?"[15] Some have argued specifically that Stendhal's remark is accurate and Fabrice is indeed at the center of the novel,[16] but critics have yet to address the hero's relationship to the continuing, widely sensed

92

awareness of something unresolved in the way the novel is put together. If Fabrice and his life are central, the work not only seems to meander, but his aunt Gina commands so much attention that it makes her nephew seem trivial. All too often, Stendhal cavalierly drops Fabrice into a convenient prison so that the author is free to pursue what might seem an unrelated topic. "But for the moment," he says for example, "we are obliged to leave Fabrice in his prison, clear up at the top of the Parma citadel; he is well guarded" (*Chartreuse*, 2.280). Sainte-Beuve's perception that "the novel is less a novel than memoirs of Fabrice and his aunt"[17] seems almost generous. Faguet was less so: "The extreme failing of *la Chartreuse de Parme* is the extreme insignificance of the main character and the small amount of interest he attracts. On the other hand, Duchess Sanseverina is a strong, memorable figure..."[18] It is difficult at first sight to consider the story of Fabrice's life as central, since Gina remains a startlingly powerful character and her activities much more important than those of the boy. As a result even good readers have been confused. "Who is the 'hero,' Gina or Fabrice?" asks Alison Finch.[19] Though textual markers regularly point to Fabrice, the volition and the activity are in fact elsewhere, and critics have found themselves paying closer attention to factors other than the hero. Barbéris says flatly, "La Chartreuse is a novel without a true hero."[20] I suspect the confusion arises because of inappropriate expectations. While readers were trained in the Aristotelian tradition to focus on action, Stendhal was exploring other possibilities.

Especially for Stendhal's period when readers expected characters to be not only suggestive of "an everyday being of flesh and bone," as Ricardou disdainfully put it,[21] but to be noticeably involved in a series of connected actions across the novel, the role of Fabrice is disconcerting because he almost never acts decisively and has little apparent will of his own. Pushed here and there, he does either as others suggest or as he is obliged. He acts, but it is usually by reaction to his environment, rather than by volition. Viewed in the light of heroes found in the works of Dumas *père*, Sue, Balzac, Hugo, and other novelists of the day, one would say he is an extraordinarily passive character. Readers who are drawn to dynamic personages find their attention divided, for while Fabrice does virtually nothing, and seldom even reveals a preference, all the others are very busy indeed. Irresolute, depending on others for direction and goals, Fabrice seems a lump, with all the character of a damp cracker.

The tremendously energetic novels of the first half of the nineteenth century, with intricate plots and numerous changes in fortune, had not on the whole prepared readers to expect the hero's beloved to play an active role in the story. Her function is rather to be loved, to be the object of love. In *La Chartreuse*, however, even Clélia provides such a strong contrast to Fabrice that his lack of self-motivation and activity is emphasized. If she were the duchess, she thinks shortly after the hero is incarcerated, "I would stab the prince, like heroic Charlotte Corday" (2.319). Of course, Clélia does not assassinate the monarch (Gina does), but she is a paragon of activity on her chosen's behalf. She warns him repeatedly when he runs the risk of being poisoned, in one case facing down a guard to do so; she tells him how to establish direct contact with her, brings him food and water, and perhaps most significantly arranges with Grillo for more reliable communication between them. In all cases, Clélia's acts need to be viewed against the realization that every gesture in Fabrice's favor constitutes both a betrayal of her father—the text specifically refers to betrayal[22]—and a personal humiliation. She later involves herself in Fabrice's escape and not only smuggles the essential ropes into the prison but cooperates as well with Ludovic in the rescue. That she consciously terms her activities crimes (2.375) makes all the more startling her vigorous efforts to free Fabrice and the contrast she establishes with her lethargic lover.

There is no question about Mosca's dynamism. Either because his enemies are attempting to injure him through Fabrice or because he acts and counsels to protect Fabrice and please la Sanseverina, Mosca is important to virtually every episode in the last twenty-three of the book's twenty-eight chapters. Ferrier insists correctly that he is not the hero of *La Chartreuse de Parme*, but a central cog in the plot.[23] Although his effectiveness remains controversial, whether he fails in virtually everything he attempts, as Weinstein argues,[24] or whether as Ferrier would have it he always succeeds (15, 29), or whether, finally, Stendhal simply did not satisfactorily integrate Mosca's supposed mistakes with his jealousy does not concern us here, since it does not affect the point at issue. In his seemingly endless undertakings, Mosca establishes a vivid contrast with Fabrice.

It is, however, Gina who constitutes a virtual whirlwind of activity and one of the most entrancing of Romantic heroines. She "suggest[s] a capacity for self-determination rare in nineteenth-century fictional women," as Finch points out (2.64). Beautiful, charming, impulsive, courageous, la Sanseverina is never mean or self-centered, but rather she acts whatever the cost for the well-being of others or for the sake of love, especially of Fabrice. "In prosperity, no one surpassed her gaiety and kindness," the narrator tells us, "as no one surpassed her courage and serenity in contrary fortunes" (2.29). As Gina del Dongo, the marquis's sister, she had a safe, comfortable position, but she threw it up to become the countess Pietranera and follow her beloved off to war. Her later decision to become the duchess Sanseverina-Taxis was only to allow her to play the roles necessary to help her lover, Mosca, and her nephew, Fabrice. Indeed, she draws the line at neither murder nor dishonor in her desire to help the latter, and she it is who becomes the guiding force in Fabrice's life, both encouraging and facilitating his preparation for the priesthood and, eventually, his escape from prison.

A selectively phrased summary of the events involving Fabrice make him sound like the typical hero of an action-packed novel. He leaves Italy in search of Napoleon and witnesses the battle of Waterloo. Having been captured subsequently, he escapes from prison (the first of several escapes), has numerous love affairs, kills one rival and seriously wounds another, is imprisoned and manages to pursue a love affair despite solitary confinement. Subsequently, he becomes an archbishop and fathers a child, before finally retiring to a monastery. This summary is, however, deceptive. On considering the events in detail, one discovers that Fabrice is anything but assertive. He reacts rather, allowing himself to be molded by other characters, by what happens, and by what he understands as his destiny.

Fabrice leaves Italy only after certain presages leave him little choice about his departure. While the importance of signs, prophecies, and predictions may not at first be apparent, as the pattern is repeated one understands the degree to which Fabrice is unable to make up his own mind, how little he controls his own destiny. His involvement in Waterloo is best characterized by his unhorsing, since he takes no effective action whatsoever. Indeed, he is never quite certain if he really had been present at the battle of Waterloo (2.289). Although it is true that he did escape from the prison of B..., he had little to do with it. The jailer's wife, "very tender" (2.54), lets him escape. La Sanseverina engineers his later flight from the Farnèse Tower. His love affairs are passed over rapidly, as they should be, given their lack of importance, or painted so as to highlight their ridiculousness. When he is attracted to La Fausta, for example, he ends in bed, not with her, but with her maid. He explains, "When I have the honor to court a beauty . . . I am able to think of her only when I see her" (2.136). "Doubtless he did not lack mistresses, but they were of no consequence for him" (2.144). His trip to Milan, carefully planned behavior, and entry into the priesthood are all according to Mosca's scheme and Gina's bidding. In the various fights or duels, which most cause the novel's resemblance to nineteenth-century adventure stories, Fabrice either acts through momentary ill-humor, as in his bar-room quarrel (2.94–95), or he merely responds to circumstances, as in his duel with the count de M... (2.242–43). In respect to the important brawl with Giletti, it is the latter who forces the fight. Fabrice scarcely defends himself until his adversary "fell on [him]" (2.194). That the woman he falls in love with is the only one he can see from his solitary prison cell is absolutely in character and by no means surprising. It is one more example of his passive acceptance of whatever crosses his path.

However one weights these events, whether going on to register the important decrease in the hero's activity as the novel progresses toward the fulfillment of his destined end as a contemplative bent on heaven, or whether one believes that the novel does everything possible to paint these events as insignificant in order to highlight his fate as a Carthusian,[25] there can be no question that if *faits et gestes* constitute the make-up of a Romantic hero, Fabrice's relative inactivity is remarkable. As an exemplar of Stendhal's celebrated cult of energy, this hero seems a failure.

Fabrice's most significant actions are in fact negative, those which he either does not take or which he takes in the wrong way. After careful thought, for example, he decides to refuse to escape from prison (2.342, 355), an unusual decision for the young man who almost always does exactly as told. Of course, he later gives in to Clélia and does indeed slip away. Thereafter, however, he silently falls into a state resembling sleep, "somewhat lethargic" (2.390). Later, when Mosca believes he can arrange to have Fabrice acquitted and tells the latter to give himself up at the city prison under his own control, the infatuated hero instead "had gone to get his old room in the citadel, all too happy to live a few steps from Clélia" (2.432). Fabrice's other activities are scarcely more encouraging. He conducts his most important love affair in the dark, and when he decides to abduct his son, the latter dies from the experience. In short, as a hero, Fabrice more closely resembles the anti-heroes of twentieth-century literature than the more energetic characters of his day. As a hero, Fabrice is progressively less effective in worldly matters, increasingly inactive, more narrowly focused on his love and, as a Carthusian, on God.

Fabrice's role becomes clearest in comparison with the other principal characters, especially with his aunt. While the psychological make-up of Mosca, Clélia, and Gina are all fixed from their introduction, Fabrice changes. The novel calls attention to the way he becomes different. After his adventures at Waterloo, for example, we read, "[T]he quality of blood he lost had delivered him from the romantic side of his character" (2.89–90). "It was as though Fabrice became another man" (2.93), we are told a few pages farther on. But it is the prison which makes the most significant alterations in his character. "[W]e will rediscover him perhaps somewhat changed" (2.280), the narrator coyly informs us after abandoning the hero to his prison. Later the differences are highlighted: "[H]e was another man" (2.317). "Fabrice had completely changed" (2.390). He has truly fallen in love, a love which will not change. Both quieter and considerably more articulate, he is capable of captivating large numbers of people by his preaching and able to keep Mosca informed of what is going on in the society around him.

He contrasts with Gina in other ways as well. While he is rather passive and ineffective,[26] she is extraordinarily active and effective. He is only somewhat successful in social circles; Gina, whose name is a diminutive of Regina or "queen," dominates every gathering and reigns as the *belle* of every ball. Although Fabrice seeks acceptance and approval from a number of groups, he is from first to last an outsider. Gina's bloodlines, as the Marquis del Dongo's sister, are impeccable, but Fabrice's birth is clouded. Though François Michel argues for his legitimacy, there is little doubt that the novel implies that he may have resulted from his mother's affair with Lieutenant Robert.[27] Still, despite his suspected bastardy and his outcast status, Fabrice regularly attempts to follow some higher rule of behavior, while Gina feels herself above the law. He adapts a number of pseudonyms, without changing his family name; her name changes regularly, without altering her true character. Gina is impulsive, he more and more clearly a contemplative. Until he falls in love and his focus changes from himself to Clélia and then to God, he is remarkably self-centered; Gina is equally notable for her selflessness. Almost all of her actions after chapter six are directed by her desire to help her nephew.

Pearson rightly refers to the novel's "emphasis on action (rather than psychology)" (217). It is, however, more important to note that the focus and degree of each of the characters' activities constitute the main differences between them and Fabrice. They clearly serve as foils to set him off. Indeed any attempt to circumscribe their activities must recognize this as their most important function, while Fabrice is directed mostly by external forces toward his own end, that is, toward his love of Clélia and his withdrawal into a Charterhouse to prepare for death. The novel's emphasis on fate and prophecy draws attention to Fabrice's predestined condition, as does his ineffectiveness and passivity, which lead nonetheless to the predictable and predicted conclusion. In visual terms, the novel presents a classic background/foreground study. The supporting characters function to highlight Fabrice, the quiet center, defining and silhouetting him. The activity of the background can be distracting, but a slight change of reader focus snaps the negative subject into view.

Emile Talbot reminds us that Romantics were establishing "a new esthetic paradigm which was part of a major shift in the thinking of Western man."[28] I would suggest that there was also a significant divergence in artists' intentions and critics' expectations, the latter trailing far behind the former. As novelists and poets struggled to find new and more effective ways of presenting their reality in a new world separated irrevocably from the past, the mode and vocabulary of neoclassicism continued to dominate criticism. Sainte-Beuve is perhaps not to be condemned for failing to recognize that Balzac, Baudelaire, and Stendhal, three of his less appreciated acquaintances, were among the greatest writers of his day (and of the last two centuries). His understanding, like that of most of his fellow critics, was given focus by Aristotle, rather than Shakespeare and Coleridge, while artists were re-evaluating humankind in line with other shifting social paradigms and in ways that involved both redefining and reconstituting art. Great artists like Stendhal were shattering canons that had lost luster and effectiveness.

For *La Chartreuse de Parme*, readers' problems may well have been not the novel, but rather the expectations Aristotle's aesthetic created. Doubtless because of the importance of tragedy to Aristotle's thought, his conceptions emphasize action. As he says in chapter two of the *Poetics*, "[I]mitative artists represent men in action," and criticism of Stendhal's novel has tended to be dominated by a belief in the primacy of action. Aristotle is unequivocal: "The plot . . . is the first essential of tragedy, its life-blood, so to speak, and character takes the second place" (ch. 6). For him, while it is true that "action is brought about by agents," it is the actions and choices that define the characters' natures (ch. 6). Many critics and not a few novelists would agree. Henry James, for example, wrote, "What is character but the determination of incident? What is incident but the illustration of character?"[29] In a more recent analysis, Mary Doyle Springer expands upon Aristotelian principles to emphasize the importance of the character's choices, speeches, and acts, and the way they are reinforced by description, diction, and episodes which put characters in opposition.[30]

In novels centering on such inanimate personages as Fabrice, definitions that depend on Aristotle may lead readers astray, for they encourage them to look for things that lie outside the author's intent and the scope of the creation. I suspect the confusion around *La Chartreuse* grows from an outdated critical mind-set in confrontation with a novel that is rooted in a new aesthetic. Stendhal seems to have sensed a way of presenting a kind of character who was significantly appropriate to his day. Rather than looking for a set of character traits that will be revealed and often developed in a narration, as is the case of literary personages in the Aristotelian tradition, it is more useful to consider "characters as an 'immanent' system, governed by compositional principles."[31]

Seymour Chatman observes that characters may or may not be produced by plot, that they may be either "teleological set[s] of traits]" or "agglomerate[s] of traits]."[32] An Aristotelian emphasis on action may be the best way to understand some literary personages, but there are many others that authors have created from values, qualities, and quantities. The latter traits may arise only through relationship, purpose, or simple inactivity. Stendhal's Fabrice, for example, is the main character because every episode turns on him and every character is focused on him. He has a purpose which he himself does not suspect and which was given not existentially but *a priori*, before his creation. In fact, the title of *La Chartreuse de Parme* announces the hero's foreordained end. Unlike another of Stendhal's characters, Julien Sorel, whose talents, ambition, and drive encourage action, but who is nonetheless destined by a hostile society for failure, and who attracts our interest because of and through what he does, Fabrice solicits our attention because of what he is. And while the hero of *La Chartreuse* has little in common with the other characters in the book, the others resemble each other in that each and every one of them is oriented—like flowers facing the sun—toward Fabrice. Their actions make sense only because of his presence. They inevitably have impact on him, and we finally understand that they are pushing him toward his predestined end in a Charterhouse. Those who remember the adventures detailed by St John of the Cross or St Teresa of Avila, where worldly action decreases as spiritual exercises increase, easily see that the ineffective activity of the first part of the novel is pointless. They are then prepared when the pace slows gradually and comes to a stop in darkness and silence.

Although I have tried to show the degree to which the anomic Fabrice differs from Julien Sorel and the majority of other Romantic heroes, it is perhaps time to point to their resemblances and consider whether they might both be an outgrowth of the same social reality. While the Corinnes, the Renés, the Adolphes, the Chattertons are set off from Fabrice by their activity, one must notice that they are singularly unsuccessful. As Sonnenfeld points out, even Julien's despairing attempt to kill Mme de Rênal is "the very parody of heroic action. . . . In this miserable nineteenth century, it is already too late for real actions, for heroism. The novel is set in an age of intrigue, of money, of corruption, not of heroism."[33] Because of their persistent failures, most students of the period consider it essential for a Romantic hero to have an impossible dream. Despite such exceptions as Fabrice, who seemingly has no will of his own and thus follows the impulsion of others' volition and of his own destiny, other Romantic principals do have a will, but their society condemns them to frustration and defeat.[34] Not infrequently their febrile actions end, like those of Adolphe, in lethargic incapacity. Indeed, the two kinds of characters—active and inactive, differentiated and undifferentiated, willful and docile, flailing about and drifting—are relatives, the offspring of the same social forces. Without exception, they are overcome by their environment, their society, their civilization, and they are unable to rise above it. No Titans these. Their only salvation is to accept, to float with the current. The renitent are condemned to fail. They are often destroyed.

La Chartreuse de Parme then provides an interesting variation on the more common Romantic hero who was committed to an impossible dream and condemned to failure by an unfeeling if not actively hostile society. It is impossible for him to choose consciously, like René, to travel widely in search of a vaguely perceived ideal. Lacking Chatterton's ability to select and stubbornly pursue a goal, too passive to echo the assertiveness of a Saint-Mégrin or a Monte-Cristo, Stendhal's Fabrice is putty in the hands of the other characters. He accepts and floats.[35] In a radically new kind of structure, others define him, vigorously taking charge of his fate. It may be that he is most adequately considered in contrast with Stendhal's earlier creation, Julien Sorel. Both have what modern psychologists would term negative father–child relationships, both begin life without a sure sense of where they should go, though Julien later gives shape to his ambitions, leaving behind his former dreams of military glory to pursue success through the church. He can never adapt to the priestly vocation, however, and he constantly goes beyond the confines of his chosen role. He molds others to his needs. Eventually, of course, he collides with an "impossible" situation and is condemned to the guillotine. In contrast, passive Fabrice dies a natural death, though one would hardly term his life an obvious success. Still, for all their differences, despite Julien's vigorous attempt to take charge of his world, despite Fabrice's acquiescence to any passing influence, both are patently overwhelmed by their environment. If Lucien Goldmann was correct to see "a transformation . . . of novelistic form which ends in the progressive dissolution and disappearance of the individual personage, of the hero" in the novel of the 1950s and 60s,[36] Fabrice and his very different but nonetheless fraternal twin, Julien, may represent first steps in the long march leading to this suppression.

When I think of characters like Fabrice, Chatterton, Indiana, I remember the terrible vision that William Owen had of his comrades that were about to die in the New Year of 1917: "I thought of the very strange look on all the faces in that camp; an incomprehensible look. . . . It was not despair, or terror, it was more terrible than terror, for it was a blindfold look, and without expression, like a dead rabbit's."[37] Romantic heroes confront the lessons of the Industrial Revolution, and they meet the gratuitous, the random, the useless, and the wasted. Having rejected the Christian God of comfort, they look to the future with empty hands and hopeless hearts. Although to a lesser degree involved in the mindless violence and bloodletting that characterize the twentieth century and inspire their later brothers and sisters who term such a world absurd, Romantic reality is a foreshadowing of what was to come. It is by no means an accident that Stendhal's *Le Rouge et le noir* constitutes one of the most important allusions in Camus's *L'Etranger*. Romantic heroes might struggle, they certainly whine, but they know in their heart of hearts that there is no hope.

Still, though both Julien and Fabrice are in their separate ways "unheroic," only Fabrice marks the early stages of auctorial revolt against the canonical Aristotelian character, since only he is defined not by his own but, rather, by the actions of others. There seems no doubt that he marks a shift in the view that the period's spokespersons had of the world. While the literature that led up to the Revolution indicates a joyous belief in human beings' abilities to change society for the better, Fabrice and his brothers and sisters seem to bring that optimism into question, to doubt the capacities of even the most capable individuals, to highlight the nascent despair that would overwhelm increasing numbers of the young and old as they drifted towards the end of the Romantic age and, indeed, the millennium.

Structural experimentation was much more radical in other hands. As I attempted to show in *Balzacian Montage*, the nineteenth-century French novelist Honoré de Balzac regularly played against the standard views of what novels were and what they should be. Perhaps his reconceptualizations grew from his well-known and deep-seated love of the Renaissance.[38] Certainly, his long novel, *Sur Catherine de Médicis* (1830–42), a short masterpiece, "Le Chef-d'œuvre inconnu" (1831), and a delightful collection of tales, the *Contes drolatiques* (1832-37) indicate an attraction of uncommon power, and, in fact, his affinity goes far deeper than mere affection or influence resulting in the ghosts of a few "borrowed" themes and stories. I want to suggest that more importantly he owed to the Renaissance a kind of occult structuring that he used

101

increasingly as the years went by and as he gained more confidence in his genius. Whether he also owed to the Renaissance his political position advocating the brutal use of governmental power is less clear, both because the Stalins, the Maos, and the Hitlers are by no means limited to the Renaissance and because he couched his political message obliquely. Today the immodest proposal that Balzac put forward in *Sur Catherine* would be termed fascist, though in fact it owes less to the political right or left than to the willingness to build a power base on a foundation of blood.

René Bray's discussion of the organization that I have in mind turned particularly on lyric poetry which, he says, though "[s]ubmitted to the general rules of poetry, . . . dispenses with any, particular regulations. . . . It is not subordinate to the precisions of reason. . . . It avoids strict rules: in particular it gives the appearance of disorder in the successions of facts and the connections between expressions, so as to impress with the passionate sweep of the genius composing it. But this disorder is nothing but a superior and hidden order. It goes beyond reason to be more thoroughly reasonable."[39] Although Bray felt that seventeenth-century literary sensibilities left this kind of arrangement behind as they turned toward classicism, several major critics have demonstrated the contrary.[40] Still, there is no doubt that it is particularly apparent in Renaissance literature. While perhaps most obvious in the elegies, odes, and other lyric forms that Bray cites, it is unquestionably an integral part of the creative world of Rabelais and Marguerite de Navarre, whose works Balzac knew well.

Sur Catherine de Médicis demonstrates the kind of hidden structure that Bray describes. It is furthermore significant that the structure is well integrated into the subject matter of the novel. The work successfully brings all aspects of the creation to focus on a single, though complex reality to create a portrait of power. Although Albert-Marie Schmidt insisted without justifying his contention that *Sur Catherine* was a "[s]ymphony formed of three distinct pieces (but rigorously composed in-between),"[41] the standard view of the novel is quite different. Claudie Bernard, for example, says, "*Sur Catherine de Médicis* does not even form a whole in itself; this stew presents Catherine to us at four sporadic points in her life."[42] Nicole Cazauran agrees: "The promises of the title are not completely honored, and we see . . . hesitations, difficulties, the ramblings of a novelist in front of a character whom he claims to have revealed in all her grandeur, when he finally constructs the work he consecrated to her."[43]

If, however, one leaves aside the external material—whether sources or the actual process of creation, which was drawn out over a dozen years and apparently haphazard—and concentrates on the final version of the novel, it seems remarkably successful at creating the image of its world.

For modern readers such an approach produces an experience of considerable power, perhaps even horror. I want to suggest that at some point before Balzac finished the creation of this signally successful though appallingly immoral work, he knew exactly what he was about. I argue not on the basis of the text's creation, but rather on what we discover from the definitive text, which leaves no doubt that Balzac was set upon breaking and casting aside the old, aesthetic molds in favor of more effective devices and structures.

Despite opening *Sur Catherine de Médicis* with an impassioned defense of Catherine, the long segment that was first called a "Preface," then an "Introduction" retains a certain distance from the object of its attention, Catherine de Médicis. She was much maligned, the narrator maintains, and turned into an ogre by those who fail to understand how important it was for someone to exercise power and by the malicious mendaciousness of the Protestants. While the narrator does not exactly dismiss the 1572 massacres of Saint Bartholomew's night, when thousands of Protestants were killed at the order of Charles IX and the instigation of Catherine, he equates them with the explosive, revolutionary bloodbath known as the Terror: "The massacres of the Revolution echo the massacres of Saint-Bartholomew. The people having become king has done to the aristocrats and king what the king and aristocrats did to the rebels of the sixteenth century" (*Sur Catherine*, 11.171). He gives Catherine credit for maintaining the crown of France, and points out that as long as she lived, the Valois family retained the throne.

The other three-quarters of the "Introduction" is taken up with what the narrator calls a "precis" of Catherine, starting with her family history and ending with the death of her husband, Henri II. Denigrated as the daughter of grocers and physicians and blamed for her husband's sterility, she saw herself publicly neglected for Henri's mistress, Diane de Poitiers. Medically resolving Henri's sterility did little for Catherine, since Henri II simply kept her pregnant and out of the way. So began a life of observation, a life behind the scenes, at first of necessity and then by choice. Although Catherine was unobtrusive, she observed the whirlwind of forces swirling about the court, and she developed a political strategy that never changed: "to oppose the great people of the kingdom to each other and to establish royal authority on the rubble" (11.197), the Guises against the Bourbons, and both against the Protestants.

The second section of the novel, *Le Martyr calviniste*, opens in 1560 with a vision of Paris. We watch as Christophe Lecamus, the twenty-two year old convert to Protestantism, agrees to carry a secret message to the queen mother. Since Catherine is "with no passion other than that for power" (11.275), the conspirators believe she will be delighted to turn to the Huguenots. Caught while hiding the material Christophe brought, Catherine saves herself by denying any knowledge of what was in the papers, and thus betrays Christophe. The courageous young man reveals nothing under torture, however, though the conspiracy is nonetheless broken and many are executed at Amboise. Eventually, with the death of Francis II, Catherine takes charge as regent during the minority of her next son, Charles IX, finally able to assuage the "thirst for dominion that devoured [her]" (11.384). The title of this section, *Le Martyr calviniste*, which was for a while a novel in its own right, makes perfect sense. The young Lecamus risks his life in the political turmoil of the day, and is richly rewarded by the queen mother. Had it been titled, *Sur Catherine de Médicis*, however, it would be more difficult to understand. Catherine is by no means central, though of course she is a necessary adjunct to the young man's story. Indeed, she is less highlighted in this second section than she was in the "Introduction."

In the third part, *La Confidence des Ruggieri*, Catherine appears almost not at all. The entire sequence seems at first to concern Charles IX in 1573, the year after the Saint Bartholomew's day massacre (11.377), as he talks of wrenching the reins of power back from his mother and as he delves into the occult sciences. Perhaps not until he confronts the astrologer–alchemist Ruggieri brothers is his powerlessness highlighted. Charles threatens to have them put to death, but the brothers are not afraid, though whether their "confidence" comes from their horoscopes or their employer, Catherine, is not clear. Certainly, the king is "annoyed to be of so little importance" (11.436). While it becomes clear that the Ruggieri brothers are not completely candid with the young king, there seems little question that the real subject of this section, as of the preceding one, is Catherine de Médicis. Through most of this portion of the text, however, she is absent. We see her through a window, as she and her twenty-four year old son, King Charles IX, watch each other. Later, she waits in vain for him to accompany her home (11.392). Then while on his way to meet some conspirators, he realizes that she might be watching him (11.400), as indeed she apparently is (11.404). Finally, she makes a sudden, ghostly appearance before him in his workshop: "[H]is mother . . . emerged like a phantom in the dusk" (11.404). Still, despite her virtual absence, we see her effects everywhere.

In the very last section, "Les Deux Rêves," Catherine appears only in Robespierre's dream. In the course of the four sections comprising *Sur Catherine de Médicis*, then, she appears less and less frequently. While the reader knows she is in the background, the narration focuses on the events and actions concerning the conspiracy. "Les Deux Rêves" assumes enormous importance as the concluding part. It is explicitly dated as having taken place in 1786, that is, some years before the French Revolution's Terror of 1792–94. When Balzac's text indicates that it was a spectral Catherine that suggested and, in effect, justified in advance Robespierre's and Marat's attempt to kill all nobles and all those in opposition to their utopian dream, one begins to understand the terrible power that she has been accumulating and exercising through the novel.

Catherine is never able to exercise authority in her own name. She always plays a subordinate role, and the novel focuses on the multiple forces that dominate her, that bear *on* (*Sur*) her, as she gradually disappears from the text, eventually resembling a specter, and finally reappearing in a dream. Nonetheless, she learns from her constant study of the court to manipulate the various factions. The text repeatedly calls attention to her "dissimulation" and to her "abbess's mask, haughty and macerated, pale and nonetheless full of depth, discrete and inquisitional" (388). Her power, and the power that she maintains in the name of her Valois sons, comes from her ability to set the opposing factions against one another. Despite her always subordinate role, however, the narrator is correct to say, "Catherine de Medici's face looked like that of a great king" (11.170), since from her subordinate position she rules over the king of France, and she manipulates Calvin (11.338). When Charles IX calls Laurent Ruggieri "the king of sorcerers," he objects: "You are the king of men, and I am the king of ideas" (11.436). Given that the speaker is in Catherine's employ, and that Charles IX seems incapable of taking charge of the kingdom, there is little doubt about who really wields the power. Despite her decreasing textual presence, as the reader progresses across the four sections, she enjoys increasing authority.

Although the potentially horrifying aspect of all this grows from the realization that Balzac is not condemning Catherine for the massacre of the Protestants or Robespierre or Marat for the Revolutionary bloodbaths, the real importance of the novel, however, lies elsewhere: in its structure. *Sur Catherine* reflects the Romantic quest for expressive ways to depict the new reality. Previously, there had been numerous experiments with the way works of art were put together. The dramaturge Hugo took great delight in indulging in prosaism, in mixing the sublime and the grotesque, in offending the rules of *bienséance* or decorum. In "Response to an Act of Accusation," he exults in what he had done, in effect, to shunt aside Aristotle's literary prescriptions. It was an open revolt against accepted canons of acceptable art. Other writers were not far behind. Stendhal seems to have organized *La Chartreuse de Parme* around a passive character who is central only because all the other characters focus on him. The novel stands in sharp contrast to Aristotle's dictum: "Imitative artists represent men in action" (ch. 2). While there is action in Stendhal's work, Fabrice, the "hero," is no more than tangentially involved. He is certainly not in control.

Still other Romantic writers attacked the accepted view of plot.[44] Through the eighteenth century there was little controversy about narrative. It was as Aristotle defined it, "the first essential" (*On the Art of Poetry*, ch. 6). Writers like Marivaux might focus on character, but the character was revealed in an Aristotelian "ordered combination of incidents" (ch. 6). With the Romantics, however, the situation changed. More or less anomic heroes like René and Adolphe do nothing of significance, and the works that represent them do little but project an image of their characters. What plot there is moves to the background so as to illuminate the particular cast of the main characters. Balzac was especially attracted to organizing his creations around thought, which Aristotle listed among the primary features of tragedy as only third in importance, after plot and character. Furthermore, while it was most common for narrative to be arranged by chronology or causality and to be at the forefront of our attention—reappearing characters that continue a preceding action help link scenes—Balzac's plots tend to begin and end at odd moments. To link episodes he depended on repeated narrative patterns, rather than narrations, on reiterated symbols, images, motifs, types, and themes.

Unlike other of Balzac's disjointed works (I think of *Histoire des Treize*, *Jésus-Christ en Flandre*, or *Autre étude de femme* that I considered at some length in *Balzacian Montage*), *Sur Catherine de Médicis* is organized by the plot of Catherine's effort to wield power. It does not resemble the common run of novels, however, since its principal narrative and character remains embedded in the background. Only after readers have advanced well into the novel do they understand the appropriateness of the work's title: Catherine is always at the center, however weighty the forces acting on her and however much she may remain behind the scenes or above the fray. This is the story of the queen's success at gaining, then exercising brute force while holding an apparently subordinate position. Seldom does the real plot rise to the surface, and then only briefly.

In a period marked primarily by change, turmoil, confusion, if not corruption, sickness, and danger, the normal institutions of public order had been demolished. The replacements seemed all too unstable. Romantic artists were confronted by a world that could not easily be represented in traditional forms. And so they experimented, adapting the tried and true, or simply turned away and began to innovate. As in Hubert Robert's *Imaginary View of the Louvre's Great Gallery in Ruins* (1796) placed at the beginning of this chapter (plate 5), artists imagined the works of the past in ruins and built highly structured masterpieces from the rubble. Increasingly they produced remarkably fresh novels like *La Chartreuse de Parme* and *Sur Catherine de Médicis*. Originality came to be one of the most highly prized virtues in the new aesthetic canon. Old conceptions of beauty seemed inadequate, distant, and cold. The awe that classical artists had endeavored to engender in the audience was no longer a word that made sense. It was necessary to break through and touch people sentimentally, essential to make them feel. As the Industrial Revolution remade the world, the Romantics struggled to find ways of describing the changes, especially insofar as those changes affected people. Literature advanced few solutions. What it did was give us a window into the sense of insecurity at the core of Romanticism.

6. Jean-Baptiste Greuze. *La Cruche cassée (The Broken Pot)*, 1771, Louvre.
© Photo RMN.

CHAPTER 5

Incest in the Mirror

Bernardin de Saint-Pierre published the sweet, strangely compelling tale of *Paul et Virginie* in 1788. His friends were not enthusiastic when he tried it out on them, but on publication it met with enormous popular acclaim. It has gone through more than two hundred editions, at least forty-five of them before 1800.[1] The story is framed conventionally with a narrator/audience who is visiting the Isle of France (now called Mauritius), and has found a peaceful spot. Although the ground is overgrown and neglected, and two nearby huts have fallen into disrepair, he is drawn there repeatedly. Suspecting a story, he asks a passing old man of "simple, noble demeanor" whether he might know something about the history of the place. It seems that two European women had lived there. One, Mme de la Tour, was a widow, left pregnant when her husband died. Disowned by her family in France because she had married a commoner, she had almost no resources until she made a friend in Marguerite, an illiterate Breton, and joined her in the peaceful basin. Marguerite was also rejected by her family, for she had an affair which resulted in an illicit baby. The fact that the father was a gentleman was, of course, no help at all when he abandoned her. Two rejected women, then, the one upper class and punished for her relationship with a commoner, the other a peasant and condemned for hers with a noble, are drawn together by their common fate. Each had an elderly slave, and they decided to make their way with what they could grow and earn by spinning cotton.

Marguerite's baby, Paul, was already born when Mme de la Tour arrived, and the latter's infant, Virginie, shortly joins the little group. Each of the mothers suckled both of the infants. "Night could not separate [the children]. It often surprised them lying in the same crib, cheek to cheek, side by side . . . asleep in each other's arms" (89). The narrative voice that takes over as the old man begins the tale compares them to "the children of Leda enclosed in the same shell" (90). The virtually inseparable

109

children were raised as brother and sister in this lushly exotic, apparently benign nature, far from the prejudices of home, and the mothers talked of marrying them. But just as the basin encompassing the little group has an opening onto the outside world, so Mme de la Tour has not cut all her ties with France. "If I were to die, what would happen to Virginie without a fortune" (92–93), she begins to wonder. She initiates a correspondence with her rich aunt in France, hoping that there will be something for her lovely daughter. In the meantime, the "naturally good" (95) children learn virtue from home and nature, while both work to help the little family survive. There is always something for others in trouble.

The first cracks in the little family's paradise are internal, when Virginie reaches adolescence.[2] Frightened by what is taking place in her as she lies in her spring, looking up at the intermingling leaves of the two trees planted when she and Paul were born, she almost understands what her mother perceives immediately: that she has fallen in love. Unfortunately, Mme de la Tour decides she and Paul are both too young and too poor to marry, and when a letter comes from the rich aunt, inviting Virginie to come to France and become her heir, Virginie is sent away. The trip over the sea fails, as one might expect from Paul's angry denunciation, which sounds very much like a traditional curse: "Barbarous mother! pitiless woman! may the ocean to which you expose her never give her back! may the waves bring my body back to you, and as it rolls with hers among the pebbles of our shores give you . . . an eternal reason for sorrow!" (153) Because faithful Virginie refuses to marry as her aunt wishes, she is disinherited and sent back to Mauritius during the dangerous season of storms. A previous hurricane had wrecked havoc with the little group's garden; this one kills Virginie. Though the boat comes within sight of land, it is caught in rough seas, and as the islanders watch, Paul tries unsuccessfully to reach Virginie.

If she had been willing to take off her heavy clothing, she might have been able to make it to shore, but she refuses to disrobe, and is drowned when she is washed overboard.[3] With "one hand on her clothing, the other on her heart, and raising serene eyes toward the sky, [Virginie had] looked like an angel taking flight toward heaven" (203). Some hours later, the old man finds the girl's body. "She was half covered with sand, in the attitude that we had seen her die. Her traits had not noticeably changed. Her eyes were closed, but her brow was serene. The pale violet tints of death were simply mixed with the pinks of modesty on her cheeks. One of her hands was on her clothing" (207). In the other was the little portrait of St Paul the Hermit that Paul had given her. Shortly, Paul, the dog Fidèle, Marguerite, Mme de la Tour, and the two slaves die as well.

110

The book held many attractions for the Romantic audience. Clearly, they could not resist either the luxuriant descriptions of a tropical paradise and of an epochal storm, or marvelous set pieces like Virginie awaiting death, or her alluring body in the sand,[4] or the old man's elegy with overtones of Job and Lamentations meant to console Paul, or themes like innocent childhood, true love, the "good savage," utopia, and a virtuous nature in opposition to a corrupt society. Chateaubriand would mimic the lush descriptions of an exotic nature and dead bodies, as well as the terminal elegy in his own, even more popular *Atala* (1801) and *René* (1802). In addition, as is to be expected of hugely successful novels whose popularity lasts for generations, *Paul et Virginie* is expertly crafted. The book breaks neatly into two parts that might be labeled "Virginie present" and "Virginie absent,"[5] two parts that also insist on the differing roles of nature. In the first half, Bernardin establishes the virtuous little society in the midst of a beneficent nature, where the illiterate children and slaves illustrate the "good savage." As pointed out previously, the two mothers are cleverly paired up by their infringements on social mores, which implicitly sets off the opposition between nature and civilization that will be more fully exploited in the second half of the novel, where the war between nature and society is both more patent and more aggressive. Hints of the evils of civilization, previously perceived in the cruel slave-master and the unfeeling governor, are magnified in the spiteful aunt. Although it is a hurricane that destroys the ship and thus the little society, there is no doubt that the aunt and civilization are responsible. Even minor detail increases the novel's coherence. Malcolm C. Cook, for example, has pointed to the novel's effective exploitation of water imagery and James W. Brown of foods.[6] And, finally, Paul's futile attempts to reach Virginie, as he repeatedly throws himself into the sea only to be washed back to shore, repeat the pattern of his trips out and back to visit the places that remind him of Virginie after the girl's departure and again after her death.

Philosophically oriented critics have castigated *Paul et Virginie* for attempting to reconcile the supposed antinomy of virtue and nature.[7] Certain that nature could never teach anyone virtue, R. A. Francis ("Failure," 60) and Bernard Bray ("Texte variable," 872–73) even perceive a fundamental incoherence in the work. Those who are more oriented toward the text will immediately dismiss such a suggestion, however, since the novel not only couples nature and virtue from beginning to end, but in addition neither puts the conjunction into question nor poses it ambiguously. It works consistently, without breaking any of the character developments, plot lines, theme or image sequences. As the secondary literature shows, most readers believe that civilization

111

has brought Virginie to reject the lessons of nature by keeping her clothing on and to prefer modest death to immodest life. It needs to be pointed out, however, that nothing indicates that she learned such exaggerated decency in France.

As Robinson observes, what Bernardin calls "'natural' is . . . understood not as what 'is' but rather as what 'ought to be'" (47). Most Romantics saw it this way. Senancour* said, for example, "I will determine what I am, I mean what I am supposed to be, and once this state is understood, I will do my utmost to conserve it during the whole of my life, convinced that nothing natural to me is either dangerous or reprehensible" (*Obermann*, 44). For Bernardin, whose admiration for Rousseau was both real and profound, a "good nature" capable of nurturing a "good savage" was certainly capable of forming a modest, decent Virginie. Such a nature is also capable of mourning her and her loved ones: "Young people so tenderly united! unfortunate mothers! dear family! these woods that gave you their shade, these springs that flowed for you, these hillsides where you rested together still lament your passing" (228). Bernardin's virtuous nature may well have been Virginie's teacher, and her modest refusal to undress is not ridiculous in the terms of this novel. It is indeed only such admirable virtue that makes her a cult figure: "We then saw troops of young women come running from the neighboring homes, so as to touch Virginie's coffin with handkerchiefs, rosaries, and wreaths of flowers, calling on her as though she were a saint. Mothers asked God for a daughter like her, boys and lovers for one who was as constant, the poor for a friend so tender, slaves for a mistress who would be as good" (210). Only someone as "reasonable, sensitive, loving, virtuous, religious" (220) as Virginie would have lived on, as she does, in the memories of the people (228). And the old man imagines he can hear her saying, "Oh Paul! life is only a trial. I was found faithful to the laws of nature, love, and virtue. I crossed the sea to obey my parents. I renounced wealth to conserve my troth, and I preferred to lose my life rather than violate decency. Heaven decided my life was sufficiently full. I have forever escaped poverty, calumny, storms, the spectacle of others' misery" (221). The little family will soon follow her example, and we understand that they are united in heaven.

Virginie and her world had to die. In the "Avant-Propos" of the 1789 edition, Bernardin insisted on the importance of her death and objected

---

* Etienne Pivert de Senancour (1770–1846) was a man of letters who wrote several novels, some essays on religion, philosophy, and history, and a considerable amount of journalism. Today, his only claim to fame rests on the quasi-autobiographical, almost plotless novel, *Obermann*.

to another version that would conclude the young people's love with marriage. He justified his position by saying that "it is necessary to teach men not only to live but also to die" (clviii). On considering the text closely, there is no question that Virginie's death is carefully prepared. Fabre even concludes, "Death is present from one end to the other of *Paul et Virginie* . . . and a naive but necessary system of premonitions leaves nothing in the dark" ("Pastorale" 172). The paradise that lovingly cradled her cannot last.[8] As in Eden, to which the little basin is compared (130), change comes, and not only is the little society doomed, but the characters are like Adam and Eve destined for death. The old man comments, "When she was born, [Virginie] was condemned to die" (218). Indeed, the girl rapidly understands the lessons of mortality. After viewing the garden around her little pool and the destruction wrought by the terrible storm, she observes to Paul, "You brought birds here; the hurricane killed them. You planted this garden; it has been destroyed. Everything on earth perishes; only heaven does not change" (137). The story itself is told near the two dilapidated huts that from the beginning mark the story with death.

Perhaps most important as a prefiguration of death, however, is the love affair itself, for it constitutes an example of an impossible love. Had Virginie not died, there is little question of what would have happened. She and Paul would have married, and, as the novel points out, their life could not have escaped from wrenching poverty and perhaps even degradation. "She had no wealth, and [was] disinherited. . . . Having returned even more delicate because of her training [than she was when she left], . . . while forcing herself to share your difficulties, you would have seen her grow weaker by the day. . . . What if one of these immoral, unethical administrators were to come [to the island]? what if, to gain some small favor, your wife were obliged to appeal to him?" (216–17). To watch fragile, beautiful Virginie give birth to unfortunate children (138) and work the land like a slave (143) is simply inconceivable. Before Virginie's years in Europe, she and Paul are too young and too poor to marry, so they need to be separated before something untoward happens (138). If the girl had succeeded in returning, they would nonetheless have been too poor. Such an end for an idyllic love cannot be.

But there is another reason that marriage is impossible. Though not related by blood, Paul and Virginie are raised as brother and sister and in effect become siblings. As John Dunkley insists, the "main and obvious function" of comparing the children to Leda's offspring "is to underline the suggested brother/sister kinship."[9] Nourished with the same milk, laid side by side in the same cradle, raised together and treated as brother and sister, they have indeed become siblings, and Paul accuses Mme de la Tour of "separating brother from sister" (152). Repeatedly, they are referred to and refer to each other as brother and sister (e.g., 89, 132, 154). For Bernardin to have married Paul and Virginie would have turned his pastoral novel into one of the erotic works that was flooding the late eighteenth-century market. It would have been a very different creation in both intent and meaning.

To the modish themes I have mentioned that explain to some degree the popularity of *Paul et Virginie*, we should add that of incest. As the century ended, the titillating aroma of incest wafted not just from Bernardin's novel but from legions of others as well. Clearly, it attracted an audience. Although some have said that "Incest is best kept within the family," I want to remove it from this intrafamilial privacy and consider it as a part of what might be called a "social disease" in the French society of the pre-Romantics and Romantics. I shall suggest that because incest—incest implied or inferred, incest averted, incest committed, incest revealed—was one of the dominant themes in the art of the day, we can conclude that Romantics were obsessed with incest and that we are probably justified in believing that it constituted a serious, widespread, and destructive problem with significant impact on the whole social organism. Such a study is not easy. As I earlier mentioned, recorded history from 1750 through 1850 has left us with little in the way of statistics about much of anything. Figures on immigration are little more than guesswork. Figures on suicide until 1825 are cobbled together from partial records, diaries, and a liberal use of Ouija boards. But these statistics are models of exactitude in comparison with what records we have concerning incest. Indeed, even today with our admirable success at designing, administering, and validating research instruments, whether questionnaires or other kinds of surveys, the test samples and statistics on incest remind one of physicians who were expected to diagnose favorite concubines by taking the sultan's pulse. As Maisch put it, "Whilst it can be said with certainty that incest occurs in all Western societies, only very unsatisfactory and barely comparable data on the frequency of its occurrence are available."[10] The most common statistical base comes from people in analysis and counseling. Kinsey built his sample from criminals and social misfits. Other sociologists pass out questionnaires to their students. The unreliability of such data is clear and needs no elaboration. Still, these samples of incest victims provide far more numerous and far more reliable data than what remains from the period that interests me, where we have virtually nothing. Jean Renvoizé has pointed out, "[W]e can never know for sure exactly what used to happen behind the bushes, in the tent or under the pile of skins. We don't know what is happening today, so how can we be certain of what happened some thousands of years ago?"[11] Here, he is commenting on anthropologists' speculations about our primitive ancestors, but the general point remains true for speculations about our grandfathers and grandmothers. It certainly holds true for the inhabitants of France two hundred years ago. We simply have no reliable records.[12]

Incest was not invented by the Romantics. The myth that assumed such importance in Freud's assessment of the human psyche was given its most important formulations in fifth century BC by Sophocles in *Oedipus Rex* and *Oedipus at Colonus*. In France the oedipal theme was most notably picked up by Corneille (1659), though there was at least one previous *Œdipe* by Jean Prévost.* And Voltaire's *Œdipe* (1718) attracted so much attention that it elicited a parody by Dominique† five months after the first performance. Concern about incest was apparently growing, since Crébillon *père*'s‡ *Rhadamiste et Zénobie* (1711) and *Sémiramis* (1717) turn on it, as does Voltaire's version of *Sémiramis* (1748) and his never performed *Les Guèbres* (1769). The title character of the Abbé Prévost's *Cleveland* (1732–39) falls in love with Cécile, whom he later discovers to be his own daughter. Nonetheless, one would hardly claim that either Oedipus or incest itself was a major subject and even less an obsession in this earlier period's literature. By the late eighteenth century, however, after Marmontel had written his "Annete et Lubin" (1761), Ducis his *Œdipe chez Admète* (1778) and *Œdipe à Colone* (1797), Mirabeau his "Le Rideau levé, ou l'Education de Laure" (1786), and Guillard and Sacchini had composed an opera titled *Œdipe à Colone* (1787), the theme of incest was a commonplace.§

---

* Jean Prévost (1580–1622) was a lawyer who wrote poetry and four tragedies that were actually performed. He is, of course, to be distinguished from the author of the *Histoire du chevalier des Grieux et de Manon Lescaut* (1731), Antoine-François Prévost (1697–1763), mentioned below and known as the Abbé Prévost.

† Dominique, whose real name was Pierre-François Biancolelli (1681–1734), wrote a number of successful plays, many of which were parodies, but was particularly appreciated for his talent as a comic actor.

‡ Prosper Jolyot de Crébillon (1674–1762), known as Crébillon *père*, was a tragedian of considerable repute. Today his sentimental tragedies, full of disguises, mistaken identities, and recognition scenes, are important primarily as precursors of Romanticism and the melodrama.

§ Jean-François Ducis (1733–1816) wrote several forgotten tragedies and adapted a number of Shakespeare's plays for the French stage. Honoré-Gabriel de Riquetti de Mirabeau (1749–91) was a famous revolutionary orator and essayist who also turned his pen to other things, like the story mentioned here. Nicolas-François Guillard (1752–1814), a librettist of some repute, joined with the equally well-known composer, Antoine-Marie-Gaspard Sacchini (1730–86), to write this opera, which was for both collaborators their masterpiece.

Even more than in the preceding chapters, with regard to incest, I turn to the period's literature less as art than as an instrument for understanding and, indeed, diagnosing one of the pathological ills of Romanticism. I am convinced that no other means serves as well to plumb the fantasies of an age, since no other artifact strives so consistently to express the inexpressible, to imply the unspeakable. Often artists were not conscious of the forces that were driving them to be what they were. Nonetheless, their paintings, poems, plays and novels leave little doubt of what people were really like in a particular period, of the impulsions that characterize them for future generations. We need to be sensitive to those images, attitudes, characters, and stories that are repeated in works by the same and different artists, that overlay one another, that then form a consistent pattern, a complex. For such purposes, the aesthetic value of a work matters little. Literature, however, is particularly important for a study of incest, since incest is a shameful, hidden reality that seldom comes to the surface except when it is read in the context of other literature and other sociological factors.

To work with Romanticism is to be immersed in the limpid pool that served Narcissus to fall in love with himself. Self-interest, self-love, self-obsession, self-centeredness, such are the most salient features of the age. No longer particularly concerned with the general needs of humankind, Romanticism was the great age of the individual, where the needs of the self were privileged. Romantics invented a particularly tautological grammar. The grammatical subject was the first person, the subjective ego, which moved in a regular way through the verb "to be" to the verbal object, the objectified ego. While Louis XIV supposedly said, "After me, the deluge!" the Romantic was far more absolute, "After me, nothing!" Though it is true that Romanticism can accurately be understood as an opposition to Classicism, the opposition of imagination, feelings, and individualism to reason, universals, and discipline, Romanticism is primarily the glorification of the self.

It is a cliché of anthropology to note that incest is virtually a universal taboo. It was a taboo for the Greeks, and it has been a taboo for the French. Exceptions are wrapped up in those moments when the society temporarily suspends the rules in celebratory festivals of worship or repentance or in otherworldly beings like gods, pharaohs, and Inca royalty (the last according to Françoise de Graffigny's* *Lettres d'une*

---

* Madame de Graffigny (1695–1758) escaped a disastrous marriage to join the group around Voltaire and Mme de Châtelet. She wrote the very popular novel mentioned here and other, less successful works like a witty pastiche of Montesquieu's *Lettres persanes* and a drama.

Péruvienne—1747). There are exceptions in fantasy life, if Freud be believed, and one is consequently not surprised to find that the lascivious fantasies of the Marquis de Sade and other pornographers include this taboo among the many violations.[13] There is no doubt that Restif de La Bretonne's fantasy life, and a significant part of his voluminous writings, are dominated by incest, especially by that of brother/sister and, later, father/daughter. As Pierre Testud clarifies, while we cannot be sure that he actually committed incest with his sister, Geneviève, there is no doubt of Restif's attraction, and his incestuous relations with his daughters Agnès and Marion are virtually certain.[14] Still, although Restif wrote several things that seem to me important in understanding the pathology of Romantic incest, he never joined Sade and Diderot in an attempt to concoct a philosophical justification. Sade has Roland explain to Justine, "[T]he more the restrictions that we break seem respectable, the more the pleasure is enhanced. How delectable are the pleasures if it is a [a man's] mother, if it is his sister, if it is his daughter."[15] In *La Philosophie dans le boudoir* (1795), Dolmancé reminds his student, Eugénie, that the families of Adam and Noah were incestuous, and far from being repulsed he claims that incest is very natural. After all, "If love . . . is born from resemblances, what could be more perfect than that between brother and sister, between father and daughter?" (3.420). Such reasoning pushes Diderot's chaplain to agree with the Tahitian, "I grant you that perhaps *incest* does not offend against anything in nature."[16] It is worth noting, however, that when Sade's *Crimes de l'amour* (1800), particularly "Emilie de Tourville" "Florville et Courval," and "Eugénie de Franval," focus on incest, the theme keys the destruction of the characters' families, the institution that the period took as the quintessential foundation of society.[17] As Queffélec argues, incest is for Sade the "prime mover for total disorganization, for a return to primordial anarchy."[18]

Despite those who would justify incest, and the fact that there was toward the end of the eighteenth century an increase in the requests for approval of marriage between cousins (in most cases to keep property in the family),[19] there is no indication that Romantics looked on incest with approval. In fact, incest was legally, morally, and ethically unacceptable. As one indication of how very unacceptable it was, it is worth remembering that the charge of incest was repeated countless times in the scabrous attacks on Marie-Antoinette. There seems little doubt that it was significant in her condemnation. As Hunt has said, "The culminating charge, of course, was incest; in the trial, this was limited to the queen's son, but in the pamphlet literature, the charges of incest included the king's brother, the king's grandfather Louis XV,

117

and her own father, who had taught her 'the passion of incest, the dirtiest of pleasures.' "[20]

One cannot consider incest without turning to Rousseau. Here, I think his relationship with Maman detailed at length in *Les Confessions* is less important than the seminal, though implicit, description of an incestuous family in *Julie, ou La Nouvelle Héloïse* (1761). As Bernard Guyon says, "*La Nouvelle Héloïse* has an exceptional position in the history of the French novel."[21] To some degree this is revealed by the sales figures, which were unusually good. Rey admits to having sold 10,000 copies in the first year, and there were over eighty editions between 1761 and 1800 (Martin 61.18). But the way its themes and devices dominated nineteenth-century literature constitutes an even more important indication of its powerful impact. As is most often the case with father–daughter incest, Julie d'Etanges's father is extremely authoritarian. His fanatical insistence on the importance of hereditary nobility reveals his insecurity most obviously. Certainly he will not entertain a marriage between the low-born Saint-Preux and his daughter. Although only a minority of incestuous fathers are violent, when M. d'Etanges becomes so agitated that he beats his daughter, one suspects his real motive may be jealousy: "[M]y father . . . whose fury was only waiting for a pretext, threw himself on your poor friend. For the first time in my life, I received a slap, and it was not the only one. Giving himself up to his anger . . . he beat me mercilessly, although my mother had thrown herself between us, had covered me with her body, and had received some of the blows meant for me" (174–75). Finally Julie falls and hits her face on a table leg. She begins to bleed, and the father's passion is spent. Tony Tanner is correct to conclude, "The attack could hardly be more sexual."[22]

If what Julie calls "[m]y fall, my blood, my tears" (2.175) does not suffice to encourage the thought of rape, Rousseau then shows us the reconciliation. M. d'Etanges pulls her onto his lap.

> All this was done so quickly, and by such a seemingly involuntary movement, that he almost seemed sorry a moment later. But I was on his lap; he could no longer change his mind, and what was even more disconcerting for him, he had to hold me in this embarrassing position. All this was done in silence, but now and then I felt his arms press against my sides with a rather poorly suppressed sigh. I do not know what false shame kept these paternal arms from abandoning themselves to these sweet embraces. There was a certain reserve that he dared not give up, a certain confusion that he dared not overcome that put between the father and his daughter this charming embarrassment that modesty and love cause in lovers. . . . I could no longer

ward off the tenderness that was overwhelming me. I pretended to slip, and to stop myself I threw an arm around my father's neck. I leaned my face against his venerable cheek, and in a moment it was covered with my kisses and bathed with my tears. I sensed from those that flowed from his eyes that he himself was relieved of a great distress. (175–76)

Later, in the postscript, Julie tells us that the next day she became so ill while in her mother's room that "I was obliged to go back to bed. I even noticed... I fear... ah my dear! I am very afraid that yesterday's fall may have had a more fatal consequence than I had thought. Thus everything is finished for me; all my hopes abandon me at the same time" (178). Here, we join Tony Tanner in understanding that Julie has miscarried her and Saint-Preux's baby.

According to recent psychologists, the father in father–daughter incest is often of the authoritarian type Rousseau describes. The offender, like M. d'Etanges, may have major difficulty in controlling his impulses and have a low tolerance for intimacy. He frequently shows poor judgment, may be abusive—perhaps physically abusive—and has frequent conflicts with people in and out of his family.[23] Certainly, the paternal characters that we meet in Gothic novels or the French *Roman noir* are most commonly of this variety, and incest is one of the most important of the infractions around which the plots turn. Literary incest may have nothing to do with blood relationships, and indeed that is not necessary. Incest has recently been defined as "any sexual activity—intimate physical contact that is sexually arousing—between nonmarried members of a family."[24] Incest, in short, may include both consanguineous and affinitative sex.

As an example, one might think of Horace Walpole's classic *Castle of Otranto*, first published in 1767 and translated into French two years later. There, Manfred, prince of Otranto, decides to impose his will on his dead son's fiancée, Isabella. Even if the prince had not already been married to Hippolita, the Anglican Church of the day would not have allowed Manfred to marry his son's fiancée.[25] The frisson comes from Manfred's determination to break the laws of heaven and earth, despite repeated warnings from family and friends, and have his incestuous way with the girl. Finally, he stabs his daughter to death, mistaking her for the stubbornly resistant Isabella; he is revealed as a false claimant for his estate; and his castle soon crumbles about him. Manfred's justification resides in his need for an heir, now that his son has died and his wife has become sterile, but the impression grows that he wants more than an heir, more than to satisfy his lust; basically narcissistic, he wants to duplicate himself.

I do not wish to suggest that the abusive father/daughter pattern is limited to the imported Gothic novel and its imitations in the *Roman noir*. I have already mentioned Sade's *Justine,* where Roland took delight in abusing his sister. Stendhal also exploited the topos in his account of "Les Cenci" (1837). According to the narrator, François Cenci's abuse of his sons and daughters, culminating in repeatedly raping his daughter while his wife looks helplessly on, should be attributed to his rebellion against heaven. In such instances incest is the "unforgivable sin," the sin that rises above all others to challenge God himself, the sin for which there was no redemption. Still, despite these home-grown examples, without any question, the British Gothic novel was a major factor in the widespread appearance of incest in France at the end of the eighteenth century. Matthew Lewis' *The Monk* (1796), translated into French in 1799, Ann Radcliffe's *The Italian* (1797), translated in 1798, Joseph Fox's *Santa-Maria, or, The Mysterious Pregnancy* (1797), translated in 1800, and many others all depend for much of their affectivity on incest.[26]

The seductive father is also common. Restif's prurient imagination provides the best model for this topos. With but few exceptions, his writings catalogue his autobiographical narrator's winsome seduction of legions of young ladies, of whom it turns out that a significant number are his daughters. On one occasion the narrator condemns another for his incestuous attraction to his cousin: "Do you believe that your mother would give her to you, if she could, without destroying both your happiness and honor!" (*Nuits,* 6.2434–35). Of course, the count is not dissuaded, a child is conceived, and a marriage takes place. Readers who are sensitive to the ways of Romantic righteousness, however, will not be surprised that the mother dies soon afterwards (6.2447–48). Restif's protagonist–narrator seems to be exempt from the sword of justice, perhaps because he claims to be unaware of the true relationships during his many incestuous seductions. Late in Restif's life he is less fastidious, and as his incestuous obsessions become increasingly acute, his writings are considerably more explicit. Even when his protagonist is involved with a young woman of no blood relationship, he cloaks the affair in simulated paternity. Expressions like: "'My dear daughter!' . . . 'My much loved papa!'" (*Nicolas,* 2.503) abound.

Romantic incest is seldom consanguineous, except when the affair will in the end be averted by the revelation of blood ties. There are exceptions. One might think of *Le Vicaire des Ardennes* (1822), a novel that Balzac almost certainly wrote but never acknowledged. Although the heroes Joseph and Mélanie are apparently not related by blood, they think of themselves as brother and sister, which raises the issue of affinity (relationship by marriage and adoption that the church also condemned). Of course, when Joseph becomes a priest and decides nonetheless to marry Mélanie, he compounds his sin and creates a parallel with the criminal love of the Marquise de Rosann and the young vicar, of whom she is in reality the mother. Joseph's passionate defense of incest reveals echoes of Diderot, if not Sade: "How, I asked myself, is my love criminal?... It isn't. Did a secret voice stop us? and if we loved each other like this, the Lord willed it! nothing happens in the universe except according to his will. . . . Besides if there was only one first man and one first woman!... whether the son marries the mother, or the father marries his daughters, *or brothers marry their sisters*: what God permitted in the past cannot be criminal now!" (*Vicaire*, 2. 99–100). Had Joseph and Mélanie been related by blood, such a defense would have been astonishing in works meant for the general market. In Balzac's *La Femme de trente ans* (1830–42), for example, when Julie learns that her daughter is having an affair with her half-brother, the shock kills her. It is inconceivable that she or any or any normal person would have defended the affair. It is significant that René's love for his sister Amélie is not consummated in Chateaubriand's famous story, however much we may join the readers of the 1820s and pity the hero. Later in the century, of course, it is no more an accident that a performance of *Phèdre* occupies an important place in Zola's *La Curée* (1872) than that the novel's incestuous heroine is named Renée.

When Etienne Jouy (known as M. de Jouy) chooses to deal openly with incest in *Cécile, ou les passions* (1827), as one would expect from an ardent social conservative and literary classicist (however Romantic the subject matter), he fills the work to overflowing with guilt. The title character bears a name that means "blind"—it is also the name of Cleveland's daughter, whom the Abbé Prévost saved from incest with a last minute revelation. Unfortunately, Jouy's Cécile is not blind. Anatole regularly addresses her as "my lovable sister" (1.149), though she is in fact the daughter of his real sister, Mme de Clénord, and there is no hesitation to condemn incest as a vile sin and crime. As his friend Charles points out, it is occasionally possible to gain ecclesiastical permission for the marriage of even such closely related relatives, given sufficient money (a common ancestor up to and including a great-grandparent require ecclesiastical dispensation), but this case would be particularly difficult, for Cécile's father would vigorously oppose it. Nonetheless, Cécile writes Anatole, "I love you" (2.78), and he responds likewise. Only a few pages later, he decides to commit suicide, and she threatens to follow his example. In the tomb of their ancestors, they feel as though they have left the land of the living.

121

"Come, Cécile, [Anatole says], pulling her up, with a distraught arm, come and receive the vows of my love on this altar for the dead.

"This love is a crime on earth, but here we are no longer in the realm of men." . . . [O]ur lips joined, our souls mingled, the incest and the sacrilege were consummated. (2.237)

No one is willing to condone their love. "Both religion and morals condemn this marriage," pronounces the family priest (3.96). Cécile herself admits to her mother that it is "a criminal passion" (3.99). But they persist. After their daughter Nathalie is born (4.2021), and Mme de Clénord dies (4.56), Cécile withdraws to a convent (4.68), only to escape and run off to the New World with Anatole.

Typically, consanguineous incest is reserved for the Gothic novel, which exploits it to elicit a sense of horror, and for pornography, which depends to a large degree upon the infraction of conventions, rules, and laws (see, for example, Fougeret de Monbron's* *Le Canapé* [1741] 103–04; Nerciat's *Félicia* [1775] 170–97, 303, 309; and Restif's *L'Anti-Justine* [1798] *passim*). Unless the incest will be averted by revelation, general literature seldom does more than hint at incestuous yearnings. When incest rises to the surface and takes on major importance, it is almost without exception either between cousins or affinitative, that is between those related by adoption. Almost always it is between those raised together from childhood.[27] Chactas, for example, is Lopez's adopted son who falls in love with Atala, whom he terms "Lopez's daughter" "Lopez," he cries, "Look at your son bury your daughter." (*Atala* [1801] 147). Of course, their love is no more consummated than that of René (1802).

Such works require a kind of stereoscopic vision, suggested by Ralph's insight into what happened to him and Indiana as he read *Paul et Virginie* to her as a child. Sir Ralph says, "When I used to read you the story of Paul and Virginie, you only half understood it. You cried, though. You had seen the story of a brother and sister, where I shivered with sympathy in considering the anguish of two lovers. The book for me was torment, for you joy" (*Indiana*, 324). Although Sir Ralph's explanation suggests that younger readers might not perceive those levels of the texts that were open to initiates, most readers were expected to enjoy the tantalizing frisson of incest, made acceptable by the lack of consanguinity, while on another plane suffering for true love denied. Innocence coincides with guilt, love with death.

---

* Louis Charles Fougeret de Monbron (1720–61) wrote a number of bitter satires and burlesques, as well as a few licentious novels.

A number of George Sand's novels play discretely on father–daughter incest. *Indiana* (1832) opens to what is apparently a typical evening at the home of Colonel Delamare, a choleric, aging industrialist suffering from rheumatism and married to a lovely young girl named Indiana. According to the narrator, she resembles a freshly opened flower in a ponderous vase (*Indiana*, 25). We learn gradually that her devoted friend, Sir Ralph, knew her as a child on *l'île* Bourbon. When her father died, he took her under his wing, determined to be a father for her. Here in France, however, though completely devoted to Indiana, the phlegmatic Sir Ralph is clearly out of his element, unable to protect the girl from her desperate search for happiness that throws her in the unworthy arms of a neighboring philanderer. Much later, after the death of her husband and much adversity, Indiana and Sir Ralph find each other once again and return to Bourbon Isle, determined to commit suicide together. Sir Ralph takes the last few moments, before they throw themselves off a promontory, to reveal that beneath his cold exterior there lies a burning love for her. When he first saw her as a child, he says, "I made you my sister, my daughter, my companion, my student, my society" (*Indiana*, 322). Although he occasionally dreamed that she would one day become his wife, he was content to be her father. "My kisses were those of a father" (*Indiana*, 324). "You were nothing but my child, or at most my little sister" (ibid.). He raised her (*Indiana*, 329). "I was happy; I was a father" (*Indiana*, 325). Unfortunately, his family forced him into an unhappy marriage. When his wife died and he came looking for Indiana, she had been married off to Delamare. But all is well, at last, for they have formed a suicide pact. Consequently, "I am now your brother, your spouse, your lover for all eternity" (*Indiana*, 336). The chapter ends without any indication that suicide can be avoided, and when the next one opens with them happily married we are left to guess what might have snatched them from the abyss into which they were ready to throw themselves. In a sort of second life, Ralph, the father, has married his child. Of course there is nothing illegal about this marriage. Ralph and Indiana are not related by blood, he is not her guardian, and she is not coerced. But the titillating breath of incest drifts across their adventure. In 1857, as the topos was losing its power to shock, Dumas would go further and allow the half-brother and sister of *Ingénue* to marry, but only in a Polish netherland far from France.[28]

Some stories are considerably more subtle. In George Sand's *La Mare au diable* (1846), Germain has been widowed for two years. His father-in-law urges him to find a new wife to help with the three children and sends him off to meet a promising young widow in another village. Mother

123

Guillette, a poor woman of the neighborhood, asks him to take her daughter to a farm where she has been placed for the year. Though referred to as "Little Marie," "little girl" (*Mare au diable*, 40), and "poor little girl" (*Mare*, 66), Marie is sixteen and the time has come for her to go to work guarding sheep. Still, as Marie herself says, "I am not a woman" (*Mare*, 67); she is "a child" (*Mare*, 89). No one worries about Germain and Marie being alone together on the trip, since he can be trusted to "respect her like a sister" (*Mare*, 44). After all he is almost thirty and "old" (70). When he later calls her "ma fille," he could be saying either "my daughter" or "my girl" (*Mare*, 58). She looks after his seven-year-old son rather like an older sister, and when she falls asleep with the boy in her arms, he calls them "my poor children" (*Mare*, 82). Naturally, given the tradition of hundreds of Romantic works, we can comfortably assume that this is the beginning of undying love. Often, as in this case, they will shortly be married. Many Romantic heroes use such formulas. Musset's André says in *Le Chandelier* (1835), for example, "[Y]ou are my daughter almost as much as you are my wife."[29] Later, he calls her "my child" (491).

Although mother/son incest is more rare in the Romantic literature, and indeed in reality,[30] it does occur. Ranked by awfulness, it is considered the worst, which perhaps explains why Oedipus has had such power on the collective imaginations of psychologists, if not the rest of society. Mentions of the "horror of incest" usually refer to mother/son incest (Renvoizé, *Incest*, 34). Literature seldom treats this variety of incest playfully. The way Louvet* deals with the cross-dressing Faublas, who calls his first conquest "little mother," is an exception.[31] A sober treatment is more common. I think, for example, of that found with Rousseau's substitute Mama (*Confessions*, 1782), or when Zola exploits Nana's incestuous affair with Georges Hugon, culminating in the boy's suicide, to mark the nadir of her destructive course (*Nana*, 1881). But authors normally struggle to make mother/son incest acceptable either by removing its sexuality, by leaving it indefinite, or by having characters avoid it by learning of their previously unknown relationship. Beaumarchais makes good use of the topos in his *Le Mariage de Figaro* (1784) when Count Almaviva and the complicitous Judge Bridoison intend to press-gang Figaro into marriage with Marceline, who turns out to be his mother. With the unveiling of the true relationships, the engaging Figaro is saved for his much loved Suzanne, and simultaneously

---

* Jean-Baptiste Louvet de Couvray (1760–97) was a revolutionary who wrote several libertine novels, the best known of which is *Les Amours du Chevalier de Faublas*.

preserved both from his ugly, old hag of a mother and from the horror of incest. In Beaumarchais's *La Mère coupable* (1792), the fear of incest is overcome only by the revelation of the parents' respective adulteries. At the other extreme, when Mme Cottin's title character in *Claire d'Albe* (1799) consummates her love with Frédéric, the young man who repeatedly refers to Claire's husband as "Father," her remorse brings death.

Stendhal's *La Chartreuse de Parme* (1839) merely hints at the possibility of incest. Fabrice and Gina, his father's sister, are very close, so very close that the local prince Ranuce-Ernest IV easily arouses Mosca's jealousy and drives him into the deepest of depressions. Mosca even considers the possibility of stabbing Fabrice to death in front of his mistress Gina. "[S]he has loved him like a son for fifteen years," thinks Mosca. "Therein lies the whole of my hope: *like a son*" (*Chartreuse*, 154). Unfortunately, Fabrice has changed a good deal since his return, and their relationship may have changed as well. It also occurs to Fabrice that Gina's feelings for him may have passed beyond the acceptable into "incest" (158). Indeed, when Gina learns of Fabrice's infatuation with Marietta, she has a surprising fit of pique. "The duchess rushed to . . . her room [where] she burst into tears. She thought there was something horrible about the thought of making love with this Fabrice whom she had seen born, and yet what did her conduct mean?" (163). Clearly, Gina, who talks of her love as though it were maternal, feels something else entirely. It is worth remembering, however, that if Fabrice's father is not the dull and cowardly Marquis del Dongo but rather the handsome and dashing French Lieutenant Robert, as the text hints, then there would be no incest, merely a perhaps unseemly difference in ages.

In George Sand's *François le champi*, to turn to another example, maternal incest is nothing if not obvious, though the author does what she can to make the close mother/son bond unobjectionable. "I will be his mother" (*François*, 247), Madeleine says of François, the abandoned child that she took in. He continually refers to her as his "dear mother" (*François*, 363); she calls him "my child" (*François*, 372). Although, as Richard B. Grant has argued, Sand struggles to desexualize the relationship, among other things by putting the planned marriage off in "a nebulous future, after the novel's close," readers will remember that early in their relationship the boy "wound around her legs like a small snake" (*François*, 245). Grant appropriately emphasizes the phallic nature of the image, for it prepares the incestuous outcome of their relationship.[32]

By far the most common examples of French literary incest are between siblings. Although psychologists long claimed that this was in reality the most common variety, it is a striking fact that their conclusion is not borne out by their data. This has been explained primarily as an indication that such incest may not cause the psychological damage that brings patients into counseling and, thus, into databases.[33] While it is unquestionably true, as Leonhardt claimed, that "For in all world literature intercourse between brother and sister—in contrast to father/daughter relationships—is portrayed as something perhaps socially undesirable, but basically moving and lovable,"[34] it seems in this case, at least, that such literature may not reflect reality. There are, of course, examples of characters like Ducray-Duminil's Chevalier Kingston whom the author reveals as "depraved" because he "had conceived an incestuous passion for his sister" (*Lolotte et Fanfan* [1788] 1.210).

Rousseau merely hints at the possibility of brother/sister incest. When the affair between Julie and Saint-Preux begins, the young man is unquestionably guilty of violating the trust accorded to him as the girl's tutor. There is no doubt that tradition condemns sexual relations within pedagogical relationships, and there is no doubt that, while perhaps understandable, perhaps even defensible, Saint-Preux's behavior is unacceptable. Later, after he has been adopted into the family, as Tony Tanner recognizes, the quickening of the passion that had long remained quiescent brings the suspicion of incest prevented only by Julie's death (Tanner, 146, 174–78).

Madame de Souza's *Eugène de Rothelin* (1808) helps to understand somewhat better the reasons why people of the Romantic period were so attracted by intrafamilial or, technically, affinitative incest and why they were so certain that it was inevitable. Eugène has fallen desperately in love with his second cousin Athénaïs de Rieux, although his father absolutely forbids him to marry her. The young people's love grows, however, and there seems little doubt that they are destined for one another, but the elder M. de Rothelin remains adamant: "Never will Athénaïs be my daughter" (*Rothelin*, 384–85, 386). He finally explains his reasons. Years before, he married Eugène's mother Amélie without knowing that she was passionately in love with her first cousin Alfred. She was indeed so much in love that she died on hearing of his death and while giving birth to Eugène. Amélie's aunt, who raised her, surely knew of this love for her son, and she should have told M. de Rothelin. Not to have done so was dishonorable.

Of course, Eugène's problems are eventually resolved so that he may marry Athénaïs. More interesting, I think, is the love of Alfred and Amélie that caused all the trouble, a love so strong that it could be denied only at the cost of their lives. The reasons for this passion are not emphasized.

Had the explanation not previously appeared in dozens upon dozens of novels, I could easily have passed it by. It comes when Alfred's mother explains that "from his tenderest years [he] was admitted to our salon. Alfred, [his sister] Sophie, Amélie remained in their apartment, and only came into mine when their father was absent. They established a sort of family off on its own" (*Rothelin*, 393).

People of eighteenth- and nineteenth-century France had a conception about what made for a perfect love that differs significantly from our own. For them true love was a matter of likeness. If a boy and girl were very similar, if they had had common experiences, if they had the same likes and dislikes, they stood a good chance of establishing the kind of love that lasted. Innumerable plays and novels avert incest only because the close blood relationship that the characters have identified as love is suddenly discovered and revealed. When Diderot's Dorval learns that Rosalie is his sister, their mutual attraction is explained (*Fils naturel*). Similarly, when Sue's Fleur-de-Marie learns that Rodolphe is her father, she understands the feelings that drew her to him (*Mystères* [1842–43] 3.169). Today, we have a different understanding. Although we do not really believe that opposites attract, we have learned that the best marriages are between people of similar cultural background who have complementary rather than similar gifts and personalities. Talkers marry listeners, leaders need followers, left-brain domination seeks right-brain talents. But the Romantics felt that the very best marriages were made of mirror images. In that age of individualism they sought in effect to marry themselves, and in marriage to replicate themselves. Today we might call it cloning. Sade's logic followed the prejudices of his day when he wrote, "If love, in a word, is born from resemblances, how could it be more perfect than between brother and sister, than between father and daughter" (*Philosophie*, 420). Restif, as well, shows rare insight in a similar passage, "Could it be true that in love, it is not the object that we love but the momentary charm that it gives our own existence. . . . So that I loved myself through Jeannette, though Mme Parangon, through Madelon Baron, through Zéphire [his daughter], through Nécard, through Louise and Thérise!... Ah! we are all Narcissuses!" (*Nicolas*, 2.213). It is surely purposeful that Mme Parangon's given name is Colette, which as Pierre Testud points out is the feminine form of Colas, the diminutive of Nicolas, Restif's given name, or that another of Restif's fictional mistresses bears the name Edmée, which is the feminine form of Edme, Restif's second given name (*Nicolas*, 1.1560–62n2). Because Restif's desire for himself was so strong, he followed the ancient pattern and used his art to create an object for his love. Ovid might well have been talking about Restif, and indeed about the whole gaggle of Romantics, when he judges Narcissus: "Foolish boy," he says. "He wants himself" (*Metamorphoses*, 3.30–31). None of them could, of course, do as René dreamed: "Oh! if I had been able to share the transports that I experienced with another! Oh God! if you had given me a woman that met my desires; if, as with our first father, you had brought me an Eve drawn from me" (*René*, 215). The object of Romantic love is not Pygmalion's Galatea, who always remained separate from her maker, or a sibling, but Narcissus who was profoundly implicated in the object of his love.

There is a very simple explanation for the plethora of images, characters, and plots that hint at, or more or less overtly play out, incestuous relationships. Given the taboo that with few exceptions hangs over incest, Romantic authors found in it the suggestion of an impossible love. An important and widely recognized characteristic of the Romantic hero is his or her insistence on becoming desperately enamored of someone whom society or family forbids. The young Saint-Mégrin of Dumas *père*'s *Henri III et sa cour* (1829) falls in love with the Duchess de Guise, wife of one of the most powerful men of the day. The title character of Hugo's *Hernani* (1830) is an outlaw who loves the fiancée of Don Ruy Gomez, a powerful duke. The impoverished poet–hero of Vigny's *Chatterton* (1835) chooses the wife of a successful industrialist. And, for one final example, Adolphe, Constant's hero of 1816, was challenged because the Count de P****'s aging mistress, Ellénore, has had two children by the count and would then never run off with her young lover. Surprisingly, and to his enormous disadvantage, Ellénore abandons her children and the safety of the count to attach herself to Adolphe.

The "success" of Constant's young hero provides a useful reminder that the Romantic hero did not always fail to achieve his impossible goal. Likewise, however impossible the condemnation of church and law made incest, Romantic literature occasionally allowed its consummation. Furthermore, as the amazing frequency of incest in the literature of the day reveals, there can be little doubt that the perversion held sway in the fantasy life of many who bought Romantic novels and admission to Romantic plays. Moreover, it seems possible, perhaps even probable that the model of incest that appears in many Romantic works reflects reality. Barbey d'Aurevilly and Fourier maintain that it was very common. Fourier adds that it was by no means unusual for men to marry into a family with many daughters, in order to make "a harem of his sisters-in-law and their friends," or for a woman to attach a lover "by giving him her daughter," but he provides no support for his claims, and we are left to wonder how common it might have been.[35] Statistics, as I previously said, were not kept in any regular fashion until 1825, and even then most sexual crimes were gathered indiscriminately under the rubric, "Rape and violations against decency."[36] Accusations of this kind of infraction rose from 271 in the period 1825–30 per 100,000 women to a high of 908 accusations in 1861–70. This has been estimated to be only thirty percent of actual crimes. Moreover, according to Chesnais, children under the age of fifteen were involved four times more often than those over fifteen.[37] As with Greuze's allegory of rape, *La Cruche cassée* (plate 6), we are left to guess whether this and other attacks were incestuous. Many undoubtedly were. Between 1848 and 1858 the numbers of children raped, most in their own homes, rose from 356 to 784 per 100,000 (Chesnais, 186). After 1880 there is a significant change for the better. Chesnais attributes this improvement to a growing sympathy for children. I shall suggest an additional reason.

I have already given a partial description of the kinds of people who typically become involved in incest and pointed out how the model fits Julie d'Etanges's authoritarian father. Let me give a more complete listing of the qualities generally found in a molester: one should include "feelings of anger, hostility, insecurity, frustration and isolation. . . . Furthermore, there are two personality traits which consistently characterize those who sexually abuse their children and which separate them from other men who may experience similar feelings of sexual stimulation with their children but do not act upon them: One problem is a lack of impulse control, either sexual or emotional. This may be the result of transient stress or may be characteristic of the individual. The second problem is a confusion of roles. The child is regarded at times as something other than a child, or as a surrogate for someone else."[38] Most people who abuse their children were themselves abused as children (Butler, 67). As for the victims of such abuse, they can most generally be diagnosed as neurotic depressives, and they all suffer from a sense of inadequacy.[39] Experts agree that incest causes almost without exception serious, long-lasting, often incapacitating, psychological damage.

I do not dwell on these traits because I want to instruct in the sordidness, the despair, and the psychological damage that pervades incest. I do so because I hope to insist that the characteristics of both the incestuous abuser and the victim I have just outlined closely parallel those of the heroes of the novels, poems, and plays that dominated the literature of France from 1750 to 1850. There are two major differences. The literary, Romantic heroes are for the most part aristocratic and exceptionally intelligent, while incest crosses society without discriminating in respect to class or IQ. Otherwise, Romantic heroes generally come, like

Adolphe, from authoritarian families, and have themselves an authoritarian personality. The ascendancy of the father was of course reflected in *ancien régime* law and the Napoleonic Code, which left women especially but children as well with few rights. And we remember that René was only one of hundreds of fictional, Romantic heroes and heroines who were lacking in direction, egotistical, depressed, dissatisfied, and lonely. That their self-centered petulance and lengthy complaints about their feelings of rejection grow doubtless from their own inadequacies is less important than that they are unable to establish viable relationships with their fellows. Did they abuse their children? Did they molest their sisters? They certainly did in the novels, poems and plays of the day.

There are other reasons for believing that the Romantic period had a significant problem with incest. Numerous, recent studies make it clear, for example, that the abodes of sex criminals are usually filled with hardcore pornography,[40] thus indicating that while there may or may not be a direct relationship of cause or perhaps even of effect, fantasy is in some way linked to actions and to reality. To this degree, recent experience would support Freud's essays linking literature with the dream life of authors. There is surely a similar relationship between people's purchases and the imaginative life they live. Previous ages had depended on generous benefactors to subvention publication. As the reading public expanded in the late eighteenth and on through the nineteenth century, publishers were much less often subventioned and were then forced to please a broad public by providing them with what they wanted. This made it possible for writers like Victor Hugo, Honoré de Balzac, and Eugène Sue to make fortunes, and it also gives us a reasonably reliable indication that readers were willing to buy what the day's authors wrote. The prevalence of incest in Romantic literature leaves no doubt that readers were clearly and indisputably, though perhaps unconsciously, attracted by the theme, since literature that represents incest sold by the cartloads.

Furthermore, we know that a number of the period's writers had seriously suspect relationships. I have already mentioned Restif de La Bretonne's life and fantasies. He is not alone. The consanguineous and affinitative incest that imbues Chateaubriand's *Atala*, *René*, and *Natchez* (1826) doubtless grows from the author's affection for his sister Lucile. Rémond has even suggested that for Chateaubriand "there is no love that is not incestuous."[41] Numerous critics have wondered about the incestuousness of George Sand's numerous affairs with younger men and about the very questionable relationship that she had with her son Maurice. In a widely quoted text that he wrote in 1835 or 1836, Stendhal's autobiographical narrator tells of his childhood desire to cover his naked mother with kisses (*Henry Brulard,* 29). The relationship of Bernardin de Saint-Pierre and his sister Catherine was particularly intense, though perhaps not physically incestuous.[42] And Balzac's affair with the older Mme de Berny whom he called "Maman" lasted for many years. There are, in short, a number of reasons for believing that the incest prevalent in Romantic literature was a major factor in society.

Still, there is a curious fact that brings the literary implication of incest into question. It comes to mind because so many Romantic novels mention that the passionate love they detail involves lovers who were raised together from their earliest years.[43] The work of E. Westermarck, Melford E. Spiro, Havelock Ellis, Robin Fox, and others, however, make love between such partners seem unlikely. As Robin Fox summarizes, "The intensity of heterosexual attraction between co-socialized children after puberty is inversely proportionate to the intensity of heterosexual activity between them before puberty."[44] Put into less dense language, he is saying simply that families that are closely knit from childhood rarely develop incestuous relationships. Twitchell puts it very simply, "Familiarity does not breed contempt; it simply does not breed at all" (247). Although the supporting evidence for this theory includes anthropological work among a number of peoples, let me merely mention the studies done on children raised in the same kibbutzim in Israel. Yonina Talmon, in particular, found not even one case of two people reared in the same peer group that had married. Moreover, she was unable to find any record of a love affair between members of the same peer group. Joseph Shepher's later consideration of the records of 2,769 kibbutz marriages comes to the same conclusion. As Fox concludes, "[B]earing in mind that the elders of these kibbutzim *wanted* their children to marry, his findings are staggering."[45] When the relationships between parent and child are investigated, however, the findings are not so clear-cut, though it now appears indisputable that paternal care-giving significantly inhibits incest.[46] It is also true that there are much higher rates of such abuse among stepfathers than among biological fathers (Williams, 102).

The kibbutz and other more recent studies might raise significant doubts about the conclusions I reached concerning incest among the Romantics were it not for what we know about the way children were raised in the eighteenth and early nineteenth centuries. If the children were raised together from their earliest years, as the novelists so often say, they would probably not have fallen in love and married. Had they been co-socialized from their tenderest years, they would undoubtedly have followed the pattern of the kibbutzim, but, as I pointed out in chapter two, most children were not raised together in the loving surroundings of their families. They were instead sent away to the wet nurse and were most often out of the home for from two to four years of age. Chesnais, as mentioned before, points to a decrease in child abuse after 1880. It is perhaps worth mentioning that the use of wet nurses had declined throughout the second half of the nineteenth century and virtually ended in the 1890s with the Pasteurian revolution that led to sterilized feeding methods. The long absences of significant portions of the paternal population as they moved around France in search of employment, which was mentioned in chapter four, would also have hindered establishing an appropriate fatherly relationship with their young children. As Roche points out, until the mid-nineteenth century the constant migrations include significant numbers of men that were alone. Later their families would more frequently accompany them.[47] In short, in addition to support from the literature of the day, the sociological data suggest a climate that would foster incest. There is a very good chance that incest was endemic in the France of the Romantics. While I would not want to suggest that the Romantic novel was responsible, there seems little doubt that it reflected an established social reality. It may even be that incest was to some degree responsible for creating readers that were willing to spend hard-earned francs to share the pathetic lot of incestuous and pathologically depressed Romantic heroes.

7. Henry Wallis. *The Death of Chatterton*, 1856, Tate Gallery, London.

CHAPTER 6

Death Wish

The Romantics were enamored of death. Even the clown Pierrot was regularly sketched hanging from a gibbet.[1] By the mid-1830s, however, literary death and especially literary suicide had become a tired cliché. As a means of arousing readers' sympathy or of shocking, suicide had lost much of its effectiveness. As a means of closure it was a bore. Real world suicides were regularly reported in the newspapers, with the official statistics and with all manner of pathetic details. Maigron gives the references to a number of "dramatic" suicides recounted in the *Constitutionnel,* and he quotes S. de Sugny's *Le Suicide* to report that from 1833 to 1836 at least, almost every morning "while drinking very hot coffee . . ., the reader can, with a little frisson, indulge in a delicious emotion."[2] In addition, hundreds of novels, stories, plays, and poems gave suicide a key role—I think of course of such early works as Chateaubriand's *Atala* (1801) and Senancour's *Obermann* (1804), but, somewhat later, of Sainte-Beuve's *Joseph Delorme,* Vigny's *Stello,* Philothée O'Neddy's* "Nuit Quatrième: Nécropolis," all published in 1829, Musset's "Le Saule," Vigny's *Chatterton,* and Hugo's *Hernani* produced in 1830, Petrus Borel's† "Champavert" of 1833, Soulié's‡ *Le Conseiller d'Etat* of 1835, and legions of others.[3] Maigron goes so far as to

---

* Philothée O'Neddy was an anagram and pseudonym of Théophile Dondey (1811–75). The author of poems, short stories, and of a work that alternated prose and verse, O'Neddy was one of the rebellious, second generation Romantics. He eventually became a drama critic.
† Petrus Borel (1809–59), who called himself the Lycanthrope (or wolf-man), was a leader in the turbulent bohemian circles where young Romantics like O'Neddy and Gautier gathered and insisted on their isolation and freedom from the middle class. He wrote poems, a volume of short stories, and a novel.
‡ Frédéric Soulié (1800–47) was the very successful author of numerous best-sellers and melodramas that are little read today.

suggest that almost all contemporary literature touched on the subject (315n1). As a topos, self-destruction had become mundane, even banal. According to an anonymous article of 1837, "many gloriously talented people" were committing suicide, and "society doesn't seem to be upset about it."[4] By 1853, the theme of self-murder had been so emptied of affectivity that Labiche could begin the comedy of *La Chasse aux corbeaux* with a ludicrous attempted suicide.

Balzac was confronted with a number of problems when he sat down in 1836 to whip out *La Vieille Fille* (he told Madame Hanska that he wrote it "in three nights"[5]). Emile de Girardin, the brilliant publisher of *La Presse* charged him with the task of providing a novel that when broken into appropriate portions would bring readers back day after day for more. Because the serialized novel or *roman feuilleton* had never before been tried in such an organ as *La Presse* and because Girardin was walking a financial tightrope, Balzac's novel had to succeed without fail. Indeed, it *was* successful, and the paper's circulation grew at a surprising rate, though, as Balzac pointed out, it "raised a storm of negative articles" (*Lettres,* 483). In fact, Nicole Mozet suggests, when the publisher later broke with Balzac because of all the complaints, Girardin was doubly right both in putting Balzac under contract and in discharging him. There is no reasonable doubt that *La Vieille Fille* brought readers to *La Presse,* or that they enjoyed reading the various episodes. And in sacrificing the novelist to their prudish complaints, Girardin could prove his sensitivity to his subscribers' demands, thus assuring their continued loyalty.[6]

Balzac's *La Vieille Fille* (1837) is nothing if not problematic. In the tempest of protests and complaints while it was appearing in *La Presse* from October 23th to November 4th of 1836, some claimed it was indecent, others that it was immoral, others obscene. The continuing attacks denegrated the characterization, the style, the descriptions, the very subject. For the ladies' paper *Psyché,* it revealed the decadence of Balzac, for the *Nouvelle Minerve* it was the production of Balzac's decrepitude. Another writer might have been encouraged when *Le Corsaire* claimed that the "deplorable obscenity" was not written by Balzac. Alphonse Karr was alone when he took an opposing position. It was, he said, "the capital production of recent days."[7] In short, Balzac had little company when, several months later, on February 10th, he wrote Mme Hanska that *La Vieille Fille* was "one of my best things" (*Lettres,* 483). Posterity has not borne him out. Only Léon Pierre-Quint has gushed, "It is one of the grandest, one of the most beautiful of Balzac's novels."[8]

Although Balzac was responsive to Girardin's need to attract subscribers for *La Presse,* the novelist never compromised with his need to satisfy his own aesthetic demands. The fabled, supposedly unreasonable Balzacian corrections on his proofs that occasionally almost doubled the length, and elicited wailing from printers, were a previously planned and contracted way for Balzac to perfect his work. He paid a substantial portion of his royalties for the privilege of using the printing press as recent writers use word processors to produce clean copy in the process of producing an acceptable final draft of the whole. Whatever he wrote had to be well done, and it had to present the society that he was slowly creating in *La Comédie humaine*.

For some time he had been concerned with the way the July Monarchy was neglecting youth and catering, indeed toadying, to the older generations. In his opinion it was a "gerontocracy." He wrote, for example, in "Ferragus" of 1834: "Today's youth is like the youth of no other epoch: it finds itself between the memories of the empire and those of the Emigration, between the former traditions of the court and the conscious considerations of the middle class. . . . Young people, uncertain in everything, blind and clairvoyant, were counted for nothing by the old men who were jealously guarding the reins of the state in their feeble hands, while the monarchy could be saved by their moving aside and by granting entrée to this young France that today the old doctrinaires, these Restoration émigrés, continue to mock" (5.801). Balzac repeatedly returned to the theme. In *Un Prince de la Bohème* of 1844, he referred to "these admirable young French people that Napoleon and Louis XIV were looking for but who have been neglected for the last thirty years by the gerontocracy beneath which everything is withering in France" (7.808). This is the real focus of *La Vieille Fille*. He wanted to show the suicidal despair of youth wasted by a monstrously self-centered society of aging, greedy, middle-class revolutionaries and self-indulgent aristocrats. Unfortunately, while it had once been possible to shock readers and quicken their sympathy by having a young hero kill him- or herself, the technique had by 1837 lost much of its power. In order to use it again, it was necessary to give renewed impact to a suicide—yet one more suicide. Balzac chose to highlight and revivify death with comedy, much as Ionesco and others would exploit the comic over a hundred years later.[9]

The novelist had a clear sense of plot as device, as an empty structure that could be filled with different types of characters working to different ends. In an earlier study, I called such structures "plot systems" or "narrative armatures."[10] Balzac was not the only one to understand that just as one has stock characters, one has stock plots and situations. Molière, for another example, saw clearly how seemingly tragic narratives could be used to comic ends. We can study the results as the dramatist walked the line between tragedy and comedy in *Don Juan, Le Misanthrope*, and *Tartuffe*. Balzac reversed the procedure, using a comic plot to communicate a sense of the tragic. As a consequence, he illuminates the wasted potential of a disintegrating society that has reached and fallen before the ultimate boundary. In *La Vieille Fille*, the novelist exploits stock characters in a situation that recalls the *fabliau*, insists with delight on the ramifications, allows us to expect a happy ending, and then suddenly confronts us with tragedy. When Athanase Granson concludes his life he writes large a conclusion to the society of a self-indulgent aristocracy, a rapacious but impotent middle class, and the pathetic incomprehension endemic in provincial France.[11]

At first, the characters are nothing if not comic. We make the acquaintance of the impoverished, aging, but still elegant beau, the Chevalier de Valois. He is an "old bachelor' (814, 819, 906), we are told, a "retired Adonis" (814). As though to encourage us to generalize, the narrator lets us know that he is only one of several buds from the still vital Valois tree. Born under the *ancien régime*, destined to die with the Restoration monarchy in 1830, this particular version of the generic tribe is delightful. One has to admire his ability not only to support himself from social gambling but also to make his benefactors believe that his quasi-prosperity comes from the repayment of an old debt dating from the emigration. His linen is always dazzlingly white, and the rouge applied tastefully; his manners are unimpeachable. "No where else does parasitism assume such gracious forms" (4.817). Despite his many effeminate traits, because he has "a prodigious nose" (4.812) we know that he is well endowed and potent. Furthermore "[T]he chevalier had the voice of his nose; his organ would have surprised by its ample and abundant sounds" (4.814). As Jameson has pointed out, "The symbolism of the Chevalier's nose, which the . . . context makes it impossible to overlook derives . . . from the oldest sexual folklore of the human race."[12] It is for good reason that the chevalier is popular with the girls who work in the laundry downstairs from his apartment. The narrator makes it clear that he is very free with them. Some years later he would have a child by Césarine (4.815), and, at the moment of what the narrator calls "the current scene" when Valois takes aim at Mlle Cormon, Suzanne, another of the girls working in the laundry, would like him to believe that because of him she is with child.

This pregnancy is a pretense that Suzanne wants to exploit for travel money. It raises another interesting issue, however. What made her think that she could get away with the blackmail? As she later admits, she is not pregnant. Furthermore, the narrator calls her "chaste Suzanne" (4.842) before he compares her to "the chaste Suzanne of the Bible that the old men had scarcely perceived" (4.845). Valois with much charm denies his part in Suzanne's pretended pregnancy: "[Y]ou would find it easier to sprinkle salt on a sparrow's tail than to make me believe that I have something to do with your affair" (4. 825). And he suggests that she give Du Bousquier a try. Moïse Le Yaouanc suggests that she uses the wiles of someone much experienced in encouraging elderly men with faded capacities to initiate some semblance of intercourse,[13] but there is no evidence of anything of the sort. In fact, Du Bousquier says very explicitly, "Devil take me if I remember having wrinkled anything other than her collaret!" (4.836). Why then does he pay her off? The novel intimates that it may be as a result of his fervent desire to believe in a revival of his former powers lost from having "pressed the orange of pleasure too much" (4.832). Certainly, if readers do not understand the importance of his bald pate beneath his toupee, his "flattened nose" (4.828), and the fact that he "did not have the voice of his muscles" (4.829), or the narrator's comparing him to a "fallen Sardanapalus" (4.831), the novel later leaves no question that he is impotent and that his wife's "faintly deliberate and sly look that distinguishes young wives in a love match" (4.925) comes from something other than coitus. Is Suzanne as ignorant as Rose Cormon of what it takes to produce a baby? Perhaps she was meant to prepare the innocence of Rose Cormon.

Du Bousquier, a former military supplier, is sufficiently big and husky to allow the delightful but stupid Mlle Cormon to believe the rumors of his successful philandering. Certainly, she wants to believe, for she desperately wants an heir. Du Bousquier has a number of things in his favor. His father, for example, was an examining magistrate, so that he is something of a country squire. Nonetheless, he has a troubled history. Lacking a fortune, he had the initiative to head for Paris, where he had considerable success during the troubled Directory, before he made the mistake of squandering his fortune in riotous living and then of gambling against Napoleon's victory at Morengo. As a result, he was ruined. After paying his enormous debts, he salvaged a small income and returned to Alençon, a reasonably well-preserved forty year old (not more than a year or two younger than Valois). Du Bousquier tried to recoup his fortunes by offering his hand to the two eligible old maids: Mlle Armande, the sister of the town's ranking aristocrat, and Mlle Cormon, the other. On being refused by both, he considers the possibilities carefully and returns to courting Rose Cormon.

The third suitor of the ample old maid is a 23-year-old boy, Athanase Granson. Son of a lieutenant-colonel killed at Iéna and an impoverished widow, Athanase has a very minor position at the local mayor's office. The narrator judges from the boy's appearance that he is exceptional. "[A]nyplace other than in the city of Alençon, his physical appearance would have earned him the assistance of superior men or women who recognize secret genius" (4.839). Unfortunately, "country life, lacking outlets, lacking approbation, lacking encouragement scribed a circle within which those thoughts that had not even come to the point of sunrise died" (ibid.). Not a man of action, he is rather contemplative, retiring, easily discouraged, waiting to be recognized for his potential. At first it was because of the money, but as time went on he fell truly in love with Mlle Cormon. "His passion was true," insists the narrator (4.840). It was "a real passion" (4.841).

The stage is set. The text of Balzac's novel mentions Cherubin, a character in a play by Beaumarchais, *Le Mariage de Figaro*, and the time he embraced Marceline. Unfortunately, as Castex points out, Cherubin never embraces Marceline, at least not in the play.[14] Balzac seems to have wanted merely to raise the possibility of a happy ending like that of *Le Mariage de Figaro*, where all ends well. Perhaps the young, pale, thin poet will move into the sunset with his buxom heiress. These three suitors are assuredly lined up to emphasize the comedy. An aging aristocrat, an impotent bourgeois speculator, and a charming young poet with black eyes "sparkling with thoughts" (4.838). If D'Aubignac was correct in 1657 to suggest that the genres of tragedy and comedy correspond respectively to noble and middle-class life, one is prepared for a comedy since *La Vieille Fille* is set in a bourgeois world.[15] Three engaging characters are in pursuit of a skittish old maid, action that readers are encouraged to settle back and enjoy. Tradition would lead us to expect that the worthy young man will win the prize, and that we will go home with a glow in our hearts. As a possible reminder of Molière, the long introduction takes readers for a tour of the imposing house built during the reign of Henri IV, to meet the people who gather nightly, and to learn the history of Mlle Cormon's problematic courtship. Only the phrase, "the poor man," which repetitively marks *Tartuffe*, is lacking when, finally, over one third of the way through the book, we meet the object of all this attention.

The tone changes somewhat when Rose actually comes on stage. She is indeed ridiculous, but it becomes increasingly difficult to deny her humanity. She is really quite engaging. "Not only did she welcome the whole town, she was charitable, pious and incapable of saying anything spiteful" (4.864). Because she wants to be loved for her own over-weight self rather than for her money, she commits her limited intelligence to testing all the suitors that have swarmed to the imposing house. All fail the tests. Too "stupid" to recognize the sincere love of Athanase Granson, she attempts to calm her tormented blood with foot baths and the confessional. "Pure as an angel, healthy as a child, and full of good will" (4.856), she was made for maternity. Furthermore, "what in her heavenly ignorance she desired above all else was children" (4.859). When 1815 arrives, Rose Cormon is forty-two years old. It will not be long before she is too old. "Her desire then gained such intensity that it approximated monomania" (4.859). As the narrator points out, her story is rather special, but "why not consider the trials of stupidity, given that we consider the trials of genius? The one is an infinitely more abundant part of society than the other" (4.863). Nonetheless, in *La Vieille Fille*, Balzac complicates the laughter cued by devices from farce by making the audience aware of the individual tragedy taking place.

Moreover, as one perceives with increasing clarity, Rose Cormon resembles provincial France. "[S]he corresponded to the general spirit and behavior of the natives who loved her as an unadulterated symbol of their lives, for she was encrusted in the habitual behavior of the provinces. ... Despite her 18,000 pounds of income from her land ... she keeps her connections with less well endowed families" (4.864). Like Rose, provincial France lacks the wisdom to choose wisely between alternate futures, and, like Rose, it consequently condemns itself to disaster.

Rose would probably have been happy with the Chevalier de Valois. He subsequently proves that he can sire a child, and he is kind, a kindness mingled with intelligence and the savoir-faire that can cover up Rose's worst faux pas. Athanase Granson would also have made her happy. Rose's fortune, moreover, would have allowed the young man to care for his mother and to do significant work that would have brought glory and honor to Alençon. But this is the story of lack of insight, of an inability to judge, in short of stupidity. "I loved the Chevalier de Valois, and I am Du Bousquier's wife!" Rose eventually understands. Athanase's love also made her feel remorseful and reproached her in her dreams (4.930). Rose Cormon picks the brutal, selfish, destructive Du Bousquier, because she thinks him particularly manly, and we slug through the ten long pages of Athanase's suicide and his mother's grief-filled efforts to bury him in sacred ground. Although, of course, "Athanase was promptly forgotten by society which wishes to and must promptly forget its mistakes" (4.921), the community was spared nothing of the disintegration of the Chevalier de Valois. His linen is soiled, his hair unkempt, he appears with missing teeth, and in disorderly apparel, and he is physically unclean (4.921). "Alençon," the narrator confides, "was witness to a continuing, different but equally pitiful suicide. . . . Poor chevalier de Valois presented a living death. He committed suicide every morning for fourteen years" (ibid.). "Finally, in the middle of the Restoration the powerless Republic won out over the valiant Aristocracy" (4.922).

Married, Du Bousquier explodes into a thoroughly unpleasant but imposing "military supplier typical of the Directoire" (4.924). He "restores" the once imposing house, painting nude women on the walls, cutting down the beloved linden trees, and replacing the comfortable yard with an English garden (4.923). Supported by the Liberals, the middle class, and the reoriented church, he works successfully to ruin the local aristocrats, while speculating with his wife's money to bring in industry. The Revolution of 1830 was for him the triumph of the Revolutionary tri-color flag. He makes a fortune and gains widespread respect, though "[he] was the household despot and completely without conjugal love" (4.929). Compelled to drink the lee of her choice, Rose is blamed by the community for their lack of children. "[S]he saw in her husband the instrument of divine anger, because she recognized her innumerable sins" (4.932). In 1830, poor Rose confided to a friend "that she couldn't stand the thought of dying a virgin" (4.836). Her poor choice of a husband causes not only Rose's despair, but also the destruction of traditional provincial culture, and the death of Athanase, Alençon's hope for the future.

Though Balzac's marvelous exploitation of comedy in conjunction with the worn-out device of suicide works very effectively, *La Vieille Fille* is not one of Balzac's masterworks. Reflective reading sheds too harsh a light on the schematic formulations analyzed by Jameson, Georges Laffly, and others that neatly oppose the virtuous potential of youth to the charming but ineffective aristocracy and the brutal greed of the middle class.[16] Readers expect more subtlety. Balzac's combination of comedy and tragedy might, however, have worked effectively on stage, with engaging dialogue and rapid changes of scene. Certainly, Ionesco has proven how successful such devices can be. It does seem, however, that Balzac was correct in his favorable assessment of the characterization of Rose Cormon.[17] She and the Chevalier de Valois are two of the novelist's most successful characters. More important, *La Vieille Fille* provides an excellent example of a way of reviving the impact of suicide. Even more significant, it proves Balzac's innovative brilliance in the techniques of fiction, skill that has too often been ignored, if not denegrated.

Nothing needed to be done to make suicide shocking when, toward the middle of the eighteenth century, French people began to kill themselves with more frequency than in preceding periods. We are not sure how much more frequently, though we know that writers of the day became aware of voluntary death as an alarming problem in the early 1780s. In 1782, for example, Mercier announced that lower-class people in particular had been killing themselves in Paris "for twenty-five years" (*Tableau*, 1.655). Just a few years later, in 1785, Mme de Genlis complained that "*Suicide* has never been more common in England than it has been in France for the last twenty-five years," and she rails not as was common against the English and their melancholy ways but against the pernicious influence of the *Philosophes*.[18] In fact there was quite a lot of talk about suicide. In 1814, claiming that he could easily prove his contention, Jouy wrote that in the preceding ten years there had been more suicides than in the entire eighteenth century.[19] The philosophically inclined tended to decriminalize if not justify it. The religiously faithful condemned and decried it. In short, suicide was a matter of continuing controversy.

It is generally believed that suicide increased through the late eighteenth and nineteenth centuries. Mercier estimated in 1782 that in a given year there were a hundred and fifty in Paris alone who took their own lives (*Tableau*, 1.656). Richard Cobb's figures from the records of the Seine district at the turn of the century make this estimate seem reasonable.[20] Barrie M. Ratcliffe calculates from data collected from 1825 onwards that in the first half of the nineteenth century, "The Seine department appeared to be responsible for a sixth of the country's suicides and had a suicide rate four times higher than the national average."[21] As he put it later in this same study, the Seine Department during the period from 1836 to 1857 accounted for 17.4 percent of the suicides of France, though with only three percent of the population (34). In 1856–60, while the suicide rate for France as a whole was eleven per hundred thousand, in the Seine department it was 35.7.[22] Ratcliffe's figures documenting a rise in the number of Parisian suicides from 415 in 1836 to a high of 710 in 1856 and 675 in 1857 are startling. Although he claims that these figures are tempered by those of the rapidly rising population in the Parisian area, they remain reasonably stable at 40.6 suicides per hundred thousand people. Most feel that the statistics for self-destruction remained distressingly high in the light of national rates that fluctuated between 7.59 in 1836–40 and 10.04 in 1851–55.[23] Certainly suicide was a significant problem in France until the rate began to decline in the mid-1890s.

There have been many attempts to explain the late eighteenth-century recrudescence and, then, dramatic increase of suicide. The more convincing explanations point to an enfeebled church, the breakdown of traditional systems of power, and the Industrial Revolution (Lieberman, "Implications"). At the end of the 18th century, the church was drastically weakened, partially because of internal corruption, partially because the state confiscated its property, partially because the Revolutionary legislators made the priests and nuns break with Rome and become state employees (the state was in desperate need of the capital to fight its various wars, and the legislators hoped that the religious workers who took care of the hospitals, orphanages, and shelters would be as faithful to the state as they were to the church and continue providing virtually unremunerated labor[24]). The influence of the intellectual elite that had long been undermining the belief in God was also significant. As a consequence, the church was unable to continue its previously effective opposition to voluntary death, based on fear of eternal damnation, which had persisted since Saint Augustin's 4th-century *City of God* had equated suicide with murder. An eternal perspective balances the view of one's own temporal importance, whereas Romantic suicide was steeped in individualism and, indeed, in egotism. To the complex of causes for the alarming number of suicides, literature makes it clear that one must add the extreme forms of individualism that made it difficult for people to see themselves as a part of the whole.

I argued earlier in chapter three that the moral and economic bankruptcy of the French aristocracy was important. It was not just that the king was executed, it was that the king and nobles were no longer capable of representing a collective ideal, thus doing away with an age old means of self-definition. While revolutionaries preached liberty for the people, the citizens, the state, their motive concepts never gained any more consistency than was necessary for demagogic rule, and individuals either continued the day-to-day struggle to live, and ignored the concepts, or translated them in predominantly idiosyncratic ways as in the bread riots of 1789, 1793, and 1795. Finally, with the Industrial Revolution, traditional family groups and other local networks disintegrated as the population shifted to the cities for work in the factories.

Although recent historians have argued that immigrants rapidly establish support groups,[25] it is also true that the rapid turnover as thousands of people arrived and left big cities and shifted from one address to another did not allow profound ties. When people were hungry, ill, depressed, they were generally alone, and, Mercier maintains, their condition often brought them to commit suicide (*Tableau*, 1.656). The machines had to be paid for, and the workers paid the price. The obvious and, indeed, the easy place to save money was in low wages. Workers seldom worked less than twelve hours a day. Laboring children often did not gain their full stature; all too frequently they died young, pathetic gnomes with big eyes, twisted backs, and bowed legs. Restif de La Bretonne's *Monsieur Nicolas* (1790–97) paints a picture of migration to and from Paris, of shallow relationships, and, with particular vividness, of the destitution brought by sickness. Previously, in small, agricultural communities, when there was a problem, there was family or neighbors, a local priest or a powerful aristocrat to help out. Now suddenly, there was no one. Particularly in the working classes, people were often lonely,[26] they had few relationships, they were malnourished, sick, overworked, brutalized in the terrible conditions that accompanied the birth of industrialization in France. Mercier calls it a "picture of somber despair" (*Tableau*, 1.655). For Durkheim, in his classic study, *Le Suicide, étude de sociologie* (1898), it was a rootless society lacking purpose, a society that was incapable of connecting anomic individuals to social groups.

While such conditions may explain the high rates of suicide among the working and migratory classes, they may or may not have much to do with voluntary death among the middle and upper classes, for which we have fewer statistics than for those at the bottom of society. Even where there are apparently reliable figures for suicide in the working classes, self-destruction has always been underreported in the middle and upper classes, and we are left almost completely in the dark for the numbers of attempted suicides. Middle- and upper-class families were very adept at covering up suicides (favored methods of carbon monoxide poisoning and excessively large doses of opium facilitated the effort). In addition, Mercier maintained that the police took care to keep the terrible facts from the public (*Tableau*, 1.656). Because self-murder was not decriminalized until the 1790s, families with heritable property found it advantageous to conceal the facts. In addition, the period before 1825 raises particular problems, since there remains no trustworthy, broadly based corpus of information about self-destruction, whether in regard to actual numbers or to the etiology.

We know that many historical notables killed themselves: P. Higonnet cites "Montagnards like Romme, Goujon, and Soubrany; Girondins like Clavière, Buzot, and Roland; *enragés* like Roux, and the Communists like Babeuf. . . . [and] many moderates and royalists like Chamfort and Le Peletier's assassin, Pâris" (87). The list might also include other well-known figures like Cabanis, Pétion and Condorcet, as well as many widowed spouses (Cabanis, Clavière, Rabaut de St Etienne, Roland). Later, such important people as Napoleon, Mme de Staël, Lamartine, Stendhal, Baudelaire let it be known that they too had been drawn to suicide. Michelet flirted with the idea throughout his life.[27] Alphonse

Rabbe's* overdose of laudanum on New Year's Day 1830 was also very likely a suicide. The list could be extended without difficulty though it would inevitably include only a very small proportion of those who attempted or actually committed suicide. The paucity of our knowledge, which is due neither to investigators' sloth nor to their carelessness, but rather to a dearth of real evidence, is filled in and partially corrected by the apparent candor of a few: the writer Nerval and painter Antoine Gros, who both killed themselves; Chateaubriand, Constant, and Musset, who considered doing so, and the hundreds of other artists who offer a contemporary recreation of the process of self-destruction. When those choosing voluntary death wrote notes, some at least were duly filed away in various archives (Lieberman recently published a few),[28] but such notes are too exceptional to provide reliable overviews.

Nonetheless, Brouc, who writes at length of the "epidemic" of suicides, felt justified in concluding that there was a positive correlation between education and self-destruction. An increase in literacy was coupled with an increase in suicide ("Considerations," 252–53). Even after suicide was decriminalized, the social stigma was very acute, since it was explained, on the one hand, as a lack of faith and, on the other, as insanity. No family concerned about business or family relations needed such disgrace. Our knowledge of the behavior of the more wealthy classes does not come uniquely from literature, however.

The preceding explanations for the rising suicide rates have been attacked of late. Motivated in part by an idealized conception of the working class, and shored up by recent studies based on newly discovered materials and rigorous methodological criticism, such historians as Barrie M. Ratcliffe have cast doubt on the whole of earlier labors by Louis Chevalier and Emile Durkheim. Ratcliffe impugns Chevalier's conclusions regarding the social deviance of immigrants by pointing out that Chevelier based his argument on statistics from 1830, an untypically disruptive year where two-thirds of the suicides were unidentified and thus, Chevalier concluded, they must have been immigrants. Ratcliffe states that from 1836 to 1857 only ten percent remained unidentified. Consequently, he reasons, immigration had little impact on the decision to kill oneself. While one may regret Chevalier's poorly chosen data, it is worth observing that even ten percent seems high and may indeed support Chevalier's conclusions, especially in the light of Cobb's sample

---

* Rabbe (1786–1830), a minor Romantic author, wrote essays colored by profound melancholy.

dating from 1795 to 1801 where only four percent remained uniden-tified.[29] Especially since it was not uncommon for Parisian families on a Sunday stroll to include visits to view the bodies at the morgue (Cobb 92) ten percent failure to recognize bodies suggests that a significant proportion of the populace was unacquainted and presumably lonely, perhaps because of the period's massive migratory practices.

While one cannot but admire the grasp that modern historians show of recent analyses and their fine surveys of newly discovered archival materials, by denigrating the reliability of the arts as windows into the period's life in order, as Ratcliffe says, to "dedramatize" this problem ("Suicides," 65, 66), they have cut themselves off from some of the more useful sources of insight into the actual lives and attitudes of pre-Romantic and Romantic people. I do not wish to neglect precisions that come from newly investigated materials. Especially during periods when figures relating to suicide are untrustworthy, our resources limited, and our vision clouded, we can ill afford to do so. Still, literature and the arts are particularly rich in all kinds of information that did not draw contem-porary disparagement because of its lack of verisimilitude and that is endorsed by the existence of a large, accepting, reading public. When they accepted descriptions of their world without complaint we are doubtless on firm ground to accept them as true or potentially true. It consequently strikes me as unsound to leave such literary passages aside because they cannot be quantified, in preference for unreliable, incom-plete data or for assumptions made on the basis of experience gained in foreign lands and different periods, where the social forces are very dissimilar. In fact, I would say that literature and the arts, tempered by what data we may have, give us the only means of penetrating many aspects of the pre-Romantic and Romantic period. Used with care, and understanding that reality is never pure, simple, or linear, literature and the arts can be illuminating. Since I have touched on the recent insights into mass migration into and out of Paris and other major cities, I might recall my discussion in chapter one, for example, of the way hopes and dreams are portrayed in Boilly's painting, *Les Déménagements* (1822), by a hearse and the ethereal vision of the Roman church, San Maria del Popolo, as a backdrop to the people moving in the Parisian Port-au-Blé. These are people whose unrealistic dreams shine on their faces but who are in fact destined for a life of deprivation and a miserable death.

As novels of the day make clear, self-destruction was well known and much discussed. Curiously, nineteenth-century specialists who studied the phenomenon explain the suicides by the despair arising from career failure, financial ruin, dishonor, misfortune, immorality, unhappy love affairs, and incurable sickness,[30] that is, in ways that are reminiscent of Classical rather than Romantic literature. It is the creative writers and artists among the Romantics who insist, probably more accurately, on melancholy, spleen, a deep-seated disgust with life, and, of course, on *ennui*. Today we would lump such explanations under the rubric of depression, a psychological malady that the ancients would have called acedia, which the thirteenth-century David of Augsburg defined as "a certain bitterness of the mind which cannot be pleased by anything cheerful or wholesome. It feeds upon disgust and loathes human intercourse. . . . It inclines to despair, diffidence, and suspicions, and sometimes drives its victim to suicide when he is oppressed by unreasonable grief. Such sorrow arises sometimes from previous impatience, sometimes from the fact that one's desire for some object has been delayed or frustrated, and sometimes from the abundance of melancholic humors."[31] As the thirteenth-century description emphasizes, such feelings are no more limited to the Romantics than was suicide. Sixteenth- and seventeenth-century Europe also suffered an increase of suicide, as does our own day (particularly among the young).

What distinguishes the Romantics is not just that depression seems to have been the dominant emotion and that many of them allowed themselves to find a solution in self-destruction, but that these essentially private emotions and acts were to a significant degree produced with an audience in mind. Romantics purposely dwelled on melancholic, morbid thoughts. They sought out cemeteries, morgues, dark and somber caves, ruins of former glories. And as work by such scholars as Armand Hoog and Robert Mauzi shows, they positively wallowed in publications that did likewise.[32] After spending a half-dozen years reading Romantic poems, novels, and plays, then comparing them to the facts of suicide, it is startlingly clear to me that as Romantics cultivated melancholy, so they cultivated death. They were very successful in creating strong emotions that they could experience. Unfortunately, these dark emotions frequently became uncontrollable depression.

Perhaps most important, novels leave no doubt that an important explanation for the high rates of suicide was a widespread difficulty in seeing oneself as essential, or even important, to the corporate body of society. As the physician Brierre de Boismont notes in 1856, "As suicides become more numerous, it seems that the causes become less serious. One would say that they have lost the imposing aspects [suicide] had in antiquity and have shrunk to the proportions of individuals" (*Du suicide*, xiii). Repeatedly, from Rousseau through the nineteenth century, writers insist that neither responsibility nor even relationship with others has sufficient power to overcome an individual's desire to quit this "vale of tears." It is not simply that at the base of the Romantic *mal du siècle*, longing for the sublime, vague religiosity, lassitude, there is, as the philosopher and essayist, Elme Caro says, a "fascination with death," a "taste for death."[33] Indeed, a surprising number of Romantics seemed to have a death wish.

Suicide occurred in plays and novels that preceded the Romantics, but it was in almost all cases a means of aesthetic closure.[34] Racine's Phèdre had in every way failed, for example, and there was nothing further that she could do. It was then time for the play to end. She commits suicide. Corneille's Cléopâtre watches her evil projects fail, and her suicide concludes the play. In short, such suicide serves rather like Mark Twain's well: " 'Rowena went out in the back yard . . . and fell down the well and got drowned. . . .' [explains the authorial voice]. It seemed a prompt good way of weeding out people that had got stalled, and a plenty good enough way for those others; so I hunted up the two boys and said 'they went out back one night to stone the cat and fell down the well and got drowned.' Next I searched around and found old Aunt Patsy Cooper and Aunt Betsy Hale where they were aground, and said 'they went out back one night to visit the sick and fell down the well and got drowned.' I was going to drown some of the others, but I gave up the idea."[35] To bring closure, the death need not even be related to anything that has preceded. Lamartine's poetaster editor comments at Jocelyn's ending his autobiographical writings with the story of an incidental death: "You would have said that death closed the book" (*Jocelyn* [1836] 253). In literature prior to the mid-eighteenth century, suicide is not particularly common, but when it does occur, it usually serves to conclude works by getting rid of characters whose function in the work has terminated.

Pre-Romanticism marks a major change, both in suicide as an indication of a character's self-evaluation and as a literary device. The shift is prepared as early as 1721 by Roxane's startling suicide in Montesquieu's *Lettres persanes*. As Julia V. Douthwaite argues, when Usbek's wives begin to write him letters and thus challenge the Persian interdiction on female speech outside the seraglio, their "appropriation of the written word affords them a modicum of autonomy. . . . [and] [s]elf-affirmation" that leads ultimately to revolt.[36] Roxane's terminal suicide marks the breakdown of Usbek's repressive system; it also reveals an unusual understanding of self-destruction. Given that Roxane destroys Usbek's property in killing herself, her suicide is on the most obvious level illegitimate. That she freely chooses death over life without her lover, and life with her master Usbek, turns her act into an even more egregious form of rebellion. Furthermore, as James F. Hamilton says, "The repetition of the first personal pronoun confirms her individual identity and exalts her self-destruction. . . . [I]t becomes an act of revolt."[37] That she uses the written word in a letter to explain her disdain, her hatred, and her revolt has further implications. Roxane's letter shows that she used her self-destruction as a weapon. Although suicide notes were exceptional, even as late as the Restoration, they are important, for as Lisa Lieberman points out, "[T]o write a note upon terminating one's existence is also to turn a private act into a public gesture, a final attempt at self-expression made with an audience very much in mind" (623). The implications of suicide as an act and as a weapon were blunted, as are so many of Montesquieu's barbs, since Roxane is not a French person, thus not civilized but rather an exotic barbarian. Nonetheless, the point was not missed by later writers. Unfortunately, Romantics forgot that when a particular act is repeatedly performed, however varied the effects, the audience will inevitably become bored and find it as hackneyed as Henry Wallis's *The Death of Chatterton* (1856, plate 7).

For Madame Riccoboni's* *Histoire du Marquis de Cressy* (1758), suicide was a conscious, public act that successfully affected another person. No longer a quiet, private deed, Mme Riccoboni recognized that it could be used to punish. Perhaps better prepared than in the *Lettres persanes*, the final suicide is nonetheless not adequately integrated into the novel's narration from the very beginning. Still, once one is introduced to the dignity and wifely devotion of Mme de Cressy, the thought that she might kill herself is unquestionably in character on learning of her husband's perfidy, of the betrayal by her close friend and protégée, Hortense de Berneil, and, worst of all, of the discovery that her valets pity her, having long known about the sordid affair between her husband and Hortense. From the first doubt to the final confrontation, the novel scrupulously records her deception and the husband's subsequent unmasking. The novelty resides in Mme de Cressy's clear comprehension of how the suicide can be used to punish her errant husband. After having had M. de Cressy serve her the tea in which she had previously mixed poison, she says, "You are going to lose a friend whose heart you have not known. . . . You have continually deceived this friend; you have neglected her; you were unfaithful to her; you have abandoned her. . . . I do not hope that you will miss her so that her memory troubles the peacefulness of

---

* Marie-Jeanne Riccoboni (1713–92) was a very successful, well-known novelist of the second half of the eighteenth century, particularly appreciated for her sentimental romances. Today, she is remembered only for her continuation of Marivaux's *Vie de Marianne*.

your life, but I do not wish to think so badly of you that I would believe that her death, caused by you yourself, would leave you completely indifferent."(*Cressy,* 74). Despite his vain attempts to save her, she dies in his arms. "I die content," she cries, "since I am dying in your arms, honored by your regrets, and bathed by your tears" (73–74). The narrator's last words insist that the marquise's weapon long continued its effect: M. de Cressy "was great, he was distinguished; he obtained all the titles, all the honors that he desired. He was rich, he was high ranking, but he was not happy" (74). For suicide to work as a weapon, the dying characters have to be quite sure of their own extraordinary importance, and they need to see themselves as having influence and power that continue beyond death. The modest will never use suicide in this fashion.

Much has been made of the effectiveness of Saint-Preux's defense of suicide in *La Nouvelle Héloïse* (1761). More, however, should be said about its crucial opposition between personal and social responsibility, its consideration of suicide as private and public action. Where Montesquieu's Roxane was a slave and belonged to Usbek, Saint-Preux maintains that because God gave him his life, he should be able to dispose of it as he wishes. Furthermore, if his life has become insupportable, it must be God who has made it so. It is then sensible to "heal yourself . . . of life" by taking it. "[T]he one who is attached to nothing, whom Heaven reduces to living alone on the earth, whose unhappy existence can produce no good, why would he not at the very least have the right to leave a place where his complaints are importunate and his pains useless?" (*Nouvelle Héloïse,* 2.383). In the next letter, Lord Edouard Bomston displaces the argument from the individual's feelings and needs, where Saint-Preux had pressed his point, to the public sphere that Saint-Preux had only mentioned in passing: because Saint-Preux has neither spouse nor parent, he claims he has no responsibility for others and is then free to decide whether further life is reasonable. Lord Edouard contradicts this position vigorously and at length. God put Saint-Preux on earth for a purpose. Not only would the young man's death bring great sorrow to Bomston and Julie, his responsibilities are by no means limited to himself. Bomston is very direct: "Don't you ever think about anything but your own problems? . . . [T]he society that preserved you, that gave you your talents, your knowledge; the country you belong to; the unfortunates that need you, do you owe them nothing?" (2.391). The decision against suicide by Prévost's Cleveland (1738) likewise turns on social ties, though they are much more personal, since they are based on paternal love: a sense of his children's need, and of his own responsibilities (*Cleveland,* 2.292–93). Bomston understands that suicide is not and can never be a private matter. It has ramifications in society. It is a social act. The point had been made before—"No man is an island, entire of itself" said John Donne; "every man is a piece of the continent, a part of the main; . . . any man's death diminishes me, because I am involved in mankind"—and the point was not lost on other, Romantic writers, no more than was Saint-Preux's insistence that the Bible did not explicitly condemn suicide and that, since God was in charge, He must be responsible for situations that render life intolerable.

The egotism that Saint-Preux reveals has been frequently discussed and thoroughly documented in respect to the Romantic hero. The trait is even more marked in consideration of suicide. Victims of Romantic self-destruction in literature (and perhaps in reality) are egregiously self-centered. They raise individualism, egotism, self-hypertrophy to new heights. Tobin Siebers goes on, however, to argue that "Rousseau's genius was to have realized that he could be his own victim and victimizer. . . . [A] logical outcome of this attitude is suicide, and in this progression we find the potential for both a great novel of suicide and much genuine self-destruction."[38] It requires a powerful sense of self for a person to be his own persecutor. In countless Romantic novels, however, we can watch as the main character displays this ego, while attempting "to build ego by sacrificing it. [Egoistic suicide] creates a cult of the self by translating negative into positive attention. The unfortunate individual who reasons, 'I will kill myself, then they will be sorry,' wishes to attain in the future by extreme measures the distinction that he or she believes is due in the present" (Siebers, 22). The Romantic outcast is a typical victim that forms a part of what Siebers calls "the poetics of suffering."

The title character of Senancour's *Obermann* (1804) emphasizes his world-weariness and suffering—"I needed happiness. I was born to suffer" (*Obermann*, 72), as he explicitly responds to Edouard Bomston's letter. "If [a person] suffers, and if he does much good at the same time, he is more satisfied than unhappy. But when the pain that he experiences is greater than the good that he works, he may leave everything: he should depart [this life] when he is useless and unhappy, if he can be sure that . . . his destiny will not change. Life was given to him without his consent; if he was moreover forced to keep it, what liberty would remain to him? . . . Suffer a great deal in order to be somewhat useful is a virtue . . . but not a duty" (172–73). Although Obermann repeatedly states that he has not decided to end his life, he is equally insistent that there is little to keep him from doing so. Even a desire to do good confronts "the perpetual incertitude of a continually agitated, precarious, subservient existence" (162). His misery, illustrated by the entire volume, grows from a life of boredom that ensues from withdrawing, like a good Romantic, from society to surround himself with nature. "I am tired of leading such a vain life" (154). "I have examined everything, known everything. If I haven't experienced everything, I have at least had a premonition of it" (161). Worst of all, lacking hope, he sees no reason to believe that his life will change (161). He brings no one joy (155), does nothing useful, and looks forward to a drearily unchanging future. Without responsibilities to either God or man, he concludes that he is free to do as he chooses. By 1827 the whole matter seemed trivial, at least to Jouy's Anatole. "By what right do people complain about life? It is a play put on for free, and no one has to remain. If you like it, stay; should the play bore you, leave the theater. If it is weakness to die because you suffer, it is madness to live in order to suffer" (*Cécile* 173–74). In short, "Saint-Preux is a thousand times more right than Lord Edouard."[39]

The way the period's novelists used religion to justify suicide is also worth considering. It is true that some writers persisted in suggesting that belief in God could save the suicidally inclined by encouraging them to turn away. Mme de Genlis, for example, portrays the unfortunate Delrive: "All of a sudden, his tears stopped.... He fixed his eyes on *the drop into the abyss*. The moonlight, reflected on the waterfall, formed brilliant strips and long furrows of light that were prolonged right up to the brink of the pit and seemed to brighten the whole of its depths. Delrive shuddered!.... This terrible abyss, he said, could in a moment be for me the impenetrable asylum of death! . . . . Nothingness is the only refuge for misfortune without resource.... Nothingness!... With these words he shivered; an unconscious movement, independent of his will, made him raise his eyes to the sky. . . . [I]n taking his eyes from the earth and looking toward heaven, he found once again the celestial image of peace. . . ." and he gets up and goes on his way ("L'Apostasie," 8.176–77). Among those who studied suicide as a social phenomenon, the weakening of religion was the most commonly cited cause. Caro, for example, claimed with legions of others that "[t]he surest guarantee against suicide. . . is the firmness of religious beliefs."[40]

It is a small step, however, to reason that if God can encourage a person to avoid suicide, then he must be to blame when one is not so persuaded. Perhaps because of Rousseau's Saint-Preux who maintains that God must be responsible for the conditions that render life unbearable, perhaps because of Gœthe's Werther who credits God with the various circumstances that facilitate his suicide ("Yes," he says for example on learning that his servant had received the fatal pistols from Charlotte's own hands, "Heaven favors my design"[41]), novelists increasingly enlisted God in the

152

suicides as an ally, perhaps even as an accomplice. *The Sorrows of the Young Werther* provided a model for the kind of egotistical, alienated, and tormented idealist who establishes his passionate involvement in his dreams from the very beginning and whose suicide is not just a device but rather the central focus of a character and a work. As with Mme Riccoboni's Mme de Cressy, Werther's death has terrible consequences for Charlotte. M. D. Farber explains, "Because Werther has internalized Charlotte, because Charlotte is inside him, fused fast with the original maternal figure, Werther can hurt Charlotte by hurting himself. This is a major aspect of the psychodynamics of the hero's self-murder" (261). But for Werther suicide becomes more than a simple weapon: it is a means of domination. Werther has no doubt that his signal suffering and suicide will gain him his desired reward from God. "I go before you," he tells Charlotte. Echoing Jesus in John 20:17, he continues, "I go to my Father, and to your Father. I will pour out my sorrows before Him, and He will give me comfort till you arrive. Then will I fly to meet you. I will claim you, and remain in your eternal embrace, in the presence of the Almighty" (115). Such a scene is enough to make one wonder who, in fact, is in charge. The visions, or fantasies, of rebirth and reunion in another life would become a commonplace as Romantics wrested control from God.

For numerous characters and, one supposes, people, the empty threat of suicide has the benefits of self-destruction without the disadvantages. After raping Mme Parangon, Monsieur Nicolas cries, "Forgive me! . . . I have resolved to die to obtain my pardon from you." Mme Parangon submits quickly, "Oh, I accuse myself as much as I do you! . . . Do not kill yourself... since I am as guilty as you... and... because a second crime will not obliterate the first" (*Nicolas*, 1.581). Later Rastignac threatens to destroy himself in the famous letter of *Le Père Goriot* (1834–35) that successfully extorts money from his family.

The casuistry reaches a zenith in Chateaubriand's *Atala* as the reader confronts the terrible dilemma of an ignorant girl whose vow to a dying mother sets her at odds with nature and her love for Chactas. The self-administered poison has several advantages. It resolves Atala's quandary. If she dies quickly, she will die a virgin and, thus, need not fear yielding to her desire. Chateaubriand, by choosing an unnamed drug that is irreversible and slow acting, remains free to explore the implications of the situation. Atala, dying from self-administered poison and worried about her guilt, asks Father Aubry whether God will forgive what she did and whether her mother is happy. The hermit priest reassures her, God "will judge you on the basis of your intentions, which were pure, and not on your act, which is reprehensible" (*Atala*, 129). Furthermore, God *could* nullify her action by stopping the mortal work of the poison. That He does not do so means that He has decided to take her to heaven. "Thank the goodness of God, then," Aubry urges her, "which takes you so rapidly from this valley of misery" (134). Although Atala has in effect asked God to remove the poison from her, after drinking it, she does as the good priest instructs and submits to His will. As a result, "I feel almost capable of making myself immortal by dint of my love. But, oh my God, may thy will be done" (136). Although surely not the Son of God, who said similar words in the Garden of Gethsemane, Atala is described as His daughter and explicitly termed a "mystical rose" (135) who has been called to her "celestial spouse" (ibid.). Aubry has effectively manipulated the theology to allow the innocent Atala to do as she wishes while leaving the responsibility with God.

Not everyone was willing to make even this nod to an increasingly distanced God of the Judeo-Christian tradition. When in *Le Paysan et la paysanne pervertis* (1783, 1787) Restif de La Bretonne's Gaudet is finally condemned to the scaffold for having flaunted the laws of God and man, he listens to the priest, then picks up a big nail, and screams at God's representative, "Look, my friend, here is the fruit that I draw from your sermon. They will not kill me, and I will have created my own fate!"—(280). Gaudet then thrusts the spike into his chest and dies. The control evidenced by Gaudet continues as an important part of suicide. These personages want to be gods, and to the degree that they had the power to decide the means and time of their own demise, they were... pathetic gods, perhaps, but gods with power not only over their own lives and deaths but over others in that their decision had continuing, significant effects.

God's implication in suicide would continue. The heroine of George Sand's *Indiana* (1832) "had made of suicide," for example, "a sort of tempting voluptuousness. One sole thought, a religious thought, had prevented her from making the final decision" (*Indiana,* 220). But as the novel demonstrates, traditional religious convictions would weaken to the point where, as Pierre Salomon has it, "Indiana, like George Sand, has been won over to the romantic religion, a religion which retains from Catholicism only those doctrines that are consoling and that no longer recognize the authority of the Church" (311n2). Unquestionably, people committed suicide because of despair, the black night of the soul, rather than because of some ethereal lucubration. Suicide notes carefully preserved in police archives prove that it was true for people, and it was true in the novels. Noun, Indiana's Creole maid, kills herself "because of despair, in one of these moments of violent crisis when extreme resolutions are the easiest" (109), the narrator explains. Later Indiana herself drifts toward a similar resolution: "absorbed in a mindless reverie, in a meditation without ideas," she moves toward the water. "At this moment her exhausted mind was governed by no conscious thought" (219–20). From the bottom rungs to well up on the societal ladder, in reality and in literature, people and characters like Athanase Granson, Balzac's genial young man who represents the future of France, feel despair and destroy themselves. The explanation offered by *Indiana*'s narrator is as good as any: they "preferred to drown themselves rather than struggle against [their] misfortune" (151). Musset's Orsini and Célio choose to die because they have been refused by their beloveds and betrayed by their friends (*Caprices de Marianne* [1833] 247–48). Célio seeks the "end of my pain" (270n1). One might rather say, however, that they feel helpless and without hope. That is certainly the case of Camille when she decides on suicide in Soulié's *Le Conseiller d'état* (1835).

Indiana also provides an example of another kind of suicide, what countless, modish young people called "thoughtful death [la mort avec réflexion]" (*Indiana*, 222) or, on other occasions, "spleen" (145). Sir Ralph explains to Indiana: "the action that we are about to commit does not result from a momentary madness but is rather the reasoned conclusion of a decision reached with a feeling of calm and reflective piousness" (312). God is mentioned, but he is mentioned in seeming ignorance of fourteen centuries of church tradition. "[I]t is important," says Ralph, "that we bring to our death the religious respect that a Catholic would feel before the sacraments of the Church" (312). "I would like to die joyous," he insists, "my brow serene, my eyes lifted to heaven," and he comes to the place where "suicide has for me taken on its most solemn and noble appearance" (312–13). Even without the aid of recent historians, suicide was well on the road to being dedramatized.

More controversy arises on suggesting that the literature might have influenced the tragic reality, but an argument about precedence seems idle. There is no doubt of a coincidental set of events: widespread, casual relationships with a distant God, the loneliness engendered by a modern industrial society, mass migrations, increasing numbers of suicides in all the classes, and legions of suicidal characters in literature. People were depressed, they felt helpless, and suicide was *à la mode*, in the way that ideas are contagious. As Maigron suggests, Romanticism contributed "certainly to making suicide stylish" (337). For many it was merely a convenient solution. Thousands upon thousands pitied the Wandering Jew who yearns in vain to be able to kill himself, for he is condemned in Edgar Quinet's *Ahasvérus* (1833) and Eugène Sue's *Le Juif errant* (1844–45) to wander without respite.

By the early 1840s, as Romanticism degenerated into what François Jost calls "[a] romantism made of misery without grandeur,"[42] suicide had become a cliché. Reybaud's Jérôme Paturot tries to convince his sensible Malvina to join him for a "[d]ouble crown" when he kills himself. He explains: "Suicide establishes a man's reputation. On one's feet, one is nothing; dead, one becomes a hero. . . . the apotheosis begins. . . . Hardly will I have left when every one of my volumes will become a monument, a work of genius. I will have advocates; I will be the center of a school; it is infallible. All suicides are successful; newspapers take them up; it becomes an emotional issue. Decidedly, I have to get ready." Malvina responds, "Talk about dumb! . . . That's it. Kick off like a seamstress with a charcoal heater" (*Paturot* [1843] 1.162). When saved from the "halo of death" (1.163) by the scheming of his faithful mistress, Paturot admits, "I was nothing but a profound egotist. I was going to sacrifice everything dear to me for some sort of sick vanity" (1.173). So much for the rapturous departure toward a better life in heaven. By 1857, one quite understands why it is almost possible to hear Flaubert's cavernous yawn behind Emma's suicide.[43] These Romantic gods had become mere men and women whose once glorious power seemed little more than a cliché. Without an audience, it seemed hardly worth wishing for death, much less killing oneself. It took some time after literature stopped glorifying self-destruction, however, before suicide rates began to change. In fact, not until a new generation arises twenty years after the Franco-Prussian War and the Roussel Law of 1874, which severely curbed wet-nursing, does suicide go into decline.

CHAPTER 7

An Ending: Julien among the Cannibals

Romantics told their story many, many times, and with minor variations it was always the same. The fact that Stendhal's *Le Rouge et le noir* is a superb work of art does not exempt it from rehashing the familiar story of the Romantic hero in an unsympathetic society. Published in 1830, the author included the subtitles *Chronicle of the XIXth Century* on the title page and *Chronicle of 1830* at the beginning of book one. While not by any means ignored, these rubrics have more importance than is normally recognized.[1] From the outset, the novel insists on the importance of Restoration society, and of Julien Sorel's story as a reflection of what was taking place in the France of 1830. History informs the text at every level. From a king's visit to Verrières, to the secret maneuvers of M. de La Mole, down to the venal tree-trimming in Verrières, what we know about the period sheds light on the incursions of external events on local and individual life. More interestingly, using the insights developed earlier in this book, it reveals the inner workings of the main character. Readers have long been puzzled, for example, by what led Julien to shoot Mme de Rênal.[2] It is hard to believe that anyone as successful at role-playing and manipulation would not have understood that a little patience, a bit of maneuvering, and the passing of time would almost certainly solve the problems raised by her denunciatory letter. After all, Mathilde was no less pregnant, and, as Hemmings points out, "M. de La Mole ought to have reflected that little weight could be given to the denunciation of a jealous, cast-off mistress."[3] We have difficulty with Julien's action that seems at best stupid, for he is brilliant, gifted, and brave, however much he is also vain, selfish, ambitious, and riddled with insecurity. Still, although it would be impossible to render everything he does acceptable in civilized society, his actions seem perfectly understandable in the terms of this society, and it is possible to admire Stendhal's characterization of Julien as what one might expect, given the powerful forces at work in Romantic France.

Thousands of young people left home the way Julien did and tried to establish a successful life. For differing reasons—some because there was no work in the region where the family lived, and the possibility if not the real threat of no food, others because of the ambitious desire to better their lot, others simply to be independent—boys, men, women, couples and children from every class moved from the farm to the city, and from small cities to larger ones. The changes were not always easy; they often brought hardship. In many cases the family's resistance prevented a child from leaving. When Nicolas's father in *La Vie de mon père* (1778) brings the young man home from Paris and insists on his marriage to an unloved local girl, he explains the reasons for his actions very simply: Nicolas will be happier if he stays with his own kind and in his own world. Overall, however, as Restif's *Monsieur Nicolas* (1790–97) demonstrates, such conservatism could not succeed universally, or even in the majority of cases. Society was changing. Indeed, society had changed, and people were forced into new roles. Although it meant that they no longer had the automatic right to step into their fathers' professions or into the network of relationships that had previously given the entire family its stability, they had no choice but to accept the changes. Forces beyond their control and for the most part beyond their comprehension had cut them loose.

As has been frequently pointed out, the Industrial Revolution brought many changes to Stendhal's fictional community of Verrières, a small town in the Jura Mountains where *Le Rouge et le noir* is set. It shows particularly in the social stratification that depends less on heredity, as under the *ancien régime*, than on wealth. Although M. de Rênal, mayor of Verrières and owner of a newly constructed home, is inordinately proud of his loudly proclaimed but far from certain aristocratic heritage, his local importance comes almost uniquely from his wealth. Our introduction to the Restoration cupidity and corruption that infuses the novel comes with the narrator hinting that M. de Rênal takes his cut from the money made from over-trimming the town's plane trees and spelling out how he has used his authority to move the local stream so as to expand his own property. The narrator implies, however, that the mayor may well be swept away by the numerous and rapacious middle-class people who follow his spoor in the chase after appointments and riches. Among the citizens of Verrières, nothing seems to remain from the "other" Revolution of 1789 but a residual fear for their money.

M. de Rênal also owns the local nail factory "that deafens the people going up the main street" (*Rouge et noir*, 1.6). Sawmills surely added to the din. "A great number" of them line the stream rushing from the mountains and traversing Verrières before spilling into the Doubs River. The local textile mill which produces printed cloth has been particularly significant in bringing wealth to the town, but all these enterprises have contributed to "an atmosphere filled with the stench of small financial interests" that asphyxiates travelers (1.8). Many are the signs indicating that the Industrial Revolution has come to Verrières. Though the material well-being of the "the majority of local inhabitants" has improved (1.6), allowing them to rise in society, it brings little but material benefits. The environmental pollution is joined by moral pollution. The people are greedy, corrupt, self-important, and limited, totally without imagination. The formula, "PRODUCE REVENUE, all by itself, represents the habitual way of thinking for three-quarters of the inhabitants" (1.14). The impact of public opinion in such a setting is inevitably pernicious. Reflecting Stendhal's prejudice against the mercantilist democracy across the sea, the narrator concludes, "As *stupid* in small French towns as it is in the United States of America" (1.10), public opinion works to punish deviations from the vapid norm. Outstanding ability like that of "old" Sorel's son Julien would not flourish.

The depth of Stendhal's portrait of this world goes beyond descriptions of a small country town and portraits of the *nouveaux riches*. While providing a detailed portrait of the pervasive insecurity that grew from this turbulant world, *Le Rouge et le noir* also plumbs the forces that created the Romantic character. Both in what he is and in what he does, Julien Sorel represents a typical person of the day, and Stendhal's novel as a whole serves to summarize those traits that seem most important in understanding the individualistic, uprooted and insecure, ambitious yet melancholy people of the late eighteenth and early nineteenth centuries. Julien Sorel reveals an acute desire to know the reality of Romantic France, for only in a clever exploitation of that world can he possibly escape his life in Verrières. Certainly, his self-centered egotism is portrayed in all its glory.

Julien has been an outcast from his youth. The smallest of Père Sorel's boys, he is simply not strong enough to do much of a sawyer's work. That he is bookish to boot explains why he is despised by everyone in his low-born family. Not surprisingly, Julien rejects his father and the life of the provinces. As the boy pursues and gains learning, he no longer wants to be a part of his heritage. His ambition grows. He wants to rise in society. Indeed, he wants to conquer society. Throughout the book he entertains thoughts and encourages suggestions that he may not be the son of his father. Were it true, he could be completely free from M. Sorel's hateful dominance, free from the whole legal system that supported, and imposed, paternity. As Peter Brooks has rightly argued, "[T]he question of authority haunts *Le Rouge et le noir*,"[4] but the novel additionally brings on a crisis of identity. Not the "Who am I?" informing *La Vie de Henry Brulard* (1835–36), but rather Julien's far more anguished "Oh God! why am I me?" (2.323).

Early on, Julien sees himself as "a sort of foundling, hated by my father, by my brothers, by my whole family" (1.62). Père Sorel's antipathy marks the boy profoundly, and he repeats, "My father has hated me from the cradle" (2.18), "He never loved me" (2.469). Naturally enough, Julien indulges in considerable day-dreaming. "'Could it be that I am the illegitimate son of some great lord exiled in our mountains by the terrible Napoleon?' Moment by moment this idea seemed less improbable to him..." (2.379). The stigma of bastardy is by no means as significant as the possibility that he may be the offspring of some philandering aristocrat. The seeds of his fantasy are sown after leaving home and learning that he truly is exceptionally intelligent. Father Pirard tells M. de La Mole that Julien might possibly be the illegitimate offspring of some wealthy man (1.364). The priest wonders later on whether the story could be true (2.13). Furthermore, because the young man soon begins to move in circles where his plebeian birth makes it difficult to serve M. de La Mole effectively, others lend substance to his fantasies. The Chevalier de Beauvoisis, who does not want it known that he fought a duel with a mere secretary, for example, spreads the rumor that Julien is the "illegitimate son of one of the Marquis de La Mole's intimate friends" (2.75–76). To Julien's surprise, the Marquis is delighted when he hears the rumor (2.77), since Julien will be more useful to him if he can function socially without raising eyebrows or causing offense. La Mole's attack of gout initiates another possibility. Because the Marquis is lonely, he imposes distinct roles on his secretary. When dressed in black, Julien will be treated and will act like the employee he is; when wearing blue, he is welcomed as an equal, as though, the Marquis says, Julien were the younger son of his old friend the Duke de Chaulnes (2.80) or, even, M. de La Mole recognizes, his own: "I am treating him like a son" (2.82). Later, in words that would be ambiguous out of context, M. de La Mole tells Pirard, "I am aware of Julien's birth, and I authorize you to stop keeping the secret of this confidential matter for me." He goes on to make it clear that he is in actuality denying the boy's heredity: "'His behavior this morning was noble,' thought the Marquis, and 'I confer a title of nobility on him'"

(2. 85). Mathilde, as well, thinks that she might claim for Julien a country squire or Spanish duke as a father (2.152). As Mossman says, "Julien Sorel first converts himself into a foundling, then manages to de-name himself, thence to acquire a new patronym in what amounts to a deconstruction of his bio-narrative."[5]

Julien's condition as, one might say, "paternally challenged" extends beyond genetics to his intellectual background. Pirard notes that he is so innocent of patristic doctrine that he hardly even knows the names of the major saints of the Catholic church (1.296). Unlike Séverin de Guys in Sophie Gay's *La Comtesse d'Egmont* (1836), Julien is not seeking his real father, but rather a new one. *Le Rouge et le noir* emphasizes the repatriarchization by first proceeding to a de-fathering: Mme de Rênal asks him, for example, "Is Julien your only name?" (1.144), and later, on his way to Paris, he is given a passport that leaves the space for a name blank (1.366). Soon, the seeds of a new heredity are planted, and for his secret journey he is given a pseudonymous passport.[6] Of course, even after he denies his real father, he is not exactly paternally deprived, since he attaches himself to a series of mentors, models and surrogate fathers. One suspects, for example, that more than the usual ecclesiastical unctuosity is involved when Father Pirard speaks repeatedly of his affection and calls him "*fili mi*" (1.356). Julien eventually acknowledges to Father Pirard, "I found a father in you" (2.18). Pirard is neither the first nor the last of these substitute fathers. Even the bishop welcomes him with "absolutely paternal kindness" (1.365). But real success does not come until M. de La Mole gives him twenty thousand francs and a new name: Julien Sorel de La Vernaye. Julien is undoubtedly less elated by the money than by the new paternity, especially when the marquis adds that M. Julien de La Vernaye receives this money from his father (2.379) and goes on to suggest a new way of looking at the head of his "previous" family. "M. de La Vernaye will perhaps decide that it is suitable to give a gift to M. Sorel, carpenter in Verrières, who looked after him during his childhood" (2.378). It has long been easy to imagine Julien raising a lamp to peer into the faces of passers-by. "Could you be my father?" he seems to be wondering. One remembers Dumas's Antony who asks, "Could you be my mother?" Julien finally succeeds in replacing his real with a substitute paternity. The "Sorel" is discarded from M. Julien Sorel de La Vernaye as though it were a bloody glove, and Mathilde thanks her father effusively for "saving" her from the Sorel name (2.375). Nonetheless, the renomination continues. After being imprisoned for murder, he signs his letter to Mathilde "J. S.", thus publically accepting his original identity and his original family (2.391).

Perhaps more important for an understanding of the novel's themes, the very possibility of illegitimacy highlights Julien's desire to free himself from his roots. Of course, he is in fact not free. According to the legal system of the day, his father could have put a stop to the boy's progress at distancing himself from his lower-class home and origins. It is not by accident that M. de Rênal makes his arrangements with M. Sorel to bring Julien into his household as a tutor for his children. Nor is Julien unaware of his father's power; nor are Julien's actions without guile when he arranges for Père Sorel to receive the directorship of the local workhouse. Julien understands that his father can be bought. Like his homonym, Julien is an apostate both to the Catholic faith that he publicly espouses, as Hemmings suggests,[7] but also, and perhaps more importantly, to the entire set of relationships that gave people definition in the preceding *ancien régime* world. He never mentions his mother, he denies his father, thus the patriarchy and his class, and he sets off to find new meaning. Consequently, he is by his own intention, at least, rootless and without identity, though despite his best efforts neither in reality nor before the law. Nonetheless, the intention has considerable importance. As I argued in chapter three, children without fathers tend to be extremely self-centered—as Father Pirard understands: Julien's ignorance of patristic doctrine explains his propensity for "self-examination, that is to say for the most appalling protestantism" (1.296). Julien exemplifies extreme individualism, and because he rejects externally imposed rules, he is in the deepest sense unruly. Individualism is an unprincipled source of power.

The fatherless also tend to lack ideals, and as the text suggests on several occasions, Julien is a moral monster. Perhaps because of the advent of behaviorism, and our hesitation to hold troubled people responsible for their reprehensible actions, perhaps because we are simply too far removed from the intellectual currents of Romanticism, modern readers have had a difficult time seeing Julien for the scoundrel he is. If, for example, he hopes for an illegitimate paternity, he explains elliptically, it is so that in hating Sorel he would not hate his father. "My hatred for my father would then be a proof... [that he is not my father]. I wouldn't be a monster [because I hated him]" (2.379). His behavior toward M. de La Mole is perhaps more to the point. The Jansenist Father Pirard leaves no doubt about Julien's debt: La Mole's offer of employment constitutes a tremendous opportunity. "If you are not a monster," the priest tells him, "you will be eternally grateful to him and his family" (2.16–17). When confronted with the choice of leaving town or proceeding in the seduction of Mathilde, and although momentarily shamed when La Mole tells him, "I like to see you" (2.165), he reminds himself of previous slights from the Duke de Chaulnes and Mme de La Mole and her friends, of his employer's advantages for procuring wealth, and of the differences in their station. "How good of me, a commoner, to have pity for someone of his rank" (2.166), he muses. He decides not to deny himself "an offered pleasure" (ibid.) and brushes off his hesitations. "My goodness! [I'm] not so dumb; everyone for himself in this desert of egotism that we call life" (ibid.) In short, when he seduces Mathilde he betrays his employer, if dressed in black, and, if in blue, he betrays his friend and his patron. On one occasion only the thought that Mathilde's father is his benefactor keeps him from killing the girl (2.206). It is not enough to keep him out of her bed.

However courageous, intelligent, and charming Julien may be, he betrays the confidence of M. de La Mole, the employer and patron who raised him above his condition, despite the fact that "[w]ithout him I would have been a scheming subordinate" (2.354). The marquis calls him a monster (2.358), and Julien accepts the epithet. He knew it was monstrous to abuse the La Moles—"I am received into a family, and as the price for the hospitality that I receive, the kindnesses that people shower on me," he dishonors their daughter (2.188). He admits to himself that he deserves M. de La Mole's reproaches (2.351). Furthermore, as a direct result of the seduction, he also abuses Father Pirard, who recommended him and whom he has called a father. Finally, although he feels occasionally sincere love for Mme de Rênal and Mathilde, he dishonors them both without distinction. There can be no doubt that he has refused to consider the obligations that he has toward employers, friends, and, eventually, the women he seduces. Nineteenth-century readers were well aware of Julien's crimes. At best, as Hippolyte Babou put it in 1846, Julien is a "sublime knave" filled with "repugnant grandeur."[8] At worst, in Sainte-Beuve's words, he seems "a small, odious monster . . . a Robespierre plunged into everyday life and domestic intrigue."[9] By comparison, Mme de Rênal's denunciation seems measured.

The hatred Julien feels toward his father is accompanied by the curious fact that he never refers to his mother. And like the Romantic hero in general, he suffers from a sense of rejection. As pointed out in chapters two and three, legions of Romantic heroes "lost [their] mother[s] at birth" and were misunderstood by cruel fathers. Although maternal and infant mortality during childbirth had varied little for several hundred years, which means that there was a far larger proportion of orphans in novels than in reality, what had changed was the way children were treated after birth. As we saw in chapter two, in the 1770s and for almost one hundred years, something like two-thirds of all children went to the wet nurse. Half died, and many of those that lived suffered from lifelong feelings of abandonment and loss. Like unbonded children who lack mothers, Julien is riddled with insecurities. He frequently feels humiliated (e.g., 1.75, 144), that others despise him (e.g., 1.53), or that they are making fun of him (e.g., 2.136, 160). Although on only one occasion do his eyes fill with "tears of shame" (Mathilde has just told him that she gave herself to him because he was the first man who happened by), he regularly despises himself (1.76, 2.134). He suffers from "the continuing feeling of his inferiority" (2.133), and even terms himself "odious" (2.308). Not surprisingly, he feels pessimistic about the possibility of a long-term relationship with Mathilde, for he recognizes that he will not be able to keep up the front he has so carefully constructed (2.323). From the beginning he has had difficulty with his persona. "From now on," he says after talking with Father Chélan, "I will only count on those parts of my character that I have tested" (1.81). Similarly, when he acts as though he were a seductive Don Juan, the role "weighed him down horribly" (1.150). And after careful plotting and persistently clumsy attempts to play the seducer, he succeeds only after abandoning his plans, bursting into tears, and throwing himself at Mme de Rênal's feet. Confronted with the evidence that Mme de Rênal loves him more than her son, he subsequently marvels, "How could I, so poor, so badly brought up, so ignorant, and sometimes so coarse have inspired such a love?" (1.195).

Because Julien has little confidence in himself, he seeks examples he can use, according to the narrator, to establish the "ideal model that he proposed to follow" (1.153). At the seminary, after he has allowed both faculty and fellow seminarians to see him in inappropriate ways, he determines, not for the first time, "to sketch a completely new character for himself" (1.309). Throughout the book he plays a series of roles, some of which he would like to be true, some to mislead those who observe him. Early on, a surgeon-major who enjoyed teaching the boy Latin and a little history, left his library of thirty or forty books to Julien. The legacy opened a literary door for the boy to expand his horizons beyond Verrières. Napoleon and Rousseau are particularly influential. Certainly, he cites both and links them repeatedly (e.g., 1.37; 2.31). The reader's first view of Julien includes a copy of the emperor's *Mémorial de Sainte-Hélène*, which serves to set in place the foundation for Julien's ethical standards of courage, intelligence, generosity, duty, honor, liberty, and the chance to accept with joy any challenges to develop and succeed. Although he mentions among other goals a bishopric and a successful military career in passing, success is never clearly defined. He simply wants to "make his fortune" (1.43, 81), though this "fortune" has less to do with money and position than with the active pursuit of a heroic self-image, which Longstaffe convincingly terms knightly and Corneillian ("Duel"). And he tests his every act in his amorous campaigns against the image of what Napoleon would have done in his more military endeavors.

The novel presents two particularly striking images that portray this ethos of a seductive warrior in priestly garb. On the one hand, Julien envisions himself as a general who has half-won a great battle (2.340); on the other, we see the booted and spurred hero wearing a cassock (1.180). Regularly Julien turns to Napoleon's *Mémorial* for inspiration and encouragement. "His only activity for the whole day," he mentions on one occasion, "was to fortify himself by the reading of the *inspired book*" (1.93; my emphasis). The "inspired" writings were not, of course, the Bible but the *Mémorial*. Discouraged by Mathilde's capriciousness, on another occasion "[h]e opened the *Mémoires dictés à Sainte-Hélène* by Napoleon with a passionate movement, and for the next two hours forced himself to read them" (2.341). Only with constant attention could he assure presenting the image of his ideal to the world at large, and he regularly "watched himself as though he were an enemy with whom he was going to have to fight" (1.93). Hemmings finds Julien's problem very simply that he is "not living his own life, but a modified *copy* of another's" (Hemmings, *Stendhal*, 116). It seems more telling to tie his persistent difficulties to the largely unsuccessful attempt at integrating the self he tries to construct from his various models with the person he believes himself in his heart of hearts to be.[10] Julien's models are particularly important in explaining why he would hurry away from virtually certain success at his long-standing dream of "making his fortune" to shoot his former mistress.

Prior to Faguet (1900), when the writings of Destutt de Tracy and Napoleon that Stendhal knew well were more than footnotes in historical overviews, no one questioned Julien's decisive act. Napoleon constitutes a significant presence in *Le Rouge et le noire*, and although Destutt de Tracy is nowhere mentioned explicitly in the novel, Stendhal specialists have long known that the *philosophe* had enormous importance to the novelist's background. His name and thought punctuates Stendhal's writings, especially those of a more personal nature like his memoirs and diaries. Certainly, Julien's ethos seems cut in large measure from the cloth of Destutt de Tracy. Accused of cowardice and mean-spirited greed, Julien apparently feels that a hero's honor and duty leave him little choice.[11] He has to react. Stendhal's nineteenth-century readers long agreed, since they followed him closely rather than criticizing vociferously. In addition, since he no longer loves Mme de Rênal, he enters what the materialist Destutt de Tracy would call a "state of war."

165

Tracy was a member of the Committee of Public Instruction under the Directory as France moved toward universal education and a secular ethos, and thus had considerable influence, but his work is little known today. According to his *Traité de la volonté et de ses effets* (1815), a human being is composed of a core personality determined by opposition to other beings and by the desires that grow from the will (*Traité*, 53). From that consciousness of him or herself and of the things that are different or other, wishes or desires grow. To desire is unfortunately to suffer; consequently, people have the right to satisfy their desires. Of course, along with the desire to satisfy oneself, there is also the fact that some desires cannot be realized and, in addition, that desires are tempered by the "most general and most imperious need of human nature, that of sympathy and commis-eration" (*Traité*, 115). Duty, the word that occurs regularly in Julien's thoughts, is nothing but the "general duty to satisfy our needs" (*Traité*, 116). "I owe it to myself," the hero says, "to be [Mme de Rênal's] lover" (1.138). In the light of Destutt de Tracy, we understand simply that he wants to seduce her. Although Julien says that he has other duties than the "duties toward himself" (1.136), Tracy would argue that all duties are egocentric: "[I]t is impossible for us not to . . . prefer our 'self' to everything that is foreign to it" (*Traité*, 512). All duties, even those that are charitable, are generated by the need to satisfy the self. Certainly, as Julien puts it, "True passions are egotistical" (1.230). Liberty is simply "the power to execute one's will, to act in conformity with one's desire" (*Traité*, 99).

When frustrated by one of the lower orders, "there is the duty to captivate or to subjugate this other will, so as to bring it to contribute to the satisfaction of our desires" (*Traité*, 112). If it is impossible to reach agreement with the other, either because it cannot understand or because it refuses to cooperate, then one resorts to persuasion or to violence (ibid.). "Would one call this a state of war? . . . It would be an exagger-ation. The state of war is where we unceasingly seek the destruction of one by the other, because we cannot assure ourselves of our own conser-vation except by the annihilation of our enemy. . . . Those whom we sacrifice to our needs are only attacked to the degree that these more or less pressing needs force us to do so. There are those who live with us in a state of peaceful subjection; others, in perfect indifference" (*Traité*, 117–18). As Tracy makes clear elsewhere, the aggressive pursuit of satis-faction will be tempered by whether or not success is possible and by our need for sympathetic relationships with others. "[T]he absolute loss of liberty is," however, "a truly infinite loss. . . . it is the extinction of all possibility of happiness for the animate being; it is the loss of the whole of it's self, for which it cannot accept any compensation" (*Traité*, 104).

Julien comes through the pages of *Le Rouge et le noir* as a bundle of contradictions. He has accepted the ethos of Napoleon and presents himself as courageous, free, intelligent, generous, honorable, and responsible, while deep down he knows nevertheless that he is "lower class" (2.165), "the son of a carpenter" (2.167), "a poor peasant from the Jura Mountains" (ibid.), in short, "of little merit" (2.323), a "scabby sheep" (1.322). Although the novel leaves no doubt of his intelligence and generosity, other traits are not so indisputable. He claims, for example, "I will never lower myself to talking about my courage . . . it would be despicable. Let people judge from the facts" (1.233), yet the fear of seeming cowardly, either to himself or to others, is enough to drive him repeatedly to extreme forms of foolhardiness. Any suggestion that he lacks the traits he attributes to himself brings on Tracy's "state of war." Whether by showing umbrage, by climbing a ladder to reach a woman's window,[12] by fighting a duel, or by subduing lackeys, he welcomes any occasion to prove his courage. "My reputation," he says, "is all that I have" (1.104). Like an existentialist in bad faith, he lives in the eyes of others, exulting for instance that Mme de Rênal has just taken his hand, so she can thus no longer despise him, and wishing that "all those proud nobles" at M. de Rênal's table could see it (1.138).

Julien's persistent need to disguise his lack of belief in the tenets of the Catholic church leads him to call himself a hypocrite (e.g., 1.302, 2.133). As Peter Brooks has pointed out, the etymology of *hypokrites* stresses Julien as a "player of roles" (71), which is unquestionably the meaning of Julien's struggle to satisfy the requirements of the public self he is constructing. The more common understanding of hypocrisy as deceptive pretense is highlighted by his allusions to Molière's Tartuffe (2.115, 167), though Tartuffe suggests two differing categories of significance. His sham religion that was adopted to trick the Orgon family comes first to mind, and there is no doubt that Julien is thinking of such religious hypocrisy. But those that know Molière's play will also think of Tartuffe when Mme de Rênal writes to denounce Julien: "Poor and avid, it is with the aid of consummate hypocrisy and by seducing a weak and unhappy woman, that this man tried to establish himself and become something. . . . Covered with the appearance of disinterestedness and by phrases from novels, his . . . unique goal is to succeed in disposing of the head of the household and of his fortune" (2.383). It is not true that Julien's seductions were pursued with the goal of gaining complete control of the household's finances. The young man's ambitions are not in the short term so venal. As Moya Longstaffe points out succinctly, Julien not only refuses the Rênal money and offers his savings to Pirard, he gives five hundred francs to Father Chélan for distribution to the poor, and he refuses financially advantageous marriages on two occasions ("Duel," 291). While Julien clearly does not seduce either Mme de Rênal or Mathilde for financial gain, any objective view of his behavior would nonetheless recall Tartuffe.

These various thematic threads leave Julien's "insane" violence against Mme de Rênal perfectly understandable. The brilliant, propertied, young nobleman that was the stuff of dreams has been actualized, validated in the eyes of others. Julien is now a wealthy, well-connected officer in the military. After a period of intense joy that he has risen above his name and station, that he has left his father and family behind, that the future is golden, Mme de Rênal's letter dashes his hopes. To tell himself, with the critic Hemmings, that the La Mole family will come around with a little time requires more cynicism than Julien has. His world has collapsed, a collapse that seems all the more discouraging since the image he thought he had succeeded in imposing on others is shattered. Another image, a negative one, a public one, has been projected. At the very least, Mme de Rênal and M. de La Mole see him as a vicious, greedy schemer, indeed, as Julien understands, a "monster." "What father would want to give his darling daughter to such a man?" (2.384). Julien's state of mind comes very close to what Tracy describes as a "loss of liberty": "truly an infinite loss for him; . . . it is the extinction of all possibility of happiness, the loss of the whole of his being, that can admit of no compensation" (*Traité*, 104). On other occasions when his constructed image has been challenged, he responds with violence. His twisted but recognizable understanding of Napoleon's ethos encourages him to respond to challenges not by defense but by attack. Destutt de Tracy would encourage him, as well. After all, Julien believes he no longer loves Mme de Rênal. As an unloved, cast-off mistress, she would fit very nicely into Tracy's category of a "lower order," and it is not surprising that Julien would move into a "state of war" and attempt to annihilate her. Tracy is discussing behavior toward other sentient, volitional beings when he argues that a rational person "has the duty to captivate or subjugate th[eir] will in order to bring them to contribute to the satisfaction of his desires; . . . he has no other means for directing their will towards the accomplishment of his desires and the satisfaction of his needs than immediate persuasion or direct violence; thus he uses and must use the one and the other depending on the occasion, without any other consideration but that of producing the effects he desires" (Tracy, 112). Persuasion is no longer possible in effacing the hatefully subversive image that Mme de Rênal projects, and Julien resorts to violence. In doing so, he acts out Tracy's philosophy.

There is another, deeper explanation provided by Romantic society. We see it today on the streets of major cities around the world in the children of one- or no-parent families. As David Blankenhorn points out, "The end of this process, the final residue from what David Gutmann calls the 'deculturation' of paternity, is narcissism: a me-first egotism that is hostile not only to any societal goal or larger moral purpose but also to any save the most puerile understanding of personal happiness. In social terms, the primary results of decultured paternity are a decline in children's well-being and a rise in male violence, especially against women. In a larger sense, the most significant result is our society's steady fragmentation into atomized individuals, isolated from one another and estranged from the aspirations and realities of common membership in a family, a community, a nation, bound by mutual commitment and shared memory."[13] If Romantic heroes had fathers, they were cruel, capricious, stupid, or brutish, and they behaved in ways that kept the children from accomplishing their greatest potential. Such fathers were regularly rejected by the main characters of Romantic literature. Many authors took the easier route and simply left the fathers out of their creations. The literary fact is unquestioned, and has been noted repeatedly. What has not been pointed out, however, is that the offspring of such paternity tend to be, like Julien, selfish and violent. Carol A. Mossman shows considerable perceptiveness when she writes, "One ill imagines a Julien Sorel denied paternal adversary. Subtract the father, and *Le Rouge et le Noir* is without its narrative springboard and deprived of its narrative dynamics" (*Matrix*, 34). Julien's relationship to his father is to a large degree the reason that Julien behaves as he does.

With narcissism and violence, as argued in chapter five, goes incest, a theme that accompanies Stendhal's allusion to Rousseau. A few lines after the reader's introduction to Napoleon, the narrator lets us know that it was from Rousseau's *Confessions* (1782, 1789) that Julien learned his snobbish refusal to eat with the servants. Furthermore, he affirms that the *Confessions* represents "the only book his imagination drew on to help him picture the world" (1.37). Although he was later to compare Rousseau to a "parvenu lackey," the philosopher remained nonetheless one of his formative and guiding stars. Julien's references to Rousseau and the more subtle allusions included in the text emphasize the hero's solitude and desire to rise in society. Most important they emphasize the sexual nature of his drive to succeed. When courting, on two separate occasions Julien steals his lines from *La Nouvelle Héloïse* (1761), and readers' responses to Stendhal's hero have surely been influenced by reminders of *La Nouvelle Héloïse* (unquestionably one of the most popular books of the period, it was republished in over 80 editions between 1761 and 1800). Furthermore, given the phonic (and visual) relationship between the names, Julie and Julien,[14] it would be difficult not to remember Rousseau's tutor, Saint-Preux, who seduces his student. Just as Saint-Preux has an affair with the pride and joy of the household where he was employed, so does Julien in both the homes of M. de Rênal and M. de La Mole. As Saint-Preux surreptitiously enters the Baron d'Etange's home at considerable danger to himself, so Julien slips into Mme de Rênal's and Mathilde's rooms. Although Julie miscarries the child, she had hoped that a pregnancy would influence her father to accept Saint-Preux as her husband. Mathilde's pregnancy does indeed have that effect, at least for a while. And to bring these parallels to an end, both Julie and Mathilde dream of dying in their lovers' arms.

Of the two texts by Rousseau, it is however the *Confessions* that raises the strongest resonances. No one who has read *Les Confessions* can (or should) fail to recall Jean-Jacques and Mme de Warens, or "Mama," on reading Julien's affair with Mme de Rênal. Julien frequently behaves like a child (his "childish pleasure" while he cuts up the letters to make the anonymous note provides one example—1.213), and Mme de Rênal calls him "[m]y child" (1.48). "She acted with him in the same intimate way she did with her children. There were days when she imagined she loved him like her own child" (1.169). While at Vergy, Julien "had lived like a true child" (1.89). Finally, he tells the court judging him that Mme de Rênal was "like a mother to me" (2.440). As mentioned before, Jean-Jacques lost his mother at birth, while Julien's exists as a noticeable emptiness, a lack, a hole in the text. Otherwise, Stendhal's main character repeats Rousseau's plot with but few variations. Both have lengthy affairs with older, maternal figures, both go off to seminary hoping one day for their own parishes, both return after an extended absence expecting to be welcomed into the maternally erotic bed. Scholars have noted many other parallels, so many in fact that it seems impossible for the allusion to be an accident.[15] Sensitive readers with the proper background will be responsive to the allusions. Jean-Jacques Rousseau's *Confessions* tells the archetypal story of the low-born arriviste who succeeds to no avail, who rises to the apex of intellectual and artistic success, yet dies, as he writes in his will, "as poor as I lived."[16] (Napoleon also climbed to dizzying heights only to be cast down in the end.) Such stories help prepare Julien's catastrophic end, an end all too typical of Romantic heroes.

The allusion to *Les Confessions* also emphasizes Julien's incestuous affair with Mme de Rênal, perhaps only to add a titillating element to the text, though more probably to further highlight the parallels with

Rousseau's adventure. The "parvenu lackey's" struggle to succeed, his many enemies, and his ultimate failure and death seem particularly important. Gilbert D. Chaitin has pointed out that if M. de La Mole is Julien's father, Mathilde would be his sister.[17] In a curiously ambiguous phrase, Stendhal also suggests that the Duke de Chaulnes, who in one fabulation was Julien's true sire, was Mathilde's father as well (Chaitin, 50 and n5). In short, *Le Rouge et le noir* emphasizes both mother/child incest and, on two occasions, that of brother/sister. Of course, as discussed at length in chapter five, incest constitutes a common factor in Romantic literature. Although Stendhal could not have failed to realize the incestuous elements in his novel, I am not so certain that he realized that Julien's incestuous proclivities are also profoundly in character for Romantic heroes in general. Of Julien's egotism there can be no doubt. Like the majority of Romantic heroes, he is so essentially self-centered that he could easily be termed narcissistic, and as Restif de La Bretonne claimed (and as is still believed), narcissism goes hand in hand with incest. Julien's character, like that of the Romantic hero in general, is so focused on itself as to approach solipsism. His incestuous nature, then, integrates him more firmly into the type and indeed into his age.

However reprehensible Julien may be, he is no worse than many other Romantic heroes, and he does face considerable danger both from the members of the class that will eventually condemn him and from the families where he works. Many devices suggest Julien's coming isolation and death. There is the oft-mentioned account that the young man finds of Louis Jenrel, who was executed in Besançon and whose name configures an easily deciphered anagram of Julien Sorel (1.45). There is the allusion to Bonaparte that illuminates the young man's attempts at heroism and which also foreshadows his isolation and death: "Julien's eye absently follows the bird of prey [circling above him][18] . . . He envied its isolation. That was Napoleon's destiny; would it one day be his?" (1.111–12). And Father Pirard's evaluation rings loud in the novel: "Your career will be difficult. I see something in you that offends ordinary people. Jealousy and calumny will follow you. Wherever Providence puts you, your colleagues will never see you without hating you, and if they feign to like you, it will be to betray you more effectively in the future" (1.338–39). Perhaps the single most noticeable trait of Romantic heroes in all the literary guises that sold so readily during the period was their isolation and loneliness. Not all were as extreme as Hernani (1830) who phrased his situation in the famous trimeter: "I am an exile! I am an outlaw! I am fated" ('*Je suis banni! Je suis proscrit! je suis funeste*'). But virtually all suffered from their inability to establish and maintain strong relationships with other people.

Readers and spectators were very attracted to these solitary creatures, or they would not have been so widespread in Romantic literature.

Le Rouge et le noir uses several allusions to make Julien's danger perceptible. References to Scribe's* libretto, *Le Comte d'Ory* (1828—2.76) and Delavigne's† *Marino Faliero* (1829—2.118) give the flavor of the epoch and warn of the dangers of illicit love. Julien's first outing in Paris is the occasion of the first reference. He goes to the opera to watch the unwanted Count d'Ory slip uninvited into the château de Formontiers and, finally become an object of ridicule. Delavigne's tragedy works on two levels. Julien takes courage from the heroic rebellion of Delavigne's Israël Bertuccio, though he seems oblivious to the tragic results of cuckolding Marino Faliero.

Another allusion to the legend of the Châtelaine de Vergy has particular importance. The story was often exploited, for example, by numerous poets from the thirteenth century onwards, by Marguerite de Navarre, by Stendhal in *De l'amour*, and by Pierre de Belloy‡ in his popular play, *Gabrielle de Vergy*. Belloy's tragedy was first performed in 1770, and Stendhal saw a performance at the Comédie Française in 1804. He also knew Carafa's opera, *Gabriella di Vergy*, that had much success in Italy after its first performance in 1816. He may have known it in one of a number of reprintings. A novelized version was moreover published in Paris in 1829. Mme de Rênal provides a summary of the story when she "ceaselessly imagined her husband killing Julien . . . and then . . . making her eat his heart" (1.221). Although Julien was happy at Vergy (e.g., 1.89), the horrifying tale comes to mind each of the numerous times that the text mentions Mme de Rênal's property, Vergy, and one can understand why Mme de Rênal would think of the story. The narrator of *Le Rouge et le noir* tells us that Vergy "is the village made famous by Gabrielle's tragic adventure" (1.85). Like the comely knight, Raoul de Coucy, who loves the lady of Vergy, Julien is in real danger from a jealous husband. Gabrielle de Vergy's insensitive, authoritarian father was responsible for her unhappy life. "In binding me to you," she tells her husband, "he made three unhappy people [you, me, and my lover]"

---

* Eugène Scribe (1791–1861) was a prolific and hugely successful dramatist who wrote vaudevilles, comedies, and historical dramas. He was known for his "well-made plays" with finely tuned plots that today seem wooden and dull.

† Casimir Delavigne (1793–1843) is another dramatist whose once popular works have not weathered the passage of time well. His tragedies and comedies formed a transition from the sober classical school to the exuberance of Romanticism.

‡ Pierre-Laurent Buirette Belloy (1727–75) was himself responsible for the "de" that adorned his name on book covers and advertisements. His tragedies had considerable success in the early nineteenth century but are virtually unknown today.

(Belloy, *Vergy* 55). Both Coucy and Julien make the husband feel importunate, and while Julien only hears the passing bullet, M. de Coucy's heart is cut from his body and brought to his mistress's lips. It provides a mortal meal in some versions of the story. Julien's danger, of course, comes not merely from M. de Rênal. As the son of a peasant, his drive to rise in society surrounds him with enemies, and he will eventually be destroyed. Belloy's Gabrielle de Vergy begins to hallucinate and screams, "Stop, Monster, Stop. —What! Your steaming hands/ Dare to bring this heart up to my bloody lips!" (*Vergy*, 111). Given the intellectual nature of the love of Julien and Mathilde, it seems appropriate that the young woman kisses his severed head rather than his heart.

As book one of *Le Rouge et le noir* is written under the sign of Vergy, so book two is under the sign of Medea. The latter's tale has been retold even more frequently than that of the pathetic Châtelaine de Vergy. Stendhal, in his *Journal Littéraire,* says that Medea reveals "the combat between the two strongest passions that perhaps exist in women: maternal love and vengeance." Such revenge as to kill one's own children is, he says, "founded on vanity." One cannot deny that Medea deserved considerable credit for Jason's successes, as does Mathilde for Julien's. When Mathilde fears the power she has given Julien over herself, she emphasizes her own vanity by recalling Medea, "*In the midst of so many perils, I remain MYSELF*" (2.175). Because Julien knows her character well, he tergiversates when breaking with her. Mathilde is his "wife" (as Medea was Jason's), and she bears what Julien regularly refers to as his "son" within her. Perhaps Julien too is sensitive to the Medea in her. If so, the danger becomes as patent to him as it is to the reader who has been privy to Mathilde's musings. Although Medea was indeed strong, Mathilde fails to mention that the mythical magician also murdered her rival and, according to Euripides, her children. Julien recognizes that because of the pride of Mathilde's family, his son's death would be welcome. At best, "negligence will be the lot of this child of unhappiness and shame" (2.422). As a result, he repeatedly suggests that Mathilde might let Mme de Rênal care for the child. After all, "in fifteen years, Mme de Rênal will adore my son, and you will have forgotten him" (2.424). While the child's fate might extend beyond the formal conclusion of *Le Rouge et le noir*, with Mme de Rênal's death we can divine the child's future. The lot of children whose wet nurses were not closely supervised was well known. Left with the Medea-like Mathilde, the child would at best become like his rejected father, another Julien Sorel struggling helplessly to rise in society. At worst, and most likely, he would be dead—again, like his father. Unlike the unhappy child left to continue her sad life beyond the death of Charles Bovary

(1857), *Le Rouge et le noir* ends, in effect, at the close of the volume. No one of the period could doubt that the child would shortly die.

Death cast a shroud over the whole period of Romanticism, not just because of the guillotine, or even because so many people were killed during the frequent wars and revolts, but rather because it was fashionable to think about death. Sunday strolls included cemeteries, ruins, and morgues. Poets vied with each other to explain their despair most clearly, and the public imitated René and Mme de Staël in considering their mortal condition. Melancholia was *à la mode*. It is no exaggeration to say that Romantics cultivated thoughts of death, indeed, they cultivated suicide. *Le Rouge et le noir* is one of many, many examples that shows characters welcoming thoughts of grim destiny and mortality.

Although near the end of book one, Mme de Rênal entertains "a vague idea that she should quit life" (1.381), it is not until book two that death and suicide become major themes. Mathilde actually takes considerable pleasure in her thoughts of death. For her it started as a celebration of the death of her heroic ancestor Boniface de La Mole, who was beheaded in 1574, and thus enjoyed a far more notable death than that of her recent relatives who allowed themselves to go like sheep to the guillotine. She is convinced that to be condemned to death is to be distinguished: "it is the only thing that can't be bought" (2.102), she says. Although Mathilde wears mourning on the anniversary of Boniface's execution, it rapidly becomes clear that her fascination with him has as much to do with death as with heroism. She soon suggests that she and Julien might follow in the Revolutionary footsteps of the Rolands—Mme Roland was guillotined, and her husband committed suicide (2.220). Later Mathilde proposes that they commit suicide together (2.410). Eventually, her contemplation of suicide gives her almost voluptuous pleasure; the very thought becomes a point of pride (2.421–22). More and more, Julien also thinks about killing himself (2.322, 388, 402). He writes a suicide note—"For a long time life has been unbearable, and I bring it to an end"—so that M. de La Mole can kill him with impunity (2.359), but Mathilde warns her father, "If he is dead, I will die" (2.361). Even Mme de Rênal shares the same mind-set, as the narrator recounts: "For a long time, she had sincerely longed for death" (2.388). And Julien sums up for them all: "Death, in itself, was not *horrible* in his eyes" (2.391). He himself seems so determined to die that M. de Frilaire suggests his execution "will be a kind of *suicide*" (2.464). Of course, he does die, and the guillotine makes it simple for Mathilde to imitate Marguerite de Navarre and kiss the severed head of her lover (2.484). Because Mme de Rênal's love for Julien is so total, she dies three days later. Only in the confused ethos of Romanticism can death be the guarantee of love.

One way to define Romanticism is simply to list all the attributes of the movement. It has been done many times. Exoticism, vague idealism, lyrical impulsions, extreme egotism, subjectivism, and so on.... every literary historian has a carefully compiled list. I have attempted to shift the focus and go beyond the surface of such elements in order to find the root causes of Romanticism. Like hundreds of novels, poems, and plays, *Le Rouge et le noir* tells the very personal story of a whole society. It is the story of insecurity, of fear, of melancholy, and a lack of certainty. As I think of the common ground for the literary archives I have explored, I see a world that confronts the hopes and vague promises of revolutionary changes with turmoil and uncertainty. Myriad heroes actively seek impossible goals, occasionally they pursue death, or in many cases drift without a firm rudder in the turbulent sea of society. Given the widespread neglect of children that was without question a reality of the day, as discussed in chapter two, the very fact of being alive was something of a miracle since approximately one of every two children died before the age of ten. Many of those that lived suffered lifelong psychological problems that were surely compounded by this tumultuously frightening world. Problematic sanitation, inadequate nutrition, and widespread disease added to the difficulties. Hope itself caused problems, for people had the vague objective of bettering their situation without the means to do it. There were no institutions capable of providing convincing ideals. A society without models or trustworthy guidelines left French people with desires but a despairing inability to reach their goals. With the full knowledge that their efforts might well be for naught, people, young and old, were left to their own devices to establish their personal ideals, morals, and dreams. Novels like *Le Rouge et le noir* repeatedly reveal that with the crisis of authority came a crisis of the individual. People no longer knew who they were. The result was constant stress and, inevitably, its faithful accompaniment, depression. Very frequently, people felt helpless, gave up, and allowed themselves to drift. The opiates that Baudelaire lists in *Les Fleurs du mal*—drugs, alcohol, sex—were no more effective at providing security and happiness for Romantics than they are today.

Martin E. P. Seligman and his colleagues have argued convincingly, using what is now an impressive body of data from experiments with animals and people and from counseling countless patients, that when sentient beings are put in situations where their expectations are repeatedly dashed, they will eventually stop trying. Perhaps the most chilling experiment was run by C. P. Richter in 1957: "Richter discovered that after he had squeezed wild rats in his hand until they stopped

175

struggling, they drowned within 30 minutes of being placed in a water tank from which there was no escape, unlike nonsqueezed rats, who swam for 60 hours before drowning. Richter could prevent sudden death . . . if he held the rat, then released it, held it again, and released it again, sudden death did not occur. Further, if, after holding it, he put the rat in the water, took it out, put it in again, and rescued it again, sudden death was prevented."[19] Seligman's conclusion is straightforward: "Most generally put, the incentive to initiate voluntary responses to control *any* outcome (e.g., food, sex, shock, termination) comes from the expectation that responding will produce that outcome. When a person or animal has learned that the outcome is independent of responding, the expectation that responding will produce the outcome wanes; therefore response initiation diminishes" (ibid., 59). Recent experiments have increased our understanding of variables, but the general conclusion has not changed appreciably.[20] The most decisive experience of helplessness comes when infants are deprived of stimulation, thus of "*control* over stimulation" (Seligman, *Helplessness,* 144). "Since helplessness in an infant . . . is the foundational motivational attitude around which later motivational learning must crystallize, its debilitating consequences will be more catastrophic" (ibid., 150 - 51). Helplessness, in short, is learned from an impossibility of achieving satisfaction, frequently from maternal deprivation, frequently from failure, always from the death of hope. The individual who feels helpless is "slow to initiate responses, believes himself to be powerless and hopeless, and sees his future as bleak" (ibid., 81). The result is depression and, sometimes, death.

Chances are good that a flesh and blood Julien exhibiting the traits of his fictional brother would have behaved as he did, even without adherence to an aggressively self-centered philosophy like that of Destutt de Tracy, in large measure because he experiences the loss of hope, probably from an early point in life. We know that for almost a hundred years the majority of his historic brothers and sisters were put in situations where maternal deprivation was the rule that left many dead and others psychologically maimed. Those who lived joined thousands of fictional and real young people who were cut loose from their roots, before suffering terribly from insecurity and loneliness. Out from under authority—the controlling influence of the local priest, the dominant aristocrat, and the family proper—people abandoned the structures of the patriarchy, replacing it with egregious, thus, unruly individualism. True, many children benefited from the expanded possibilities of education—by 1850, illiteracy was no longer a problem in France. True, some exceptionally talented men and women were able to rise to wealth and influence in the post-Revolutionary society. Influenced by widespread sickness and malnutrition in overpopulated cities and by loneliness, however, many Romantics fell into a perpetual state of depression. Indeed, melancholy became a virtue. It meant that the sufferer had significant feelings. With values focused on themselves, like Julien, they were capable of heroic deeds and great crimes. Romantic literature regularly toyed with thoughts of incest. The self and self-gratification had become the greatest good. Although the prevailing spirit of the times encouraged attempts to escape from unsatisfying situations, successful and unsuccessful escape generally resulted in depression. Failure, of course, was sufficient cause for suicide, a resolution that brought no solutions. Romanticism, then, should be defined as a dominant, society-wide sense of helplessness and depression, accompanied by extreme individualism, marked by turmoil in the personal, public, and natural world, and characterized by excessive self-awareness, acute recognition of an alienating world, and desire to find escape.

Among French people of the late eighteenth and early nineteenth centuries that I have tried to describe, there were surely many exceptions that will not fit the mold I have identified. There are always some who seem untouched by their times. From another perspective, were one to focus on the exceptional, dealing for instance only with the geniuses who rose above the conditions of the day, there would be a somewhat different picture. Other differences would occur, should I give the political history, or recount the wars, or detail the revolts. There are many kinds of history and many archives. Still, the sustained literary market provided by a reading public from all classes gives strong support for the portrayal I have presented. For a hundred years people bought and continued to buy the novels, poems, plays that detail the characters and problems considered in the above pages. Because the Romantic I have uncovered is remarkably present in the several hundred works that I have read for this project, I believe that the literary Romantic was a distillation of historical Romantics. If a writer created a particular fiction, if a publisher was willing to gamble his financial investment of time, equipment, and personnel to bring it to print, and if people actually purchased the result, one might even claim for literature the trait of replicability that scientists demand of their experiments. Art uncovers a society's unconscious reality in all its glory and shame. One looks especially for elements that are repeated, sometimes obsessively, in the same and different works by the same and different artists. I have then tried to see how the constants fit with other things we know about the period. Granted, my archive is fiction. One must read between the lines and in a large context that includes other data and interpretations. Though some of the works are less successful from an aesthetic point of view, all are useful to reveal the social realities of the period. It is indisputable that the fictions of a group, whether major or minor works, define and to some degree both create the outlook of its members and determine their future, but I have been more concerned with the way and degree to which stories reveal a people for what and whom they are. Consequently, I am not surprised when Stendhal says, "M. [Destutt] de Tracy was telling me that you can't get closer to reality than in the novel" (*Rouge et noir,* 1.389).

Notes

CHAPTER 1: MOVING

1 Moreau, *Le Romantisme* (Paris: del Duca, 1957). The search for the most typical Romantic is, of course, a vain enterprise, though I would agree with Henri Peyre that one can perhaps come closest to such a *rara avis* with the pre-Romantics: "It was Rousseau, in his *Nouvelle Héloïse*, and in some very moving letters written shortly before or after the composition of this novel . . . and in a few authors considered of minor importance today, but more representative of the mood of the epoch, who have expressed almost all the sentiments regarded as romantic since that time"—*What Is Romanticism?*, tr. Roda Roberts (University AL: U of Alabama P, 1977) 19.

2 Maurice Cranston, for whom Rousseau was "the first of the Romantics"—*The Romantic Movement* (Oxford: Blackwell, 1994) 1—does suggest others, though he would agree that Chateaubriand and Staël are very important (77–98). Philippe Van Tieghem insists as well on the importance of Chateaubriand, Staël, and Rousseau—*Le Romantisme français* (Paris: Presses Universitaires de France, 1966) 6–8.

3 Dating Romanticism is problematic if not impossible, as it depends on the way one defines the movement or, as Irving Babbitt put it, on the elements that are taken to be primary—*Rousseau and Romanticism* (1919; Boston: Houghton Mifflin, 1947) 2–3. Laurence M. Porter discusses some of the problems of dating in his suggestive, "The Present Directions of French Romantic Studies, 1960–1975," *Nineteenth-Century French Studies,* 6.1–2 (1977–78): 1–20, which includes a substantial, useful bibliography. For bibliography on Romanticism, the new addition to the [*Cabeen*] *Critical Bibliography of French Literature, The Nineteenth Century*, ed. David Baguley, vol. 5 (Syracuse: Syracuse UP, 1994) esp. part 1, is essential.

4 Febvre, *Le Problème de l'incroyance au XVIe siècle: La Religion de Rabelais* (Paris: Albin Michel, 1942) 2.

5 As Michelle Perrot said briefly, "[N]ovels . . . may be consulted as legitimate historical sources because they reveal more fully than other sources the ideals of private life that fascinated their perspicacious authors"—"The Family

Triumphant," *From the Fires of Revolution to the Great War*, ed. Michelle Perrot, tr. Arthur Goldhammer, vol. 4 of *A History of Private Life* (Cambridge: Harvard UP, 1990) 134. For some suggestive essays, see, e.g., Febvre, "Une Vue d'ensemble. Histoire et psychologie," *Combats pour l'histoire* (Paris: Armand Colin, 1953), 207–20, as well as his, "La Sensibilité et l'histoire: Comment reconstituer la vie affective d'autrefois?" ibid., 221–38; Louis Chevalier, *Classes laborieuses et classes dangereuses à Paris, pendant la première moitié du XIXe siècle*, Pluriel (1958; Paris: Hachette, 1984) esp. 69–259; Robert Mandrou, *Introduction to Modern France, 1500–1640: An Essay in Historical Psychology*, tr. R.E. Hallmark. New York: Holmes & Meier, 1976; Emmanuel Le Roy Ladurie, "L'Ethnographie à la Rétif," *Le Territoire de l'historien*, 2 vols. (Paris: Gallimard, 1978) 2.337–97; H. Aram Veeser, ed., *The New Historicism* (New York: Routledge, 1989). Literature as a tool to read the hearts and minds of a people has its dangers, of course. It remains true, as Chevalier warned, that "you have to know how to interpret it"—*Classes laborieuses et classes dangereuses*, 115.

6   May, *Le Dilemme du roman au XVIIIe siècle: Etude sur les rapports du roman et de la critique (1715–1761)* (New Haven: Yale UP, 1963) 15–74.

7   Sigmund Freud, *The Interpretation of Dreams* (1900), *The Basic Writings of Sigmund Freud*, tr. A.A. Brill (New York: Modern Library, 1938) 311.

8   Freud, "The Relation of the Poet to Day-Dreaming" (1908), *Collected Papers* (1925; London: Hogarth, 1957) 173–83; "Twenty-Third Lecture: General Theory of the Neurosis: The Development of the Symptoms" (1917), *A General Introduction to Psychoanalysis.*, tr. G. Stanley Hall (New York: Boni & Liveright, 1920) 311–27.

9   E.g., Charles Mauron. *L'Inconscient dans l'œuvre et la vie de Racine* (Aix-en-Province: Faculté des Lettres, 1957) 180–81.

10 Lucien Goldmann, *Racine*, tr. Alastair Hamilton (1956; Cambridge: Rivers Press, 1972) 57.

11 James Smith Allen, *Popular French Romanticism: Authors, Readers, and Books in the 19th Century* (Syracuse: Syracuse UP, 1981); Françoise Parent-Lardeur, *Lire à Paris au temps de Balzac. Les Cabinets de lecture à Paris, 1830–1850* (Paris: Ecole des Hautes Etudes en Sciences Sociales, 1981).

12 If Eugen Weber is correct, as he has persuasively argued, that by and large much of rural France prior to 1870 was not really "French" in the terms we usually use—*Peasants into Frenchmen: The Modernization of Rural France: 1870–1914* (Stanford: Stanford UP, 1976)—my conclusions may be overly influenced by the city of Paris, which was the publishing and intellectual center of France, where most authors lived and most books were published, though sales and book rentals had considerable importance in the rest of France (see the references in note 10, above). Still, Paris was even more than today the unquestioned focus and center of France, the reflection and the impulsion of much that happened in the country. See, Prendergast's discussion in *Paris and the Nineteenth Century* (Oxford: Blackwell, 1992) 6–11. Other reservations are of course possible. Since most authors came

from the upper middle class, literature is probably not as representative of the lower, working classes as one might wish, a reservation advanced, for example, by Edward Shorter, "Différences de classe et sentiment depuis 1750: L'Exemple de la France," *Annales Economies Sociétés Civilisations* 29 (1974): 1034. And as has been repeatedly pointed out, for example by Georges Benrekassa, "Le Typique et le fabuleux: Histoire et roman dans la *Vie de mon père*," *Revue des Sciences Humaines* 44.172 (1978): 31–56, an author's work inevitably reflects and is thus distorted by the author's psychological or physical reality. Literature must be used with great discretion. It must be tested against other sources. Still, it represents another useful tool that should not be neglected.

Unable to read all the creative works of the period, I have been satisfied with a sample. I hope, nonetheless, that like the psychiatrist who cannot know patient's every single thought, I have isolated significant repetitions. I have attempted to establish a representative selection, though I have emphasized novels, since they have proven more abundant in the patterns and commentary that interest me here. Occasionally my selections were made from perusing the lists provided in such studies as Priscilla Clark [Ferguson]'s *The Battle of the Bourgeois: The Novel in France, 1789–1848* (Paris: Didier, 1973), and Glyn Holmes' *The 'Adolphe Type' in French Fiction in the First Half of the Nineteenth Century* (Sherbrooke, Québec: Editions Naaman, 1977). I am also indebted to suggestions after the papers and lectures where I tried out the various ideas that have occupied me during the course of this project. On more than one occasion, I have succumbed to happy accident as my eye has fallen on a title in some bibliography, essay, or library (Arthur Koestler would attribute such good fortune to the ministry of a "library angel"). I have tried to include at least one work by the major French writers of the period and by the better known, frequently published, secondary authors, though I have been content with a sample of creations by the little or unknown. In pursuing this reading, I have often been impressed with the regular repetition of the motifs I discuss in these pages.

13 As indicated in the front matter, the novels, poems, plays, essays, and autobiographies of the period that I have used are considered "primary sources" and are listed with bibliography at the end of the volume. Elsewhere they are indicated parenthetically in the text.

14 These works and others like them are engagingly described by Priscilla Parkhurst Ferguson, *Paris as Revolution: Writing the Nineteenth-Century City* (Berkeley: U of California P, 1994) 36–75.

15 E.g., May, *Le Dilemme du roman, passim*; Thomas M. Kavanagh, *Enlightenment and the Shadows of Chance: The Novel and the Culture of Gambling in Eighteenth-Century France* (Baltimore: Johns Hopkins UP, 1993) 120–21.

16 Ribner, "Paintings of Terrorized *parlementaires* for the Bourbon Conseil d'état," *The Play of Terror in Nineteenth-Century France*, ed. John T. Booker and Allan H. Pasco (Newark: U of Delaware P, 1996).

17 Barnett Singer goes so far as to call the *mal du siècle* "a middle-class luxury"—

181

Village Notables in Nineteenth-Century France: Priests, Mayors, Schoolmasters (Albany: SUNY P, 1983) 106.

18 *Génie du Christianisme, Œuvres complètes*, vol. 2 (Paris: Garnier, n.d.) 2.219.

19 Frederick Garber, "Self, Society, Value, and the Romantic Hero," *The Hero in Literature*, ed. Victor Brombert (New York: Fawcett, 1969) 213–27. In regard to the apparent inability to distinguish between self and other, René Wellek has suggested that the "essence and nature" of Romanticism is "to identify subject and object, to reconcile man and nature, consciousness and unconsciousness by poetry which is 'the first and last of all knowledge' "— "Romanticism Re-examined," *Romanticism Reconsidered: Selected Papers from the English Institute*, ed. Northrop Frye (New York: Columbia UP, 1963). Regarding the differentiating/undifferentiating self, Nancy Chodorow offers a good review of the relevant psychological theories in her consideration of gender as relation and process—"Gender, Relation, and Difference in Psychoanalytic Perspective," *The Future of Difference*, ed. Hester Eisenstein and Alice Jardine (Boston: G.K. Hall, 1980) 3–19. Otherwise, this summary description of the Romantic hero uses the work of many critics and intellectual historians, among which I might mention: Lloyd Bishop, *The Romantic Hero and his Heirs in French Literature* (New York: Peter Lang, 1984); Barbara T. Cooper, "Breaking Up/Down/Apart: 'L'Eclatement' as a Unifying Principle in Musset's *Lorenzaccio*," *Philological Quarterly* 65.1 (1986): 103–12; Lilian R. Furst, *The Contours of European Romanticism* (London: Macmillan, 1979); Albert Joseph George, *The Development of French Romanticism: The Impact of the Industrial Revolution on Literature* (Syracuse: Syracuse UP, 1955); Glyn Holmes, *The 'Adolphe Type'*; Armand Hoog, "Un Cas d'angoisse préromantique," *Revue des Sciences Humaines* 67 (1952): 181–92; Robert Mauzi, "Les Maladies de l'âme au XVIIIᵉ siècle," *Revue des Sciences Humaines* 100 (1960): 459–93; Georges Poulet, "Timelessness and Romanticism," *Journal of the History of Ideas* 15 (1954): 3–22; George R. Ridge, *The Hero in French Decadent Literature* (Athens: U of Georgia P, 1961); William Rose, *From Goethe to Byron: The Development of* Weltschmerz *in German Literature* (London: Routledge, 1924); Raney Stanford, "The Romantic Hero and That Fatal Selfhood," *Centennial Review* 12.4 (1968): 430–54; Peter L. Thorslev, Jr. *The Byronic Hero: Types and Prototypes* (Minneapolis: U of Minnesota P, 1962), though I have drawn on others that are mentioned throughout this study in relation to more specific problems.

20 E.g., Peyre, *What Is Romanticism?*, 73–75. Musset was, of course, not the first to make such a suggestion, merely the most eloquent. Similar explanations occur elsewhere. See, for example, Adolphe Custine's hero regretting that he "would not be able to take part in the exploits that used to bring luster to my country, and I quivered with indignation on thinking that there would no longer be any nations left to subjugate when I became old enough to join the army"—*Aloys ou le religieux du Mont Saint-Bernard* (1829) 37–38.

21 See ch. 3 below, and Barnett Singer's consideration of rural priests after the Revolution: *Village Notables*, 9–36, 89–107.

22 Hufton, *Women and the Limits of Citizenship in the French Revolution* (Toronto: U of Toronto P, 1992).

23 See, e.g., George Levitine, *Girodet-Trioson: An Iconographical Study* (New York: Garland, 1978) 236–38. Madelyn Gutwirth, "The Engulfed Beloved: Representations of Dead and Dying Women in the Art and Literature of the Revolutionary Era," *Rebel Daughters*, ed. Melzer and Rabine, 198–227.

24 I am painting here with a broad brush and sweeping strokes. None of the changes that interest me took place overnight or in an uncomplicated way. Emmanuel Le Roy Ladurie, as a problematic example, is right to point to an "anti-capitalistic" result of the Revolution when previously large, aristocratic estates were broken up into small, peasant land-holdings—"La Crise et l'historien," *Territoire*, 2.445.

25 Michael W. Flinn, *The European Demographic System, 1500–1820* (Baltimore: Johns Hopkins UP, 1981) 65. For a detailed consideration of French migration, which picks up significantly in the second half of the eighteenth century, see, Jacques Dupâquier, *Histoire de la population française* 2 (Paris: Presses Universitaires de France, 1988) 99–174.

26 André Corvisier, "Service militaire et mobilité géographique au XVIIIe siècle," *Annales de Démographie Historique,* 1970: 193.

27 Daniel Roche, "Nouveau Parisiens au XVIIIe siècle," *Cahiers d'histoire* 24 (1979): 12.

28 Lareynie came from Montpellier—Ourliac, *Suzanne*, 1.87.

29 Abel Chatelain, "Les Migrations temporaires françaises au XIXe siècle: Problèmes. Méthodes. Documentation," *Annales de Démographie Historique,* 1967: 11–27.

30 Jan de Vries, *European Urbanization 1500–1800* (Cambridge: Harvard UP, 1984) 259.

31 Picard, *Le Gil Blas de la Révolution* 1.142. Cf. Flinn, 68–69, Roche, 13.

32 Roche, 8; Louis Henry, "Deux analyses de l'immigration à Paris. 1) Le Volume de l'immigration à Paris de 1740 à 1792," *Population* 26.6 (1971): 1073–85; Alain Blum and Jacques Houdaille, "12 000 Parisiens en 1793: Sondage dans les cartes de civisme," *Population* 41.2 (1986): 274–76.

33 Jean Chagniot, *Paris au XVIIIe siècle, Nouvelle Histoire de Paris* (Paris: Hachette, 1988) 218–19. For a consideration of the attempts to find ways of accurately estimating the population of France and its cities from the fifteenth century through the eighteenth, see Dupâquier, 2.1–98. Most statistics prior to 1825 are problematic. Le Roy Ladurie, for example, gives an interesting case study of attempts to estimate crop yields after 1700: "Les Comptes fantastiques de Gregory King," *Le Territoire de l'histoirien*, 1.252–70.

34 Roche, 16–17; Blum and Houdaille, 281–92.

35 Quoted from Susan L. Siegfried's translation in "Boilly's *Moving House: 'An Exact Picture of Paris'?*" *The Art Institute of Chicago Museum Studies,* 15.2 (1989): 130. Boilly repeated *Les Déménagements* sometime around 1840, with several notable changes. I limit my discussion to the version of 1822.

36 Compare figures 4 and 5 of Susan L. Siegfried, "Boilly's *Moving House: 'An*

Exact Picture of Paris'?" *Art Institute of Chicago Museum Studies* 15.2 (1989): 132–33.

37 Eliel, "Louis Boilly, précurseur de l'esthétique moderne," *Louis Boilly 1762 - 1845* (Paris: Musée Marmottan, 1984) 16–18. The fact that the wealthy and influential were often spared this fate was well known. See Lamothe-Langon's angry denunciation of prefectural corruption: *Monsieur le Préfet* (1824) 3.6–10.

38 Hallam, "The Two Manners of Louis-Léopold Boilly and French Genre Painting in Transition," *Art Bulletin* 63 (1981):618–33.

39 Georges Bernier, cataloguer, "Louis-Leopold Boilly 1761–1845," *Art in Early XIX Century France: Consulat—Empire - Restoration: A Loan Exhibition for the Benefit of the Lycée Français of New York* (New York: Wildenstein, 1982) n. pag.

40 For the identification of the church, see Bernier. On the controversy that has arisen since the identification of the church, see Siegfried, "Exact Picture," 126–37; Siegfried, "The Artist as Nomadic Capitalist: The Case of Louis-Léopold Boilly," *Art History* 13.4 (1990): 516–41; John Stephen Hallam, *The Genre Works of Louis-Léopold Boilly* (Ann Arbor: 1979)114; and Carol S. Eliel, *Form and Content in the Genre Works of Louis-Léopold Boilly* (Ann Arbor: 1985) 179n77.

41 Mercier, *Tableau de Paris* 1.110; Chauvet, *Essai sur la propreté de Paris* (Paris: Chez l'Auteur, 1797) 38. For the summary description of Parisian streets that follows, I have depended primarily on Mercier's *Tableau*. See, especially, "Ruisseaux" (1.110–11), "Boucheries" (1.112–14), "Pont-Royal" (1.140–42), "Réverbères" 1.175–76, "Balcons" 1.916–18, "Boueurs" 1.1237–40, "Décrotteurs" (1.1255–59), "Portes Cochères" (2.834–36), "La Fête de saint Martin" (2.913–14), "Les Gouttières" (2.1068–70), "Latrines" (2.1071–74), but I am also indebted to: Chauvet, mentioned above; Donald Reid, *Paris Sewers and Sewermen: Realities and Representatives* (Cambridge: Harvard UP, 1991); J.-H. Ronesse, *Vues sur la propreté des rues de Paris* (n.p.: n. p., 1782); Alain Corbin, *The Foul and the Fragrant: Odor and the French Social Imagination* (Cambridge: Harvard UP, 1986) esp. 25, 34, 59–60, 94; Pierre Saddy, "Le Cycle des immondices," *Dix-Huitième Siècle* 9 (1977): 203–14; Alexandre Parent-Duchâtelet, "Essai sur les cloaques ou égouts de la ville de Paris" (1824), *Hygiène publique,* 2 vols. (Paris: J.B. Baillière, 1836) 1.183–225; Owen and Caroline Hannaway, "La Fermeture du cimetière des Innocents," *Dix-Huitième siècle* 9 (1977): 181–91.

42 *Mystères de Paris* (1.57); Sue also mentions the Brasserie Passageway, a "humid, muddy [*boueuse*], dark, sad passageway, where the sun almost never penetrates" (3.90). Ronesse emphasized the insalubrity of these narrow, dark streets (12, 23), which were an important feature decried by reformers like Louis-René Villermé—"Sur les cités ouvrières" *Annales d'Hygiène public et de médecine légale,* 43 (1850): 241–61. See, also, Restif de la Bretonne, *Les Nuits de Paris* (1788–94) t. 5, pt. 10, night 159, p. 2392; Mercier, *Tableau,* 2.914; *Le Nouveau Paris,* 3.98.

43 *Tableau,* 1.1255; Chauvet, 14. There is some controversy about the etymology of *Lutèce*. See, e.g., the note to Mercier's claim (*Tableau,* 1.1830–31), and also

both Walther von Wartburg's *Französisches etymologisches wörterbuch* under *lutare* and *luteus*, and André Cherpillod, *Dictionnaire étymologique des noms géographiques* (Paris: Masson, 1986) under *Lutèce*.

44 The comment, which dates from 1888, is quoted from Pierre Pierrard, *La Vie ouvrière à Lille sous le Second Empire* (Paris: Bloud et Gay, 1965) 46. For a detailed consideration of the streets of Lille, see ibid., 49–55. Stendhal describes the streets of Nancy: "Narrow, poorly paved streets . . . had nothing remarkable except for the abominable uncleanness; down the middle flowed a stream of muddy water that looked [to Lucien] like a decoction of clay." Then, the hero is splashed by "black, foul smelling water" (*Lucien Leuwen* [1834–35; 1894] 1.793). When Lucien marks his first vision of Madame de Chasteller with a fall that deposited both horse and rider in the *boue*, the fact that the dried residue on his uniform was later described as "white" does not necessarily mean that it was less vile than the black stuff of the streets of Paris, though it almost certainly was (*Lucien*, 1.794).

45 Julius R. Ruff, *Crime, Justice and Public Order in Old Regime France: The Sénéchaussées of Libourne and Bazas, 1696–1789* (London: Croom Helm, 1984) 80.

46 "Projet d'épilogue pour la seconde édition des *Fleurs du mal*" (180), and "Reliquat et dossier des *Fleurs du mal*" (177).

CHAPTER 2: THE UNROCKED CRADLE

1 Shattuck, *The Forbidden Experiment: The Story of the Wild Boy of Aveyron* (New York: Farrar Straus Giroux, 1980) 193. See also n2, below.

2 Harlan Lane's *The Wild Boy of Aveyron* (Cambridge: Harvard UP, 1976) 20–21.

3 Isabelle Brouard-Arends, *Vies et images maternelles dans la littérature française du dix-huitième siècle*, Studies on Voltaire and the Eighteenth Century, no. 291 (Oxford: Voltaire Foundation, 1991) 287.

4 E.g., Dorval's mother "gave me life and died shortly afterwards" (Diderot, *Fils naturel* [1757] 66); the parents of Marmontel's Annete and Lubin of 1761 are dead (2.218), Jenny's parents refuse to recognize her in Madame Riccoboni's *Histoire de Miss Jenny* (1764), and Sophie is a foundling in the same author's later *Lettres d'Elisabeth Sophie de Vallière* (1772). Voltaire's Arzame says, "[m]y unfortunate mother/When I was in the cradle completed her destined course" (*Guèbres* [1769] 1.5). The mother of Louvet's Faublas died during his childhood—"My mother died too soon" (*Une Année* [1787] 419). Hyacinthe's mother died "in giving life to this child" (Ducray-Duminil, *Victor* [1797] 2.239). From early in her life, Mme de Staël's Delphine (1802) was an orphan. The father of Fiévée's Frédéric tells him: "I never knew my mother; my birth cost her life" (*Frédéric* [1802] 2.112). The latter novel's

Adèle, whom Frédéric eventually marries, was abandoned near the Place des Victoires when she was four or five (2.172). In this novel of rejection, despite the discovery of their parents, neither Adèle nor Frédéric are ever wholly accepted. Adèle eventually takes the name of her employer; Frédéric has himself adopted by the Montlucs. Eugène's mother in Madame de Souza's *Eugène de Rothelin* (1808) likewise "died in bringing him into the world" (244). The heroines of Mlle Palaiseau's *Histoire de Mesdemoiselles de Saint-Janvier* (1812) were orphaned early on in a slave up-rising. The hero of Custine's *Aloys ou le religieux du Mont Saint-Bernard* (1829) says, "I knew neither my father, who died a victim of the factional fury, nor my mother who could not be consoled for the loss of her husband (11–12). He eventually realizes that he has fallen in love with the mother of the woman he is supposed to marry. Albert de Surville, the love of Pascaline's life, was orphaned in the first few years of his life (Estournelles, *Pascaline* [1821]). The Beaumont girls lost their mother when they were infants (Picard, *Gil Blas* [1824] 1.31). The mothers of both of the main characters, Edgar and Valentine, are dead in Delphine Gay's *Le Lorgnon* of 1830. The main character of Albitte's *Une Vie d'homme* (1832) is an orphan. Stephen's mother died in his childhood in *Sous les tilleuls* (1832) (270). Eugénie Grandet's cousin Charles has lost his mother (1833). Amaury was orphaned early on in Sainte-Beuve's *Volupté* (1834) (1.184). Neither Emma nor Olbreuse have mothers in Sophie Pannier's *L'Athée* (1836). In *La Comtesse d'Egmont* (1836), Septimanie's mother died shortly after her birth (3–4), and Séverin's parents abandoned him. Both of the main characters of Ourliac's *Suzanne* (1840) were abandoned: Peters when he was two and Suzanne when she was between three and four years old. The title character of *Hyacinthe, l'apprenti* (1841) is an orphan. In Suë's *Les Mystères de Paris* (1842–43), Le Chourineur and Fleur-de-Marie were abandoned. George Sand's *La Mare au Diable* (1846) opens with the recently widowed main character being encouraged to find a new wife to help care for his three young children, and the title character of Sand's *François le champi* (1848) is an orphan. Flaubert's *Salammbô* (1862) and Deslauriers of *L'Education sentimental* (1869) lack mothers. Jean-Marc, narrator–protagonist of Maxime du Camp's *Mémoires d'un suicidé* (1853) lost his as well during his childhood. And so on.

5 Glyn Holmes, *The 'Adolphe Type' in French Fiction in the First Half of the Nineteenth Century* (Sherbrooke, Québec: Editions Naaman, 1977) 140.

6 In France, per thousand people there were 27.7 deaths in 1800, 26.0 in 1815, 25.0 in 1830, 23.6 in 1848, 23.6 in 1869, 22.6 in 1884, and, for comparison, 10.6 in 1975—B.R. Mitchell, *European Historical Statistics: 1750–1975*, 2nd ed. (London: Macmillan, 1981) 93–95.

7 Although reliable figures are very difficult to come by, Roger Schofield calculates that something like ten mothers per thousand childbirths died within sixty days of birth in Europe from 1600 through about 1850—"Did the Mothers Really Die? Three Centuries of Maternal Mortality in the World We Have Lost," *The World We Have Gained: Histories of Population and Social*

Structure: Essays Presented to Peter Laslett on His Seventieth Birthday, ed. Lloyd Bonfield, et al. (Oxford: Basil Blackwell, 1986), 231–60. He feels "a woman on average would have run a 6 to 7 percent risk of dying in childbed [that is, within sixty days of giving birth to one of her children] at some time in her procreative career"—(259). Hector Gutierrez and Jacques Houdaille, arrive at somewhat different figures for rural France from 1700 to 1829; they indicate 11.5 deaths per thousand occurred because of childbirth—"La Mortalité maternelle en France au XVIIIe siècle," *Population* 38.6 (1983): 975–93. The calculations given for this period by J.-P. Bardet, et al., are similar to those of Gutierrez and Houdaille in Rouen and Vexin—"La Mortalité maternelle autrefois: Une Etude comparée (de la France de l'ouest à l'Utah)," *Annales de démographie historique*, 1981, 31–48. For purposes of comparison, in France between 1975 and 1977, there were only 0.163 maternal deaths per 1,000 live births (Gutierrez and Houdaille, 978), while in England and Wales in 1980, there was a 0.1 maternal mortality rate per 1,000 births (Schofield, 231). In the United States, "[m]aternal mortality declined from 9.6 per 100,000 births in 1978 to 7.8 in 1985" (i.e., 0.096 per 1,000 in 1978 to 0.078 in 1985)— Richard W. Wertz and Dorothy C. Wertz, *Lying-In: A History of Childbirth in America*. 2nd ed. New Haven: Yale UP, 1989), 303.

8   See, n7 above.
9   Lloyd Bishop, *The Romantic Hero and His Heirs in French Literature* (New York: Peter Lang, 1984) 37.
10 Delécluze's *Souvenirs de soixante années* (1862) is quoted by Armand Hoog, "Who Invented the 'Mal du siècle'?" *Yale French Studies* 13 (1954): 49–50. In fact, as Hoog has claimed, Romanticism has its roots set so deeply in the eighteenth century, that we might better do away with the concept of pre-Romanticism—"Un Cas d'angoisse préromantique," *Revue des Sciences Humaines* 67 (1952): 181.
11 M. A. Ribble, "Infantile Experience in Relation to Personality Development," *Personality and Behavior Disorders*, ed. J. M. Hunt (New York: Ronald, 1944) 2.621–51; "Anxiety in Infants and Its Disorganizing Effects," *Modern Trends in Child Psychiatry*, ed. N.D.C. Lewis and B.L. Pacella (New York: International Universities Press, 1945).
12 H. Bakwin, "Emotional Deprivation in Infants," *Journal of Pediatrics* 35 (1949): 512–21.
13 Mary D. Ainsworth, "The Effects of Maternal Deprivation: A Review of Findings and Controversy in the Context of Research Strategy," *Deprivation of Maternal Care: A Reassessment of Its Effects* (Geneva: World Health Organization, 1962) 97–165. Early findings have not been contradicted by recent studies. Burton L. White says, for example: "A child who does not have the opportunity for the establishment of a good parent–child relationship during the first three years of life, or who has that relationship interrupted for three or more months (after the first six months of life), suffers rather serious negative consequences. No relationship at all leads to an emotional cripple who will never be socially normal throughout his life. An interrupted relationship of three months or longer

once the child is six months old leads to emotional distress whose intensity and longevity is linked directly to such factors as the length of the separation"— *Educating the Infant and Toddler* (Lexington, MA: D.C. Heath, 1988) 39.

14 See, e.g., Robert Wright, "The Biology of Violence," *New Yorker* 13 March 1995, 68–77 (cited by Norman N. Holland in his presentation "Brains and Literature," Modern Language Association Meeting, Chicago, IL, 30 December 1995); Jane M. Healy, *Endangered Minds: Why our Children Don't Think* (New York: Simon & Schuster, 1990) 155, 169, 237–39, 361; Naomi Segal, *Narcissus and Echo* (Manchester: Manchester UP, 1988) 52. Extensive bibliography exists on the results of maternal deprivation. See, e.g., Andrew B. Crider, George R. Goethals, Robert D. Kavanaugh, Paul R. Solomon. *Psychology.* 4th ed. (New York: Harper Collins, 1993) 349–51.

15 Lawrence Stone, *The Family, Sex and Marriage in England 1500–1800.* (London: Weidenfeld and Nicolson, 1977) 431–32; Edward Shorter, *The Making of the Modern Family* (New York: Basic Books, 1975) 182. According to Valerie Fildes, wet-nursing was never so widespread in England as in other countries—*Wet Nursing: A History from Antiquity to the Present* (Oxford: Basil Blackwell, 1988) 79. Furthermore, "In Germany there was a steady decline in the number of wet nurses employed: in the mid-eighteenth century they formed 4–5 per cent of the population of Hamburg; by the end of the nineteenth century they formed 0.01 per cent of the populace" (ibid., 207).

16 George D. Sussman, *Selling Mothers' Milk: The Wet-Nursing Business in France: 1715–1914* (Urbana: U of Illinois P, 1982), 308, 313.

17 Quoted from Sussman, *Selling* 307.

18 See, e.g., Keith R. Bradley, "Wet-Nursing at Rome: A Study in Social Relations," *The Family in Ancient Rome: New Perspectives,* ed. Beryl Rawson (Ithaca: Cornell Univ. Press, 1986), 201–29; and Fildes, 1–25, 34–35, 68.

19 See also Sussman, *Selling,* 88; Maurice Crubellier, *L'Enfance et la jeunesse dans la société française, 1800–1950* (Paris: Armand Colin, 1979), 41–42; Fanny Faÿ-Sallois, *Les Nourrices à Paris au XIXe siècle* (Paris: Payot, 1980) 156, 228–29, 235; Brouard-Arends, *Vies et images maternelles,* 50–52. Restif de la Bretonne mentions these beliefs in a veiled way, veiled I suspect not so much because of taste as because further explanation was at the time unnecessary: "[M]y mother could not nurse me; my father was opposed to it, doubtless for good reasons. . . . The maid Lolive, the wife of Lemoine, weaned her already strong daughter Nannette in receiving me, but the dear woman could not resist her husband's desire that had been constrained for eighteen months. They felt obliged to wean me at six months..."—*Monsieur Nicolas,* 1.20.

20 Senior, "Aspects of Infant Feeding in Eighteenth-Century France," *Eighteenth-Century Studies* 16 (1983): 375–77. Restif maintains that Parisian and upper-class women should not breast feed their own children. Given their exalted passions, their milk would be overheated—*Les Nuits,* night 184, 2513–15.

21 Philippe Ariès, *L'Enfant et la vie familiale sous l'Ancien Régime* (Paris: Seuil, 1973), 53. See also Brouard-Arends's recent consideration where she reaches similar conclusions: *Vies et images maternelles,* 49–50; Edward Shorter,

"Différences de classe et sentiment depuis 1750: L'Exemple de la France," *Annales Economies Sociétés Civilisations* 29 (1974): 1034. The relationship between high infant mortality and maternal indifference has been observed elsewhere—Ellen K. Coghlin, "Mother Love and Infant Death in a Brazilian Shantytown" (a review essay of Nancy Scheper-Hughes's *Death Without Weeping*), *The Chronicle of Higher Education*, June 10, 1992: 7–9. Ariès's argument elicited considerable debate. In general, it was maintained that, while he might be correct for the society as a whole, contemporary diaries make it clear that there were many exceptions. Rosemary Lloyd gives a good summary of this controversy—*The Land of Lost Content: Children and Childhood in Nineteenth-Century French Literature* (Oxford: Clarendon, 1992) 8. Lloyd argues overall that childhood was not really discovered until late in the nineteenth century. Montaigne mentions the loss of "two or three" of his children while at the nurse's, though he professes some distress: "I lost two or three children while they were with the wet nurse, if not without regrets, at least without anger"—Michel de Montaigne, *Essais, Œuvres complètes*, Bibliothèque de la Pléiade (Paris: Gallimard, 1962) 1.14.61. It may dramatize children's scant value when we note that he apparently did not remember that, in fact, five of his six children died at the wet nurse's (ibid., 2.8.369 and n1). For purposes of comparison, in 1985 neonatal mortality (deaths under 28 days) in the United States were 7 per 1,000 (Wertz 303).

22 Sussman, *Selling*, 20; see also 110–12, 127. Faÿ-Sallois has similar estimates (57). Sussman's figures for 1801–2 show a sharp drop in wet-nursing to 51 percent (110), which can probably be explained by the government's use of depreciated Revolutionary money to pay nurses (Faÿ-Sallois, 32–33). Louis Sébastien Mercier discusses these issues repeatedly: e.g., *Tableau de Paris*, ed. Jean-Claude Bonnet, 2 vols. (1781–88; Paris: Mercure de France, 1994). See especially "Bureau des nourrices et recommandaresses" (1.871–72), "Réponse au *Courrier de l'Europe*" (1.995), "Accouchée" (1.1288–91), "Hôtel des Enfants-Trouvés" (2.147–52), "Enfants abandonnés" (2.1376–79). Etienne de Jouy describes a state run Agency for Nurses (*Bureau des Nourrices*)—*Guillaume Le Franc-Parleur*, 2 vols. (Paris: Pillet, 1815) 1.198–210.

23 The fictional character Thérèse, who saw her child twice in two years, is probably not uncommon (Picard, *Gil Blas*, 2.7), as Brouard-Arends describes: *Vies et images maternelles*, 47.

24 Galliano, "La Mortalité infantile (indigènes et nourrisons) dans la banlieu sud de Paris à la fin du XVIIIᵉ siècle (1774–1794)," *Annales de Démographie Historique* 1966: 150.

25 Sussman, *Selling*, 67. From 1779 to 1789, 42 percent of abandoned children died in Reins, 82 percent in Paris—Antoinette Chamoux, "L'Enfance abandonnée à Reims à la fin du XVIIIᵉ siècle," *Annales de Démographie Historique*, 1973: 277; 80 percent in Rouen—J.-P. Bardet, "Pour que vivent les enfants trouvés, " *Annales de Démographie Historique*, 1973: 395. Chamoux published a number of interesting selections concerning infant mortality

dating from the late eighteenth century and collected by a surgeon named Tenon, who was an administrator in the *Assistance publique* (health and social security services)—"Mise en nourrice et mortalité des enfants légitimes," *Annales de Démographie Historique,* 1973: 418–22. Among other observations, he notes that in Lyon from 1785 to 1788 only 16 percent of the babies nursed by their mothers died, while two-thirds of those commercially nursed did so (421). Though these figures seem plausible, I should perhaps insist that, while all statistics from this period need to be viewed judiciously if not skeptically, estimates of infant mortality are particularly untrustworthy—see Jacques Dupâquier, *Histoire de la population française* 2 (Paris: Presses Universitaires de France, 1988) 221–34.

26 Houdaille, "La Mortalité des enfants dans la France rurale de 1690–1779," *Population* 39.1 (1984): 77–106.

27 Duché, "De l'industrie des nourrices et de la mortalité des petits enfants dans le département de l'Yonne," *Annuaire de l'Yonne,* 1868: 165.

28 Donzelot, The *Policing of Families,* tr. Robert Hurley (1977: tr. New York Pantheon, 1979) 11. See also Daniel Roche, "Nouveaux Parisiens au XVIIIe siècle," *Cahiers d'Histoire,* 24.3 (1979): 8.

29 Faÿ-Sallois, 13n1, 73; Fildes, 192; Yvonne Knibiehler, "La Maternité en question," *L'Histoire des mères du moyen-âge à nos jours* (n.p.: Montalba, 1980) 230; André Armengaud, "Les Nourrices du Morvan au XIXe siècle," *Annales de Démographie Historique,* 1964: 131–39.

30 Fildes says that infant mortality in foundling homes during the first twelve months "ranged from 41 to 90 per cent with an estimated average of 60 per cent for France as a whole" (149). See also table 10.1 on p. 156. From 1750 to 1789, Louis Henry estimates that 66 percent of foundlings died yearly— "Deux analyses de l'immigration à Paris. 1) Le Volume de l'immigration à Paris de 1740 à 1792," *Population* 26.6 (1971): 1083–84. According to Léon Lallemand, 92 percent of the children abandoned in 1797 died in hospice, but, given the conditions for those that lived to be sent to a wet nurse, the actual death rate probably reached 96 or 97 percent—*Histoire des enfants abandonnées et délaissés: Etudes sur la protection de l'enfance aux diverses époques de la civilisation* (Paris: Alphonse Picard, 1885) 261. Of the 104 children abandoned in 1801 in Toulon only three lived (Lallemand, 164). In 1846, 66 percent died nationwide—André Armengaud, "L'Enfant dans la société du XIXe siècle," *Annales de Démographie Historique,* 1973: 308. Combeferre maintains in Victor Hugo's *Les Miserables* (1862) that 55 percent of all foundlings die (4.89; quoted by Chevalier, "Description littéraire," 178). In Year IX (1801–2), something like 62,000 babies were abandoned, 106,000 in 1821, 131,000 in 1833 (Faÿ-Sallois, 66).

31 "For a while, women wanted to nurse, but it was only a fad, and it passed"— Mercier, *Tableau de Paris,* 1.1290. Tenon estimated that from 1770 to 1776, when the influence of *Emile* was high (Martin, Mylne, and Frautschi list 20 editions of the novel between 1762 and 1774—62.33), Paris's wet-nursing bureaus nonetheless recruited 10,000 nurses, with private parties finding

another 5,000 (Faÿ-Sellois, 29). Charles Fourier claims that the women converted by Rousseau to nursing their own babies were in the wealthiest classes and totaled "only an eighth of mothers"—*Théorie de l'unité universelle*, 5.48. Although Mercier claims in 1798 that "maternity becomes another degree of enhancement for our French women: all nourish, all take pride in being mothers, and all feel that the only good nurse is the true mother" (*Nouveau Paris*, 3.192–93), clearly, the influence of Rousseau's *Emile* should not be exaggerated. As Nancy Senior concludes, "[I]ts immediate impact in terms of numbers was small"—"Infant Feeding," 369. See, also, Maurice Crubellier, *L'Enfance et la jeunesse dans la société française, 1800–1950* (Paris: Armand Colin, 1979), 39; Sussman, *Selling*, 27. Curiously, despite the apparent brevity of the renewal of maternal breast-feeding, it was common in novels by female authors from 1760 to 1790 (Brouard-Arends, 339–47), and it became a popular symbol of the relationship between the revolutionary state and its citizens—see Mary Jacobus, "Incorruptible Milk: Breast-Feeding and the French Revolution," *Rebel Daughters: Women and the French Revolution*, ed. Sara E. Melzer and Leslie W. Rabine (New York: Oxford UP, 1992) 54–75.

32 Athénaïs Mialaret is quoted from Erna O. Hellerstein, et al., eds, *Victorian Women: A Documentary Account of Women's Lives in Nineteenth-Century England, France, and the United States* (Stanford: Stanford UP, 1981) 25.

33 Quoted from Eugen Weber, *Peasants into Frenchmen: The Modernization of Rural France: 1870–1914* (Stanford: Stanford UP, 1976) 183n. Actually, by 1870 French society was well on the way to returning to maternal nursing. As already mentioned, by the 1840s, the wealthier classes were doing so. Then, in 1869 the Academy of Medicine held a series of sessions to respond to increasingly strident attacks on commercial nursing, claiming that the hecatomb which had claimed the lives of 138,481 infants in 1831 had left 182,189 dead in 1862 (Faÿ-Sallois, 72–76). 1862 seems to have been the high point, after which popular pressure, more stringent regulation, and better sanitation had significant effect in discouraging wet-nursing.

34 Under the rubric of what nineteenth-century physicians called "nostalgia," Michael S. Roth gives several examples of children who suffered from being taken from their nurse—"Returning to Nostalgia," *Home and Its Dislocations in Nineteenth-Century France*, ed. Susanne Nash (Albany: State U of New York P, 1993) 25–26, 28.

35 Fuchs, *Abandoned Children: Foundlings and Child Welfare in Nineteenth-Century France* (Albany: State U of New York P, 1984) 266.

36 Pauvert, *Sade vivant*, vol. 1 (Paris: Robert Laffont, 1986) 27. Brouard-Arends considers Sade's visions of mothers at some length: *Vie et images maternelles*, 360–71.

37 Flaubert, doubtless because he was the offspring of a doctor, was nursed by his mother.

38 Flaubert, *Madame Bovary*, 409. Claudine Gothot-Mersch, in her study of *La Genèse de* Madame Bovary (Paris: José Corti, 1962), remarks that Flaubert's notes ("Put the child with the wet nurse—filthy house the child stinks") make

it seem that the visit was invented in order "to describe the sordid surroundings where the Bovary's little girl had to live. . . . [A]t first he thought only of the way the middle class abandon their newborns" (191).

39 Dumas *père*, *Les Morts vont vite*, 2.4.

40 Balzac, *Lettres à Madame Hanska*, ed. Roger Pierrot, 4 vols. (Paris: Les Bibliophiles de l'Originale, 1967–71) 3.128. Gérard de Nerval's tragedy was the more common one. Given his well-known troubles and suicide, the resulting maternal deprivation seems indisputable: "I never saw my mother. Her portraits were either lost or stolen. I only know that she resembled an engraving of the period in the manner of Prud'hon or Fragonard that was called *Modesty*. The fever which killed her touched me on three occasions, at times that form regular, periodic divisions of my life"—"Promenades et souvenirs," 1.135.

41 Chateaubriand, *Mémoires d'outre-tombe*, vol. 1, part 2, book 1, ch. 11, pp. 42–44. Sainte-Beuve's Amaury, in *Volupté* (1834), remembers: "After having read the beautiful story of *René* one evening, I wrote an agitated judgment in my notebook . . . : 'I read *René* and I trembled; I recognized myself completely. . . .' How many others, over the last twenty years, have likewise trembled and believed that they were confronting themselves in this immortal portrait!" (1.243).

42 Elme Caro, "Le Suicide dans ses rapports avec la civilisation," *Nouvelles Etudes morales sur le temps présent* (Paris: Hachette, 1869) 49.

CHAPTER 3: DODDERING PATERNITIES

1 Jaucourt, "Père," *Encyclopédie, ou Dictionnaire raisonné des sciences, des arts et des métiers*, ed. Diderot and D'Alembert, 17 vols. (Paris: Briasson, 1751–65) 12.339.

2 See David J. Denby's *Sentimental Narrative and the Social Order in France, 1760–1820* (Cambridge: Cambridge UP, 1994), and Edward Shorter, "Différences de classe et sentiment depuis 1750: L'Exemple de la France," *Annales Economies Sociétés Civilisations* 29 (1974): 1034–57.

3 J. Mulliez reviews the legal situation in: "La Volonté d'un homme," *Histoire des pères et de la paternité*, ed. Jean Delumeau and Daniel Roche (Paris: Larousse, 1990) 279–312.

4 Jeffrey Merrick, "Sexual Politics and Public Order in Late Eighteenth-Century France: The *Mémoires secrets* and the *Correspondance secrète*," *Journal of the History of Sexuality* 1 (1990): 68. See also Isabelle Brouard-Arends, *Vies et images maternelles dans la littérature française du dix-huitième siècle*, Studies on Voltaire and the Eighteenth Century, no. 291 (Oxford: Voltaire Foundation, 1991) 283, 321, 403–4; and Robert Mandrou, *Introduction to Modern France*

1500–1640: An Essay in Historical Psychology, trans. R.E. Hallmark (New York: Holmes & Meier, 1976) 83–89.

5 J.-C. Bonnet, "De la famille à la patrie," *Histoire des pères*, ed. Delumeau and Roche, 256. Extreme examples of pseudonyms and actually taking on other identities occur, for example, in Louvet's *La Fin des amours de Faublas* (1790), where Faublas is termed "the young man with fifty names" (2.857); and *passim* in Rétif's *Le Palais-Royal* (1790) and Balzac's *Splendeurs et misères* (1738–47). The importance of names is otherwise emphasized in such plays as Dumas *père*'s *Antony* (1831), where the title character's lack of a family name fills him with anguish. In *Sans nom* (1837), one of the parodies that marked *Antony*'s success, Félix Bonhomme wants to discard his patronymic for something more appealing: "I deny my family and name myself... Ant[ony]... Oh! better than that!... I have it.... . . . I am *the man without a name...* that is even more picturesque"—quoted from Barbara Cooper, "Parodie et pastiche: La Réception théâtrale d'*Antony*," *Œuvres et Critiques* 21.1 (1996): 125. On the instability of identity, see also Cooper's "The Return of Martin Guerre in an Early Nineteenth Century French Melodrama," *Melodrama: the Cultural Emergence of a Genre*, ed. Michael Hays and Anastasia Nikolopoulou (New York: St. Martin's Press, 1996) 113.

6 In a recent interview by Annette Tapert published in the November 1995 issue of *Town & Country*, Countess Jacqueline de Ribes is quoted as saying: "In France, honoring religion and tradition and family is still, after all, the responsibility of the aristocracy." Despite the current crisis in the French church and the almost invisible French aristocracy, the statement constitutes a remarkable reapparition of the close ties binding church and nobility that came under attack at the end of the eighteenth century.

7 A. Cabantous, "La Fin des patriarches," *Histoire des pères*, ed. Delumeau and Roche, 323. Cities had numerous unattached males, and as Richard D.E. Burton explains in his excellent book, *The Flaneur and His City: Patterns of Daily Life in Paris 1815–1851* (Durham: U of Durham P, 1994) 16–22, the marked increase in numbers of cafés and restaurants can be directly tied to this phenomenon. Unlike eighteenth-century salons, cafés were "predominantly, even exclusively, male institutions" that attracted both married and unmarried men.

8 See, e.g., Joan Hinde Stewart, *Gynographs: French Novelists by Women of the Late Eighteenth Century* (Lincoln: U of Nebraska P, 1993) 1–3; Georges May, *Le Dilemme du roman au XVIIIᵉ siècle: Etude sur les rapports du roman et de la critique (1715–1761)* (New Haven: Yale UP, 1963) esp. 204–46; Jouy, *Chaussée d'Antin* 1.78–86; Christine Planté, *La Petite Sœur de Balzac* (Paris: Seuil, 1989).

9 See Susan Dunn, *The Deaths of Louis XVI: Regicide and the French Political Imagination* (Princeton: Princeton UP, 1994) 70; the entire development is of considerable interest, 67–92.

10 See, e.g., Lynn Hunt, *The Family Romance of the French Revolution* (Berkeley: U of California P, 1992); J.-C. Bonnet, "La Malédiction Paternelle," *Dix-Huitième*

Siècle 12 (1980): 195–208; Joan B. Landes, "Representing the Body Politic: The Paradox of Gender in the Graphic Politics of the French Revolution," *Rebel Daughters: Women and the French Revolution*, ed. Sara E. Melzer and Leslie W. Rabine (New York: Oxford, 1992) 15.

11 Marcel David, *Fraternité et Révolution française* (Paris: Aubier, 1987) 276.

12 M. Sonnet, "Les Leçons paternelles," *Histoire des pères*, ed. Delumeau and Roche, 264–65; Cabantous, 323–25; Hunt, *Family Romance*, 22, 40. See also the documentation concerning orphans in my preceding chapter. Most often, as I say, the father is simply not there. Stephen's childhood passed, for example, far from his father (*Sous les tilleuls* [1832] 60). Saint-Estève draws more universal conclusions: "There are no fathers in nature . . . there are only mothers. Fathers are a social fiction" (Pannier, *L'Athée* [1836] 1.21).

13 The serious effects of inadequate parenting are clear. See, e.g., Michele D. Wilson and Alain Joffe, "Adolescent Medicine," *Journal of the American Medical Association* 7 (June 1995): 1656–59; Deborah A. Cohen, Jean Richardson, Laurie LaBree, "Parenting Behaviors and the Onset of Smoking and Alcohol Use: A Longitudinal Study," *Pediatrics* 94.3 (September 1994): 368–75; Stephen Nagy, Anthony G. Adcock, and M. Christine Nagy, "A Comparison of Risky Health Behaviors of Sexually Active, Sexually Abused, and Abstaining Adolescents," *Pediatrics* 93.4 (April 1994): 570–75.

14 Norberg, " 'Love and Patriotism': Gender and Politics in the Life and Work of Louvet de Couvray," *Rebel Daughters*, ed. Melzer and Rabine, 47–48.

15 David Blankenhorn, *Fatherless America: Confronting Our Most Urgent Social Problem* (New York: Basic Books, 1994) 9–48.

16 Alexandre Parent-Duchâtelet had heard an estimate of 60,000—*De la prostitution dans la ville de Paris*, 3d ed., 2 vols. (1836; Paris: Baillière, 1857) 1.29. Although Parent-Duchâtelet recognized that the figure was too high, the figure of officially registered prostitutes was undoubtedly too low— in 1830 there were, depending on the month, between 2965 and 3084 registered prostitutes. It was the unknown number of *insoumises* or unregistered practitioners that made the figures unreliable. He quotes a M. Boucher with the suggestion that before the Revolution there were probably between 15,000 and 30,000 prostitutes in Paris (1.28). Police computations varied: in 1762 the official estimate was 25,000, in 1810 perhaps as high as 18,000, in 1825 over 15,000, and various pamphlets estimated the number at 20,000 for 1830 after the July Revolution (1.27–29). C. J. Lecour comments on these figures some years later, and suggests that "the figures vary depending on the evaluator's point of view"—*La Prostitution à Paris et à Londres, 1789–1870* (Paris: Asselin, 1870) 119. As for him, he would say, primarily on the basis of the numbers of unregistered prostitutes arrested annually, that the actual figure is in the neighborhood of 30,000 year in and year out (119–20).

17 Perrot, "The Family Triumphant," *From the Fires of Revolution to the Great War*, ed. Michelle Perrot, tr. Arthur Goldhammer, vol. 4 of *A History of Private Life*, (Cambridge: Harvard UP, 1990) 98–165; the quotation is from p. 100.

18 3.130. See my discussion of paternity in *Le Père Goriot: Balzacian Montage: Configuring* La Comédie humaine (Toronto: U of Toronto P, 1991) 22–35.

19 Mulliez, 283. See also, particularly in respect to the rights of women, Jean-François Tetu, "Remarques sur le statut juridique de la femme au XIXe siècle," *La Femme au XIXe siècle: Littérature et idéologie,* ed. R. Bellet (Lyon: PU de Lyon, 1979), 5–17. The civil influence on marriage began in the sixteenth century, to a significant degree because of the Reform: André Armengaud, *La Famille et l'enfant en France et en Angleterre du XVIe au XVIIIe siècle: Aspects démographiques* (Paris: Société d'Edition d'Enseignement Supérieur, 1975) 24–25.

20 Merrick, *The Desacralization of the French Monarchy in the Eighteenth Century* (Baton Rouge: Louisiana State UP, 1990) 132.

21 Merrick, "Patriarchalism and Constitutionalism in Eighteenth-Century Parlementary Discourse," *Studies in Eighteenth-Century Culture* 20 (1990): 318–25; Gail Bossenga, *The Politics of Privilege: Old Regime and Revolution in Lille* (Cambridge: Cambridge UP, 1991) 201–5.

22 Olwen Hufton, "The Reconstruction of a Church 1796–1801," *Beyond the Terror: Essays in French Regional and Social History, 1794–1815,* ed. Gwynne Lewis and Colin Lucas (Cambridge: Cambridge UP, 1983) 21–52. The quotation is from p. 21. For a sense of the way the church was increasingly viewed, the commentary of the eighteenth-century artisan Jacques-Louis Ménétra is also instructive: *Journal of My Life,* ed. Daniel Roche, tr. Arthur Goldhammer (New York: Columbia UP, 1986). Roche's commentary on Ménétra's religion is useful (338–58).

23 *Desacralization,* 43. See also Armengaud, *Famille,* 68.

24 See my discussion of this work in *Balzacian Montage* (Toronto: U of Toronto P, 1991) 83–88.

25 Antoine de Baecque, "The 'Livres remplis d'horreur': Pornographic Literature and Politics at the Beginning of the French Revolution," *Erotica and the Enlightenment,* ed. Peter Wagner (Frankfurt am Main: Peter Lang, 1991) 130–31. For further consideration of this material, see also his "Pamphlets: Libel and Political Mythology," *Revolution in Print: The Press in France, 1775–1800,* ed. Robert Darnton and Daniel Roche (Berkeley: U of California P, 1989) 165–76; Lynn Hunt, "The Many Bodies of Marie Antoinette: The Problem of the Feminine in the French Revolution," *Eroticism and the Body Politic* (Baltimore: Johns Hopkins UP, 1991) 108–30; and her edition, *The Invention of Pornography: Obscenity and the Origins of Modernity, 1500–1800* (New York: Zoine Books, 1993); Robert Darnton, *The Literary Underground of the Old Régime* (Cambridge: Harvard UP, 1982) 1–40; and Darnton's *The Forbidden Best-Sellers of Pre-Revolutionary France* (New York: W. W. Norton, 1995); Jacques Revel, "Marie-Antoinette in Her Fictions: The Staging of Hatred," *Fictions of the French Revolution,* ed. Bernadette Fort (Evanston: Northwestern UP, 1991) 111–29; Chantal Thomas, *La Reine scélérate: Marie-Antoinette dans les pamphlets.* (Paris: Seuil, 1989); Peter Wagner, "Anticatholic Erotica in Eighteenth-Century England," *Erotica and the Enlightenment,* ed. Peter Wagner (Frankfurt am Main: Peter Lang, 1991)

166–209; and Wagner, *Eros Revived: Erotica of the Enlightenment in England and America* (London: Secker & Warburg, 1988). For a brief history of slanderous publications attacking powerful individuals, with a particularly interesting segment on the *mazarinades*, see, Darnton, *Forbidden Best-Sellers,* 198–206.

26 Quoted by Merrick, *Desacralization,* 36–37. Chantal Thomas mentions that Talleyrand's library included one hundred and five of these pamphlets— *La Reine scélérate,* 73–74. As Robert Darnton puts it after considering *Anecdotes sur Mme la comtesse du Berry* of 1775, such publications convey a clear message, "The French could no more see their king as a father than as a god. He had lost the last shreds of his legitimacy"—*Forbidden Best-Sellers* 166.

27 Darnton, *Literary Underground,* 21–40, 199–208. See also Antoine de Baecque, "Pamphlets: Libel and Political Mythology," *Revolution in Print,* ed. Darnton and Roche, 165–76.

28 Angus Martin, Vivienne G. Mylne, Richard Frautschi, *Bibliographie du genre romanesque français: 1751–1800* (London: Mansell, 1977) 261, item no. 83.47.

29 Restif de La Bretonne, *Les Contemporaines,* 3 vols. (Paris: Les Yeux ouverts, 1962) 3.5.

30 See, e.g., Claude Tillier's *Mon oncle Benjamin* (1843) 37–40, 264.

31 Edward Sullivan, "The Novelist's Undeclared Assumptions: Balzac and Stendhal," *Laurels* 54.1 (Spring 1983): 49.

32 Enrico de' Negri, "The Legendary Style of the *Decameron,*" *Romanic Review* 43 (1952): 166–89.

33 Michelet, *L'Amour* (1858), *Œuvres complètes,* vol. 18 (Paris: Flammarion, 1985) 47; for a similar statement, see 170.

34 Claverie, "Thérèse Raquin ou les Atrides dans la boutique du Pont-Neuf," *Cahiers Naturalistes* 36 (1968): 147.

35 Richard B. Grant, "The Rise and Fall of Romantic Sainthood: Chateaubriand to George Sand," paper presented at the Colloquium in Nineteenth-Century French Studies, October 12, 1990.

36 Jonathan P. Ribner, *Broken Tablets: The Cult of the Law in French Art from David to Delacroix* (Berkeley: U of California P, 1993) 41, fig. 24. Of course, this medallion is exceptional only in its obviousness. While more subtle, the taste of Ingres's *Napoleon enthroned* is no less questionable. As Claude Keisch explains in Walter Markov's *Grand Empire: Virtue and Vice in the Napoleonic Era* (New York: Hippocrene Books, 1990) 42, "This most solemn of all the representations of the emperor alludes to older paintings of God and Christ sitting in judgement upon the world."

37 Peyre, *What Is Romanticism?* tr. Roda Roberts (University: U of Alabama P, 1977) 73–75.

38 Barrès, *Les Déracinés,* 2 vols. (1897; rpt. Paris: Plon, 1922) 2.188. Similar cries were heard much earlier. Sophie Pannier's Saint-Estève says, for example, "Today all social reality is in contradition with its own maximes. . . . Society then needs a morality that is in harmony with its standards of behavior" (*L'Athée* [1836] 1.19).

39 Edgar Quinet, *La Révolution*, 3 vols. (1865; Paris: Germer-Baillière, 1877–79) 2.153. Quoted by Dunn, *Deaths*, 167.

40 Glyn Holmes' long consideration of Romantic ideals gives many examples, several of which I have used: *The "Adolphe Type" in French Fiction in the First Half of the Nineteenth Century*. (Sherbrooke, Quebec: Naaman, 1977) 159–98.

41 Although Susan Dunn is correct to maintain that Balzac opposed the death penalty (*Deaths*, 110–11), for example, it is important to realize that her textual support comes from "Souvenirs d'un paria," a work published in 1830, and that Balzac became increasingly conservative, and sanguinary, through the rest of his career.

42 Gutwirth, "The Engulfed Beloved: Representations of Dead and Dying Women in the Art and Literature of the Revolutionary Era," *Rebel Daughters*, ed. Melzer and Rabine, 198–227.

43 Brooks, *The Melodramatic Imagination: Balzac, Henry James, Melodrama, and the Mode of Excess* (New Haven: Yale UP, 1976) 24–55.

44 Constant, "Préface," *Mélanges de littérature et de politique, Œuvres*, ed. Alfred Roulin, Bibliothèque de la Pléiade (Paris: Gallimard, 1957) 801; quoted by Margaret Waller, *The Male Malady: Fictions of Impotence in the French Romantic Novel* (New Brunswick: Rutgers UP, 1993) 93.

45 Coleridge, *Biographical Literaria, or Biographical Sketches of My Literary Life and Opinions* (1817; London: J. M. Dent, 1975) 154.

46 Furst, *The Contours of European Romanticism* (London: Macmillan, 1979) 42–43.

47 Saint-Amand, *The Libertine's Progress: Seduction in the Eighteenth-Century French Novel*, rev. ed., tr. Jennifer Curtiss Gage (Hanover: Brown/U Press of New England, 1994) 114–15.

CHAPTER 4: THE UNHEROIC MODE

1 Lioure, *Le Drame*. (Paris: Armand Colin, 1963) 8.

2 Madelénat, *L'Epopée* (Paris: P.U.F., 1986) 18. For a brief but remarkable overview of the epic as a historical genre, see, Van Kelly, "Criteria for the Epic: Borders, Diversity, and Expansion," *Epic and Epoch: Essays on the Interpretation and History of a Genre*, ed. Steven M. Oberhelman, Van Kelly, and Richard J. Golsan (Lubbock: Texas Tech UP, 1994) 1–21.

3 Steiner, *The Death of Tragedy* (New York: Alfred A. Knopf, 1961) 247.

4 Durand, "*Lucien Leuwen* ou l'héroïsme à l'envers," *Stendhal Club* 3 (15 avril 1959): 203.

5 Jean-François Marmontel, "Epopée," *Eléments de littérature* (1787), *Œuvres complètes de Marmontel*, 14 vols. (Paris: Verdière, 1818–20) 13.347.

6 György Lukács, *The Theory of the Novel,* tr. Anna Bostyock (Cambridge: M.I.T. Press, 1971) 88.

7 Honig, *Dark Conceit: The Making of Allegory* (1959; Cambridge: Walker de Berry, 1960) 181.

8 Maxime du Camp was one of very few exceptions. In his preface to the *Chants modernes* (1855), he asks, "Where are the writers? . . . Science does wonders, industry accomplishes miracles, and we remain impassive. They discover steam, we sing about Venus, . . . they discover electricity, we sing of Bacchus, ... It is absurd!"—Claude Pichois, *Littérature et progrès: Vitesse et vision du monde, essai* (Neuchâtel: La Baconnière, 1973) 39. In fact, Pichois points out, it was du Camp's verses that were absurd. Flaubert dismissed them as a "a bunch of rather dishonorable twaddle" (ibid., 40). Still, du Camp was at least partially correct. Few poets were attracted to modernity.

9 Pichois's discussion of the chronological progression in images of machines, moving from a sense of progress to the one of despair, is very instructive. See esp., *Littérature et progrès*, chs. iii and v.

10 Raymond Giraud, *The Unheroic Hero in the Novels of Stendhal, Balzac and Flaubert* (New Brunswick, NJ: Rutgers UP, 1957) 85. Giraud's comments are intended for the Stendhalian hero in general, though they grow specifically from *Lucien Leuwen,* a novel which has considerable relevance to my discussion. Gilbert Durand is probably correct to suggest that readers have not appreciated *Lucien Leuwen* because the hero is so decidedly unheroic—*"Lucien Leuwen* ou l'Héroïsme à l'envers," *Stendhal Club* 3 (15 avril 1959): 201–25—though, as Robert J. Niess has shown, people of the day no longer believed that a true leader/hero was possible—"Sainte-Beuve and Balzac: *Volupté* and *Le Lys dans la vallée*," *Kentucky Romance Quarterly* 1 (1973): 113–24.

11 Honoré de Balzac, "Etudes sur M. Beyle (Frédéric Stendalh [*sic*]" (1840), rpt. *La Critique stendhalienne de Balzac à Zola: Textes choisis et présentés,* ed. Emile Talbot (York, SC: French Literature Publications, 1979) 64. Louis Kronenberger takes a similar position in "Stendhal's *Charterhouse*," *Encounter* 27 (July 1966): 32–38.

12 Emile Zola, "Stendhal" (1880), rpt. Talbot's *Critique stendhalienne,* 264. Pierre-Louis Rey wonders whether it might be a "thrown together novel"—La Chartreuse de Parme: *Stendhal. Analyse critique* (Paris: Hatier, 1973) 24.

13 Caro, "Stendhal: Ses Romans" (1855), *Etudes morales sur le temps présent,* rpt. Talbot's *Critique,* 191. A. Lytton Sells takes a similar position in *"La Chartreuse de Parme*: The Problem of Style," *Modern Language Quarterly* 11 (1950): 486–91, and in his subsequent *"La Chartreuse de Parme*: The Problem of Composition," *Modern Language Quarterly* 12 (1951): 204–15.

14 Most recently, see my *Novel Configurations: A Study of French Fiction,* 2nd ed. (Birmingham: Summa, 1994) 27–50, but the position is not uncommon. Maurice Bardèche says, for example: *"[L]a Chartreuse* is not *a drama,* as Balzac thought every novel should be, it is *a life.* It is admirable as *life* but not as *drama.* And the novel's unity is a unity of *character,* so to speak, and not a *unity of action"—Stendhal romancier* (Paris: La Table Ronde, 1947) 417.

15 Stendhal, "La Réponse de Stendhal: Second Brouillon" (17–28 octobre 1840), *La Chartreuse de Parme*, ed. Victor Del Litto and Ernest Abravanel, 2 vols. (Geneva: Cercle du Bibliophile, 1969) 524–27.

16 For references to participants in the continuing controversies, see Sells' "Problem of Composition," 205–8; Hans B. Johansen, "Notes sur la structure de *la Chartreuse de Parme*," *Actes du 4ᵉ Congrès des Romanistes Scandinaves. Revue Romane*, Numéro Spécial 1 (1967): 196. Elsewhere, the latter argues explicitly that Fabrice constitutes the novel's "spine" and that he begins life looking for satisfaction in the external world, only to "end by finding happiness in an inner life. This passage from external life to inner life is the general direction of his destiny"—*Stendhal et le roman: Essai sur la structure du roman stendhalien* (Aran: Grand Chêne, 1979) 44. F. W. J. Hemmings, after citing the various, conflicting themes which have been indicated as the subject of the novel, suggests that the book's artistic unity is to be found in the "passage from dream to reality" (227). "[It] is made of *contrast* and *balance*" (230)—"L'Unité artistique de *La Chartreuse de Parme*," *Communications présentées au Congrès Stendhalien de Civitavecchia* [1964], ed. V. Del Litto, Publications de l'Institut Français de Florence, 1ᵉʳᵉ série—Collection d'études d'histoire, de critique et de philologie—no. 16 (Firenze: Sansoni Antiquariato, 1966) 224–31.

17 C.A. Sainte-Beuve, "M. de Stendhal: Ses Œuvres complètes" (2 janvier 1854), *Causeries du Lundi*, rpt. Talbot's *Critique*, 166.

18 Faguet, "Stendhal" (1892), *Politiques et moralistes du dix-neuvième siècle*, 3ᵉ série (Paris: Société Française d'Imprimerie et de Librairie, 1899) 56.

19 Finch, *Stendhal*: La Chartreuse de Parme (London: Edward Arnold, 1984) 21. Hemmings argues that Fabrice is detached, a spectator rather than an actor— *Stendhal: A Study of His Novels* (Oxford: Oxford UP, 1964) 184–86. Roger Pearson points out analogously, "[T]here is little analysis of the central hero Fabrice: he seems merely to act, indeed often only to re-act, and the elements of development, or education, may appear to be minimal. Also one may wonder if he is in fact to be regarded as the central character"—*Stendhal's Violin* (Oxford: Clarendon P, 1988) 206. And as René Servoise says, Stendhal occasionally becomes so involved with telling Gina's story that he seemingly forgets Fabrice—"Les Arcanes de *La Chartreuse de Parme*," *Nouvelle Revue des Deux Mondes* November 1981: 354. Michel Guérin, recognizing the problem, argues that it is both "Fabrice's novel," "the story of the duchess" and neither; rather, "the hero of *La Chartreuse de Parme* is *La Chartreuse de Parme*!"—*La Politique de Stendhal* (Paris: P. U. F., 1982) 177–78.

20 Pierre Barbéris, *Sur Stendhal* (Paris: Editions sociales/Messidor, 1982) 168.

21 Ricardou, "Discussion," after Nathalie Sarraute's "Ce que je cherche à faire," *Nouveau roman: Hier, aujourd'hui*, ed. Jean Ricardou and Françoise van Rossom-Guyon, 2 vols. (Paris: 10/18, 1972) 2.43.

22 319, 347, 350, 357, 391. For a consideration of Clélia's wrenching experience, see, Philippe Berthier, *Stendhal et la sainte famille* (Geneva: Droz, 1983) 12–13.

23 Ginette Ferrier, "Sur un personnage de *La Chartreuse de Parme*: Le Comte Mosca," *Stendhal Club* 13 (1971): 29.

24 Leo Weinstein, "Stendhal's Count Mosca as a Statesman," *PMLA* 80 (1965): 210–16. If Weinstein is correct, Stendhal may have chosen Mosca's name, which means "fly" in Italian, to remind readers of the fly's pretentious but ineffective activity in La Fontaine's "Le Coche et la mouche." Gina's use of "Le Jardinier et son seigneur" (425) may be enough to bring the fabulist's oeuvre to the reader's mind. Geoffrey Strickland associates the fly with "ruse"—*Stendhal: The Education of a Novelist* (Cambridge: Cambridge UP, 1974) 240—though C.W. Thompson remembers the Stendhal's aversion to these insects—*Le Jeu de l'ordre et de la liberté dans* La Chartreuse de Parme (Aran: Grand-Chêne, 1982) 142. For a view of a more successful Mosca, see, e.g., Ann Jefferson, "Représentation de la politique, politique de la représentation: *La Chartreuse de Parme*," *Stendhal Club* 27.107 (1985): 200–13. Pierre B. Daprini has I think a more satisfying conception of Mosca, not so much as a success or failure, but rather as a function motivated by usefulness and enlightened self-interest—"Le Moraliste sans foi ou la structure anthropologique de *La Chartreuse de Parme*," *Stendhal Club* 25.98 (1983): 283–96. It is also possible that Mosca's many failures are more suitably synthesized in Guérin's conclusion: Mosca "ironically manifests the insufficiencies of politics"—*Politique*, 230.

25 For the purposes of this study, I accept the argument that the novel turns around Fabrice and his destined end as a Carthusian on his way to eternal joy, a position which can be traced through the following critics: Victor Brombert points out that Stendhal's prison functions principally to encourage self-discovery—*Stendhal: Fiction and the Themes of Freedom* (Chicago: U of Chicago P, 1968) 173. In this regard, see, as well, François Landry, *L'Imagination chez Stendhal* (Lausanne: L'Age d'Homme, 1982), 236. H.W. Wardman argues that Fabrice "is fitted only for the contemplative life"—"*La Chartreuse de Parme*: Ironical Ambiguity," *Kenyon Review* 17 (1955): 463. The images of withdrawal, silence, and renunciation mentioned by Finch (18) deserve more development. I have gone on to conclude, "Fabrice, like Petrarch, has the encouraging hope of eternal life with his beloved"—*Novel Configurations: A Study of French Fiction*, 2nd ed. (Birmingham: Summa, 1994) 45.

26 "Fabrice is almost passive. Diverse things happen to him. It is not what happens to someone that is interesting, it is what he does"—Faguet, 56.

27 François Michel, *Etudes stendhaliennes*, 2nd ed. (Paris: Mercure de France, 1972) 58. Guérin argues that the text means to leave the question of Fabrice's legitimacy somewhat vague—*Politique*, 186–88.

28 Emile Talbot, *Stendhal and Romantic Esthetics* (Lexington, KY: French Forum, 1985) 9.

29 Henry James, "The Art of Fiction," *The Art of Fiction and other Essays*, ed. Morris Roberts (New York: Oxford Univ. Press, 1948) 13.

30 Mary Doyle Springer, *A Rhetoric of Literary Character: Some Women of Henry James* (Chicago: Univ. of Chicago Press, 1978), 14 and *passim*. Vladimir Propp's seminal study of narrative functions in Russian folk tales is also solidly in the Aristotelian tradition, as is Claude Bremond's *Logique du récit*

(Paris: Seuil, 1973). Likewise for Mary McCarthy's very interesting redefinition of characters as "human vectors with acceleration and force"— "Characters in Fiction," ed. Shiv K. Kumar and Keith McKean, *Critical Approaches to Fiction* (New York: McGraw-Hill, 1968) 80. We have, says Walter Allen, "the strong sense . . . that in some mysterious way it should be possible, in imagination, to walk around [a novel's character] and inspect from every angle, as though he were a person in life"—"Narrative Distance, Tone, and Character," *Theory of the Novel*, ed. Halperin, 328. Though Kenneth Burke is by no means limiting himself to physical perspectives, his point of view is similar when he says, "[I]t is by the approach through a variety of perspectives that we establish a character's reality"—*A Grammar of Motives* (New York: Prentice-Hall, 1945) 504. An excellent defense of regarding characters as "semblances" appears in Seymour Chatman's *Story and Discourse: Narrative Structure in Fiction and Film* (Ithaca: Cornell UP, 1978) 134–38.

31 The point of view is attributed to Bernard Seuffert's "Beobachtungen über dicterische Komposition" (1909) by Lubomir Dolezel, "Narrative Composition: A Link Between German and Russian Poetics," *Russian Formalism*, ed. S. Bann and J. E. Bowlt (New York: Barnes & Nobel, 1973) 77.

32 Chatman's essay shrewdly builds on other theorists (e.g., Barthes, Todorov, Bradley) to make a significant contribution—*Story and Discourse*, esp. 107–38. Earlier versions are worth consulting as well, since Chatman did not integrate all elements of his thought into the book. See, e.g., his discussion of "function": "The Structure of Fiction," *University Review* 37 (Spring 1971): 209–10, n22.

33 Albert Sonnenfeld, "Ruminations on Stendhal's Epigraphs," *Pre-Text, Text, Context: Essays on Nineteenth-Century French Literature*, ed. Robert L. Mitchell (Columbus: Ohio State UP, 1980) 109.

34 There are, of course, other variations. Wendelin Guenthner reminded me of Lucien Leuwen, for example, who "heroically" pursues bourgeois goals and who, on failing, seems doubly ridiculous—see, in this regard, Durand's previously cited article on *Lucien Leuwen* (n. 4) and K. G. McWatters, "Lucien Leuwen et l'armée impossible," *Le Plus Méconnu des romans de Stendhal: Lucien Leuwen*. Paris; SEDES, 1983) 141–53.

35 C.W. Thompson puts it more positively: "Fabrice habitually follows the easy path"—*Jeu de l'ordre*, 174.

36 Lucien Goldmann, *Pour une sociologie du roman* (Paris: Gallimard, 1964) 32–37.

37 Quoted from A. Alvarez, *The Savage God: A Study of Suicide* (1971; New York: Norton, 1990) 261.

38 See, e.g., Maurice A. Lecuyer, *Balzac et Rabelais* (Paris: Les Belles Lettres, 1956); Maurice Serval, "Autour d'un roman de Balzac: *Le Lys dans la vallée*," *Revue d'Histoire Littéraire* 33 (1926): 370–89, 565–94; Nancy K. Miller, "Tristes Triangles: *Le lys dans la vallée* and Its Intertext," *Pre-text/Text/Context: Essays on Nineteenth-Century French Literature*, ed. Robert L. Mitchell

(Columbus, Ohio State Univ. Press, 1980), 67–77; Raymond Lebègue, "De Marguerite de Navarre à Honoré de Balzac," *Comptes rendus de l'Académie des Inscriptions et Belles-Lettres* July 1957: 251–56.

39 René Bray, *La Formation de la doctrine classique en France* (Lausanne: Payot, 1931) 352–53. As Van Kelly suggested to me, Renaissance writers may well have learned this kind of structure from Ovid's *Metamorphoses*.

40 J.D. Hubert, *Essai d'exégèse racinienne: Les Secrets témoins* (Paris: Nizet, 1956); David Lee Rubin, *Higher, Hidden Order: Design and Meaning in the Odes of Malherbe* (Chapel Hill: U of NC P, 1972); *The Knot of Artifice: A Poetic of the French Lyric in the Early 17th Century* (Columbus: Ohio State UP, 1981; *A Pact with Silence: Art and Thought in La Fontaine's* Fables (Columbus: Ohio State UP, 1991).

41 Albert-Marie Schmidt, "Préface," *Sur Catherine de Médicis* by Balzac, vol. 11 of *L'Œuvre de Balzac* (Paris: Club Français du Livre, 1955) 9. For a similar and equally unsupported statement, see Albert Prioult, *Balzac avant* La Comédie humaine: *Contribution à l'étude de la genèse de son œuvre* (Paris: G. Gourville, 1936) 290.

42 Claudie Bernard, "Balzac et le roman historique: *Sur Catherine de Médicis*: une Histoire paradoxale," *Poétique* 71 (1987): 335; see also Peter G. Christensen: "Balzac is not able to achieve a unified narrative, only a four-part hybrid"—"Yeats and Balzac's *Sur Catherine de Médicis*," *Modern Language Studies* 19.4 (1989): 112.

43 Nicole Cazauran, *Catherine de Médicis et son temps dans* La Comédie humaine (Geneva: Droz, 1976) 484. Elsewhere, she terms the novel a collection of "disparate stories" (357).

44 See, e.g., Albert J. George, "Théophile Gautier and the Romantic Short Story," *L'Esprit Créateur* 3 (1963): 110–17.

CHAPTER 5: INCEST IN THE MIRROR

1 Paul Toinet, Paul et Virginie, *répertoire bibliographique et iconographique* (Paris: Maisonneuve et Larose, 1963); Angus Martin, Vivienne G. Mylne, Richard Frautschi, *Bibliographie du genre romanesque français: 1751–1800* (London: Mansell, 1977) 88.101.

2 Racault suggests that Virginie's bath "marks the rupture of paradisiacal harmony"—"Système de la toponymie et organisation de l'espace romanesque dans *Paul et Virginie*," *Studies on Voltaire and the Eighteenth Century*, no. 242 (Oxford: Voltaire Foundation, 1986) 392.

3 Readers generally explain her refusal to disrobe as ill-placed modesty learned in "civilized" France. Jean Fabre points to a plausible analogy in comparing Virginie to Eve. Virginie has experienced the "sacrilegious world. . . . and her

last movement of modesty recreates the first gesture of Eve when she saw she was nude and understood that Paradise was lost"—*Lumières et romantisme: Energie et nostalgie de Rousseau à Mickiewicz* (Paris: Klincksieck, 1963) 188.

4   The Romantic fascination with dead bodies that frequently verges on necrophilia punctuates the literature, with notable examples in *Atala* and *Le Rouge et le noir*. See, Doris Kadish's analysis of Girodet's *Atala au tombeau* in, *Politicizing Gender: Narrative Strategies in the Aftermath of the French Revolution* (New Brunswick: Rutgers UP, 1991) 81–88.

5   Philip Robinson, *Bernardin de Saint-Pierre*: Paul et Virginie, Critical Guides to French Texts (London: Grant & Cutler, 1986) 60–74. Robert Mauzi— "Préface," *Paul et Virginie*, by Bernardin de Saint-Pierre (Paris: Garnier-Flammarion, 1966) 21–22—and, later, Robinson, have also suggested quadrapartite structures. Joyce O. Lowrie's suggestion of a "tri-partite structure of Paradise, Fall, and Alienation or Death"—"The Structural Significance of Sensual Imagery in *Paul et Virginie*," *Romance Notes* 12 (1971): 351—strikes me as less functional on the structural level than on the semantic.

6   Malcolm C. Cook, "Harmony and Discord in *Paul et Virginie*," *Eighteenth-Century Fiction* 3.3 (April 1991): 212; James W. Brown, "The Ideological and Aesthetic Functions of Food in *Paul et Virginie*," *Eighteenth-Century Life* 4.3 (1978): 61–67.

7   E.g., Mauzi, "Préface," 12; Francis, 54–60; Bernard Bray, "*Paul et Virginie*, Un Texte variable à usages didactiques divers," *Revue d'Histoire Littéraire de la France* 89.5 (1989): 856–78; Alain Billault, "Les Amants dans l'île: Longus, Bernardin de Saint-Pierre, Mishima," *Bulletin de l'Association Guillaume Budé* 1 (1985): 80–81; Edouard Guitton, ed., "Introduction," *Paul et Virginie*, by Bernardin de Saint-Pierre (Paris: Imprimerie Nationale, 1984) 40. The other major problem has been generic, since Bernardin clearly exploited the traits of the neighboring genres of pastoral, idyll, and moral tale. Jean Fabre, responded to the controversy with a learned essay that primarily considers the pastoral—Bernardin repeatedly called his work a pastoral (see Fabre, 185–86)—and concludes: "[F]or us, *Paul et Virginie* is a novel" (176). See also Robinson, 30–32.

8   Several critics have considered the novel's relationship to the extensive utopic literature of the century, in particular the reasons for the failure of utopias. R.A. Francis points out that such Arcadias based on innocence (in contrast to utopias which he believes to be based on conscious choice) cannot continue in the face of such internal change as growing up, since "they leave childhood innocence behind them"—"Bernardin de Saint-Pierre's *Paul et Virginie* and the Failure of the Ideal State in the Eighteenth-Century French Novel," *Nottingham French Studies* 13.2 (1974): 56, 58. The second, destructive force is "external pressure from a corrupt or hostile society," the third from the forces of nature or accident, and, finally, the simple passage of time and mortality (58). Behind these sums of destruction is the fact that ideal states are by definition static, and when described in a novel which is dynamic, they cannot prevail (Francis, 57). Jean-Michel Racault offers refinements on this understanding of destructive elements—"*Paul et Virginie* et l'utopie de la

'petite société' au mythe collectif," *Studies on Voltaire and the Eighteenth Century*, no. 242 (Oxford: Voltaire Foundation, 1986): 252–59.

9 Dunkley, "*Paul et Virginie*: Aesthetic Appeal and Archetypal Structures," *Trivium* 13 (1978): 99–100, his discussion of the problem continues through p. 102. For other briefer mentions of the incest theme, see, e.g., Racault, "Virginie entre la nature et la vertu: Cohésion narrative et contradictions idéologiques dans *Paul et Virginie*," *Dix-Huitième Siècle* 18 (1986): 397; Carolyn A. Durham, "Fearful Symmetry: The Mother–Daughter Theme in *La Religieuse* and *Paul et Virginie*," *Fearful Symmetry: Doubles and Doubling in Literature and Film*, ed. Eugene J. Crook (Tallahassee, UP of Florida, 1981) 39; Guitton, "Introduction," 34–35.

10 Herbert Maisch, *Incest*, tr. Colin Bearne (1968; New York, Stein and Day, 1972) 86–90, the quotation is from p. 86. See also Mary de Young, *The Sexual Victimization of Children* (Jefferson, NC: McFarland, 1982) 1–5.

11 Jean Renvoizé, *Incest: A Family Pattern* (London: Routledge & Kegan Paul, 1982) 32.

12 Michelle Perrot says, "[C]ensorship of these matters was so powerful that the veil is only occasionally lifted"—"Roles and Characters," *From the Fires of Revolution to the Great War*, ed. Michelle Perrot, tr. Arthur Goldhammer, vol. 4 of *A History of Private Life* (Cambridge: Harvard UP, 1990) 222.

13 Henry Miles estimates that incest was the third most common fantasy of the Victorian pornographers—*Forbidden Fruit: A Study of the Incest Theme in Erotic Literature* (London: Luxor P, 1973) 6. For a brief listing of incest in 18th- and 19th-century English literature, see, Montague Summers, *The Gothic Quest: A History of the Gothic Novel* (London: Fortune P, 1938) 391–92. It was also an important part of the *Sturm und Drang* literature, and, of course, of Byron's and Shelley's writings.

14 Pierre Testud, *Rétif de La Bretonne et la création littéraire* (Geneva: Droz, 1977) 636–52.

15 Sade, 3.282. Sade repeats the gist of several of the statements cited below in his *Aline et Valcour* (1795, composed during his 1784–89 stay at the Bastille) 5.121–22.

16 Diderot, *Supplément au Voyage de Bougainville*, ed. P. Vernière, *Œuvres philosophiques* (Paris: Garnier, 1956) 496. According to Vernier, Diderot probably first drafted the text in 1772 and revised it sometime in 1778–79, though it was not published until after his death. As Georges Benrekassa explains, however, Diderot's position on incest varies widely: *Le Concentrique et l'excentrique: Marges des lumières* (Paris: Payot, 1980) 197–201. Charles Fourier goes somewhat further in his analysis of biblical incest. He concludes that God must have approved of the incestuous relations of Cain, Abel, and Seth, since He could have avoided the need by creating a second "first" couple. While recognizing that incest is no longer permitted, Fourier opens the possibility that at some future time, God may reintroduce the old statutes—*Théorie de l'unité universelle* (1822), *Œuvres complètes*, 2nd ed., 6 vols. (Paris: Société pour la Propagation et pour la Réalisation de la Théorie de Fourier, 1841–48) 4.81–84.

17 Michelle Perrot, "The Family Triumphant," *From the Fires of Revolution*, ed. Michelle Perrot 4.98–165.

18 Lise Queffélec, "Figuration de la violence dans le roman de l'avant à l'après 1789: Sade, Rétif, Dumas," *Revue d'Histoire Littéraire de la France* 90.34–5 (1990): 671–72.

19 Edward Shorter, "Différences de classe et sentiment depuis 1750: L'Exemple de la France," *Annales Economies Sociétés Civilisations* 29 (1974): 1041; André Armengaud, *La Famille et l'enfant en France et en Angleterre du XVIe au XVIIIe siècle: Aspects démographiques* (Paris: Société d'Edition d'Enseignement Supérieur, 1975) 17.

20 Lynn Hunt, "The Many Bodies of Marie Antoinette: Political Pornography and the Problem of the Feminine in the French Revolution," *Eroticism and the Body Politic*, ed. Lynn Hunt (Baltimore: Johns Hopkins UP, 1990) 123.

21 "Introduction," *Julie, ou La Nouvelle Héloïse*, 2.xviii.

22 Tony Tanner, *Adultery in the Novel: Contract and Transgression* (Baltimore: Johns Hopkins UP, 1979) 124. I follow Tanner's argument in regard to the incest motif in *Julie*. A similar scene occurs in Pigault-Lebrun's *Adélaïde de Méran* (1815) 19.153–54.

23 See, e.g., Lorna M. Anderson and Gretchen Shafer, "The Character-Disordered Family: A Community Treatment Model for Family Sexual Abuse," *American Journal of Orthopsychiatry* 49.3 (July 1979): 436–45. See also Renvoizé, *Incest*, 85–87. For additional studies of the characteristics of such offenders, which occasionally differ from those I cite in relation to M. d'Etanges, see Melodye L.F. Dabney, *Incest Annotated Bibliography: Offenders, Victims, Families, Treatment Programs (Strategies)* (Eugene, OR: Melodye L. F. Dabney, 1983) 1–13.

24 Blair Justice and Rita Justice, *The Broken Taboo: Sex in the Family* (New York: Human Sciences Press, 1979) 25. For a brief discussion of other definitions, see Mary de Young, 1–2.

25 The relevant page from a 1760 *Book of Common Prayer* is reproduced in Appendix A of Sandra Dianne Sandell, " 'A Very Poetic Circumstance': Incest and the English Literary Imagination 1770–1830," diss. U of Minnesota, 1981, 176. If Manfred had not already been married to Hippolita, his marriage to Isabella would not have been a crime in France, except insofar as he was coercing the girl to submit to his will.

26 The list is easily extended, for incest is suggested as well in Defoe's *Moll Flanders* (published 1721/translated 1761), Fielding's *Joseph Andrews* (1742/1743), Frances Burney's *Evelina* (1778/1784), Mackenzie's *The Man of the World* (1773/1775), and so on: see James B. Twitchell, *Forbidden Partners: The Incest Taboo in Modern Culture* (New York: Columbia UP, 1987) 162. Ellen Moers notes that childhood roughhousing of female authors of Gothic fantasies with their brothers "took on outsize proportions and powerful erotic overtones in their adult imaginations"—*Literary Women* (New York: Oxford UP, 1985) 105.

27 I think, for example, of Duclos's *Histoire de Madame de Luz* (1741), whose

many calamities would have doubtless been forestalled had she been allowed to marry the love of her life, M. de Saint-Geran, who "loved her almost from the time he was born" (31); of the many afflictions of Louis d'Erbeuil who loved and, with the required papal dispensation, married his cousin Julie (Lesuire, *Aventurier français* [1783]); of Ducray-Duminil's Victor who falls passionately in love with the daughter of the family that adopted him (*Victor* [1797]); of Ducray-Duminil's convoluted novel *Cœlina* whose title character adored, and eventually married, her cousin, Stephany, with whom she was raised (1799); of Henri who was brought up with and weds Thérèse's daughter (*Gil Blas de la Révolution* [1824]); of the title character of Estournelles's *Pascaline* (1821), who loves Albert de Surville, her childhood companion; of Brigaut who loves Pierrette, his "adopted, little sister" (*Pierrette* [1840] 4.98), although the narrator tells us, "It is extremely rare for passion between children of differing sex to persist" (4.98); and of La Louve whose story exemplifies life among the dregs of society: "Yes, there are lots of dens where children and adults, girls and boys, legitimate or bastards, bedded down on the same straw mattress like animals, . . . continually have before their eyes abominable examples of drunkenness, violence, debauchery, and murders... Yes, and too frequently even... INCEST!!! incest committed at the tenderest age comes to add one more horror to these horrors" (Sue, *Mystères* [1842–43] 2.279–80). La Louve was the mistress of her adopted mother's son and was eventually raped by this same woman's lover. I have, of course, already mentioned that Madame de Duras's novellas, *Ourika* and *Edouard,* both concern affinitative incest.

28 Lise Queffélec considers three of Dumas *père*'s novels where incest plays a significant role: *Les Mémoires d'un médecin* (1846–53), *Ingénue,* and *Création et Rédemption* (1872). She points out that for Dumas, incest was a figure for historical violence—"Figuration," 673–78.

29 The passage appears in the first published version: Alfred de Musset, *Théâtre complet,* Bibliothèque de la Pléiade (Paris: NRF, 1958) 1444. Similarly, Lamartine's priest, Jocelyn, refers to Laurence as his sister—*Jocelyn* (1836) 105, 106, 107, 134, 233—and to himself as both her father and mother (94, 102).

30 E.g., Karin C. Meiselman, *Incest: A Psychological Study of Causes and Effects with Treatment Recommendations* (San Francisco: Jossey-Bass, 1978) 298–99; M. de Young, 66; Maisch, 97.

31 *Une Année* [1787] e.g., 505–10. The humorously equivocal nature of this relationship is highlighted on several occasions, as for example when the Marquise de B*** tells him, falsely, that she is pregnant. "'Pregnant!' I repeated with a joyous cry. 'Pregnant; I am a father! . . . Mama! My dear mama! I have always loved you. You become even more dear than ever before'" (ibid., 664).

32 Richard B. Grant, "George Sand's *François le champi* and the Incest Motif," paper presented at the Colloquium in Nineteenth-Century French Studies held at the University of Nebraska on 23 October 1986. References to *François le champi* are to the Garnier edition mentioned above.

33 Meiselman, 75–79; Twitchell, *Forbidden Partners* 249; Robin Fox, *The Red Lamp of Incest: An Enquiry into the Origins of Mind and Society* (Notre Dame: U of Notre Dame P, 1983) 49–51, 162–63.

34 R.W. Leonhardt, quoted from Maisch, 20.

35 Barbey, *Diaboliques* (1874) 2.229; Charles Fourier, *Le Nouveau Monde industriel et sociétaire* (Paris: Bossange père, 1829) 284–86; *Théorie de l'unité universelle* (1822), *Œuvres complètes*, 2nd ed. 6 vols. (Paris: Société pour la Propagation et pour la Réalisation de la Théorie de Fourier, 1841–48) 4.103.

36 Jean-Claude Chesnais, *Histoire de la violence en Occident de 1800 à nos jours*, Collection Pluriel (Paris: Robert Laffont, 1981) 182–83. André-Michel Guerry's figures are higher than those of Chesnais that I cite farther on in this paragraph. He says that there were 130 cases of "rape and violations of decency against children [under fifteen]" brought to court yearly from 1825 to 1830 in France—*Essai sur la statistique morale de la France* (Paris: Crochard, 1833) 5.

37 Chesnais, 182–86. Earlier, Mercier tells of a doctor who assured him that he had been asked to cure the venereal disease of several little girls of three, four, five, and six years of age (*Tableau*, 2.1410).

38 Sandra Butler, *Conspiracy of Silence: The Trauma of Incest* (San Francisco: New Glide Publications, 1978) 65.

39 See, e.g., Jean Benward and Judianne Densen-Gerber, "Incest as a Causative Factor in Antisocial Behavior: An Exploratory Study," *Contemporary Drug Problems* 4.3 (Fall 1975): 323–40; and Vernon R. Wiehe, *Sibling Abuse: Hidden Physical, Emotional, and Sexual Trauma* (Lexington, MA: D. C. Heath, 1990) 109–33. For a useful bibliography concerned with the victims of incest, see Dabney, 14–47.

40 W.L. Marshall, "Pornography and Sex Offenders," *Pornography: Research Advances and Policy Considerations*, ed. D. Zillmann and J. Bryant (Hillsdale, NJ: Lawrence Erlbaum, 1989) 185–214, offers a survey of much relevant research. See, also, D. Carter, R. Prentky, R. Knight, P. Vanderveer, and R. Boucher, "Use of Pornography in the Criminal and Developmental Histories of Sexual Offenders," *Journal of Interpersonal Violence* 2 (1987): 196–211; M. Silbert and A. Pines, "Pornography and Sexual Abuse of Women," *Sex Roles* 10 (1984): 857–68; James V.P. Check and Ted H. Guloien, "Reported Proclivity for Coercive Sex Following Repeated Exposure to Sexually Violent Pornography, Nonviolent Dehumanizing Pornography, and Erotica," *Pornography: Research Advances*, 159–84; E. Donnerstein, "Pornography: Its Effect on Violence Against Women," *Pornography and Sexual Aggression*, ed. N. Malamuth and E. Donnerstein (New York: Academic Press, 1984) 53–81; D. Linz, E. Donnerstein, and S. Penrod, "The Effects of Multiple Exposures to Filmed Violence Against Women," *Journal of Communication* 34.3 (1984): 130–47.

41 Jean-Pierre Rémond, "Il n'y a d'amour qu'incestueux donc impossible," *Quinzaine Littéraire* 245 (1976): 7.

42 Lieve Spaas, "Catherine et Bernadin de Saint-Pierre: L'Œdipe adelphique,"

Eros Philadelphe: Colloque de Cerisy, ed. Wanda Bannour and Philippe Berthier (Paris: Félin, 1992) 85–104. See, also, her *Lettres de Catherine de Saint-Pierre à son frère Bernardin* (Paris: Harmattan, 1996).

43 As a counterbalance for the prevailing trend in pre-Romantic and Romantic work, I have found several suggestions that early co-socialization may not lead to amorous attraction. Benrekassa, for example, quotes a passage of 1783 by Diderot : "People raised together from childhood, accustomed to seeing each other without break, contract indifference which grows from habitual experience from this familiarity, rather than a keen feeling of sympathy that brings together two people who have never seen each other before"— *Concentrique*, 201. Crébillon *fils*, discusses a similar indifference in *Les Orphelins* (1754) 2.2, as does Estournelles in *Pascaline* (1821) 1.3, 13, and Sandeau in *Mademoiselle de La Seiglière* (1848) 86, 91, 93.

44 Robin Fox, *The Red Lamp of Incest: An Inquiry into the Origins of Mind and Society* (Notre Dame: U of Notre Dame P, 1983) 50; Edward Westermarck, *The History of Human Marriage* (New York: Macmillan, 1891; Havelock Ellis, *The Psychology of Sex: A Manual for Students*, 2nd ed. (New York: Emerson Books, 1964) 92–96; Melford E. Spiro, *Children of the Kibbutz* (Cambridge: Harvard UP, 1958); J.R. Fox, "Sibling Incest," *British Journal of Sociology* 13 (1962): 128–50; A.P. Wolf, "Adopt a Daughter-in-Law, Marry a Sister: A Chinese Solution to the Problem of the Incest Taboo," *American Anthropologist* 70 (1968): 864–74; Wolf, "Childhood Association and Sexual Attraction: A Further Test of the Westermarck Hypothesis," *American Anthropologist* 72 (1970): 503–15. This impressive body of work elicited a number of objections, primarily on the basis of methodology. Some suggested, however, that there would be no taboo if there were a natural aversion (e.g., Maisch, 45–46), which strikes me as unconvincing unless one takes "natural" for "genetic" which was not the meaning of any of the above work. There is also a natural aversion to matricide which is reflected in a taboo, for example. Society's apparent need for the taboo grows from the fact that mothers are occasionally murdered by their children, a practice that society explicitly discourages. More important objections have arisen when the conclusions growing from work on affinitative or consanguineous siblings was expanded to parent and child, as in the work of P.L. van den Berghe, "Human Inbreeding Avoidance: Culture in Nature," *Behavioral and Brain Sciences* 6 (1983): 91–123; and H. Parker and S. Parker, "Father–Daughter Sexual Abuse: An Emerging Perspective," *American Journal of Orthopsychiatry* 56 (1986): 531–49.

45 I summarize Talmon's and Shepher's work from Fox, *Red Lamp*, 47–48.

46 Boris Cyrulnik, "Le Sentiment incestueux," *De l'inceste*, ed. Françoise Heritier (Paris: Odile Jacob, 1994) 44–62; Linda M. Williams and David Finkelhor, "Parental Caregiving and Incest: Test of a Biosocial Model," *American Journal of Orthopsychiatry* 65.1 (1995): 101–13.

47 Chesnais, 183; Daniel Roche, "Nouveaux Parisiens au XVIIIe siècle," *Cahiers d'Histoire* 24.3 (1979): 3–20.

CHAPTER 6: DEATH WISH

1   Claude Book-Senninger, *Théophile Gautier: Auteur dramatique* (Paris: Nizet, 1972) 285.

2   Louis Maigron, *Le Romantisme et les mœurs* (1910; rpt. Geneva: Slatkine Reprints, 1977) 333.

3   The list could easily be lengthened in major and minor writers. When shamed by the girl he seduced, L.-D.-M.-E. threw himself into the river and drowned—Restif, "La Fille Séduite," *Contemporains* [1780]. After running her lover through with his sword, Clara Kingston drives the same sword into her own heart (Ducray-Duminil, *Lolotte et Fanfan* [1789] 1.251). Faublas's beloved Eléonore de Lignolle drowns herself in the Seine in *La Fin des amours du chevalier de Faublas* (1790). Emilie's scoundrel of a brother kills himself in *Emilie de Varmont* (1791). Both Trugulin and his son commit suicide in Ducray-Duminil's *Cœlina* (1799). Madame de Staël's Delphine of 1802 takes poison. Both M. Spronck and Charles Munster choose "voluntary death" (65) in Nodier's *Le Peintre de Saltzbourg* (1803). Octave de Malivert kills himself slowly and deliciously in Stendhal's *Armance* (1827). William Richard shoots himself in Ricard's *La Grisette* (1827). Maria wraps her arms around Virmer, who has just refused to marry her, and throws them both off a cliff in Albitte's *Une Vie d'homme* (1831). Hugo's Quasimodo commits suicide in *Notre-Dame de Paris* (1831). Alphonse Karr's Magdeleine hangs herself in *Sous les tilleuls* (1832). Charles' father kills himself in Balzac's *Eugénie Grandet* of 1833. Sand's *Lélia* (1833) has several suicides, and Ida Gruget commits suicide in Balzac's "Ferragus" (1834). *Jacques* (1834), and Musset's *Lorenzaccio* (1834) culminate in suicide. Both Esther and Lucien kill themselves in Balzac's *Splendeurs et Misères des courtisanes* (1834–47). Musset's Cœlio throws himself into the assassin's arms when he mistakenly believes that Octave has betrayed him with Marianne (*Caprices de Marianne*— 1834). M. de Saint-Hilaire refers to several suicides in his successful attempt to dissuade his son from doing likewise—Alletz, "Désenchantement" (1835). Louis de Gisors successfully seeks death in battle in Sophie Gay's *La Comtesse d'Egmont* (1836). Julie's father kills himself in Guttinguer's *Arthur* (1836). Clémence de Bergenheim throws herself off a balcony and drowns in Charles de Bernard's *Gerfaut* (1838). Lamiel remains in the Palais de Justice that she burns down to revenge Valbayre and dies—Stendhal, *Lamiel* (1839–40); Fernand d'Aquilar poisons himself in Camille Bodin's *Berthe et Louise* (1843); Bernard Stamply commits suicide in Sandeau's *Mademoiselle de La Seiglière* (1848); M. de Favras drinks poison in Dumas père's *Le Collier de la reine* (1849–50). Maxime du Camp's *Mémoires d'un suicidé* dates from 1853. Javert used the Seine for his suicide in Hugo's *Les Misérables* (1862). And so on. This is just a sampling. A list of works where suicide is considered, discussed, threatened, or attempted would be even longer, and would include Prévost's *Manon Lescaut* (1731), Duclos's *Histoire de Mme de Luz* (1741), Graffigny's

Lettres d'une péruvienne (1747), Lesuire's *L'Aventurier français* (1782), Ducray-Duminil's *Victor* (Year V or 1797), Pigault-Lebrun's *Monsieur Botte* (Year XI or 1803), Estournelles's *Pascaline* (1821), Ricard's *Le Portier* (1827), Jouy's *Cécile* (1827), Stendhal's *Le Rouge et le noir* (1831), Boulay-Paty's *Elie Mariaker* (1834), Alletz's "La Séduction" (1835), Fromentin's *Dominique* (1863), and many others. Gérald Antoine's edition of Sainte-Beuve's *Joseph Delorme* includes a list of different works where suicide plays a significant part (168n121).

4   "Un Mal du siècle—Le Suicide," *L'Independant, Furet de Paris* 10 (26 January 1837) 1.

5   Letter of 6 October 1836, *Lettres à Madame Hanska,* ed. Roget Pierrot, 4 vols. (Paris: Delta, 1967) 1.445.

6   Mozet, ed., "Introduction," *La Vieille Fille, La Comédie humaine,* by Honoré de Balzac, ed. Pierre-Georges Castex, 12 vols., Bibliothèque de la Pléiade (Paris: Gallimard, 1976–81) 4.795–96.

7   For this summary, I have used Patricia Kinder's "Un Directeur de journal, ses auteurs et ses lecteurs en 1836: Autour de *La Vieille Fille,*" *L'Année Balzacienne* 1972: 173–200.

8   Quoted from Bardèche, ed., "Notice," *La Vieille Fille, Œuvres complètes,* vol. 6 (Paris: Club de l'Honnête Homme, 1956) 558.

9   Armine Mortimer has in addition shown how Balzac turned a comic detail into the image of the whole—"Balzac's Vieille Fille and Her Corset," Paper presented at the Colloquium in Nineteenth-Century French Studies, October 22, 1994.

10 Pasco, *Balzacian Montage: Configuring* La Comédie humaine (Toronto: U of Toronto P, 1991) 11, 92–94.

11 Cf., "Why add this story [of Athanase Granson]? You can take this protuberance away without affecting the life of the plot!"—Henri Queffélec, "Préface," *La Vieille Fille, L'Œuvre de Balzac,* ed. Albert Béguin and Jean A. Ducourneau, vol. 1 (Paris: Formes et Reflets, 1949) 897; Maurice Bardèche, who cites Paul Souday's similar position, writes for himself: "What about Athanase Granson's destiny? . . . Why give him such an important development when there was no need? We don't understand what [Balzac] wanted to do in incorporating a character and an event that he fails to integrate into the story, that remains foreign to the characters and to their interests without moreover succeeding in setting up a contrast, and that, in the light of Balzac's understanding of the laws of composition and the conception of a subject, leave the impression of a mistake"—"Notice," *La Vieille Fille, Œuvres complètes de Balzac,* tome 6 (Paris: Club de l'Honnête Homme, 1956) 557. While I would agree that Balzac was not completely successful in a sympathetic characterization of Athanase, I trust I can show why Athanase remains an important part of *La Vieille Fille.*

12 Fredric Jameson, "The Ideology of Form: Partial Systems in *La Vieille Fille,*" *Sub-stance* 15 (1976): 34.

13 Le Yaouanc, "Le Plaisir dans les récits balzaciennes," *L'Année Balzacienne*

1973: 209. Albert Béguin, also, terms her a "professional of love" (quoted from Philip Berthier, ed. *La Vieille Fille, Le Cabinet des antiques* (Paris: Garnier-Flammarion, 1987) 382. Though she eventually becomes such, there is reason to believe that she was a rank amateur in Alençon.

14 Pierre-Georges Castex, ed., *La Vieille Fille*, by Honoré de Balzac (Paris: Garnier, 1957) 62n1.

15 See Edouard Morot-Sir, "La Dynamique du théâtre et Molière," *Romance Notes* 15, supplement no. 1 (1973): 39. Morot-Sir argues that "*comic form* reveals a certain concept of an *obstacle* to destiny, something *off-beat* or *troublesome* . . . and manifests itself in a complicitous relationship between love and cunning. There is, then, good and bad *deceitfulness*, justifiable and dishonorable *deception*, that, moreover, rules both friend and foe. Its motivating force, which becomes the essence of the comic, is the play of ignorance and deceit. The behavior of 'the one who does not know' makes us laugh." *La Vieille Fille* would illustrate Morot-Sir's view nicely, at least up to the point where Rose makes her decision.

16 Jameson, 29–49; Laffly, "La Politique dans *La Vieille Fille*," *Ecrits de Paris*, novembre 1970: 66–75; Robert Kopp, "Préface," *La Vieille Fille*, by Balzac, Folio (Paris: Gallimard, 1978); Lise Queffélec, "*La Vieille Fille* ou la science des mythes en roman-feuilleton," *L'Année Balzacienne* 1988: 163–77.

17 *Lettres à Madame Hanska* of 1 February 1837, 1.483, and 4 May 1843, 2. 210.

18 "Deux Réputations," 148. The *Mémoires secrets* also point to the years 1760–70 as the time when suicides began to increase both in numbers and in their often spectacular character—Robert Fave, *La Mort dans la littérature et la pensée françaises au siècle des lumières* (Lyon: PU de Lyon, 1978) 473. According to Merrick the Parisian publisher Siméon-Prosper Hardy "reported large numbers of suicides in the second half of the eighteenth century. Hardy attributed the alleged epidemic of self-destruction to the 'decay of religion and morality' in his time"—*The Desacralization of the French Monarchy in the Eighteenth Century* (Baton Rouge: Louisiana State UP, 1990) 41n20. See also Merrick's "Patterns and Prosecution of Suicide in Eighteenth-Century Paris," *Historical Reflections/Réflexions Historiques* 16 (1989): 1–53.

19 Etienne de Jouy, *Franc-Parleur*, 1.73. See also e.g., Patrice Higonnet, "Joint Suicide in Eighteenth-Century French Literature and Revolutionary Politics," *Fictions of the French Revolution*, ed. Bernadette Fort (Evanston: Northwestern UP, 1991) 87–110; Gita May, "Staël and the Fascination of Suicide: The Eighteenth-Century Background," *Germaine de Staël: Crossing the Borders*, ed. Madelyn Gutwirth, et al. (New Brunswick: Rutgers UP, 1991) 168–76; and Priscilla Parkhurst Ferguson, "Suicide, société et sociologie de Durkheim à Balzac," *Nineteenth-Century French Studies* 3 (1973): 200–12, as well as her more recent, *Paris as Revolution: Writing the Nineteenth Century* (Berkeley: U of California P, 1994) 101–4.

20 As Cobb explains, the data of October 1795 to 1801 that he studies from the Basse-Geôle (the riverside quarters) are far too incomplete to be more than

an indication. In 1795, for example, when for the third year in a row Paris had 30,000 deaths, suicides were termed "particularly numerous," but only a few were registered and no exact figures were given. "The totals for the Year III [1795–96] (9) and for Year IV (18) are so fragmentary as to be quite unrepresentative of the gravity of [the] crisis. . . . The Year V accounts for 29 suicides, there are 44 suicides in the Year VI, 50 in each of the Years VII and VIII, 74 in a little over eleven months of the Year IX"—*Death in Paris* (Oxford: Oxford UP, 1978) 7.

21 Ratcliffe, "Suicides in the City: Perceptions and Realities of Self-Destruction in Paris in the First Half of the Nineteenth Century," *Historical Reflections* 18.1 (1992): 3. The figures on suicide, as Ratcliffe insists, are by no means completely reliable, even after 1825 when officials attempted to pursue reliable investigations and keep consistent records. In 1833, André-Michel Guerry had even stronger reservations about the accuracy of his estimates (6,900 suicides or almost 1,800 per year between 1827 and 1830): "It would be a serious mistake to consider these numbers as entirely correct; they are probably too low"—*Essai sur la statistique morale de la France* (Paris: Crochard, 1833) 61. Alain Corbin then exaggerates when he claims, "Thanks to detailed official investigations, we know exactly what people killed themselves in nineteenth-century France"—Michelle Perrot, ed., *From the Fires of Revolution to the Great War*, tr. Arthur Goldhammer, vol. 4 of *A History of Private Life* (Cambridge: Harvard UP, 1990) 647.

22 Ratcliffe, "Suicides," 66n158. According to Lisa Jo Lieberman, citing Gaston Garrisson, by 1880 it was seventeen per hundred thousand—"Une Maladie épidémique: Suicide and Its Implications in Nineteenth-Century France," diss. Yale U, 1987, 2. See also, for more detail, 58–63. Lieberman's dissertation is a superb survey of nineteenth-century sources dealing with suicide in France.

23 Ratcliffe, "Suicides," 34–39. Lieberman claims that "[t]aking population growth into account, the number of suicides in France from the last years of the Restoration through the first decade of the Third Republic increased by a factor of three" (2). Her figures are in line with others cited here: "Between 1827 and 1830, an average of five out of every 100,000 inhabitants took their lives each year; by 1880, the total had reached seventeen" (ibid.). Of course, as M. Brouc makes clear in 1836, the rates in Paris were considerably higher: "From 1794 to 1823, in Paris there were on average 233 suicides per year. This period of 29 years did not have an equal number of suicides for its different periods. From 1794 to 1804, there were 107 suicides per year, while from 1814 to 1823, this number was at 334. . . . [F]rom 1830 to 1835 inclusively . . . this number was 3823 suicides per year. . . . M. Guerry concludes that from 1827 to 1830 there was one suicide per 3000 inhabitants of the Seine Department, while from 1830 to 1835, we have found . . . one suicide per 2,094 inhabitants. The progression is then real"—"Considerations sur les suicides de notre époque," *Annales d'hygiène publique et de médecine légale* 16 (1836): 224–25. According to M. Petit, cited by Alexandre Brierre de

Boismont in 1865, from 1835 to 1846 on average 3002 killed themselves each year—*Du suicide et de la folie suicide* (Paris: G. Baillière, 1865) 486–87.

24 Olwen H. Hufton, *Women and the Limits of Citizenship in the French Revolution* (Toronto: U of Toronto P, 1992) 53–88.

25 David Garrioch, *Neighbourhood and Community in Paris, 1740–1790* (Cambridge: Cambridge UP, 1986) 254–55.

26 Corbin insists on the importance of loneliness—in Perrot's ed., *From the Fires of Revolution*, 646–49. See, however, Thomas Brennan, *Public Drinking and Popular Culture in Eighteenth-Century Paris* (Princeton: Princeton UP, 1988).

27 See *Mother Death: The Journal of Jules Michelet: 1815–1850*, tr. and ed. by Edward K. Kaplan (Amherst: U of Massachusetts Press, 1984).

28 Lieberman, "Romanticism and the Culture of Suicide in Nineteenth-Century France," *Comparative Studies in Society and History* 33.3 (1991): 623–29.

29 Ratcliff, "Suicide," 31. Cobb, 6, 111–12nG. Elsewhere, Ratcliffe's figures are even more notable, since the percentages of unrecognized corpses are higher, thus, perhaps, suggesting that if they were unrecognized they must be immigrants: "In the period 1811–30, 62.4 percent of bodies were identified, while the percentage rose to 86.8 percent in 1837–46"—Ratcliff, "Classes laborieuses et classes dangereuses à Paris pendant la première moitié du XIXe siècle?: The Chevalier Thesis Reexamined," *French Historical Studies* 17 (1991): 592n79. Applying the half-full/half-empty principle may put these numbers in proper perspective: From 1811 to 1830, 37.6% of bodies were not recognized, while the figure dropped to the still significant 13.2% in 1837–46.

30 E.g., Jouy, *Franc-Parleur*, 80–81; Brierre de Boismont, *Du suicide et de la folie-suicide*, 21–26. Corbin is right to judge that these explanations are "not very convincing"—in Perrot's ed., *From the Fires of Revolution*, 646—but they can be evaluated in the light of considerable other material.

31 Quoted from Seymour Perlin, *A Handbook for the Study of Suicide* (New York: Oxford UP, 1975) 12–13.

32 Armand Hoog, "L'Ame préromantique et les instincts de mort; II: La Poésie de la mort dans le silence de la littérature (1798–1808)," *Bulletin de la Faculté des Lettres de Strasbourg* 1952: 149–60; Robert Mauzi, "Les Maladies de l'âme au XVIIIe siècle," *Revue des Sciences Humaines* 100 (1960): 459–93.

33 Caro, "Le Suicide dans ses rapports avec la civilisation," *Nouvelles Etudes morales sur le temps présent* (Paris: Hachette, 1869) 51–53.

34 A point made by James Hiddleston, "Literature and Suicide," *The Play of Terror in Nineteenth-Century France.*, ed. John T. Booker and Allan H. Pasco (Newark: U of Delaware P, 1996) 209–25.

35 Twain, "Preface," *Those Extraordinary Twins*, *The Complete Novels of Mark Twain*, ed. Charles Neider, vol. 2 (Garden City: Doubleday, 1964) 611.

36 Douthwaite, *Exotic Women: Literary Heroines and Cultural Strategies in Ancien Régime France* (Philadelphia: U of Pennsylvania P, 1992) 95. Margaret R. Higonnet discusses suicide as a means of self-staging: "[B]y unmaking herself, she also remakes herself"—"Suicide as Self-Construction," *Germaine de Staël: Crossing the Borders*, 69–81 (the quotation is from 78).

37 Hamilton, "Reason and Sentiment in Montesquieu's Understanding of Suicide," *American Society Legion of Honor Magazine* 47 (1976): 108.

38 Siebers, "The Werther Effect: The Esthetics of Suicide," *Mosaic* 26 (Winter 1993): 17.

39 Ibid. Baudelaire, haunted himself by the thought of suicide, called Rousseau's argument against self-destruction a piece of "stupidity [*sottise*]"—"Plans et projets," *Œuvres complètes,* 518. Restif felt suicide was "natural for the thinking being" when "pain has been substituted for the pleasure of existing" (1.946).

40 *Etudes morales,* 102; See also, e.g., Brierre de Boismont, 480; Lieberman, "Implications," 5, 21, 68–73.

41 Wolfgang Goethe, *The Sorrows of the Young Werther,* 118. Translated into French as early as 1776, the short novel is generally believed to have had extraordinary influence on the Romantic temperament. Though the device of sharing the guilt by receiving the means of death from the hands of another was previously exploited by Mme Riccoboni, she did not bring God into the equation. *Werther* is also credited (or blamed) for an explosion of suicides across Europe. Jouy mentions it as an important factor in a suicide (*Franc-Parleur,* 1.75). M.D. Farber's conclusion is more balanced. He concludes that "Gœthe's novel played some kind of role in the suicidal conduct of numerous Europeans during the late eighteenth and early nineteenth centuries. I say some kind of role simply because we cannot attribute an individual's suicide to the influence of a book, unless, of course, we make it very clear that we are regarding the book as an efficient rather than a formal or final cause, in line with Aristotle's useful analysis of causation"—"The Suicide of Young Werther," *Psychoanalytic Review* 60.2 (1973): 239–40. Two other extremes may be exemplified, on the one hand, by Ratcliffe who goes too far in "dedramatizing" suicide, and, on the other, by Louis Maigron, *Le Romantisme et les mœurs: Essai d'étude historique et sociale d'après des documents inédits* (Paris: Champion, 1910) 312–50, whose efforts to sound the alarm seem overly strident, though with statistics that are quite similar to those of Ratcliffe. The suggestion that God is responsible for the suicide continues through the Romantic period. In 1835, Camille de Lubois says, for example, "If I am committing a crime in killing myself, God will doubtless absolve me, since he didn't give me the strength to bear my life any more"—*Le Conseiller d'état,* 2.263.

42 Jost, "Littérature et suicide de Werther à Madame Bovary," *Revue de Littérature Comparée* 42 (1968): 192.

43 Hiddleston's analysis of Emma's suicide is excellent.

CHAPTER 7: AN ENDING—JULIEN AMONG THE CANNIBALS

1   A bibliography of work that considers the historical substance in *Le Rouge et le noir* would include a significant portion of the novel's secondary sources, though particularly interesting considerations are to be found in: e.g., Erich Auerbach, *Mimesis: The Representation of Reality in Western Literature*, Anchor Books (Garden City: Doubleday, 1957) 400–13; Henri Martineau, "Introduction," *Le Rouge et le noir*, by Stendhal (Paris: Garnier, 1960) i–xxx; Stirling Haig, *Stendhal:* The Red and the Black (Cambridge: Cambridge UP, 1989) 14–26.

2   For useful summaries of this controversy, see, Haig, *Stendhal*, 84–87; Christopher Prendergast, *The Order of Mimesis: Balzac, Stendhal, Nerval, Flaubert* (Cambridge: Cambridge UP, 1986) 143–44; and Moya Longstaffe, "L'Ethique du duel et la couronne du martyre dans *Le Rouge et le noir*," *Stendhal Club* 72 (1976): 283–88.

3   F.W.J. Hemmings, *Stendhal: A Study of His Novels* (Oxford: Clarendon P, 1964) 124.

4   Brooks, "The Novel and the Guillotine; or, Fathers and Sons in *Le Rouge et le noir*," *Reading for the Plot: Design and Intention in Narrative* (New York: Knopf, 1984) 62–89, the quotation is from 62.

5   Carol A. Mossman, *The Narrative Matrix: Stendhal's* Le Rouge et le noir (Lexington: French Forum, 1984) 60.

6   2.276. The theme of onomastic instability continues with other characters. Julien refers to Mathilde as Mme Dubois, for example (2.287). Later, when M. de La Mole arranges to bury Julien's patronym, Mathilde thanks him for saving her from the Sorel name (2.375).

7   F.W.J. Hemmings, "Julien Sorel and Julian the Apostate," *French Studies* 16 (1962): 229–44.

8   Babou, "Stendhal," *Les Sensations d'un juré* (Paris: A Lemerre, 1875) 21.

9   Sainte-Beuve, "M. de Stendhal: Ses *Œuvres complètes*," *Causeries du lundi*, 9ᵉ série, 3ᵉ édition (Paris: Garnier, 1869) 330.

10 What I am suggesting here is somewhat different than the phenomenon that Victor Brombert signals: "The protagonists' need to find shelter from outer encroachments develops inner resources of reverie and unconstraint. Often, characters involved in an apparently absorbing dialogue pursue an independent interior discourse"—*Stendhal: Fiction and the Themes of Freedom* (Chicago: U of Chicago P, 1968) 84. I am interested rather in the being Julien believes himself to be, however much he would like to be different, and the being he constructs for the benefit of others. Mary Eloise Ragland-Sullivan's Lacanian reading of the hero's inner and outer selves brought into irreconcilable conflict when Mme de Rênal pronounces his inner self a lie is closer to what I have in mind—"Julien's Quest for "Self": *Qui suis-je?*" *Nineteenth-Century French Studies* 8 (Fall–Winter 1979–80): 1–13.

11 See the excellent argument by Henriette Bibas, "Le Double dénouement et la

215

morale du *Rouge*," *Revue d'Histoire Littéraire de la France* 49 (1949): 21–36; and, especially, Longstaffe, "Duel," 283–306.

12 Harry Levin argues that ladders symbolize Julien's rise in society—"*The Red and the Black*: Social Originality," *Stendhal's* The Red and the Black, ed. Harold Bloom (New York: Chelsea House, 1988) 29.

13 David Blankenhorn, *Fatherless America: Confronting Our Most Urgent Social Problem* (New York: Basic Books, 1995) 4.

14 Hemmings, "Apostate," 230.

15 E.g., Victor Brombert, "Stendhal lecteur de Rousseau," *Revue des Sciences Humaines* 92 (1958): 463–82; Hava Sussmann, "Julien Sorel dans le sillage de Jean-Jacques Rousseau à Turin," *Lettres Romanes* 40.2 (1986): 127–32; and Michel Connon, "Pères, mères et fils dans le roman stendhalien," *Stendhal Club* 27 (1985): 163–76.

16 Jean-Jacques Rousseau, *Œuvres completes*, ed. Bernard Gagnebin, Robert Osmont, Marcel Raymond, Bibliothèque de la Pléiade, vol. 1 (Paris: Gallimard, 1959) 1224.

17 Gilbert D. Chaitin, *The Unhappy Few: A Psychological Study of the Novels of Stendhal* (Bloomington: Indiana UP, 1972) 58.

18 On the names of *Le Rouge*, see esp., Jean-Jacques Hamm, "Hypothèses sur quelques noms propres de *Rouge et noir*," *Stendhal Club* 18 (1976): 228–34; and Anthony Purdy, "Un Cheval nommé Sorrel et une taupe régicide. Réflexions onomastiques sur *Le Rouge et le noir*," *Stendhal Club* 22 (1980): 144–52. For another passage where Julien is compared to a "bird of prey," cited like the preceding one by Hamm, see 1.126.

19 Quoted from Seligman, *Helplessness: On Depression, Development, and Death* (New York: W. H. Freeman, 1975) 49.

20 E.g., Christopher Peterson, Steven F. Maier, Martin E.P. Seligman, *Learned Helplessness: A Theory for the Age of Personal Control* (New York: Oxford UP, 1993); Mario Mikulincer, *Human Learned Helplessness: A Coping Perspective* (New York: Plenum P, 1994).

BIBLIOGRAPHY OF PRIMARY SOURCES
18TH AND 19TH CENTURY FRENCH LITERARY WORKS

Agoult, Marie de Flavigny [pseud. Daniel Stern]. *Esquisses morales et politiques.* Paris: Paguerre, 1849.

Albitte, Gustave. *Une Vie d'homme* (1832). Paris: Charles Gosselin, 1832.

Alletz, Edouard. "Le Désenchantement." *Maladies du siècle.* Paris: C. Gosselin, 1835. 105–204.

— "L'Isolement." *Maladies du siècle.* 23–103.

— "La Séduction." *Maladies du siècle.* 205–303.

Arnaud, François-Thomas-Marie de Baculard d'. *Fanni ou la nouvelle Paméla, histoire anglaise.* 3d edition. 1764; Paris: L'Esclapart and la veuve Duchesne, 1767.

Aunet, Léonie. *Voyage d'une femme au Spitzberg.* Paris: Hachette, 1854.

Augier, Emile. *Le Ciguë, Comédie en deux actes et en vers.* Paris: Second Théâtre Français, 1844.

Balzac, Honoré de. *Le Curé de village* (1841). *La Comédie humaine.* 12 vols. Bibliothèque de la Pléiade. Paris: Gallimard. 1976–81. 9.641–872.

— "La Duchesse de Langeais" (1834). *La Comédie humaine* 5.905–1037.

— *Les Employés* (1838). *La Comédie humaine.* 7.897–1117.

— *Eugénie Grandet* (1833). *La Comédie humaine.* 3.1027–1199.

— *La Femme de trente ans* (1830–42). *La Comédie humaine.* 2.1039–1214.

— "Ferragus " (1834). *La Comédie humaine.* 5.787 - 903.

— "La Fille aux yeux d'or" (1834–35). *La Comédie humaine.* 5.1039–1112.

— "Jésus-Christ en Flandre" (1830–31). *La Comédie humaine.* 10.311–27.

— *Illusions perdues* (1837–43). *La Comédie humaine.* 5.123–732.

— *Le Lys dans la vallée* (1836). *La Comédie humaine.* 9.969–1229.

— "La Maison Nucingen" (1838). *La Comédie humaine.* 6.329–92.

— *Lettres à Madame Hanska.* Ed. Roget Pierrot. 4 vols. Paris: Delta, 1967.

— *Mémoires de deux jeunes mariées* (1842). *La Comédie humaine.* 1.195–403.

— *La Peau de chagrin* (1831). *La Comédie humaine.* 10.57–294.

— *Le Père Goriot* (1834 - 35). *La Comédie humaine.* 3.37–290.

— *Pierrette* (1840). *La Comédie humaine.* 4.29–163.

— *Splendeurs et misères des courtisanes* (1838 - 47). *La Comédie humaine.* 6.429–935.

— *Sur Catherine de Médicis* (1830 - 42). *La Comédie humaine.* 11.167–457.

— "El Verdugo" (1830). *La Comédie humaine.* 10.1133–43.

[—]. *Le Vicaire des Ardennes.* By Horace de Saint-Aubin. 1822; Paris: Bibliophiles de l'Originale, 1962.

— *La Vieille Fille* (1837). *La Comédie humaine.* 4.811–936.

Barbey d'Aurevilly, Jules-Amédée. *Les Diaboliques* (1874). *Œuvres romanesques complètes.* Ed. Jacques Petit. 2 vols. Bibliothèque de la Pléiade. Paris: Gallimard, 1964, 1966. 2.9–264.

Barrès, Maurice. *Les Déracinés.* 2 vols. 1897; Paris: Plon, 1922.

Baudelaire. *Les Fleurs du mal* (1857). *Œuvres complètes.* Ed. Y.-G. Le Dantec, revised by Claude Pichois. Bibliothèque de la Pléiade. Paris: Gallimard, 1961.

Beaumarchais, Pierre-Augustin Caron de. *La Folle Journée, ou Le Mariage de Figaro* (1784). *Théâtre, lettres relatives à son théâtre.* Ed. Maurice Allem and Paul-Courant. Bibliothèque de la Pléiade. Paris: Gallimard, 1957. 231–364.

— *L'Autre Tartufe, ou La Mère coupable* (1792). *Théâtre.* 457–528.

Bernard, Charles de. *Gerfaut* (1838). Paris: Michel Lévy, 1856.

Belloy, Pierre de. *Gabrielle de Vergy, Tragédie.* Paris: Duchesne, 1770.

Bodin, Camille [pseud. Jenny Bastide]. *Berthe et Louise* (1843). *La Semaine Littéraire du Courrier des Etats-Unis* 2.48–53 (1843): 3–51.

— *Etrennes morales: Dix ans de la vie d'une jeune fille.* Paris: Aubert, [1840].

Borel, Petrus. *Champavert: Contes immoraux.* 1833; Paris: Editions des Autres, 1979.

Boulay-Paty, Evariste. *Elie Mariaker.* Paris: H. Dupuy, 1834.

Chateaubriand, François-René. *Atala* (1801). *Atala, René, Les Aventures du Dernier Abencérage.* Paris: Garnier, 1962.

— *Génie du Christianisme, Œuvres complètes,* vol. 2 (Paris: Garnier, n.d.).

— *Mémoires d'outre-tombe.* 1849–50; Paris: Ministère de l'Education Nationale, 1972.

— *René* (1802). *Atala, René.*

Constant, Benjamin. *Adolphe.* Ed. Jacques-Henri Bornecque. 1816; Paris: Garnier, [1960].

Cottin, Madame. *Claire d'Albe* (1799). *Œuvres complètes.* Vol. 1. Paris: J.L.F. Foucault, 1920. 81–224.

Crébillon *fils*, Claude Prosper Jolyot de. *Les Egarements du cœur et de l'esprit. Romanciers du XVIIIe siècle.* Vol. 2. Ed. René Etiemble. Bibliothèque de la Pléiade. Paris: Gallimard, 1965. 5–188.

— *Les Heureux Orphelins, histoire imitée de l'anglais.* 4 vols. Brussels: Vasse, 1754.

— *La Nuit et le moment, ou les matines de Cythère.* 1755; Bruxelles: J. Rozez, 1869.

Crébillon *père*, Prosper Jolyot. *Rhadamiste et Zénobie* (1711). *Théâtre complète.* Nouvelle édition. Paris: Laplace, Sanchez, n.d. 141–82.

— *Sémiramis* (1717). *Théâtre complète.* 183–229.

Custine, Adolphe. *Aloys ou le religieux du Mont Saint-Bernard.* Paris: Vezard, 1829.

Delavigne, Casimir. *Marino Faliero* (1829). *Œuvres complètes.* Vol. 2. Paris: Firmin-Didot, 1888. 1–109.

Diderot, Denis. *Les Bijoux indiscrets* (1748). *Œuvres romanesques.* Ed. Henri Bénac. Paris: Garnier, 1962. 1–233.

— *Le Fils naturel* (1757). *Œuvres complètes.* Ed. Jacques Chouillet and Anne-Marie Chouillet. Vol. 10. Paris: Hermann, 1975. 13–81.

— *Le Neveu de Rameau* (1761–76). *Œuvres romanesques.* 395–492.

— *Le Père de famille, Comédie* (1758). *Œuvres complètes.* 10.190–306.

— *Supplément au Voyage de Bougainville* (1796). Ed. P. Vernière. *Œuvres philosophiques.* Paris: Garnier, 1956.

Du Camp, Maxime. *Mémoires d'un suicidé.* 1853; Paris: Librairie Nouvelle, 1855.

Duclos, Charles. *Les Confessions du comte de **** (1742). *Œuvres de Duclos.* 3 vols. Paris: A. Belin, 1820–21.

— *Histoire de Mme de Luz.* (1741); London, 1782.

Ducis, Jean-François. *Œdipe chez Admète* (1778). *Œuvres.* Paris: Ledentu, 1859. 62–83.

— *Œdipe à Colone* (1797). *Œuvres.* 207–24.

Ducray-Duminil, François-Guillaume. *Cœlina, ou l'enfant du mystère.* Year VII; 1799; Paris: Le Prieur, 1818.

— *Lolotte et Fanfan.* 2 vols. 1788; Paris: Maradan, 1789.

— *Victor ou l'enfant de la forêt.* 4 vols. 1797; Paris: Le Prieur, 1821.

Dumas *père*, Alexandre. *Antony* (1831). *Nineteenth Century French Plays.* Ed. Joseph L. Borgerhoff. New York: Appleton-Century-Crofts, 1959. 153–78.

— *Le Collier de la reine.* 2 vols. 1849–50; Lausanne: Rencontre, 1965, 1967.

— *Le Comte de Monte-Cristo.* Ed. J.-H. Bornecque. 2 vols. 1841–45; Paris: Garnier, 1962.

— "Eugène Sue." *Les Morts vont vite.* 2 vols. Paris: Michel Lévy, 1861.

— *Henri III et sa cour* (1829). *Nineteenth Century French Plays.* Ed. Joseph L. Borgerhoff. 118–52.

Duras, Claire de. *Edouard* (1825). *Œuvres de Mme Elie de Beaumont, de Mme de Genlis, de Fiévée et de Mme de Duras.* Paris: Garnier, 1865. 411–505.

— *Olivier ou le secret* (1822; 1971). Ed. Denise Virieux. Paris: J. Corti, 1971.

— *Ourika* (1824). *Œuvres de Mme Elie de Beaumont . . . et de Mme de Duras.* 371–410.

Estournelles, Louise d'. *Pascaline.* 2 vols. Paris: Ch. Villet, 1821.

Fiévée, Joseph. *La Dot de Suzette* (1798). Paris: Maradan, Year VI (1798).

— *Frédéric.* 3 vols. Year VII, 1799; Paris: Maradan, Year VIII (1800).

— "L'Innocence." *Six Nouvelles.* 2 vols. Paris: Perlet, 1803. 1.209–90.

— "La Jalousie." *Six Nouvelles.* 1.1–105.

Flaubert, Gustave. *L'Education sentimentale* (1869). *Œuvres.* 2 vols. Bibliothèque de la Pléiade. Paris: Gallimard, 1951. 2.31–457.

— *Madame Bovary* (1857). *Œuvres.* 1.326–645.

— *Salammbô* (1862). *Œuvres.* 1.741–1028.

Foa, Eugénie. *Rachel.* 1833; Paris: Henry Dupuy, 1833.

Fougeret de Monbron, Louis Charles. *Le Canapé, couleur de feu.* Amsterdam: Compagnie des Libraires, 1741.

— *Margot la ravaudeuse.* 1750; Hambourg: n.p. 1800.

Fromentin, Eugène. *Dominique.* 1863; Paris: Nelson, 1959.

Gautier, Théophile. "Jettatura" (1859). *Romans et contes.* Paris: Charpentier, 1919.

Gay, Delphine. *Le Lorgnon* (1830). *Œuvres complètes de Madame Emile de Girardin.* 6 vols. Paris: Henri Plon, 1860–61. 2.1–126.

Gay, Sophie. *Anatole.* 1815; Paris: Michel Lévy, 1864.

— *La Comtesse d'Egmont.* Paris: Dumont, 1836.

— *Léonie de Montbreuse.* 2 vols. 1813; Paris: Michel Lévy, 1864.

Genlis, Madame de. "L'Apostasie, ou La Dévote." *Nouveaux Contes moraux et nouvelles historiques* (1802–3). *Œuvres.* Vol. 8. Paris: Lecointe et Durey, 1825.

— "Les Deux Réputations." *Contes moraux.* Paris: Libraires Associés, 1785.

Gide, André. *Les Faux-Monnayeurs* (1925). *Romans, récits et soties, œuvres lyriques.* Bibliothèque de la Pléiade. Paris: Gallimard, 1958. 931–1248.

— *Le Prométhée mal enchaîné* (1899). *Romans, récits et soties.* 301–41.

Goethe, Wolfgang. *The Sorrows of the Young Werther.* Tr. Eric Lane. 1774; London: Dedalus, 1987.

Graffigny, Françoise de. *Lettres d'une Péruvienne.* 1748; New York: MLA, 1993.

Guttinguer, Ullric. *Arthur.* Paris: E. Renduel, 1837.

Hugo, Victor. *Hernani* (1830). *Théâtre complet.* Vol. 1. Bibliothèque de la Pléiade. Paris: Gallimard, 1963.

— *La Légende des siècles* (1859–83). Ed. André Dumas. Paris: Garnier, 1964.

— *Les Misérables.* 4 vols. Paris: Nelson, n.d.

— *Notre-Dame de Paris* (1831). *Notre-Dame de Paris 1482; Les Travaileurs de la mer.* Bibliothèque de la Pléiade. Paris: Gallimard, 1975. 1–557.

Huysmans, Joris-Karl, *A rebours.* 1884; rpt. Paris: Fasquelle, 1968.

Jouy, Etienne. *Cécile, ou les passions* (1827). Paris: n.p., 1827.

Jouy, Monsieur [Etienne] de. *Guillaume Le Franc-Parleur.* 2 vols. Paris: Pillet, 1815.

Karr, Alphonse. *Sous les tilleuls* (1832). *Œuvres complètes.* Paris: Calmann Lévy, 1881.

Krudner, Madame de. *Valérie.* 1803; Paris: A Quantin, 1878.

Labiche, Eugène. *La Chasse aux corbeaux* (1853). *Théâtre d'Eugène Labiche.* Ed. Henry Gidel. Vol. 1. Paris: Garnier, 1991. 635–714.

Lamartine, Alphonse de. *La Chute d'un ange.* Ed. Marius-François Guyard. 1838; Genève: Droz, 1954. 1145–1319.

— *Jocelyn: Episode: Journal trouvé chez un curé de village.* Ed. Jean des Cognets. 1836; Paris: Garnier, 1960.

Lamothe-Langon, Etienne Léon de. *Monsieur le Préfet.* 4 vols. Paris Ladvocat, 1824.

Latouche, Hyacinthe. *Olivier.* 1823; Paris: U. Canel, 1826.

Lesuire, Robert-Martin. *L'Aventurier français ou Mémoires de Grégoire Merveil.* 2 vols. London and Paris: Quillau, 1782.

— *Suite de l'Aventurier français, ou Mémoires de Grégoire Merveil, marquis d'Erbeuil.* 2 vols. London: Quillau, 1783.

Louvet de Couvay, Jean-Baptiste. *Emilie de Varmont, ou le divorce nécessaire, et les amours du curé Sévin.* Paris: Bailly, 1791.

— *Une Année de la vie de Faublas* (1787). *Romanciers du XVIIIᵉ siècle.* Ed. Etiemble. 2 vols. Bibliothèque de la Pléiade. Paris: Gallimard, 1965. 2.419–720.

— *Six semaines de la vie du chevalier de Faublas* (1788). *Romanciers du XVIIIe siècle*. 2.721–846.

— *La Fin des amours du chevalier de Faublas* (1790). *Romanciers du XVIIIe siècle*. 2.847–1222.

Marivaux. *La Vie de Marianne, ou les aventures de Madame la comtesse de ****. (1731–42). Ed. Frédéric Deloffre. Paris: Garnier, 1963.

Marmontel, Jean-François. "Annete et Lubin, histoire véritable" (1761). *Contes moraux.* Vol. 2. Paris: J. Merlin, 1765. 201–20.

Masson, Michel. *Hyacinthe, l'apprenti, ou Une Enigme sans mot.* Bruxelles: Meline, Cans, 1841.

Maupassant, Guy de. "Aux champs" (1882), "Le Champ d'oliviers" (1890), "Un Fils" (1882), and "La Mère aux monstres" (1883). *Contes et nouvelles.* Ed. Louis Forestier. 2 vols. Bibliothèque de la Pléiade. Paris: Gallimard, 1974, 1979.

Ménétra, Jacques-Louis. *Journal of My Life.* Ed. Daniel Roche. Tr. Arthur Goldhammer. New York: Columbia UP, 1986.

Mercier, Louis-Sebastian. *Le Nouveau Paris.* 6 vols. Paris: Fuchs, C. Pougens, et C.-F. Cramer, Year VII (1798).

— *Tableau de Paris.* Ed. Jean-Claude Bonnet. 2 vols. 1781–88; Paris: Mercure de France, 1994.

Michelet, Jules. *L'Amour* (1858). *Œuvres complètes.* Vol. 18. Paris: Flammarion, 1985.

— *Mother Death: The Journal of Jules Michelet: 1815–1850.* Translated and edited by Edward K. Kaplan. Amherst: U of Massachusetts Press, 1984.

Mirabeau, Honoré-Gabriel-Riquetti [also attributed to the Marquis de Sentilly]. "Le Rideau levé, ou l'Education de Laure" (1786). *L'Œuvre du comte de Mirabeau.* Ed. Guillaume Apollinaire. Paris: Bibliothèque des Curieux, 1921. 263–75.

Montesquieu, Robert de. *Lettres persanes.* Ed. Paul Vernière. 1721; Paris: Garnier, 1960.

Musset, Alfred de. *Les Caprices de Marianne* (1833). Ed. Maurice Allem. *Théâtre complet.* Bibliothèque de la Pléiade. Paris: Gallimard, 1958. 227–74.

— *Confessions d'un enfant du siècle.* Ed. Maurice Allem. 1836; Paris: Garnier, 1968.

— *Lorenzaccio* (1834). *Théâtre complet.* 49–203.

— "Le Saule" (1830). *Premières Poésies: 1829–1835.* Paris: Garnier, 1967.

Nerciat, André-Robert Andréa de. *Félicia, ou mes fredaines.* 1775; Paris: Arcanes, 1954.

Nerval, Gérard de. "Promenades et souvenirs" (1854–55). *Œuvres.* 2 vols. Bibliothèque de la Pléiade. Paris: Gallimard, 1960. 1.119–45.

Niboyet, Eugénie. *Catherine II et ses filles d'honneur.* Paris: Dentu, 1847.

Nodier, Charles. "Jean-Francois les bas-bleus" (1833). *Contes.* Ed. P.-G. Castex. Paris: Garnier, 1961. 362–76.

— *Le Peintre de Saltzbourg* (1803). *Romans.* Paris: Charpentier, 1884.

O'Neddy, Philothée. "Nuit Quatrième: Nécropolis" (1829). *Feu et flamme.* 1833; Paris: Presses Françaises, 1926.

Ourliac, Edouard. *Suzanne*. Vol. 1. Paris: Desessart, 1840.

Palaiseau, Mademoiselle de. *Histoire de Mesdemoiselles de Saint-Janvier*. Paris: J.J. Blaise, 1812.

Pannier, Sophie. *L'Athée*. 2 vols. 1835; Paris: Fournier, 1836.

Picard, Louis-Benoit. *Le Gil Blas de la Révolution, ou les Confessions de Laurent Giffard*. 5 vols. 1824; Paris: Baudouin Frères, 1824.

Pigault-Lebrun. *Adélaïde de Méran* (1815). *Œuvres complètes*. 20 vols. Paris: J.N. Barba, 1822–24. 19.5–498 and 20.1–189.

— *Angélique et Jeanneton de la Place Maubert*. 2 vols. Paris: J.N. Barba, Year VII (1799).

— *L'Enfant du carnaval* (1796). *Œuvres complètes*. Vol. 1. Paris: J.-N. Barba, 1822.

— *Monsieur Botte* (1803). 4 vols. Paris: J.-N. Barba, Year XI (1803).

Prévost, Antoine-François, Abbé. *Le Philosophe anglais ou Histoire de Monsieur Cleveland* (1732–39). Ed. Philip Stewart. *Œuvres de Prévost*. Ed. Jean Sgard. 8 vols. Grenoble: PU de Grenoble, 1978.

Proust, Marcel. *A la recherche du temps perdu*. Ed. Jean-Yves Tadié. 4 vols. Bibliothèque de la Pléiade. Paris: Gallimard, 1987–89.

Quinet, Edgar. *Ahasvérus ou le Juif errant* (1833). Vol. 7. *Œuvres complètes*. Paris: Pagnerre, 1858.

— *Génie des religions* (1842). Paris: Hachette, n.d.

— *Merlin l'enchanteur*, 2 vols. 1860; Geneva: Slatkine Reprints, 1977.

Restif de La Bretonne, Nicolas-Edme. *L'Anti-Justine, ou les délices de l'amour* (1798). *Œuvres érotiques*. Paris: Fayard, 1985. 281–537.

— *Les Contemporaines*. 3 vols. 1780–85; Paris: Les Yeux ouverts, 1962.

— *Monsieur Nicolas ou le cœur humain dévoilé* (1790–97). Ed. Pierre Testud. 2 vols. Bibliothèque de la Pléiade. Paris: Gallimard, 1989.

— *Les Nuits de Paris, ou le spectateur nocturne*. 8 vols. London, Paris: n.p., 1788–94.

— *Le Paysan et la paysanne pervertis*. 1783, 1787; Paris: Œuvres Représentatives, 1932.

— *Le Palais-Royal*. 3 vols. 1790; Geneva: Slatkine, 1988.

— *La Vie de mon père*. 1778; Paris: Jules Tallandier, 1929.

Reybaud, Louis. *Jérôme Paturot à la recherche d'une position sociale*. 2 vols. 1843; Paris: Paulin, 1846–47.

Ricard, Auguste. *La Grisette, roman de moeurs*. 4 vols. 1827; Paris: Tétot, 1829.

— *Le Portier: Roman de mœurs*. 3 vols. Paris: Lecointe, 1827.

Riccoboni, Madame. *Histoire du Marquis de Cressy* (1758). *Œuvres de Madame Riccoboni*. Paris: Garnier, 1865. 1–74.

Rousseau, Jean-Jacques. *Les Confessions* (1782, 1789). 4 vols. *Œuvres complètes*. Ed. Bernard Gagnebin, et al., Bibliothèque de la Pléiade. Paris: Gallimard, 1959–69. 1.1–656.

— *Emile* (1762). *Œuvres complètes*. 4.55–924.

— *Julie, ou La Nouvelle Héloïse* (1761). *Œuvres complètes*. 2.1–792.

Sade, Donatien A. F. *Crimes de l'amour* (1800). Vols. 3–5. *Œuvres complètes du marquis de Sade*. Paris: Cercle du Livre Précieux, 1966.

— *Justine, ou les malheurs de la vertue* (1791). *Œuvres complètes*. Vols. 6–7.

— *La Philosophie dans le boudoir* (1795). *Œuvres complètes*. Vol. 3.

Sainte-Beuve, Charles Augustin. *Vie, poésies et pensées de Joseph Delorme*. Ed. Gérald Antoine. 1829; Paris: Nouvelles Editions Latines, 1956.

— *Volupté* (1834). Ed. Maurice Regard. 2 vols. Paris: Imprimerie Nationale, 1984.

Saint-Pierre, Jacques-Henri Bernardin de. *Paul et Virginie* (1788). Ed. Pierre Trahard. Paris: Garnier, 1964.

Sand, George. *François le champi* (1848). *La Mare au diable; François le Champi*. Ed. P. Salomon and J. Mallion. Paris: Garnier, 1962.

— *Indiana* (1832). Ed. Pierre Salomon. Paris: Garnier, 1962.

— *La Mare au Diable* (1846). *La Mare au diable; François le Champi*.

Sandeau, Jules. *Mademoiselle de La Seiglière*. 1848; Paris: Nelson, 1933.

Scribe, Eugène. *Le Comte Ory* (1828). *Théâtre*. Vol. 4. Paris: Michel Lévy, 1856. 39–72.

Senancour, Etienne Pivert de. *Obermann*. 1804; Paris: Charpentier, 1882.

Soulié, Frédéric. *Le Conseiller d'Etat*. (1835). Brussels: J. P. Meline, 1835.

Souza, Madame de. *Eugène de Rothelin* (1808). Vol. 3. *Œuvres completes*. Paris: Alexis Eymery, 1821–22. 3.167–419.

Staël, Madame de. *Corinne ou l'Italie*. 1807; Paris: Garnier, n.d.

— *De l'Allemagne*. 1808–10; Paris: Firmin-Didot, 1882.

— *Delphine*. Ed. Simone Balayé and Lucia Omacini. 1802; Paris: Droz, 1987

Stendhal. *Armance* (1827). *Romans et nouvelles*, 2 vols. Ed. Henri Martineau, Bibliothèque de la Pléiade. Paris: Gallimard, 1952. 1.23-192.

— "Les Cenci" (1837). *Romans et nouvelles*. 2.678–702.

— *La Chartreuse de Parme* (1839). *Romans et nouvelles*. 2.21–525.

— *Journal (1818–1842)*, *Œuvres intimes*, ed. Henri Martineau, 2 vols., Bibliothèque de la Pléiade. Paris: Gallimard, 1955. 1.399–1389.

— *Lamiel* (1839–40; 1889). *Œuvres complètes*. Ed. Victor Del Litto and Ernest Abravanel, vol. 44. Geneva: Slatkine, 1986.

— *Lucien Leuwen* (1834–35; 1894). *Romans et nouvelles*. 1.765–1413.

— *Le Rouge et le noir* (1830). *Œuvres complètes*. Ed. Victor Del Litto. Vols. 1–2. Genève: Slatkine Reprints, 1986.

— *Vie de Henry Brulard*, Paris: Gallimard, 1961.

Sue, Eugène. *Le Juif errant*. 1844; Paris: R. Simon, n.d.

— *Les Mystères de Paris*. 4 vols. 1842–43; Paris: Charles Gosselin, 1843.

— *Thérise Dunoyer* (1842). *Œuvres illustrées*. Vol. 2. Paris: n. p., n. d. 1–64.

Tencin, Madame de. *Mémoires du comte de Comminge* (1735). *Œuvres de Mesdames de Fontaines et de Tencin*. Paris: Garnier, n.d. 129–81.

Tillier, Claude. *Mon Oncle Benjamin*. 1843; Paris: Nelson, n.d.

Tracy, Antoine-Louis-Claude Destutt de. *Traité de la volonté et de ses effets*. 2nd ed. 1818; Paris: Slatkine 1984.

Viennet, Jean. *Journal de Viennet, Pair de France, témoin de trois règnes: 1817 - 1848*. Paris: Amiot-Dumont, 1955.

Vigny, Alfred de. *Chatterton* (1830). *Nineteenth Century French Plays*. Ed. Joseph L. Borgerhoff. New York: Appleton-Century-Crofts, 1959. 246–70.

— "Le Déluge" (1826). *Poèmes antiques et modernes*. *Œuvres complètes*. Ed. François Germain and André Jarry. Bibliothèque de la Pléiade. Vol. 1. Paris: Gallimard, 1986. 32–41.

— "La Maison du Berger" (1844). *Les Destinées. Œuvres complètes.* 1.119–28.

— *Les Consultations du docteur Noir; Première Consultation: Stello* (1832). *Stello; Daphné.* Ed. François Germain. Paris: Garnier, 1970. 1–210.

Voltaire. *Les Guèbres, ou la tolérance* (1769). *Œuvres complètes.* Nouvelle édition. 52 vols. Paris: Garnier frères, 1877–85. 6.504–67.

— *Œdipe* (1718). *Œuvres complètes.* 2.59–117.

— *Sémiramis* (1748). *Œuvres complètes.* 4.506–67.

Zola, Emile. *La Curée* (1872). *Les Rougon–Macquart.* Ed. Henri Mitterand. 5 vols. Bibliothèque de la Pléiade. Paris: Gallimard, 1960–67. 1.317–599.

— *Nana* (1881). *Les Rougon–Macquart.* 2.1093–485.

— *Thérèse Raquin.* 1867; rpt. Paris: Calmann-Lévy, n.d.

— *La Terre* (1887). *Les Rougon–Macquart.* 4.365–811.

BIBLIOGRAPHY OF SECONDARY SOURCES

Ainsworth, Mary D. "The Effects of Maternal Deprivation: A Review of Findings and Controversy in the Context of Research Strategy." *Deprivation of Maternal Care: A Reassessment of Its Effects.* Geneva: World Health Organization, 1962. 97–165.

Allen, James Smith. *Popular French Romanticism: Authors, Readers, and Books in the 19th Century.* Syracuse: Syracuse UP, 1981.

Allen, Walter. "Narrative Distance, Tone, and Character." *Theory of the Novel: New Essays.* New York: Oxford UP, 1974. 323–37.

Alvarez, A. *The Savage God: A Study of Suicide.* 1971; New York: Norton, 1990.

Anonymous. "Un Mal du siècle—Le Suicide." *L'Independant, Furet de Paris* 10 (26 January 1837) 1.

Ariès, Philippe. *L'Enfant et la vie familiale sous l'Ancien Régime.* Paris: Seuil, 1973.

Aristotle. *On the Art of Poetry. Classical Literary Criticism.* Trad. T. S. Dorsch. Harmondsworth, Middlesex: Penguin, 1965.

Armengaud, André. "L'Enfant dans la société du XIXe Siècle." *Annales de Démographie Historique* 1973: 303–12.

— *La Famille et l'enfant en France et en Angleterre du XVIe au XVIIIe siècle: Aspects démographiques.* Paris: Société d'Edition d'Enseignement Supérieur, 1975.

— "Les Nourrices du Morvan au XIXe siècle." *Annales de Démographie Historique* 1964: 131–39.

Auerbach, Erich. *Mimesis: The Representation of Reality in Western Literature.* Anchor Books. Garden City: Doubleday, 1957.

Babou, Hippolyte. *Les Sensations d'un juré.* Paris: A Lemerre, 1875.

Baecque, Antoine de. *La Caricature révolutionnaire.* Paris: P du C.N.R.S., 1988.

— "Pamphlets: Libel and Political Mythology." *Revolution in Print: The Press in France: 1775–1800.* Ed. Robert Darnton and Daniel Roche. Berkeley: U of California P, 1989. 165–76.

— "The 'Livres remplis d'horreur': Pornographic Literature and Politics at the Beginning of the French Revolution." *Erotica and the Enlightenment.* Ed. Peter Wagner. Frankfurt am Main: Peter Lang, 1991. 123–65.

Baguley, David, ed. [*Cabeen*] *Critical Bibliography of French Literature: The Nineteenth Century.* Vol. 5. Syracuse: Syracuse UP, 1994.

Bakwin, H. "Emotional Deprivation in Infants." *Journal of Pediatrics* 35 (1949): 512–21.

Balzac, Honoré de. "Etudes sur M. Beyle (Frédéric Stendalh [sic])" (1840). Rpt. *La Critique stendhalienne*. Ed. Talbot. 15–68.

Barbéris, Pierre. *Sur Stendhal*. Paris: Editions sociales/Messidor, 1982.

Bardèche, Maurice, ed. "Notice." *La Vieille Fille. Œuvres complètes*. By Balzac. Vol. 6 (Paris: Club de l'Honnête Homme, 1956) 551–63.

— *Stendhal romancier*. Paris: La Table Ronde, 1947.

Bardet, Jean-Pierre, et al. "La Mortalité maternelle autrefois: Une Etude comparée (de la France de l'ouest à l'Utah)," *Annales de Démographie Historique* 1981: 31–48.

Bardet, Jean-Pierre. "Pour que vivent les enfants trouvés." *Annales de Démographie Historique* 1973: 395–400.

Bayley, John. "Character and Consciousness." *New Literary History* 5 (1974) 225–35.

Benrekassa, Georges. *Le Concentrique et l'excentrique: Marges des lumières*. Paris: Payot, 1980.

— "Le Typique et le fabuleux: Histoire et roman dans la *Vie de mon père*." *Revue des Sciences Humaines* 44.172 (1978): 31–56.

Bernard, Claudie."Balzac et le roman historique: *Sur Catherine de Médicis*: Une Histoire paradoxale." *Poétique* 71 (1987): 333–55.

Bernier, Georges, cataloguer. "Louis-Leopold Boilly 1761–1845." *Art in Early XIX Century France: Consulat—Empire–Restauration: A Loan Exhibition for the Benefit of the Lycée Français of New York*. New York: Wildenstein, 1982.

Berthier, Philippe, ed. *La Vieille Fille, Le Cabinet des antiques*. By Balzac. Paris: Garnier-Flammarion, 1987.

— *Stendhal et la sainte famille*. Geneva: Droz, 1983.

Bibas, Henriette. "Le Double dénouement et la morale du *Rouge*." *Revue d'Histoire Littéraire de la France* 49 (1949): 21–36.

Billault, Alain. "Les Amants dans l'île: Longus, Bernardin de Saint-Pierre, Mishima." *Bulletin de l'Association Guillaume Budé* 1 (1985): 73–86.

Bishop, Lloyd. *The Romantic Hero and His Heirs in French Literature*. New York: Peter Lang, 1984.

Blankenhorn, David. *Fatherless America: Confronting Our Most Urgent Social Problem*. New York: Basic Books, 1995.

Blum, Alain, and Jacques Houdaille. "12 000 Parisiens en 1793: Sondage dans les cartes de civisme." *Population* 41.2 (1986): 259–302.

Bøggild, Bente. "Une Analyse de Paul et Virginie." *(Pré)publications* 94 (1985): 1–35.

Bonnet, J.-C. "De la famille à la patrie." *Histoire des pères*. Ed. Delumeau and Roche. 235–58.

— "La Malédiction Paternelle." *Dix-Huitième Siècle* 12 (1980): 195–208.

Book-Senninger, Claude. *Théophile Gautier: Auteur dramatique*. Paris: Nizet, 1972.

Bossenga, Gail. *The Politics of Privilege: Old Regime and Revolution in Lille*. Cambridge: Cambridge UP, 1991.

Bradley, Keith R. "Wet-Nursing at Rome: A Study in Social Relations." *The*

Family in Ancient Rome: New Perspectives. Ed. Beryl Rawson. Ithaca: Cornell Univ. Press, 1986. 201–29.

Bray, Bernard. "Paul et Virginie, Un Texte variable à usages didactiques divers." *Revue d'Histoire Littéraire de la France* 89.5 (1989): 856–78.

Bray, René. *La Formation de la doctrine classique en France.* Lausanne: Payot, 1931.

Bremond, Claude. *Logique du récit.* Paris: Seuil, 1973.

Brennan, Thomas. *Public Drinking and Popular Culture in Eighteenth-Century Paris.* Princeton: Princeton UP, 1988.

Brierre de Boismont, Alexandre. *Du suicide et de la folie-suicide considérés dans leurs rapports avec le statistique.* Paris: G. Baillière, 1856.

Brombert, Victor. "Stendhal lecteur de Rousseau." *Revue des Sciences Humaines* 92 (1958): 463–82.

— *Stendhal: Fiction and the Themes of Freedom.* Chicago: U of Chicago P, 1968.

Brooks, Peter. *Reading for the Plot: Design and Intention in Narrative.* New York: Knopf, 1984.

— *The Melodramatic Imagination: Balzac, Henry James, Melodrama, and the Mode of Excess.* New Haven: Yale UP, 1976.

Brouard-Arends, Isabelle. *Vies et images maternelles dans la littérature française du dix-huitième siècle. Studies on Voltaire and the Eighteenth Century.* No. 291. Oxford: Voltaire Foundation, 1991.

Brouc, Martial. "Considerations sur les suicides de notre époque." *Annales d'hygiène publique et de médecine légale* 16 (1836): 223–62.

Brown, James W. "The Ideological and Aesthetic Functions of Food in Paul et Virginie." *Eighteenth-Century Life* 4.3 (1978): 61–67.

Burke, Kenneth. *A Grammer of Motives.* New York: Prentice-Hall, 1945.

Burton, Richard. *The* Flaneur *and His City: Patterns of Daily Life in Paris 1815–1851.* Durham: U of Durham P, 1994.

Cabantous, A. "La Fin des patriarches." *Histoire des pères.* Ed. Jean Delumeau and Daniel Roche. 323–48.

Caro, Elme. "Le Suicide dans ses rapports avec la civilisation." *Nouvelles Etudes morales sur le temps présent.* Paris: Hachette, 1869. 1–103.

— "Stendhal: Ses Romans" (1855). *Critique stendhalienne.* Ed. Talbot. 173–96.

Castex, Pierre-Georges, ed. *La Vieille Fille.* By Balzac. Paris: Garnier, 1957.

Cazauran, Nicole. *Catherine de Médicis et son temps dans* La Comédie humaine. Geneva: Droz, 1976.

— "Sur l'apologie balzacienne de la saint-Barthélemy." *Revue d'Histoire Littéraire* 73.5 (1973): 859–75.

Chagniot, Jean. *Paris au XVIIIe siècle: Nouvelle Histoire de Paris.* Paris: Hachette, 1988.

Chaitin, Gilbert D. *The Unhappy Few: A Psychological Study of the Novels of Stendhal.* Bloomington: Indiana UP, 1972.

Chamoux, Antoinette. "L'Enfance abandonneé à Reims à la fin du XVIIIe siècle." *Annales de Démographie Historique* 1973: 263–85.

— "Mise en nourrice et mortalité des enfants légitimes." *Annales de Démographie Historique* 1973: 418–22.

Chatelain, Abel. "Les Migrations temporaires françaises au XIXe siècle: Problèmes. Méthodes. Documentation." *Annales de Démographie Historique* 1967: 11–27.

Chatman, Seymore. "The Structure of Fiction." *University Review* 37 (Spring 1971): 199–214.

— *Story and Discourse: Narrative Structure in Fiction and Film.* Ithaca: Cornell UP, 1978.

Chauvet, Pierre. *Essai sur la propreté de Paris.* Paris: Chez l'Auteur, Year V (1797).

Check, James V.P., and Ted H. Guloien. "Reported Proclivity for Coercive Sex Following Repeated Exposure to Sexually Violent Pornography, Nonviolent Dehumanizing Pornography, and Erotica." *Pornography: Research Advances and Policy Considerations.* Ed. D. Zillmann and J. Bryant. Hillsdale, New Jersey: Lawrence Erlbaum, 1989. 159–84

Cherpack, Clifton. "Paul et Virginie and the Myths of Death." *PMLA* 90.2 (1975): 247 - 55.

Chesnais, Jean-Claude. *Histoire de la violence en Occident de 1800 à nos jours.* Collection Pluriel. Paris: Robert Laffont, 1981.

Chevalier, Louis. *Classes laborieuses et classes dangereuses à Paris, pendant la première moitié du XIXe siècle.* Pluriel. 1958; Paris: Hachette, 1984.

Chodorow, Nancy. "Gender, Relation, and Difference in Psychoanalytic Perspective." *The Future of Difference.* Ed. Hester Eisenstein and Alice Jardine. Boston: G.K. Hall, 1980. 3–19.

Christensen, Peter G. "Yeats and Balzac's *Sur Catherine de Médicis.*" *Modern Language Studies* 19.4 (1989): 11–30.

Claverie, Michel. "Thérèse Raquin ou les Atrides dans la boutique du Pont-Neuf," *Cahiers Naturalistes* 36 (1968): 138–47.

Cobb, Richard. *Death in Paris.* Oxford: Oxford UP, 1978.

Coghlin, Ellen K. "Mother Love and Infant Death in a Brazilian Shantytown" (a review essay of Nancy Scheper-Hughes's *Death Without Weeping*). *The Chronicle of Higher Education,* June 10, 1992: 7–9.

Connon, Michel. "Pères, mères et fils dans le roman stendhalien." *Stendhal Club* 27 (1985): 163–76.

Cook, Malcolm C. "Harmony and Discord in *Paul et Virginie.*" *Eighteenth-Century Fiction* 3.3 (April 1991): 205–16.

Cooper, Barbara T. "Breaking Up/Down/Apart: 'L'Eclatement' as a Unifying Principle in Musset's *Lorenzaccio.*" *Philological Quarterly* 65.1 (1986): 103–12.

— "Parodie et pastiche: La Réception théâtrale d'*Antony.*" *Œuvres et Critiques* 21.1 (1996): 112–31.

— "The Return of Martin Guerre in an Early Nineteenth Century French Melodrama." *Melodrama: the Cultural Emergence of a Genre.* Ed. Michael Hays and Anastasia Nikolopoulou. New York: St. Martin's Press, 1996. 103–20.

Corbin, Alain. *From the Fires of Revolution to the Great War.* Ed. Michelle Perrot. Trans. Arthur Goldhammer. Vol. 4 of *A History of Private Life.* Cambridge: Harvard UP, 1990. 457–613.

Coulet, Henri. "Des Grieux et Manon, Paul et Virginie entre nature et civilisation." *Littératures* 23 (automne 1990): 103–15

Cranston, Maurice. *The Romantic Movement*. Oxford: Blackwell, 1994.

Crider, Andrew B., George R. Goethals, Robert D. Kavanaugh, Paul R. Solomon. *Psychology*. 4th ed. New York: Harper Collins, 1993.

Crubellier, Maurice. *L'Enfance et la jeunesse dans la société française, 1800–1950*. Paris: Armand Colin, 1979.

Cushman, Philip. "Why the Self is Empty: Toward a Historically Situated Psychology." *American Psychologist* 45.5 (May 1990): 599–611.

Cyrulnik, Boris. "Le Sentiment incestueux." *De l'incest*. Ed. Françoise Heritier. Paris: Odile Jacob, 1994. 23–70.

Daprini, Pierre B. "Le Moraliste sans foi ou la structure anthropologique de *La Chartreuse de Parme*." *Stendhal Club* 25.98 (1983): 283–96.

Darnton, Robert. *The Forbidden Best-Sellers of Pre-Revolutionary France*. New York: W.W. Norton, 1995.

— *The Literary Underground of the Old Regime*. Cambridge: Harvard UP, 1982.

David, Marcel. *Fraternité et Révolution française*. Paris: Aubier, 1987.

— *Le Printemps de la fraternité: Genèse et vicissitudes 1830–1875*. Paris: Aubier, 1992.

de Vries, Jan. *European Urbanization 1500–1800*. Cambridge: Harvard UP, 1984.

DeJean, Joan. "The Politics of Pornography: L'Ecole des Filles." *The Invention of Pornography: Obscenity and the Origins of Modernity, 1500–1800*. Ed. Lynn Hunt. New York: Zone Books, 1993. 109–123.

Delécluze, Etienne. *Souvenirs de soixante années*. Paris: Lévy, 1862.

Delumeau, Jean, and Daniel Roche, eds. *Histoire des pères et de la paternité*. Paris: Larousse, 1990.

Denby, David J. *Sentimental Narrative and the Social Order in France, 1760–1820*. Cambridge: Cambridge UP, 1994.

Diderot, Denis, and Jean Le Rond d'Alembert, eds. *Encyclopédie, ou Dictionnaire raisonné des sciences, des arts et des métiers*. 17 vols. Paris: Briasson, 1751–65.

Dolezel, Lubomir. "Narrative Composition: A Link Between German and Russian Poetics." *Russian Formalism*. Ed. S. Bann and J.E. Bowlt. New York: Barnes & Nobel, 1973. 73–84.

Donnerstein, E. "Pornography: Its Effect on Violence Against Women," *Pornography and Sexual Aggression*. Ed. N. Malamuth and E. Donnerstein. New York: Academic Press, 1984. 53–81.

Donzelot, Jacques. *The Policing of Families*. Trans. Robert Hurley. 1977; New York Pantheon, 1979.

Douthwaite, Julia V. *Exotic Women: Literary Heroines and Cultural Strategies in Ancien Régime France*. Philadelphia: U of Pennsylvania P, 1992.

Duché, Emile. "De l'industrie des nourrices et de la mortalité des petits enfants dans le département de l'Yonne." *Annuaire de l'Yonne* 1868: 160–81.

Dunkley, John. "Paul et Virginie: Aesthetic Appeal and Archetypal Structures." *Trivium* 13 (1978): 95–112.

Dunn, Susan. *The Deaths of Louis XVI: Regicide and the French Political Imagination*. Princeton: Princeton UP, 1994.

Dupâquier, Jacques. *Histoire de la population française*. Vol. 2. Paris: Presses Universitaires de France, 1988.

Durand, Gilbert. *"Lucien Leuwen* ou l'héroïsme à l'envers," *Stendhal Club* 3 (15 avril 1959): 201–25.

Durham, Carolyn A. "Fearful Symmetry: The Mother–Daughter Theme in *La Religieuse* and *Paul et Virginie.*" *Fearful Symmetry: Doubles and Doubling in Literature and Film.* Ed. Eugene J. Crook. Tallahassee, UP of Florida, 1981. 32–40.

Durkheim, Emile. *Le Suicide, étude de sociologie* (1898). Nouv. éd. Paris: F. Alcan, 1930.

Eliel, Carol S. *Form and Content in the Genre Works of Louis-Léopold Boilly.* Ann Arbor: 1985.

— "Louis Boilly, précurseur de l'esthétique moderne." *Louis Boilly 1762–1845.* Paris: Musée Marmottan, 1984.

Fabre, Jean. "Paul et Virginie, pastorale." *Lumières et romantisme: Energie et nostalgie de Rousseau à Mickiewicz.* Paris: Klincksieck, 1963. 167–99.

Faguet, Emile. "Stendhal" (1892). *Politiques et moralistes du dix - neuvième siècle.* 3e série. Paris: Société Française d'Imprimerie et de Librairie, 1899. 1–64.

Farber, M. D. "The Suicide of Young Werther." *Psychoanalytic Review* 60.2 (1973): 239–76.

Fave, Robert. *La Mort dans la littérature et la pensée françaises au siècle des lumières.* Lyon: PU de Lyon, 1978. 469–96.

Faÿ-Sallois, Fanny. *Les Nourrices à Paris au XIXe siècle.* Paris: Payot, 1980.

Febvre, Lucien. "La Sensibilité et l'histoire: Comment reconstituer la vie affective d'autrefois?" *Combats pour l'histoire.* Paris: Armand Colin, 1953. 221–38.

— "Une Vue d'ensemble. Histoire et psychologie." *Combats pour l'histoire.* 207–20

— *Le Problème de l'incroyance au XVIe siècle: La Religion de Rabelais.* Paris: Albin Michel, 1942.

[Ferguson], Priscilla Clark. *The Battle of the Bourgeois: The Novel in France, 1789–1848.* Paris: Didier, 1973.

Ferguson, Priscilla Parkhurst. *Paris as Revolution: Writing the Nineteenth-Century City.* Berkeley: U of California P, 1994.

[Ferguson], Priscilla P. Clark. "Suicide, société et sociologie de Durkheim à Balzac." *Nineteenth-Century French Studies* 3 (1973): 200–12.

Ferrier, Ginette. "Sur un personnage de *La Chartreuse de Parme*: Le Comte Mosca." *Stendhal Club* 13 (1971): 9–43.

Fildes, Valerie. *Wet Nursing: A History from Antiquity to the Present.* Oxford: Basil Blackwell, 1988.

Finch, Alison. *Stendhal: La Chartreuse de Parme.* London: Edward Arnold, 1984.

Findlen, Paula, "Humanism, Politics and Pornography in Renaissance Italy." *The Invention of Pornography: Obscenity and the Origins of Modernity, 1500 - 1800.* Ed. Lynn Hunt. New York: Zone Books, 1993. 49–108.

Flahaut, François. "*Paul et Virginie* lu comme un mythe." *Revue philosophique de la France de l'Etranger* 3 (1968): 361–79.

Flinn, Michael W. *The European Demographic System, 1500–1820.* Baltimore: Johns Hopkins UP, 1981.

Forster, E.M. *Aspects of the Novel*. Harvest Books. New York: Harcourt, Brace, 1954.

Fort, Bernadette, ed. *Fictions of the French Revolution*. Evanston: Northwestern UP, 1991.

Fourier, Charles. *Le Nouveau Monde industriel et sociétaire*. Paris: Bossange père, 1829.

— *Théorie de l'unité universelle* (1822). *Œuvres complètes*. 2nd ed. 6 vols. Paris: Société pour la Propagation et pour la Réalisation de la Théorie de Fourier, 1841–48.

— *Traité de l'association domestique agricole*. 2 vols. Paris: Bossange, 1822.

Fox, Robin. *The Red Lamp of Incest: An Inquiry into the Origins of Mind and Society*. Notre Dame: U of Notre Dame P, 1983

Francis, R.A. "Bernardin de Saint-Pierre's *Paul et Virginie* and the Failure of the Ideal State in the Eighteenth-Century French Novel." *Nottingham French Studies* 13.2 (1974): 49–60.

Freud, Sigmund. *The Interpretation of Dreams* (1900). *The Basic Writings of Sigmund Freud*. Trans. A.A. Brill. New York: Modern Library, 1938.

— "The Relation of the Poet to Day-Dreaming" (1908). *Collected Papers*. 1925; London: Hogarth, 1957. 173–83.

— "Twenty-Third Lecture: General Theory of the Neurosis: The Development of the Symptoms" (1917). *A General Introduction to Psychoanalysis*. Trans. G. Stanley Hall. New York: Boni & Liveright, 1920. 311–27.

Frye, Northrop ed. *Romanticism Reconsidered: Selected Papers from the English Institute*. New York: Columbia UP, 1963.

Fuchs, Rachel G. *Abandoned Children: Foundlings and Child Welfare in Nineteenth-Century France*. Albany: State University of New York Press, 1984.

Furst, Lilian R. *The Contours of European Romanticism*. London: Macmillan, 1979.

Galliano, Paul. "La Mortalité infantile (indigènes et nourrisons) dans la banlieu sud de Paris à la fin du XVIIIe siècle (1774–1794)." *Annales de Démographie Historique* 1966: 139–53.

Garber, Frederick. "Self, Society, Value, and the Romantic Hero." *The Hero in Literature*. Ed. Victor Brombert. New York: Fawcett, 1969. 213–27.

Garrioch, David. *Neighbourhood and Community in Paris, 1740–1790*. Cambridge: Cambridge UP, 1986.

George, Albert J. *The Development of French Romanticism: The Impact of the Industrial Revolution on Literature*. Syracuse: Syracuse UP, 1955.

— "Théophile Gautier and the Romantic Short Story." *L'Esprit Créateur* 3 (1963): 110–17.

Giraud, Raymond. *The Unheroic Hero in the Novels of Stendhal, Balzac and Flaubert*. New Brunswick, NJ: Rutgers Univ. Press, 1957.

Goldmann, Lucien. *Pour une sociologie du roman*. Paris: Gallimard, 1964.

— *Racine*. Trans. Alastair Hamilton. 1956; Cambridge: Rivers Press, 1972.

Goodden, Angelica. "Tradition and Innovation in *Paul et Virginie*: A Thematic Study." *Modern Language Review* 77.3 (1982): 558–67.

Gouesse, Jean-Marie. "Parenté, famille et mariage en Normandie aux XVIIe et XVIIIe siècles: Présentation d'une source et d'une enquête." *Annales Economies Sociétés Civilisations* 27 (1972): 1139–54.

Grant, Richard B. "The Rise and Fall of Romantic Sainthood: Chateaubriand to George Sand. " Paper presented at the Colloquium in Nineteenth-Century French Studies, October 12, 1990.

Greaves, A. E. *Stendhal's Italy: Themes of Political and Religious Satire.* Exeter: U of Exeter P, 1995.

Guérin, Michel. *La Politique de Stendhal.* Paris: P.U.F., 1982.

Guerry, André-Michel. *Essai sur la statistique morale de la France.* Paris: Crochard, 1833.

Guise, René. "Balzac et le roman feuilleton." *L'Année Balzacienne* 1964: 283–338.

Guitton, Edouard, ed. "Introduction." *Paul et Virginie.* By Bernardin de Saint-Pierre. Paris: Imprimerie Nationale, 1984. 9–59.

Gutierrez, Hector, and Jacques Houdaille. "La Mortalité maternelle en France au XVIIIe siècle." *Population* 38.6 (1983): 975–93.

Gutwirth, Madelyn. "The Engulfed Beloved: Representations of Dead and Dying Women in the Art and Literature of the Revolutionary Era." *Rebel Daughters: Women and the French Revolution.* Ed. Sara E. Melzer and Leslie W. Rabine. New York: Oxford UP, 1992. 198–227.

Haig, Stirling. *Stendhal: The Red and the Black.* Cambridge: Cambridge UP, 1989.

Hallam, John Stephen. *The Genre Works of Louis-Léopold Boilly.* Ann Arbor: 1979.

— "The Two Manners of Louis-Léopold Boilly and French Genre Painting in Transition." *Art Bulletin* 63 (1981): 618–33.

Hamilton, James F. "Reason and Sentiment in Montesquieu's Understanding of Suicide." *American Society Legion of Honor Magazine* 47 (1976): 101–14.

— "Stendhal's *Le Rouge et le noir* and Rousseau's *Emile*: Contrary Experiments." *Nineteenth-Century French Studies* 6 (1978): 199–212.

— "The Anxious Hero in Chateaubriand's *René.*" *Romance Quarterly* 34 (1987): 415–24.

Hamm, Jean-Jacques. "Hypothèses sur quelques noms propres de *Rouge et noir.*" *Stendhal Club* 18 (1976): 228–34.

Healy, Jane M. *Endangered Minds: Why our Children Don't Think.* New York: Simon & Schuster, 1990.

Hélin, Etienne. "Une Sollicitude ambiguë: L'Evacuation des enfants abandonnés." *Annales de Démographie Historique* 1973: 225–29.

Hemmings, F.W.J. "Julien Sorel and Julian the Apostate." *French Studies* 16 (1962): 229–44.

— *Stendhal: A Study of His Novels.* Oxford: Clarendon P, 1964.

— "L'Unité artistique de La Chartreuse de Parme." *Communications présentées au Congrès Stendhalien de Civitavecchia* [1964]. Ed. V. Del Litto. Publications de l'Institut Français de Florence, 1ère série—Collection d'études d'histoire, de critique et de philologie—no. 16. Firenze: Sansoni Antiquariato, 1966. 224–31.

Henry, Louis. "Deux analyses de l'immigration à Paris. 1) Le Volume de l'immigration à Paris de 1740 à 1792." *Population* 26.6 (1971): 1073–85.

Hiddleston, James. "Literature and Suicide." *The Play of Terror in Nineteenth-Century France*. Ed. John T. Booker and Allan H. Pasco. Newark: U of Delaware Press, 1996. 209–25.

Higonnet, Margaret R. "Suicide as Self-Construction." *Germaine de Staël: Crossing the Borders*. Ed. Madelyn Gutwirth, et al. New Brunswick: Rutgers UP, 1991. 69–81.

— "Joint Suicide in Eighteenth-Century French Literature and Revolutionary Politics." *Fictions of the French Revolution*. Ed. Bernadette Fort. 87–110.

Holmes, Glyn. *The "Adolphe Type" in French Fiction in the First Half of the Nineteenth Century*. Sherbrooke, Quebec: Naaman, 1977. 159–98.

Honig, Edwin. *Dark Conceit: The Making of Allegory*. 1959; Cambridge: Walker de Berry, 1960

Hoog, Armand. "L'Ame préromantique et les instincts de mort; II: La Poésie de la mort dans le silence de la littérature (1798–1808)." *Bulletin de la Faculté des Lettres de Strasbourg* 1952: 149–60.

— "Un Cas d'angoisse préromantique." *Revue des Sciences Humaines* 67 (1952): 181–98.

— "Who Invented the 'Mal du siècle'?" *Yale French Studies* 13 (1954): 49–50.

Houdaille, Jacques. "La Mortalité des enfants dans la France rurale de 1690–1779." *Population* 39.1 (1984): 77–106.

Hubert, J.D. *Essai d'exégèse racinienne: Les Secrets témoins*. Paris: Nizet, 1956.

Hufton, Olwen H. *Women and the Limits of Citizenship in the French Revolution*. Toronto: U of Toronto P, 1992.

Hunt, Lynn, ed. *The Invention of Pornography: Obscenity and the Origins of Modernity, 1500–1800*. New York: Zone Books, 1993.

— "Introduction: Obscenity and the Origins of Modernity, 1500–1800." *The Invention of Pornography*. Ed. Lynn Hunt. 9–45.

— "Pornography and the French Revolution." *The Invention of Pornography*. Ed. Lynn Hunt. 301 - 39.

— *The Family Romance of the French Revolution*. Berkeley: U of California P, 1992.

— "The Many Bodies of Marie Antoinette: Political Pornography and the Problem of the Feminine in the French Revolution." *Eroticism and the Body Politic*. Ed. Lynn Hunt. Baltimore: Johns Hopkins UP, 1990. 109–30.

Jacobus, Mary. "Incorruptible Milk: Breast - Feeding and the French Revolution." *Rebel Daughters*. Ed. Melzer and Rabine. 54–75.

James, Henry. "The Art of Fiction." *The Art of Fiction and Other Essays*. Ed. Morris Roberts. New York: Oxford UP, 1948.

Jameson, Fredric. "The Ideology of Form: Partial Systems in *La Vieille Fille*." *Sub-stance* 15 (1976): 29–49.

Jaucourt, Chevalier de. "Père." *Encyclopédie*. Ed. Diderot and D'Alembert 12.338–39.

Jefferson, Ann. "Représentation de la politique, politique de la représentation: *La Chartreuse de Parme*." *Stendhal Club* 27.107 (1985): 200–13.

Johansen, Hans B. "Notes sur la structure de *la Chartreuse de Parme*." *Actes du 4e Congrès des Romanistes Scandinaves. Revue Romane* Numéro Spécial 1 (1967): 194–206.

— *Stendhal et le roman: Essai sur la structure du roman stendhalien.* Aran: Grand Chêne, 1979.

Jost, François. "Littérature et suicide de *Werther* à *Madame Bovary.*" *Revue de Littérature Comparée* 42 (1968): 161–98.

Kadish, Doris Y. *Politicizing Gender: Narrative Strategies in the Aftermath of the French Revolution.* New Brunswick: Rutgers UP, 1991.

Kavanagh, Thomas M. *Enlightenment and the Shadows of Chance: The Novel and the Culture of Gambling in Eighteenth-Century France.* Baltimore: Johns Hopkins UP, 1993.

Kelly, Van. "Criteria for the Epic: Borders, Diversity, and Expansion." *Epic and Epoch: Essays on the Interpretation and History of a Genre.* Ed. Steven M. Oberhelman, Van Kelly, and Richard J. Golsan. Lubbock: Texas Tech UP, 1994. 1–21.

Kermode, Frank. *The Sense of an Ending.* New York: Oxford UP, 1967.

Kinder, Patricia. "Un Directeur de journal, ses auteurs et ses lecteurs en 1836: Autour de La Vieille Fille." *L'Année Balzacienne* 1972: 173–200.

Knibiehler, Yvonne. "La Maternité en question." *L'Histoire des mères du moyen-âge à nos jours.* N.p.: Montalba, 1980. 262–364.

Kopp, Robert, ed. *La Vieille Fille.* By Balzac. Folio. Paris: Gallimard, 1978.

Kronenberger, Louis. "Stendhal's *Charterhouse.*" *Encounter* 27 (July 1966): 32–38.

Lachaise, Claude. *Topographie médicale de Paris.* Paris: J. B. Baillière, 1822.

Ladurie, Emmanuel Le Roy. "Les Comptes fantastiques de Gregory King," *Le Territoire de l'historien.* 2 vols. Paris: Gallimard, 1978. 1.252–70.

— "La Crise et l'historien." *Le Territoire de l'historien.* 2.429–49.

— "L'Ethnographie à la Rétif." *Le Territoire de l'historien.* 2.337–97.

Laffly, Georges. "La Politique dans *La Vieille Fille.*" *Ecrits de Paris* novembre 1970: 66–75.

Lallemand, Léon. *Histoire des enfants abandonnées et délaissés: Etudes sur la protection de l'enfance aux diverses époques de la civilisation.* Paris: Alphonse Picard, 1885.

Landes, Joan B. "Representing the Body Politic: The Paradox of Gender in the Graphic Politics of the French Revolution." *Rebel Daughters.* Ed. Melzer and Rabine. 15–37.

Landry, François. *L'Imagination chez Stendhal.* Lausanne: L'Age d'Homme, 1982.

Lane, Harlan. *The Wild Boy of Aveyron.* Cambridge: Harvard UP, 1976.

Le Yaouanc, Moïse. "Le Plaisir dans les récits balzaciennes," *L'Année Balzacienne* 1973: 201–33.

Lebègue, Raymond. "De Marguerite de Navarre à Honoré de Balzac." *Comptes rendus de l'Académie des Inscriptions et Belles-Lettres* July 1957: 251–56.

Lecour, C. J. *La Prostitution à Paris et à Londres, 1789–1870.* Paris: Asselin, 1870.

Lecuyer, Maurice A. *Balzac et Rabelais.* Paris: Les Belles Lettres, 1956.

Levin, Harry. "*The Red and the Black*: Social Originality." *Stendhal's* The Red and the Black. Ed. Harold Bloom. New York: Chelsea House, 1988. 25–33.

Levitine, George. *Girodet-Trioson: An Iconographical Study.* New York: Garland, 1978.

Lieberman, Lisa Jo. "Romanticism and the Culture of Suicide in Nineteenth-Century France." *Comparative Studies in Society and History* 33.3 (1991): 623–29.

— "Une Maladie épidémique: Suicide and Its Implications in Nineteenth-Century France," diss. Yale U, 1987.

Lioure, Michel. *Le Drame*. Paris: Armand Colin, 1963.

Lloyd, Rosemary. *The Land of Lost Content: Children and Childhood in Nineteenth-Century French Literature*. Oxford: Clarendon, 1992.

Longstaffe, Moya. "L'Ethique du duel et la couronne du martyre dans *Le Rouge et le noir*." *Stendhal Club* 72 (1976): 283–306.

Lowrie, Joyce O. "The Structural Significance of Sensual Imagery in *Paul et Virginie*." *Romance Notes* 12 (1971): 351–56.

Lukács, György. *Studies in European Realism*. London: Hillway, 1950.

— *The Theory of the Novel*. Trans. Anna Bostyock. Cambridge: M.I.T. Press, 1971.

Madelénat, Daniel. *L'Epopée*. Paris: P.U.F., 1986.

Maigron, Louis. *Le Romantisme et les mœurs: Essai d'étude historique et sociale d'après des documents inédits*. 1910; rpt. Geneva: Slatkine Reprints, 1977. 312–50.

Maisch, Herbert. *Incest*. Trans. Colin Bearne. 1968; New York, Stein and Day, 1972.

Mandrou, Robert. *Introduction to Modern France, 1500–1640: An Essay in Historical Psychology*. Trans. R.E. Hallmark. New York: Holmes & Meier, 1976.

Marmontel, Jean-François. "Epopée." *Eléments de littérature* (1787). *Œuvres complètes*. 14 vols. Paris: Verdière, 1818–20. 13.347–80.

Marshall, W.L. "Pornography and Sex Offenders." *Pornography: Research Advances and Policy Considerations*. Ed. D. Zillmann and J. Bryant. Hillsdale, New Jersey: Lawrence Erlbaum, 1989. 185–214.

Martin, Angus, Vivienne G. Mylne, Richard Frautschi. *Bibliographie du genre romanesque français: 1751–1800*. London: Mansell, 1977.

Martineau, Henri. "Introduction." *Le Rouge et le noir*. By Stendhal. Paris: Garnier, 1960. i–xxxiv.

Mauron, Charles. *L'Inconscient dans l'œuvre et la vie de Racine*. Aix-en-Province: Faculté des Lettres, 1957.

Mauzi, Robert. *L'Idée du bonheur dans la littérature et la pensée françaises au XVIIIᵉ siècle*. 1979; Paris: Albin Michel, 1994.

— ed. "Préface." *Paul et Virginie*. By Bernardan de Saint-Pierre. Paris: Garnier-Flammarion, 1966. 11–24.

— "Les Maladies de l'âme au XVIIIᵉ siècle." *Revue des Sciences Humaines* 100 (1960): 459–93.

May, Georges. *Le Dilemme du roman au XVIIIᵉ siècle: Etude sur les rapports du roman et de la critique (1715 - 1761)*. New Haven: Yale UP, 1963.

May, Gita. "Staël and the Fascination of Suicide: The Eighteenth-Century Background." *Germaine de Staël: Crossing the Borders*. Ed. Madelyn Gutwirth, et al. New Brunswick: Rutgers UP, 1991. 168–76.

McCarthy, Mary. "Characters in Fiction. " Ed. Shiv K. Kumar and Keith McKean. *Critical Approaches to Fiction*. New York: McGraw-Hill, 1968. 79–95.

McWatters, K. G. *"Lucien Leuwen* et l'armée impossible." *Le Plus Méconnu des romans de Stendhal: Lucien Leuwen.* Colloque de la Société des Etudes Romantiques. Paris; SEDES, 1983. 141–53.

Meiselman, Karin C. *Incest: A Psychological Study of Causes and Effects with Treatment Recommendations.* San Francisco: Jossey-Bass, 1978.

Melzer, Sara E., and Leslie W. Rabine, eds. *Rebel Daughters:Women and the French Revolution.* New York: Oxford UP, 1992.

Ménétra, Jacques-Louis. *Journal of My Life.* Trans. Arthur Goldhammer. Ed. Daniel Roche. New York: Columbia UP, 1986.

Merrick, Jeffrey W. *The Desacralization of the French Monarchy in the Eighteenth Century.* Baton Rouge: Louisiana State UP, 1990.

— "Patriarchalism and Constitutionalism in Eighteenth-Century Parlementary Discourse." *Studies in Eighteenth-Century Culture* 20 (1990): 317–30.

— "Patterns and Prosecution of Suicide in Eighteenth-Century Paris." *Historical Reflections/Réflexions Historiques* 16 (1989): 1–53.

— "Sexual Politics and Public Order in Late Eighteenth-Century France: The *Mémoires secrets* and the *Correspondance secrète.*" *Journal of the History of Sexuality* 1 (1990): 68–84.

Michel, François. *Etudes stendhaliennes.* 2nd ed. Paris: Mercure de France, 1972.

Mikulincer, Mario. *Human Learned Helplessness: A Coping Perspective.* New York: Plenum P, 1994.

Miller, Nancy K. "Tristes Triangles: *Le Lys dans la vallée* and Its Intertext." *Pre-text/Text/Context: Essays on Nineteenth-Century French Literature.* Ed. Robert L. Mitchell. Columbus, Ohio State UP, 1980. 67–77.

Mitchell, B.R. *European Historical Statistics: 1750–1975.* 2nd ed. London: Macmillan, 1981.

Moreau, Pierre. *Le Romantisme.* Paris: del Duca, 1957.

Morot-Sir, Edouard. "La Dynamique du théâtre et Molière." *Romance Notes* 15, supplement no. 1 (1973): 15–49.

Mortimer, Armine. "Balzac's *Vieille Fille* and Her Corset." Paper presented at the Colloqium in Nineteenth-Century French Studies, October 22, 1994.

Mossman, Carol A. *The Narrative Matrix: Stendhal's* Le Rouge et le noir. Lexington: French Forum, 1984.

Mozet, Nicole, ed. "Introduction." *La Vieille Fille. La Comédie humaine.* By Honoré de Balzac. Ed Pierre-Georges Castex. Vol. 4. Bibliothèque de la Pléiade. Paris: Gallimard, 1976. 795–810.

Mudrick, Marvin. "Character and Event in Fiction." *Critical Approaches to Fiction.* Ed. Shiv K. Kumar and Keith McKean. New York: McGraw-Hill, 1968. 97–112.

Mulliez, J. "La Volonté d'un homme." *Histoire des pères.* Ed. Delumeau and Roche. 279–312.

Mylne, Vivienne. *The Eighteenth-Century French Novel: Techniques of Illusion.* 2nd ed. Cambridge: Cambridge UP, 1981.

Nash, Susanne, ed. *Home and Its Dislocations in Nineteenth-Century France.* Albany: State U of New York P, 1993.

Niess, Robert J. "Sainte-Beuve and Balzac: *Volupté* and *Le Lys dans la vallée.*" *Kentucky Romance Quarterly* 1 (1973): 113–24.

Norberg, Kathryn. "'Love and Patriotism': Gender and Politics in the Life and Work of Louvet de Couvrai." *Rebel Daughters.* Ed. Melzer and Rabine. 38–53.

Parent-Duchâtelet, Alexandre-J.-B. *De la prostitution dans la ville de Paris.* 2nd ed. 2 vols. 1836; Paris: Baillière, 1837.

— "Essai sur les cloaques ou égouts de la ville de Paris" (1824). *Hygiène publique.* 2 vols. Paris: J. B. Baillière, 1836. 1.183–225.

Parent-Lardeur, Françoise. *Lire à Paris au temps de Balzac. Les Cabinets de lecture à Paris, 1830–1850.* Paris: Ecole des Hautes Etudes en Sciences Sociales, 1981.

Parker, H., and S. Parker. "Father–Daughter Sexual Abuse: An Emerging Perspective." *American Journal of Orthopsychiatry* 56 (1986): 531–49.

Pasco, Allan H. *Allusion: A Literary Graft.* Toronto: U of Toronto P, 1994.

— *Balzacian Montage: Configuring* La Comédie humaine. Toronto: U of Toronto P, 1991.

— *Novel Configurations: A Study of French Fiction.* 2nd ed. Birmingham: Summa, 1994

Pauvert, Jean-Jacques. *Sade vivant.* Vol. 1. Paris: Robert Laffont, 1986.

Pearson, Roger. *Stendhal's Violin.* Oxford: Clarendon Press, 1988.

Perlin, Seymour. *A Handbook for the Study of Suicide.* New York: Oxford UP, 1975.

Perrot, Michelle. "The Family Triumphant." *From the Fires of Revolution to the Great War.* Trans. Arthur Goldhammer. Ed. Michelle Perrot. Vol. 4 of *A History of Private Life.* Cambridge: Harvard UP, 1990. 98–165.

— "Roles and Characters." *From the Fires of Revolution.* Ed. Michelle Perrot. 167–259.

Peterson, Christopher, Steven F. Maier, Martin E.P. Seligman. *Learned Helplessness: A Theory for the Age of Personal Control.* New York: Oxford UP, 1993.

Pichois, Claude. *Littérature et progrès: Vitesse et vision du monde, essai.* Neuchâtel: La Baconnière, 1973.

Pierrard, Pierre. *La Vie ouvrière à Lille sous le Second Empire.* Paris: Bloud et Gay, 1965.

Planté, Christine. *La Petite Sœur de Balzac.* Paris: Seuil, 1989.

Porter, Laurence M. "The Present Directions of French Romantic Studies, 1960–1975." *Nineteenth-Century French Studies* 6.1–2 (1977 - 78): 1–20.

Poulet, Georges. "Timelessness and Romanticism." *Journal of the History of Ideas* 15 (1954): 3–22.

Prendergast, Christopher. *Paris and the Nineteenth Century.* Oxford: Blackwell, 1992.

— *The Order of Mimesis: Balzac, Stendhal, Nerval, Flaubert.* Cambridge: Cambridge UP, 1986.

Prioult, Albert. *Balzac avant* La Comédie humaine: *Contribution à l'étude de la genèse de son œuvre.* Paris: G. Gourville, 1936.

Propp, Vladimir. *Morphologie du conte.* 1928; Paris: Seuil, 1970.

Purdy, Anthony. "Un Cheval nommé Sorrel et une taupe régicide. Réflexions onomastiques sur *Le Rouge et le noir.*" *Stendhal Club* 22 (1980): 144–52.

Queffélec, Henri. "Préface." *La Vieille Fille. L'Œuvre de Balzac*. Ed. Albert Béguin and Jean A. Ducourneau. Vol. 1. Paris: Formes et Reflets, 1949. 893–901.

Queffélec, Lise. "*La Vieille Fille* ou la science des mythes en roman-feuilleton." *L'Année Balzacienne* 1988: 163–77.

Racault, Jean-Michel. "*Paul et Virginie* et l'utopie: de la 'petite société' au mythe collectif." *Studies on Voltaire and the Eighteenth Century*. No. 242. Oxford: Voltaire Foundation, 1986. 419–71.

— "Système de la toponymie et organisation de l'espace romanesque dans *Paul et Virginie*." *Studies on Voltaire and the Eighteenth Century*. No. 242. Oxford: Voltaire Foundation, 1986. 377–418.

— "Virginie entre la nature et la vertu: Cohésion narrative et contradictions idéologiques dans *Paul et Virginie*." *Dix-Huitième Siècle* 18 (1986): 389–404.

Ragland-Sullivan, Mary Eloise. "Julien's Quest for 'Self': Qui suis-je?" *Nineteenth-Century French Studies* 8 (Fall–Winter 1979–80) 1–13.

Ratcliff, Barrie M. "Classes laborieuses et classes dangereuses à Paris pendant la premiere moitié du XIXe siècle?: The Chevalier Thesis Reexamined." *French Historical Studies* 17 (1991): 1–70.

— "Suicides in the City: Perceptions and Realities of Self-Destruction in Paris in the First Half of the Nineteenth Century." *Historical Reflections* 18.1 (1992): 1–70.

Reid, Donald. *Paris Sewers and Sewermen: Realities and Representations*. Cambridge: Harvard UP, 1991.

Renvoizé, Jean. *Incest: A Family Pattern*. London: Routledge & Kegan Paul, 1982.

Revel, Jacques. "Marie-Antoinette in Her Fictions: The Staging of Hatred." *Fictions of the French Revolution*. Ed. Bernadette Fort. 111–29.

Rey, Pierre-Louis. La Chartreuse de Parme: Stendhal. *Analyse critique*. Paris: Hatier, 1973.

Ribble, M.A. "Anxiety in Infants and Its Disorganizing Effects." *Modern Trends in Child Psychiatry*. Ed. N.D.C. Lewis and B.L. Pacella. New York: International Universities P, 1945.

— "Infantile Experience in Relation to Personality Development." *Personality and Behavior Disorders*. Ed. J. M. Hunt. Vol. 2. New York: Ronald, 1944. 2: 621–51.

Ribner, Jonathan P. *Broken Tablets: The Cult of the Law in French Art from David to Delacroix*. Berkeley: U of California P, 1993.

— "Paintings of Terrorized parlementaires for the Bourbon Conseil d'état." *The Play of Terror in Nineteenth-Century France*. Ed. John T. Booker and Allan H. Pasco. Newark: U of Delaware Press, 1996.

Ricardou, Jean. "Discussion" after Nathalie Sarraute's "Ce que je cherche à faire." *Nouveau roman: Hier/aujourd'hui*. Ed. Jean Ricardou and Françoise van Rossom-Guyon. 2 vols. Paris: 10/18, 1972.

Rich, Adrienne. *Of Woman Born: Motherhood as Experience and Institution*. New York: Norton, 1976.

Ridge, George R. *The Hero in French Decadent Literature*. Athens: U of Georgia P, 1961.

Robbe-Grillet, Alain. *Pour un nouveau roman.* Collection Idées. Paris: N.R.F., 1963.

Robinson, Philip. *Bernardin de Saint-Pierre: Paul et Virginie.* Critical Guides to French Texts. London: Grant & Cutler, 1986.

Roche, Daniel. "Nouveaux Parisiens au XVIIIe siècle." *Cahiers d'Histoire* 24.3 (1979): 3–20.

Ronesse, J.-H. *Vues sur la propreté des rues de Paris.* N.p.: n.p., 1782.

Rose, William. *From Goethe to Byron: The Development of Weltschmerz in German Literature.* London: Routledge, 1924.

Roth, Michael S. "Returning to Nostalgia." *Home and Its Dislocations.* Ed. Susanne Nash. 25–43.

Rubin, David Lee. *A Pact with Silence: Art and Thought in La Fontaine's Fables.* Columbus: Ohio State UP, 1991.

— *Higher, Hidden Order: Design and Meaning in the Odes of Malherbe.* Chapel Hill: U of NC P, 1972.

— *The Knot of Artifice: A Poetic of the French Lyric in the Early 17th Century.* Columbus: Ohio State UP, 1981.

Ruff, Julius R. *Crime, Justice and Public Order in Old Regime France: The Sénéchaussées of Libourne and Bazas, 1696–1789.* London: Croom Helm, 1984.

Saddy, Pierre. "Le Cycle des immondices." *Dix-Huitième Siècle* 9 (1977) 203–14.

Saint-Amand, Pierre. *The Libertine's Progress: Seduction in the Eighteenth-Century French Novel.* Rev. ed. trans. Jennifer Curtiss Gage. Hanover: Brown/U Press of New England, 1994.

Sainte-Beuve, Charles Augustin. "M. de Stendhal: Ses Œuvres complètes" (2 janvier 1854). *Critique stendhalienne.* Ed. Talbot. 143–71.

Sarraute, Nathalie. *L'Ere du soupçon: Essais sur le roman.* Paris: Gallimard, 1956.

Sartre, Jean-Paul. "M. François Mauriac et la liberté." *Situations I: Essais critiques.* Paris: Gallimard, 1947. 33–52.

Schmidt, Albert-Marie. "Préface." *Sur Catherine de Médicis.* By Balzac. Vol. 11. *L'Œuvre de Balzac.* Paris: Club Français du Livre, 1955. 9–14.

Schofield, Roger. "Did the Mothers Really Die? Three Centuries of Maternal Mortality in the World We Have Lost." *The World We Have Gained: Histories of Population and Social Structure: Essays Presented to Peter Laslett on His Seventieth Birthday.* Ed. Lloyd Bonfield, et al. Oxford: Basil Blackwell, 1986.

Segal, Naomi. *Narcissus and Echo.* Manchester: Manchester UP, 1988.

Seligman, Martin E.P. *Helplessness: On Depression, Development, and Death.* New York: W.H. Freeman, 1975.

Sells, A. Lytton. "*La Chartreuse de Parme:* The Problem of Style." *Modern Language Quarterly* 11 (1950): 486–91.

— "*La Chartreuse de Parme:* The Problem of Composition." *Modern Language Quarterly* 12 (1951): 204–15.

Senior, Nancy. "Aspects of Infant Feeding in Eighteenth-Century France." *Eighteenth-Century Studies* 16.4 (1983): 367–88.

Serval, Maurice. "Autour d'un roman de Balzac: *Le Lys dans la vallée.*" *Revue d'Histoire Littéraire* 33 (1926): 370–89, 565–94.

Servoise, René. "Les Arcanes de *La Chartreuse de Parme*." *Nouvelle Revue des Deux Mondes* November 1981: 352–56.

Shattuck, Roger. *The Forbidden Experiment: The Story of the Wild Boy of Aveyron*. New York: Farrar Straus Giroux, 1980.

Shorter, Edward. "Différences de classe et sentiment depuis 1750: L'Exemple de la France." *Annales Economies Sociétés Civilisations* 29 (1974): 1034–57.

— *The Making of the Modern Family*. New York: Basic Books, 1975.

Siebers, Tobin. "The Werther Effect: The Esthetics of Suicide." *Mosaic* 26 (Winter 1993): 15–34.

Siegfried, Susan L. "Boilly's Moving House: 'An Exact Picture of Paris'?" *The Art Institute of Chicago Museum Studies* 15.2 (1989): 126–37.

— "The Artist as Nomadic Capitalist: The Case of Louis-Léopold Boilly." *Art History* 13.4 (1990): 516–41.

Singer, Barnett. *Village Notables in Nineteenth-Century France: Priests, Mayors, Schoolmasters*. Albany: SUNY P, 1983.

Sonnenfeld, Albert. "Ruminations on Stendhal's Epigraphs." *Pre-Text, Text, Context: Essays on Nineteenth-Century French Literature*. Ed. Robert L. Mitchell. Columbus: Ohio State UP, 1980. 99–110.

Sonnet, M. "Les Leçons paternelles." *Histoire des pères*. Ed. Delumeau and Roche. 259–78.

Spaas, Lieve. "Catherine et Bernadin de Saint-Pierre: L'Œdipe adelphique." *Eros Philadelphe: Colloque de Cerisy*. Ed. Wanda Bannour and Philippe Berthier. Paris: Félin, 1992. 85–104.

— *Lettres de Catherine de Saint-Pierre à son frère Bernardin*. Paris: Harmattan, 1996.

Springer, Mary Doyle. *A Rhetoric of Literary Character: Some Women of Henry James*. Chicago: U of Chicago P, 1978.

Stanford, Raney. "The Romantic Hero and That Fatal Selfhood." *Centennial Review* 12.4 (1968): 430–54.

Steiner, George. *The Death of Tragedy*. New York: Alfred A. Knopf, 1961.

Stone, Lawrence. *The Family, Sex and Marriage in England 1500–1800*. London: Weidenfeld and Nicolson, 1977.

Strickland, Geoffrey. *Stendhal: The Education of a Novelist*. Cambridge: Cambridge UP, 1974.

Sullivan, Edward. "The Novelist's Undeclared Assumptions: Balzac and Stendhal." *Laurels* 54.1 (Spring 1983): 49–57.

Sussman, George D. *Selling Mothers' Milk: The Wet-Nursing Business in France: 1715–1914*. Urbana: U of Illinois P, 1982.

— "The Wet-nursing Business in Nineteenth-Century France," *French Historical Studies* 9.2 (1976): 304–28.

Sussmann, Hava. "Julien Sorel dans le sillage de Jean-Jacques Rousseau à Turin." *Lettres Romanes* 40.2 (1986): 127–32.

Talbot, Emile, ed. *La Critique stendhalienne de Balzac à Zola: Textes choisis et présentés*. York, SC: French Literature Publications, 1979.

— *Stendhal and Romantic Esthetics*. Lexington, KY: French Forum, 1985.

— *Stendhal Revisited*. New York: Twayne, 1993.

Tanner, Tony. *Adultery in the Novel: Contract and Transgression*. Baltimore: Johns Hopkins UP, 1979.

Tetu, Jean-François. "Remarques sur le statut juridique de la femme au XIXe siècle." *La Femme au XIXe siècle: Littérature et idéologie*. Ed. R. Bellet. Lyon: PU de Lyon, 1979. 5–17

Thomas, Chantal. *La Reine scélérate: Marie-Antoinette dans les pamphlets*. Paris: Seuil, 1989.

Thompson, C.W. *Le Jeu de l'ordre et de la liberté dans* La Chartreuse de Parme. Aran: Grand-Chêne, 1982.

Thorslev, Peter L., Jr. *The Byronic Hero: Types and Prototypes*. Minneapolis: U of Minnesota P, 1962.

Toinet, Paul. *Paul et Virginie, répertoire bibliographique et iconographique*. Paris: Maisonneuve et Larose, 1963.

Trahard, Pierre, ed. *Paul et Virginie* (1788). By Bernardin de Saint-Pierre. Paris: Garnier, 1964.

Trotsky, Leon. *Literature and Revolution*. London: Allen & Unwin, 1925.

Twitchell, James B. *Forbidden Partners: The Incest Taboo in Modern Culture*. New York: Columbia UP, 1987.

Van Tieghem, Philippe. *Le Romantisme français*. Paris: Presses Universitaires de France, 1966.

van den Berghe, P.L. "Human Inbreeding Avoidance: Culture in Nature." *Behavioral and Brain Sciences* 6 (1983): 91–123.

Veeser, H. Aram, ed. *The New Historicism*. New York: Routledge, 1989.

Viennet, Jean. *Journal de Viennet, Pair de France, témoin de trois règnes: 1817–1848*. Paris: Amiot-Dumont, 1955.

Villermé, Louis-René. "Sur les cités ouvrières." *Annales d'Hygiène Publique et de Médecine Légale* 43 (1850): 241–61.

Wagner, Peter. "Anticatholic Erotica in Eighteenth-Century England." *Erotica and the Enlightenment*. Ed. Peter Wagner. Frankfurt am Main: Peter Lang, 1991. 166–209.

— *Eros Revived: Erotica of the Enlightenment in England and America*. London: Secker & Warburg, 1988.

— ed. *Erotica and the Enlightenment*. Frankfurt am Main: Peter Lang, 1991.

Waller, Margaret. *The Male Malady: Fictions of Impotence in the French Romantic Novel*. New Brunswick: Rutgers UP, 1993.

Wardman, H.W. "*La Chartreuse de Parme*: Ironical Ambiguity." *Kenyon Review* 17 (1955): 449–71.

Weber, Eugen. *Peasants into Frenchmen: The Modernization of Rural France: 1870–1914*. Stanford: Stanford UP, 1976.

Weil, Rachel. "Sometimes a Scepter Is Only a Scepter: Pornography and Politics in Restoration England." *The Invention of Pornography: Obscenity and the Origins of Modernity, 1500–1800*. Ed. Lynn Hunt. New York: Zone Books, 1993. 123–53.

Weinstein, Leo. "Stendhal's Count Mosca as a Statesman." *PMLA* 80 (1965): 210–16.

Wellek, René. "Romanticism Re-examined." *Romanticism Reconsidered: Selected Papers from the English Institute*. Ed. Northrop Frye. New York: Columbia UP, 1963.

Wertz, Richard W., and Dorothy C. Wertz. *Lying-In: A History of Childbirth in America*. 2nd ed. New Haven: Yale UP, 1989.

White, Burton L. *Educating the Infant and Toddler*. Lexington, MA: D.C. Heath, 1988.

Wiehe, Vernon R. *Sibling Abuse: Hidden Physical, Emotional, and Sexual Trauma*. Lexington, MA: D. C. Heath, 1990. 109–33.

Williams, Linda M., and David Finkelhor. "Parental Caregiving and Incest: Test of a Biosocial Model." *American Journal of Orthopsychiatry* 65.1 (1995): 101–13.

Wolf, A.P. "Adopt a Daughter-in-Law, Marry a Sister: A Chinese Solution to the Problem of the Incest Taboo." *American Anthropologist* 70 (1968): 864–74.

— "Childhood Association and Sexual Attraction: A Further Test of the Westermarck Hypothesis." *American Anthropologist* 72 (1970): 503–15.

Wright, Robert. "The Biology of Violence." *New Yorker* 13 March 1995: 68–77.

Zola, Emile. "Stendhal" (1880). *Critique stendhalienne*. Ed. Talbot. 233–67.

Index

aesthetic innovation: xvi, 84–107.
Ainsworth, Mary D.: 41.
Albitte, Gustave: 185n4, 209n3.
allegory: 90.
Allen, James Smith: x, 180n11.
Allen, Walter: 201n30.
Alletz, Edouard: 8, 77, 209–10n3.
Alvarez, A.: 201n37.
Anderson, Lorna M.: 205n23.
Antoine, Gérald: 210n3.
Aprile, Max: x.
Ariès, Philippe: 43, 188–89n21.
aristocrats: see monarchy.
Aristotele: 88, 89, 93, 98, 99, 106, 214n41.
Armengaud, Yvonne: 190nn29, 30, 195n19, 195n23, 205n19.
Arnaud, François-Thomas-Marie de Baculard d': 25.
Auerbach, Erich: 215n1.
Augustine, Saint: 143.

Babbitt, Irving: 179n3.
Babeuf, François Noël: 144.
Babou, Hippolyte: 163.
Baculard d'Arnaud: see Arnaud.
Baecque, Antoine de: 68, 69, 195n25, 196n27.
Baguley, David: 179n3.
Bakwin, H.: 41, 187n12.
Ballio, Joseph: 21.
Balzac, Honoré de: 5, 8–9, 15, 18, 22, 24, 25–26, 27–28, 35, 43, 48–49, 50, 52, 55, 63, 64, 66, 70–71, 74, 80–81, 90, 91–92, 92–93, 120–21, 130, 131, 153, 155, 185n4, 193n5, 197n41, 198n14, 206n27, 209n3; *Sur Catherine de Médicis*: 101–07; *La Vieille Fille*: 71, 135–41.

Barbéris, Pierre: 93.
Barbey d'Aurevilly, Jules: 26, 128.
Bardèche, Maurice: 198n14, 210n8, 210n11.
Bardet, Jean-Pierre: 189n25.
Barrès, Maurice: 76.
Barthes, Roland: 201n32.
Baudelaire, Charles: 23, 25, 91, 144, 175, 214n39.
Beaumarchais, Pierre-Augustin Caron de: 69, 71, 124–25, 139.
Béguin, Albert: 211n13.
Belloy, Pierre de: 172–73.
Benrekassa, Georges: 181n12, 204n16, 208n43.
Benward, Jean: 207n39.
Bernard, Charles de: 209n3.
Bernard, Claudie: 102.
Bernier, Georges: 184nn39–40.
Berthier, Philippe: 199n22.
Bibas, Henriette: 215–16n11.
Billault, Alain: 203n7.
Bishop, Lloyd: 38, 182n19.
Blankenhorn, David: 169, 194n15.
Blum, Alain: 183n32, 34.
Boccaccio, Giovanni: 73.
Bodin, Camille: 55, 79, 209n3.
Boilly, Louis-Léopold: frontispiece, 18–21, 20, 23, 146, 183–84nn35–40.
Bonnet, J.-C.: 57, 193nn5, 10.
Book-Senninger, Claude: 209n1.
Borel, Petrus: 134.
Bossenga, Gail: 195n21.
boue: 22–29, 70, 81.
Boulay-Paty, Evariste: 25, 67, 210n3.
Bradley, Keith R.: 188n18.
Bray, Bernard: 111, 203n7.
Bray, René: 102.
Bremond, Claude: 200–01n30.

Brennan, Thomas: 13, 213n26.
Brierre de Boismont, Alexandre: 147, 211–12n23, 213n30, 214n40.
Brombert, Victor: 200n25, 215nn10, 15.
Brooks, Peter: 78, 160, 167.
Brouard-Arends, Isabelle: 34, 188nn19, 21, 189n23, 191nn31, 36, 192n4.
Brouc, Martial: 145, 211n23.
Brown, James W.: 111.
Burke, Kenneth: 201n30.
Burney, Frances: 205n26.
Burton, Richard: x, 193n7.
Butler, Sandra: 129, 207n38.
Buzot, François: 144.
Byron, George Gordon: 38, 39, 204n13.

Cabanis, Pierre Jean Georges: 144.
Cabanis, Madame: 144.
Cabantous, A.: 59, 194n12.
Camus, Albert: 77, 101.
Carafa, Michele: 172.
Caro, Elme: 51, 92, 148, 152.
Carter, D.: 207n40.
Cazauran, Nicole: 102, 202n43.
Chagniot, Jean: 183n33.
Chaitin, Gilbert D.: 171.
Chamfort, Sébastien Roch Nicolas: 144.
Chamoux, Antoinette: 189n25.
Chateaubriand, François-René: 1–2, 7, 11, 34, 38, 39, 45, 49, 50, 99, 100, 111, 121, 123, 128, 130, 145, 153, 174, 179n2.
Chatelain, Abel: 183n29.
Châtelet, Madame de: 116.
Chatman, Seymour: 99, 201n30, 201n32.
Chauvet, Pierre: 22, 184nn41, 43.
Check, James V.P.: 207n40.
Cherpillod, André: 185n43.
Chesnais, Jean-Claude: 129, 132, 207n36.
Chevalier, Louis: 145–46, 180n5, 190n30.
child, child care: see maternal deprivation.
child abuse: see incest.
Chodorow, Nancy: 182n19.
Chon, F.: 24.
Christensen, Peter G.: 202n42.
church: xv, xvi, 58, 64–66, 67, 71, 74–76, 80–82.

classics debased: 84–92.
Claverie, Michel: 73.
Clavière, Etienne: 144.
Cobb, Richard: xv, 142, 145–46.
Code civil: 58, 63, 75, 130.
Cognets, Jean des: 87.
Cohen, Deborah A.: 194n13.
Coleridge, Samuel Taylor: 79, 98.
Collective mentality: xii–xvii, 2–6, 29, 32–33, and *passim*.
comedy: 88.
Comte, August: 10.
Connon, Michel: 215n15.
Condorcet, Marie Jean Antoine Nicolas de: 60, 144.
Constant, Benjamin: 2, 8, 51, 55, 79, 99, 100, 128, 130, 145.
Cook, Malcolm C.: 111.
Cooper, Barbara T.: x, 182n19, 193n5.
Corbin, Alain: 184n41, 211n21, 213n26, 213n30.
Corneille, Pierre: 115, 148.
Corvisier, André: 16.
Cottin, Madame Sophie: 34, 125.
Cranston, Maurice: 179n2.
Crébillon *fils*, Claude Prosper Jolyot de: 34, 208n43.
Crébillon *père*, Prosper Jolyot: 115.
Crider, Andrew B.: 188n14.
Crubellier, Maurice: 188n19, 191n31.
Custine, Adolphe: 182n20, 186n4.
Cyrulnik, Boris: 208n46.

Dabney, Melodye L.F.: 205n23, 207n39.
Danton, Georges Jacques: 60, 68.
Daprini, Pierre B.: 200n24.
Darnton, Robert: xiii, 195–96n25, 196nn26.
David, Jacques Louis: 6.
David, Marcel: 61.
David of Augsburg: 147.
death: see suicide.
Defoe, Daniel: 33, 205n26.
de' Negri, Enrico: 196n32.
Densen-Gerber, Judianne: 207n39.
depression: see Romanticism and depression.
de Vries, Jan: 18, 183n30.
de Young, Mary: 204n10, 205n24, 206n30.

Diderot, Denis: 34, 59, 60, 73, 117, 121, 127, 185n4.
disease: xvi, 11, 13, 16, 36, 147, 177.
Dominique: 115.
Donaldson-Evans, Mary: x.
Donne, John: 151.
Donnerstein, E.: 207n40.
Donzelot, Jacques: 44.
Douthwaite, Julia V.: 148.
Du Camp, Maxime: 11, 55, 186n4, 198n8, 209n3.
Duché, Emile: 44.
Ducis, Jean-François: 115.
Duclos, Charles: 205–06n27, 209n3.
Ducray-Duminil, François-Guillaume: 31–33, 35, 57, 59, 126, 185n4, 206n27, 209–10n3.
Dumas *père*, Alexandre: 35, 47, 48, 50, 70, 100, 123, 128, 161, 193n5, 206n28, 209n3.
Dunkley, John: 113.
Dunn, Susan: 76, 77, 193n9, 197nn39, 41.
Dupâquier, Jacques: xv, 18, 183n25, 183n33, 190n25.
Durand, Gilbert: 89, 201n34.
Duras, Madame Claire de: 55, 206n27.
Durham, Carolyn A.: 204n9.
Durkheim, Emile: 12, 144, 145–46.

Eliel, Carol S.: 19, 184nn37, 40.
Ellis, Havelock: 131, 208n44.
Empson, William: 92.
epic: 86–90.
Estournelles, Louise d': 61, 185n4, 206n27, 208n43, 210n3.
Etiemble: 86.
Euripides: 173.

Fabre, Jean: 202–03n3, 203n7.
Faguet, Emile: 93, 165, 200n26.
family: see paternity.
Farber, M.D.: 153, 214n41.
Fave, Robert: 211n18.
Faÿ-Sallois, Fanny: 188n19, 189n22, 190nn29, 30, 191nn31, 33.
Febvre, Lucien: 2, 3, 180n5.
Ferguson, Priscilla Clark: 181nn12, 14, 211n19.
Ferrier, Ginette: 94.
Fielding, Henry: 205n26.

Fiévée, Joseph: 34, 35, 39, 57, 72, 185n4.
Fildes, Valerie: 48, 188n15, 190nn29, 30.
Finch, Alison: 93, 94, 200n25.
Flaubert, Gustave: 9, 42, 47, 61, 156, 186n4, 191–92nn37, 38, 198n8.
Flinn, Michael W.: 16, 183n31.
Fougeret de Monbron, Louis Charles: 122.
Fourier, Charles: 128–29, 191n31, 204n16.
Fox, Joseph: 120.
Fox, Robin: 131, 207n33, 208n44.
Francis, R.A.: 111, 203n8.
Frautschi, Richard: see Martin, Angus.
Freud, Sigmund: 4–5, 117, 130.
Fromentin, Eugène: 8, 210n3.
Fuchs, Rachel G.: 47.
Furst, Lilian R.: 7, 79, 182n19.

Galliano, Paul: 44.
Garber, Barnett: 8.
Garrioch, David: 213n25.
Garrisson, Gaston: 212n22.
Gautier, Théophile: 48, 84–85.
Gay, Delphine: 186n4.
Gay, Sophie: 46, 54–58, 161, 186n4, 209n3.
Genlis, Madame de: 142, 152.
George, Albert J.: 10, 182n19, 202n44.
Gérard, François Pascal 1.
Gide, André: 87, 88.
Girardin, Emile de: 135.
Giraud, Raymond: 9l, 198n10.
Girodet-Trioson, Anne Louis: 1–2, 78.
Goethe, Wolfgang: 11, 38, 39, 40, 152, 153, 214n41.
Goldmann, Lucien: 4–5, 52, 100.
Gothot-Mersch, Claudine: 191–92n38.
Goujon, J. M. C. A.: 144.
Graffigny, Françoise de: 116–17, 209–10n3.
Grant, Richard B.: x, 125, 196n35.
Greuze, Jean-Baptiste: 30, 108, 129.
Gros, Antoine: 145.
Guenthner, Wendelin: 201n34.
Guérin, Michel: 199n19, 200n24.
Guerry, André-Michel: 207n36, 211nn21, 23.
Guillard, Nicolas-François: 115.

Guitton, Edouard: 203n7.
Gutierrez, Hector: 187n7.
Guttinguer, Ullric: 209n3.
Gutwirth, Madelyn: 77, 183n23.
Guyon, Bernard: 118.

Haig, Stirling: 215nn1, 2.
Hall Family Foundation: ix; Joyce & Elizabeth Hall Center for the Humanities: ix.
Hallam, John Stephen: 21, 184n40.
Hamilton, James F.: 149.
Hamm, Jean-Jacques: 215n18.
Hannaway, Owen and Caroline: 184n41.
Hapsburg, Maria Theresa: 43.
Hardy, Siméon-Prosper: 211n18.
Healy, Jane M.: 188n14.
Helvétious, Claude Adrien: 72.
Hemmings, F. W. J.: 157, 165, 199nn16, 215n14.
Henry, Louis: 18, 183n32, 190n30.
Hiddleston, James: 213n34, 214n43.
Higonnet, Margaret R. 213n36.
Higonnet, Patrice: 144, 211n19.
Hoffmann, E. T. A.: 6.
Holland, Norman N.: 188n14.
Holmes, Glyn: 36, 181n12, 182n19, 197n40.
Honig, Edwin: 90.
Hoog, Armand: 147, 182n19, 187n10.
Houdaille, Jacques: 44, 183nn32, 34, 187n7.
Hubert, J.D.: 202n40.
Hufton, Olwen H.: 14, 65, 212n24.
Hugo, Victor: 77, 84–85, 87, 128, 130, 134, 190n30, 209n3.
Hunt, Lynn: 60–61, 64, 68, 117, 193n10, 194n12, 195n25.
Huysmans, Joris-Karl: 36.

incest: xvi, 62, 109–32, 169–71.
individual, individualism: 6, 9–10, 13, 55, 73–74, 79, 80–81, 90, 116, 143, 162.
illness: see disease.
Ionesco, Eugène: 136, 141.

Jacobus, Mary: 191n31.
James, Henry: 98.
Jameson, Fredric: 137, 141.
Jaucourt, Chevalier de: 54.

Jefferson, Ann: 200n24.
Joffe, Alain: 194n13.
Johansen, Hans B.: 199n16.
Jost, François: 156.
Jouy, Monsieur Etienne de: xiii, 5, 55, 120–21, 142, 152, 189n22, 193n8, 210n3, 213n30, 214n41.
Justice, Blair, and Rita Justice: 205n24.

Kadish, Doris: 203n4.
Kanter, Sanford: 46.
Kaplan, Edward K.: 213n27.
Karr, Alphonse: xvi, 78, 135, 186n4, 194n12, 209n3.
Kavanagh, Thomas M.: 181n15.
Keisch, Claude: 196n36.
Kelly, Van: x, 197n2, 202n39.
Kinder, Patricia: 210n7.
Kinsey, Alfred Charles: 114.
Knibiehler, Yvonne: 190n29.
Kock, Paul de: 85–86.
Koestler, Arthur: 181n12.
Kopp, Robert: 211n16.
Kronenberger, Louis: 198n11.

La Fontaine, Jean de: 200n24.
Ladurie, Emmanuel Le Roy: 180n5, 183nn24, 33.
Laffly, Georges: 141.
Lallemand, Léon: 190n30.
Lamartine, Alphonse de: 7, 35, 77, 87, 88, 144, 148, 206n29.
Lamothe-Langon, Etienne Léon de: 81, 184n37.
Landes, Joan B.: 194n10.
Landry, François: 200n25.
Lane, Harlan: 185n2.
Lebègue, Raymond: 202n38.
Lecour, C. J.: 194n16.
Lecuyer, Maurice A.: 201n38.
LeNoir, Jean-Charles-Pierre: 43.
Leonhardt, R.W.: 126.
Le Peletier, Louis Michel: 144.
Lesuire, Robert-Martin: 25, 206n27, 210n3.
Levin, Harry: 216n12.
Levitine, George: 183n23.
Lewis, Matthew: 120.
Le Yaouanc, Moïse: 138.
Lieberman, Lisa Jo: 143, 145, 149, 211n22, 211n23, 214n40.

Linaeous, Carolus: 33.
Linz, D.: 207n40.
Lioure, Michel: 85.
Lloyd, Rosemary: 189n21.
Longstaffe, Moya: 164–65, 167, 215n2.
Louis XV: xiv, 67–69, 117; see also monarchy.
Louis XVI: xiv, 67–69, 70, 76; see also monarchy.
Louvet de Couvay, Jean-Baptiste: 64, 124, 185n4, 193n5, 206n31, 209n3.
love, sentimental or "romantic": 54–55, 59, 61, 85.
lower class: 50.
Lowrie, Joyce O.: 203n5.
Lukács, György: 52, 89.

Mackenzie, Henry: 205n26.
Madelénat, Daniel: 86, 90.
Maier, Stephen: 215n20.
Maigron, Louis: 134–35, 155, 214n41.
Maisch, Herbert: 114, 206n30, 207n34, 208n44.
Mandrou, Robert: 3, 58, 180n5, 192–93n4.
Marguerite de Navarre: 102, 174.
Marie-Antoinette: xiv, 67–68, 70, 117.
Marivaux: 18, 34, 50, 106.
Marmontel, Jean-François: 89, 115, 185n4.
Marshall, W.L.: 207n40.
Martin, Angus: 118, 196n26, 202n1.
Martineau, Henri: 215n1.
Masson, Michel: 186n4.
maternal deprivation: xv, 13, 17–18, 31–52, 61, 163–64; see, also, paternity.
Maupassant, Guy de: 36.
Mauron. Charles: 4–5, 180n9.
Mauzi, Robert: 147, 182n19, 203n5, 203n7.
May, Georges: 4, 181n15, 193n8.
May, Gita: 211n19.
McCarthy, Mary: 201n30.
McWatters, K. G.: 201n34.
Medea: 173–74.
Meiselman, Karin C.: 206n30, 207n33.
melancholy: see Romanticism and depression.
Melzer, Sara: x.
Ménétra, Jacques-Louis: 195n22.

mentalités: see, Collective mentality.
Mercier, Louis Sébastien: xiii, 5, 22–23, 24, 45, 68, 73, 79, 142, 144, 184nn41, 43, 189n22, 190–91n31, 207n37.
Merrick, Jeffrey: 64, 65–66, 66–67, 192n4, 195n21, 196n26, 211n18.
Methodology for this study: xiii–xv, xvi, 3–5, 73–74, 113–14, 116, 146–47, 177–78, 181n12, 183n23.
Mialaret, Athénaïs: 45.
Michel, François: 97.
Michelet, Jules: 37, 45, 60, 73, 76, 77, 144.
middle class: 1, 10, 50.
migration: xv, 13–29, 143, 145–46.
Mikulincer, Mario: 215n20.
Miles, Henry: 204n13.
Miller, Nancy K.: 201n38.
Mirabeau, Honoré-Gabriel-Riquetti: 64, 115.
Mitchell, B.R.: 186n6.
Moers, Ellen: 205n26.
Molière: 66, 136–37, 139, 167.
monarchy: xiv, xv, 1, 10, 38, 58, 60, 66, 67–72, 74, 75, 80, 84–85, 87, 88, 143–44.
Montaigne, Michel de: 60, 189n21.
Montesquieu, Robert de: 116, 148, 150–51.
Moreau, Pierre: 1.
Morot-Sir, Edouard: 211n15.
Mortimer, Armine: 210n9.
Mossman, Carol A.: 161, 169.
Mozet, Nicole: 135, 210n6.
Mulliez, J.: 56, 60, 64, 192n3.
Musset, Alfred de: 11, 26, 40, 77, 124, 134, 145, 155, 182n20, 206n29, 209n3.
Mylne, Vivienne G.: see Martin, Angus.

Nagy, Stephen: 194n13.
names: 57, 97, 160–62, 193n5, 215n6.
Napoleon: 62, 63, 68, 76, 82, 85, 95, 138, 144, 164–68, 171.
Narcissus, narcissism: 127–28.
narrative armature: 136.
Nerciat, André-Robert Andréa de: 67, 122.
Nerval, Gérard de: 91, 145, 192n40.
Niess, Robert J.: 198n10.
Nodier, Eugénie: 209n3.
Norberg, Kathryn: 61.

Oedipus: 33, 77–78, 115.
O'Neddy, Philothée: 134.
onomastics: see names.
orphans: see maternal deprivation.
Ourliac, Edouard: 8, 14, 17, 183n28, 186n4.
Ovid: 201n39.

Palaiseau, Mademoiselle de: 186n4.
Pannier, Sophie: 186n4, 194n12, 196n38.
Parent-Duchâtelet, Alexandre: 22, 194n16.
Parent-Lardeur, Françoise: 180n11, 184n41.
parental deprivation: see maternal deprivation, and paternity.
Pâris, Philippe-Nicolas-Marie de: 144.
Parker, H., and S. Parker: 208n44.
Pascal, Blaise: 60.
Pasco, Allan H.: 136, 195n18, 195n24, 198n14, 200n25.
paternity, patriarchy: xv, 13, 54–82, 159–65, 169–70, 195n18.
Pauvert, Jean-Jacques: 47.
Pearson, Roger: 97, 199n19.
Perlin, Seymour: 213n31.
Perrot, Michelle: 63, 179n5, 204n12, 205n17.
Peterson, Christopher: 215n20.
Pétion, Jérôme: 144.
Petit, M.: 211n23.
Peyre, Henri: 179n1, 182n20.
Picard, Louis-Benoit: 14, 17, 80, 186n4, 189n23, 206n27.
Pichois, Claude: xx, 198nn8, 9.
Pierrard, Pierre: 185n44.
Pierre-Quint, Léon: 135.
Pigault-Lebrun: 42, 47, 54, 59, 69, 205n22, 210n3.
Planté, Christine: 193n8.
plot systems: 136.
Pope, Whitney: 12.
Pornography: 66–71, 130.
Porter, Laurence M.: x, 179n3.
Poulet, Georges: 182n19.
Prendergast, Christopher: 180n12, 215n2.
Prévost, Abbé Antoine-François: 57, 115, 121, 150–51, 209n3.
Prévost, Jean: 115.

priest: see church.
Prioult, Albert: 202n41.
Propp, Vladimir: 200n30.
Proust, Marcel: 36.
pseudonymes: see names.
Purdy, Anthony: 215n18.

Queffélec, Henri: 210n11.
Queffélec, Lise: 117, 206n28, 211n16.
Quinet, Edgar: 76, 86–87, 155.

Rabaut de St Etienne, Jean Paul: 144.
Rabbe, Alphonse: 144–45.
Rabelais: 88, 102.
Racault, Jean-Michel: 202n2, 203n8, 204n9.
Racine: 85, 148.
Radcliffe, Ann: 120.
Ragland-Sullivan, Mary Eloise: 215n10.
Ratcliffe, Barrie M.: 142, 145–46, 211n22, 211n23, 214n41.
Realism: 4–6, 19, 37.
Reid, Donald: 184n41.
Rémond, Jean-Pierre: 130.
Renvoizé, Jean: 114, 124, 205n23.
Restif de La Bretonne, Nicolas-Edme: xiii, 5, 17, 18, 43, 59, 60, 67, 69, 71, 117, 120, 122, 127, 130, 144, 153, 154, 158, 171, 184n42, 188nn19, 20, 193n5, 209n3, 214n39.
Revel, Jacques: 195n25.
Reybaud, Louis: 79–80, 156.
Ribble, M. A.: 40, 187n11.
Ribner, Jonathan P.: 6, 196n36.
Ricard, Auguste: 19, 24, 26, 35, 209n3, 210n3.
Ricardou, Jean: 93.
Riccoboni, Madame Marie-Jeanne: 149, 153, 185n4, 214n41.
Richter, C. P.: 175–76.
Ridge, George R.: 182n19.
Robert, Hubert: 83, 107.
Robinson, Philip: 112, 203nn5, 7.
Roche, Daniel: 17, 18, 132, 183nn31, 32, 34, 190n28, 195n22.
Roland, Jean Marie: 144.
Roland, Jeanne Manon Phlipon: 144.
Romantic hero: xv, 1–3, 6–9, 13, 37–40, 41–42, 50, 51–52, 84–86, 89, 92–102, 84–107, and passim.
Romanticism: 1–2, 9–29, 74–75, and

passim; dating: 9–10, 11–14;
definition: xv, xvi–xvii, 2, 11–13, 177;
and depression: xvi, 8–9, 13, 38–39,
62, 143, 147–56, 174–77.
Romme, Charles Gilbert: 144.
Ronesse, J.-H.: 22, 23, 184nn41, 42.
Rose, William: 7. 182n19.
Roth, Michael S.: 191n34.
Rousseau, Jean-Jacques: xiv, 3, 32, 33,
34, 35, 37, 39, 40, 42, 45, 50, 54, 60,
73, 112, 118–19, 124, 126, 147,
150–51, 152, 164–65, 169–70,
179nn1, 2, 191n31.
Roux, Jacques: 144.
Rubin, David Lee: 202n40.
Ruff, Julius R.: 185n45.

Sacchini, Marie-Gaspard: 115.
Saddy, Pierre: 184n41.
Sade, Donatien A. F.: 47, 73, 81, 86,
117, 120, 121, 127, 191n36, 204n15.
Saint-Amand, Pierre: 81.
Saint-Pierre, Jacques-Henri Bernardin
de: 55, 109–14, 122–23, 131.
Sainte-Beuve, Charles Augustin: 1, 50,
93, 98, 134, 163, 186n4, 192n41,
210n3.
Salomon, Pierre: 154.
Sand, George: xiv, 36, 46, 47, 101,
122–24, 125, 130, 154–55, 186n4,
209n3.
Sandeau, Jules: 6–7, 55, 208n43, 209n3.
Sandell, Sandra Dianne: 205n25.
Scheper-Hughes, Nancy: 189n21.
Schmidt, Albert-Marie: 102.
Schofield, Roger: 186n7.
Scribe, Eugène: 172.
Segal, Naomi: 188n14.
Seligman, Martin E.P.: 175–77, 215n19,
215n20.
Sells, A. Lytton: 198n13, 199n16.
Senancour, Etienne Pivert de: 50, 112,
134, 151–52.
Senior, Nancy: 43, 191n31.
Serval, Maurice: 201n38.
Servoise, René: 199n19.
Seuffert, Bernard: 201n30.
Shafer, Gretchen: 205n23.
Shakespeare, William: 98, 115.
Shattuck, Roger: 33.
Shelley, Percy Bysshe: 204n13.

Shepher, Joseph: 131.
Shorter, Edward: 181n12, 188nn15, 21,
192n2, 205n19.
sickness: see disease.
Siebers, Tobin: 151.
Siegfried, Susan L.: 19, 183nn35, 36,
184n40.
Silbert, M.: 207n40.
Singer, Barnett: 181n17, 182n21.
Sonnenfeld, Albert: 99.
Sonnet, M.: 194n12.
Sophocles: 115.
Soubrany, Pierre Auguste de: 144.
Souday, Paul: 210n11.
Soulié, Frédéric: 134, 155, 214n41.
Souza, Madame de: 42, 126–27, 186n4.
Spaas, Lieve: 207–08n42.
Spiro, Melford E.: 131, 208n44.
Springer, Mary Doyle: 98.
Staël, Madame Anne Louise Germaine
Necker de: 1–2, 50, 85, 99, 144, 174,
185n4, 209n3.
Stanford, Raney: 182n19.
Steiner, George: 88.
Stendhal: 7, 9; 25, 27, 28–29, 50, 91,
120, 131, 185n44, 209–10n3; *Le
Rouge et le noir*: 26, 99–101, 125,
157–78; *La Chartreuse de Parme*:
92–101, 107, 144.
Stewart, Joan Hinde: 193n8.
Stone, Lawrence: 188n15.
Stowe, Harriet Beecher: 52.
Strickland, Geoffrey: 200n24.
structural innovation: xvi, 84–107.
Sue, Eugène: 23, 26 , 48, 88, 127, 130,
155, 184n42, 186n4, 206n27.
Sugny, S. de: 134.
suicide: xiv, xvi, 7, 28, 38, 40, 54, 73, 89,
114, 123, 124, 134–56, 170, 174–77.
Sullivan, Edward: 73, 196n31.
Summers, Montague: 204n13.
Sussman, George D.: 43, 44, 188nn16,
17, 19, 189n25, 191n31, 215n15.
Sussmann, Hava: 216n15.

Talbot, Emile: 98.
Talleyrand, Charles Maurice de: 60,
196n26.
Talmon, Yonina: 131.
Tanner, Tony: 118–19, 126.
Tapert, Annette: 193n6.

Telemachus: 56.
Tencin, Madame Claudine-Alexandrine Guérin de: 57.
Tenon, M.: 190nn25, 31.
Testud, Pierre: 117, 127.
Tetu, Jean-François: 195n19.
Thomas, Chantal: 195n25, 196n26.
Thompson, C.W.: 200n24, 201n35.
Thorslev, Jr., Peter L.: 182n19.
Tillier, Claude: 75, 196n30.
Toinet, Paul: 202n1.
Toqueville, Alexis de: xv.
Trotsky, Leon: 52.
Tracy, Antoine-Louis-Claude Destutt de: 165–68, 176, 178.
tragedy: 84–86, 87.
Trotsky, Leon: 52.
Twain, Mark: 148.
Twitchell, James B.: 205n26, 207n33.

unbonded child: see maternal deprivation.

Van Tieghem, Philippe: 3, 179n2.
van den Berghe, P.L.: 208n44.
Veeser, H. Aram: 180n5.
Vergy, Châtelaine de: 172–73.
Vernière, P.: 204n16.
Viennet, Jean: 85.
Vigny, Alfred de: 11, 50, 91, 99, 100, 101, 128, 134.

Villermé, Louis-René: 184n42.
violence: 58, 62–63, 75–76.
Voltaire: 72, 85, 115, 116. 185n4.
Vries, Jan de: 183n30.

Wagner, Peter: 67, 195–96n25.
Wallace, William Ross: 52.
Waller, Margaret: 197n44.
Wallis, Henry: 133, 149.
Walpole, Horace: 119.
Wardman, H.W.: 200n25.
Weber, Eugen: xiii, 180n12, 191n33.
Weinstein, Leo: 94, 200n24.
Wellek, René: 182n19.
Wertz, Richard W. and Dorothy C.: 187n7, 189n21.
Westermarck, Edward: 131, 208n44.
White, Burton L.: 187n13.
White, Hayden: 4.
Wiehe, Vernon R.: 207n39.
Williams, Linda M.: 131, 208n46.
Wilson, Michele D.: 194n13.
Wolf, A.P.: 208n44.
Wright, Robert: 188n14.

Zola, Emile: 16, 73, 86, 87–88, 90, 92, 121, 124.
Zumthor, Paul: 86.